*Bring That Beat Back*

# Bring That Beat Back

## How Sampling Built Hip-Hop

### NATE PATRIN

University of Minnesota Press

Minneapolis

London

Published by the University of Minnesota Press
111 Third Avenue South, Suite 290
Minneapolis, MN 55401-2520
http://www.upress.umn.edu

Printed in the United States of America on acid-free paper

The University of Minnesota is an equal-opportunity educator and employer.

25  24  23  22  21  20    10  9  8  7  6  5  4  3  2  1

---

Library of Congress Cataloging in Publication Data
Patrin, Nate, author.
Bring that beat back : how sampling built hip-hop / Nate Patrin.
LCCN 2019033190 (print) | ISBN 978-1-5179-0628-3 (pb)
Description: Minneapolis : University of Minnesota Press, [2020] | Includes
    bibliographical references and index.
Subjects: LCSH: Rap music—History and criticism. | Rap music—Production
and direction—History.
Classification: LCC ML3531 .P4 2020 (print) | DDC 782.421649—dc23
LC record available at https://lccn.loc.gov/2019033190

To my brother Damian,
who knew I'd like *De La Soul Is Dead*

# Contents

# Introduction
## The Art of the Loop

ON APRIL 17, 1966, Steve Reich took a young man's traumatized voice and transformed it into harrowing music. Daniel Hamm was one of six black Harlem teenagers accused of being complicit in the stabbing death of used clothing store merchant Margit Sugar two years before, and the Harlem Six, as they'd come to be known, were beaten so regularly and brutally by police and prison guards that they became indelible symbols for civil rights. In his essay "A Report from Occupied Territory," published in *The Nation* on July 11, 1966, James Baldwin put the situation into the starkest of words: "People are destroyed very easily. Where is the civilization and where, indeed, is the morality which can afford to destroy so many?"

But it was a recording from before that stabbing, after Hamm and another teenager were arrested under flimsy pretext during a fracas around an overturned fruit stand, that symbolized just how deeply that destruction would resonate. Reich had completed an early example of tape manipulation as music in 1965 when he pitted two identical but asynchronous recordings of a Pentecostal street preacher against each other for the piece "It's Gonna Rain," loops clicking in and out of orbit until meaning gave way to words, words gave way to rhythms, rhythms gave way to noise. It left enough of an impression that activist and author Truman Nelson—whose 1968 book *The Torture of Mothers* examined the tragic repercussions of the Harlem Six case—lent Reich twenty hours' worth of tape-recorded interviews involving Hamm, with the purpose of turning the collected recordings into a condensed recollection of their mistreatment at the hands of the police. Reich agreed to do the work for free—just as long as he could use one of the clips to make another loop-experiment track.

That track became "Come Out," a thirteen-minute recording that manipulated a four-second line from Hamm's testimony about proving to a hospital that he'd been beaten by police: "I had to, like, open the bruise up, and let some of the bruise blood come out to show them." Those last five words were isolated by Reich, played through two different audio channels, and looped end to end as they gradually fell out of sync, creating a multilayered echo effect—*comeouttoshowthemcome outtoshowthem*—a slowly expanding droning chorus of rhythmic vocal patterns until the mechanical nature of the recording and the living, breathing voice are thoroughly intertwined.

Thirty-seven years later, and nearly three decades after Hamm was finally found not guilty after spending eight years in prison, his voice was heard again—the same source, but to a vastly different end, in a song called "America's Most Blunted," produced by Oxnard, California, beat-maker/MC Madlib for Madvillain, his team-up with rapper MF Doom. Hamm's lines emerge in the first thirty or so seconds of the song from a fog of aluminum thunderstorm sound effects taken from the Detroit soul group Dramatics' February 1972 #1 soul single "In the Rain." Hamm's line flips quickly to a truncated piece of the phase-shifting portion from Reich's "Come Out" before being accompanied by a reverbed guitar strum—also from "In the Rain"—and then abruptly being cut off by a ragged cough, bong-rip sound effects, and a snippet of a comedy monologue about the benefits of "listening to music while stoned." It was a strange opening flourish, but by the 2003 release date of Madvillain's "Money Folder" b/w "America's Most Blunted" single, it wasn't as avant-garde as Steve Reich was in the '60s—it was just hip-hop.

How did we get from there to here? Incorporating found sound and manipulating it into another form entirely wasn't an unheard-of practice before hip-hop started—everything from Buchanan and Goodman's 1956 single "The Flying Saucer" and its "news report" pop-song punchlines to the Beatles' conceptual sound collage "Revolution 9" in 1968 prefigured the idea that repurposing preexisting sounds and music could create new pieces of music in themselves. But these were typically works of comedy or uncommercial experiments, often meant to parody, belittle, or transcend the idea of actually being popular music. Sampling, however—especially as it existed in the context of hip-hop as it rose to prominence in the 1980s—has done more than any musical movement originated in the twentieth century to maintain a continuum of popular music as a living document, and in the process it's become one of the most successful (and commercial) strains of postmodern art.

It's a deceptively simple technique. At its most basic, you simply take a piece of a preexisting recording and manipulate it—making it repeat on a loop, altering the pitch, cutting it into pieces, and reassembling it—to make something new. But from the very start, it was laden with complex and ever-mutating consequences in the worlds of cultural exchange, the music business, intellectual property, archival history, and even basic songwriting. By the end of the 1980s, the spread of sampling and its ability to dictate musical trends had become as crucial as the pop charts and the press in determining what pieces of music from bygone eras had the means to join a historical canon. Yet as time wore on and trends in both production and copyright law made the original sampling methods obsolete, new ways had to be found of incorporating it—and newer meanings were found in those juxtapositions.

So the story of sampling in hip-hop isn't quite as straightforward as your typical music history lesson. It has clear origin points—particularly the turntable-manning, record-spinning hip-hop DJs of 1970s New York, whose real-time remixing of largely contemporaneous or otherwise recent songs emphasized and extended snapshot moments of a particularly strong beat. But where those points go is rarely a straight line, or a parabola, or even a constellation. Sampling was built off word of mouth, broken secrets, technological experiments, fierce competition, artful introspection, happy accidents, memetic replication, strokes of good luck, DIY necessity, collector impulse, and unbridled fandom. And an entirely new movement could turn on the whims of one taste-making entity, an idiosyncratic figure or two or even a crew that amassed experience and knowledge the same way they stocked their record crates.

If there's one thing that ties together all these different threads, it's the power of recontextualization: of taking something that was neglected by the masses or oversaturated through fame and giving it a renewed presence in music that highlighted a new way of hearing it. Hip-hop reframed music as the meritocracy that charts, labels, and the industry couldn't: it created a place where the semi-forgotten soul singer Syl Johnson was every bit as central as an icon like James Brown, where once-anonymous session players became as prized as the charismatic front men they played for, where critically derided or neglected genres—fusion jazz, arena rock, smooth '80s R&B—could all find a place in a new revolution. Just as long as it could move the rhythm, the track, and the body from simple head nods to all-out dance sessions, it didn't matter whether it originated from an ultra-scarce private press 7-inch single or the highest-selling blockbuster albums of all time: just start with the beat and go from there.

Sampling, above all, has a way of warping time and space in the pursuit of an empathetic form of creation. It takes a snapshot of a particularly stirring piece of music and lets listeners hear it anew, nodding to the work of an original creator and the vision of its hip-hop reinterpreter all at once. Even the smallest fragments of sound can become something revolutionary, and the creators of these one-bar-loop symphonies can bring people to musical epiphanies by the time you count to four.

*Bring That Beat Back* examines the history of sampling in hip-hop through the lens of four different artists: Grandmaster Flash as the popular face of the music's DJ-born origins, Prince Paul as an early champion of sampling's potential to elaborate on and rewrite music history, Dr. Dre as the superstar who personified the rise of a stylistically distinct regional sound while blurring the lines between sampling and composition, and Madlib as the underground experimentalist and record-collector antiquarian who constantly broke the rules of what the mainstream expected from hip-hop. From these four artists' histories, and the stories of the people who collaborated, competed, and evolved with them, this book aims to provide a foundational introduction to a side of music that's often been belittled, insulted, or taken for granted: the aesthetic and reconstructive power of one of the most revelatory forms of pop culture to ever emerge from postwar twentieth-century America. And you can nod your head to it.

Part I

# The Grandmaster

Grandmaster Flash at the UIC Pavilion in Chicago, 1982. Photograph by Paul Natkin / Getty Images.

# 1 | *Wheels of Steel*
## How DJs Became Artists

**The dawn of hip-hop turns the DJ into a performer and curation into an artform, one break at a time.**

BEFORE EVERYTHING ELSE—the sampler, the remix, the entire concept of hip-hop—there was the DJ. Here you have a figure who stands overlooking a dancefloor with a few crates full of records, watching people react and move to whatever gets put on the turntable. And that turntable can manipulate people. Find a hot song, and you can pack the floor. Isolate the best part of that song, and you can build a peak. Make a thing out of finding that best part—manipulate it, reshape it, distort it, rewind it, extend it beyond any preconceived notion of just how long that groove was able to go—and the head-to-feet connection gets all wrapped up in a feedback loop that makes moving to a beat feel like an epiphany.

The idea of the disc jockey as an in-house attraction dates back to the discotheques of Europe, though it's more accurate to say that the records the DJ played were the actual draw. In postwar France, the novelty of bars that featured jukeboxes in the early '50s soon evolved into trendy hangouts for European jet-setters, hitting a fever pitch in the early '60s when the Twist craze spiked demand for dancefloor space. But New York is where it really became an art form. While the transatlantic high society celebrities and beautiful people that populated early European-style mid-'60s discotheques in NYC were getting down to Motown hits in pop art palaces like Arthur and the Electric Circus, the club scene's tendency to lean on shutting up and playing the hits had shifted by the turn of the '70s to something a bit more personality-driven and idiosyncratic.

Francis Grasso, a resident DJ at the Hell's Kitchen gay nightclub the Sanctuary, pulled off an important twofer. First, he played and subsequently popularized imports and obscurities, giving the people not just what they wanted, but what they didn't *know* they wanted even more. Then he mixed it all together in a sort of musical narrative journey that incorporated one of the earliest known forms of beatmatching. His selections didn't merely segue from one outro to the next intro—they were layered and juxtaposed in a more streamlined fashion. In some cases, Grasso would spin two copies of the same record, holding one at a specific cue and waiting for just the right moment to let it spin back up again, all to make the grooves of his favorite hard-hitting funk and rock jams last as long as he felt was necessary to keep people dancing.

If Grasso's technique was the prototype for what New York night-clubs eventually turned into disco, it was also widely shared as a common ancestry with the DJs that hip-hop founding fathers would take their cues from a few years down the line. One pre-hip-hop favorite was Cameron Flowers, better known as Grandmaster Flowers, a DJ who opened for James Brown at Yankee Stadium in 1969 and spent much of the '70s throwing mobile DJ parties in the outer boroughs. As under-credited as he is today, Flowers was one of New York's most widely traveled DJs, renowned for his top-notch mixing skills and his ability to cater to both "bourgie" Manhattan disco audiences and inner-city crowds that gathered in public recreation-field "park jams." Not many recordings exist of his sets, and the ones that do come from the late '70s when he was competing against the newer generation of hip-hop DJs, but you can hear why old heads swear up and down by his mixes.

DJ Hollywood, another disco-crossover DJ who flourished beginning in the early '70s, spun at some of Harlem's biggest clubs, where he earned such a rep that he could make 8-track tapes of one-off mixes and sell them for $12 apiece (more than $70 in current money). And his place in history was assured when he became recognized as the first DJ to incorporate the same poetic "rhythm talk" stage patter that black radio DJs like WWRL's "Soul Server" Hank Spann and WBLS's Frankie Crocker used, focusing on riding the beat with a more continuous flow of rhymes and leading call-and-response segments with the crowd. There are still debates as to who the first actual rapper was, but it's safe to say Hollywood helped plant the roots for a form of rapping that audiences would come to know by the end of the '70s. And it's still worth noting that DJing and MCing weren't always mutually exclusive parts of a performance.

Yet something separated the Manhattan, Brooklyn, and Queens DJs from the ones who would eventually turn the Bronx into hip-hop's most formative battleground. After the Cross-Bronx Expressway severed the middle-class lifelines that kept the borough together, decades' worth of underfunded public housing, neglectful landlords, and street gang violence had come to define the Bronx as a no-man's land. If an emerging subculture was going to flourish in the Bronx, it would carry a similar air of youthful restlessness in the face of this decaying but loyalty-demanding homestead—somewhere between an escape, a rebellion, and a celebration.

The uptown clubs where DJs like Hollywood spun catered to a more adult clientele, one with money and tastes that ran toward the opulent orchestral soul of Isaac Hayes, Barry White, and the groups of Philadelphia International Records like the O'Jays and Harold Melvin & the Blue Notes. But Bronx audiences skewed younger, tougher, and more intensely competitive: they didn't just dance to be seen or pick up partners, but also danced to battle, whether they represented a gang like the Savage Skulls or just a tight-knit crew of locals into the graffiti scene. And the cuts they demanded were heavier, nastier, and rocked harder than the rest: fuzzed-out, Latin percussion–laced anthems by cult funk artists like the Jimmy Castor Bunch ("It's Just Begun"), Mandrill ("Fencewalk"), and Dennis Coffey ("Scorpio"). All it took was one DJ to capitalize on this demand—and an almost complete unknown did just that, combining right-place-right-time luck with a powerful command of the crowd and a monster sound system.

• • •

Clive Campbell was part of the wave of Caribbean immigrants who arrived in New York between the mid-'50s and late '60s, a Kingston-born kid who landed in the Bronx at twelve years old and aimed to follow in the footsteps of his father's own soundman business. By high school, he'd fashioned himself a memorable alias, combining the name he used tagging graffiti ("Kool," from the cigarette brand a suave James Bond–style spot advertised on TV) and a nickname earned on the basketball court ("Herc," from his formidable height and Herculean prowess in the paint). And though his predecessors and rivals outside the Bronx will enthusiastically contest this, DJ Kool Herc offered one of the rare occasions where the birth of a subculture can be directly traced to a single specific date, place, and time: 9:00 p.m., August 11, 1973, at 1520 Sedgwick Avenue, right off the expressway that tore the Bronx apart.

Herc charged admission for a rec room party held in conjunction with his sister Cindy, a special "Back to School Jam" ("25 cents for ladies, 50 cents for fellas") organized to raise funds so Cindy could buy some fly new clothes for the upcoming semester. The eighteen-year-old Herc had worked hard to downplay his roots due to local mockery; before the outlaw cachet of Bob Marley and *The Harder They Come* made being a rasta cool, local gang members were said to be throwing Jamaican kids into trash cans. But he still felt echoes of the massive sound systems he heard from blocks away as a kid back in Kingston, and started his set off with a few reggae tracks. The mostly high-school-aged crowd remained unmoved, so Herc had to switch his style up quick.

Fortunately for his young DJ career, Herc had learned from studying dancefloor showdowns elsewhere that the kids wanted breaks. The "break" is what people now call the part of a record where the music gets heaviest on percussion, unaccompanied or otherwise, and acts almost like a signal to throw down and show your best moves. Unlike the grown-up crowds that the no-sneakers-allowed clubs catered to, the younger dancers lived and died by the break, using it as a key moment to show off the most elaborate maneuvers they could muster: upright dance moves wildly transitioning into body-upending, floor-hitting horizontal contortions that took style to new acrobatic lengths. So Herc gave them breaks: stretching seconds into minutes, a handful of bars into a whole breakdown, a mix into a stream of consciousness. He used the same technique that most DJs from Grasso onward did—cueing up a second copy of the same record to keep the break going in a loop once the first record reached the end of the breakdown—and added his own DJ patter over the mix through an echo chamber, giving the party the feel of a cavernous outdoor sound system transplanted from a Kingston yard into a Bronx rec room.

Some cuts could do the job on their own: Booker T. & the M.G.'s 1971 instrumental "Melting Pot," a popular choice held down by a ruthless here-comes-the-cavalry Al Jackson Jr. drumbeat, was pretty much nothing *but* eight-plus minutes' worth of break. But Herc's big innovation was to string together a series of different songs' breaks into what he called the "Merry-Go-Round," a combination of technique and selection that proved to be the foundation of hip-hop beats. The running order of the Merry-Go-Round and what tracks it used could vary depending on whether the crowd was feeling it, but it usually had some common threads. For James Brown's "Give It Up or Turnit a Loose," from 1970's *Sex Machine,* Herc focused square on a break about two-thirds of the way through that was almost entirely clapping, Johnny Griggs's conga drums, and James shouting ("Clap your hands / stomp your feet / in the jungle, brother") before the rolling-thunder drums of Clyde Stubblefield burst in. There was "The Mexican," an up-tempo prog rock–goes–funky number with Ennio Morricone spaghetti western flourishes, by English obscurities and Pink Floyd labelmates Babe Ruth; the drums were powerful but it had a monster of a bassline during the break, too.

Herc also swore by a couple cuts by Michael Viner's Incredible Bongo Band, an MGM studio group first formed to soundtrack the preposterous 1972 race-relations sci-fi flick *The Thing with Two Heads.* (Tagline: "They transplanted a WHITE BIGOT'S HEAD onto a SOUL BROTHER'S BODY!") "Bongo Rock '73," more popularly known as just "Bongo Rock," was a key selection, with blistering Latin rhythms turning the titular drum into the sounds of a dance-provoking avalanche of percussion. But often Herc would mix it or just swap it out entirely for another track from the same 1973 album *Bongo Rock,* a version of the Shadows' rock instrumental "Apache" that had even heavier, more frantic beats—the atom bomb in Herc's arsenal that every other DJ had to stock up on in their own arms race in order to keep pace. "Apache" would eventually become one of the most recognizable beats to ever emerge out of hip-hop's new canon of dance music, going on to be sampled or otherwise interpolated in well over five hundred acknowledged songs. As revolutions went, Herc's Merry-Go-Round was pretty seat-of-the-pants, but it proved to be a powerful blueprint to follow.

Following, however, proved easier than copying. As far as his selections went, Herc made a point of removing the labels from his records—soaking them off with hot water usually did the trick—and keeping them in nondescript sleeves so nobody else could capitalize on his discoveries. And even if word got out, who could compete with his sound system? What money Herc made typically went toward his tools of the trade—new records, bigger speakers, more top-of-the-line turntables—until he manned a mobile unit that outdid any sound system in New York City and most of them in Jamaica for good measure. In '74, he'd moved

from the rec room to block parties and park jams, and from there to a
steady gig doing sets at clubs like the Twilight Zone, the Hevalo, and the
Executive Playhouse until he ruled the Bronx nightlife in '76 with early-
adopter MC Coke La Rock bigging him up on the mic.

Herc called his crew of assorted MCs and b-boys the Herculords,
and his system the Herculoids: the speakers were colossal Shure col-
umns taller than most of the people in the crowd, while the amplifiers
were a pair of Macintosh MC-2300 solid state amps (the same kind the
Grateful Dead used in 1974 for their gargantuan "Wall of Sound" PA system). And most crucially, the turntables were state-of-the-art Thorens,
$1,000 apiece and shrouded in exotic German-import mystery—a brand
nobody else had, with one fateful advantage. Whereas most turntables
of the day spun with a belt-driven mechanism that made cutting and
cueing a bit stiff, the direct-drive Thorens were easy to spin up or spin
back manually, were far more vibration- and skip-resistant, and could
stop and start on a dime. This gave Herc a head start on other DJs who
had to wait until the more affordable and available Technics 1200 caught
on in the wider market, at which point it was still nearly impossible to
match his system in power.

One of Herc's peers, said to be an attendee at the famous 1520 Sedgwick party, was a fellow child of West Indian immigrants who went by
the name Afrika Bambaataa—a legendary DJ in his own right. Bambaataa's crew-turned-movement, the Zulu Nation, transformed the
reformed gang the Black Spades into a battalion of hip-hop activists
that organized parties and cultural events throughout the Bronx, then
all of New York, until their Afrocentric perspective permeated global
hip-hop thoroughly by the end of the '80s. Whereas Herc set himself
apart as the DJ with the best sound system, the up-and-coming Bambaataa, who played his first gig at the Bronx River Community Center
in November of '76, made his name through his eclecticism. Bam didn't
just unearth breaks from funk and R&B, he subscribed to disco pools
and caught on to what was going on in the more esoteric corners of clubland, while simultaneously raiding the annals of classic rock and new
wave for breaks—Kraftwerk rubbing elbows with the Rolling Stones,
the Beatles with the B-52s.

DJ sets were one thing, but the competitive post-gang nature of the
Bronx demanded DJ *battles,* and a battle at the Webster Avenue Police
Athletic League best personified Herc and Bam's different approaches

in one outlandish showdown circa 1977. As Zulu Nation member and DJ Jazzy Jay recalled it, Herc took so long to set up his massive system that Bambaataa's crew used it as an excuse to keep their set going into overtime, playing well past the slot they'd been allotted and showing off all the rare and obscure breaks in Bam's crates. Herc was clearly annoyed, but he couldn't say he didn't warn them: he turned his Echoplex up and began to intone, over and over: "Bambaataa, could you please turn your system down?" And with every time the request was ignored, Herc just cranked it louder, made the echo boom deeper, sent the reverb shaking further, repeating "Bambaataa, turn your system down" with the voice of a soundclash god, one man's booming system versus another's bottomless crates. The Zulu Nation did their best to hold their ground, but as Jay put it, "We started reaching for knobs, turning shit up, speakers started coughing. And then [Herc] comes on with 'The Mexican' . . . By about sixteen bars into the song, we just gave up, turned off all the fucking amps. Turned everything off. And the drums didn't even come in yet. When the drums came in, all the walls . . . just like VROOM. That was it." The Herculoids had spoken. And their heirs were listening.

• • •

Joseph Saddler was born in Barbados on New Year's Day 1958, a party rocker's equivalent to entering the world on Christmas. As a toddler, he'd peek in on the New Year's house parties his parents would throw at their recently settled Bronx home and learn to associate his birthday with the sounds of their revelry—which meant the sounds of James Brown, of Chuck Berry, of Miles Davis. Like most of his pioneer-generation hip-hop peers, his education came through his parents' records, usually listened to during family get-togethers, but sometimes surreptitiously when his father wasn't home. As a kid, Joseph wasn't just fascinated by the music itself: it was the *how* of it all, the strange mystery of what happened when you dropped a skinny little needle on the grooves set in a round platter and made the speakers bump. The sounds were endlessly compelling, not just as works of music, but elements of technology, a feat of engineering that fatefully stuck with Joseph throughout his life.

Joseph was a gearhead, a compulsive experimenter who was relentlessly eager to find out how everything worked—which usually involved taking apart some appliance or another and examining it in an attempt to figure out what each inscrutable piece of electronics was responsible for doing. By his mid-teens, Joseph had enrolled in Samuel Gompers High School, a vocational technical school intended to educate and prepare students for a future in skilled trades. To his teachers, Joseph came across as an inquisitive enthusiast, likely bound for a career as an electrical engineer. But the knowledge that Joseph took to heart went toward a different goal—to construct his own sound system from scratch.

The South Bronx would provide. The battered, abandoned cars that littered the streets may have had their radios jimmied out long before Joseph got to them, but a surprising number still had intact speakers and yards of audio cable left attached. Broken electronics were dumped in abandoned lots by garbagemen or other people uninterested in disposing of them properly, and Joseph pulled it all apart to salvage any working components he could. He even picked up a janky belt-driven Thorens turntable for nothing when a local connect ditched it in the trash after failing to sell it on the street. Not every DIY project was a resounding success: one day Joseph brought home some plastic meat-shipping containers that he planned on converting into speaker cabinets, but put off washing out the remnants of bacon residue and stunk up the whole house. But by the time he relocated his gear to the basement of a brownstone owned by a friend's father, he had built a remarkable Frankenstein's monster of a system—an array of speakers hung from the ceiling off wires like flies in a spiderweb—that was suitable enough to impress his friends.

It wasn't as though it was easy for Joseph to impress people otherwise. His efforts to get down like the b-boys that were creating the new style of dance in the Bronx resulted in pratfall-style injury, and his short-lived tagalong experience with graffiti left him with almost nothing—save, at least for the first time in broad daylight, an alias: FLASH 163. (A friend from the same street, fatefully named Gordon, picked up on the shared reference of the Flash Gordon science fiction character and figured Joseph ran fast enough to make the aka doubly fitting.) But the atmosphere was perfectly charged for a Bronx teenager to find one foot or another in the hip-hop world, and those who went looking would find both feet in Kool Herc's territory soon enough.

A prime opportunity came in the spring of '74 at a free park jam at the Cedar Park Rec Center—Herc's main venue once he'd found his parties too big for 1520 Sedgwick. It was an hour-plus walk from where Joseph lived on East 163rd Street, but it didn't take him the entirety of his westward journey to hear it: two blocks away, he recognized the break from "The Mexican," booming through the loudest, most authoritatively deep speakers he or anyone else in the Bronx had ever heard. By the time he arrived at the park proper, he saw Herc surrounded by his Herculords, a titan among selecters, layering break over break, bellowing his name through the Echoplex, driving all the b-boys into a frenzy. The songs Herc played that Joseph knew became revelatory in their stacked-speaker stature, and the ones he didn't know hinted at the possibilities of a far bigger world than the one he'd found in his father's formative record collection. Joseph didn't dance. But he witnessed.

Soon he'd have a new sound system: a group of local toughs called the Casanovas, impressed with his record selection during an impromptu park jam of his own, gifted him a top-notch setup that they had mysteriously come across shortly after it had been stolen from the renowned Bronx club Hunts Point Palace. And to find the choicest material to play on that system, Joseph would make treks to Manhattan in search of obscure breaks, whether they came from under-the-radar funk acts that other DJs hadn't caught onto yet or rock bands they hadn't even thought to look for. Searching not just for songs but for breaks, for pieces to make into a new whole, would be a mode of record collecting and curation that would soon become one of hip-hop's greatest contributions to music: sticking to genre conventions or known quantities would get you left in the dust. Real DJs ignored the big names on the front of the record for the small ones on the back. Certain previously semi-anonymous session players became must-haves. Did Bernard Purdie play drums? Was Chuck Rainey on bass? Cop that shit.

By 1975, the newly self-christened DJ Flash had the kind of gear and record crates that would make him a contender—but in the Bronx, contending wasn't the same as reigning. His system was professional grade, but Herc's was a world-beater. His selections were choice, but Bam's record pool connections would soon prove tastemaking. And so, if Flash couldn't dominate through his speakers or his wax, he'd have to find a third way: to floor people with pure technique. Herc had his own, to be sure, but as Flash studied his inspiration, he began to notice not just what Herc did well—creating a flow from one record to the next that set actual moods or told musical stories—but what he did that Flash could do better.

Herc could segue from one record to the next all right, but his mixing wasn't as concerned with matching up beats per minute or making things sound seamless. Flash felt his sense of timing could tighten up. And so the kid who spent most of his life studying the effects of rotation on recorded music came of age analyzing just how he could manipulate this rotation to warp time and space: turn a few bars' worth of music into a whole breakdown, seconds into minutes, a fleeting thought into an entire thesis. Every hip-hop DJ strove to do this. Flash just needed to figure out how to do it *tight*.

It seems obvious in retrospect: all Flash really had to do was let one copy of the record play out, cue up the other copy right to the point the break would come in, and spin that record there with his hand until he cued up the right spot, at which point he let go right on the beat, repeating with the other copy back and forth between the two turntables. He needed direct-drive turntables and a quick-switching crossfader between them to work, as well as immaculate timing, manual dexterity, and ability to visually isolate where on the record the break was. Flash's preferred method, to denote in grease pencil where the breaks began using the positions of a clock face, proved to be the most useful.

It allowed for more precision than merely picking up and dropping the needle back on the wax. But it also needed to break an unwritten rule for DJs to never touch the actual grooved surface of the record. And in breaking that rule, Flash's "Quik Mix Theory" opened the door for another innovation that became the hip-hop DJ's most uniquely characteristic maneuver. Flash claims he stumbled across it in '75 during a practice session when he played a mix of "It's Just Begun" and the Commodores' "Assembly Line" for two of his b-boy friends, missed a cue by a fraction of a second, and manually pushed the record back into place in time with the beat: a *zuka-zuka* sound that became its own additional form of percussion. For Flash, it was initially just a one-beat sort of flourish, a showoff way to keep the timing while winding back to the cue point.

Theodore Livingston, aka Grand Wizzard Theodore, was a friend and apprentice of Flash a few years his junior, whose own claim to discovery was a different stroke of accidental luck that same year: when his mom burst in his bedroom to complain about his loud stereo, Theodore put his hand on the record to stop it, but idly moved the record back and forth as she spoke to him; fascinated by the sound that resulted, he eventually found a way to use this technique in his own DJ sets, but in a more elaborate, drawn-out way that was a miniature showcase in itself. Flash picked up on Theodore's innovation and took it up himself, a trick in his repertoire that would soon come to eclipse every other ace up his sleeve.

But Flash discovered that his way of DJing wouldn't make for an instant phenomenon. After the friends who witnessed that primordial scratch talked him up all around the neighborhood, he debuted his Quik Mix Theory technique at what is now known as Behagen Playground to a crowd of hundreds. And nobody danced. Flash was devastated. For the next month, he considered his DJ career all but dead, especially as word spread that his whole style of scratching would destroy records and made him out to be an incompetent amateur.

Eventually Flash's absence at the park jams was enough to spur the neighborhood's resident community lookout, a mother/mentor figure to the kids known as Miss Rose, to get in touch with a man she figured could help break Flash out of his malaise. This man was a DJ, but unlike Herc, he prioritized Flash's idea of smooth-flowing beatmatching over the power of a massive sound system. And Flash caught on, even before he spoke to the DJ, that his whole style was on point and more than compatible with Flash's own vision for what he wanted to achieve on the turntables. This man's name was Pete DJ Jones. And he played disco.

• • •

Hip-hop and disco have often seemed at odds—the street-tough Bronx versus bourgie Manhattan, Adidas versus Gucci, James Brown versus KC and the Sunshine Band—but even at their most strained relationship, they're still brothers from another mother. While Herc and Flash were extending breaks on wax for b-boys in the park, Tom Moulton was editing up tapes for the crowds at Fire Island's Sandpiper club, seamlessly stringing together danceable up-tempo soul cuts and using his lingering name recognition from his old record industry gig to ask record labels for instrumentals he could futz with. Moulton liked the tracks, he just wanted them to be a bit longer; after some experimenting, he found out that the only way he could really pull that off was to lengthen the instrumental break. By 1975, the same year Flash met Jones, Moulton was engineering his way to a new musical rearrangement mode eventually called the "remix," turning singles into such marathon expeditions of extended dance grooves that the DJ's industry standard format had to inevitably gravitate to the album-sized 12-inch single.

And so Flash's disco-world apprenticeship to Pete DJ Jones was, if a bit fish-out-of-water at first, still a schooling in a parallel world whose rules could largely apply to his own. Many of the ideas Flash had either come to independently or did for the first time in a hip-hop context were disco simpatico: the idea of matching beats per minute, his "peeka-boo" method of previewing the cue point of the record he had lined up next through a pair of headphones, and his crates. They were closer to the glamorous Manhattan crowd's preferences, but still part of what would become the lineage of hip-hop's own sound.

Funky disco purveyors like Hamilton Bohannon and Brooklyn's own B. T. Express were big, but the Philadelphia sound was *huge,* and even a couple years after it dropped, MFSB's string-driven, intensely groov-ing "Love Is the Message"—a Tom Moulton favorite—was the sound of every dancefloor ninety-something miles east of Philly, whether it lit up or not. And "The Mexican" worked with the Manhattan disco scene, too, just like it did in the Bronx, echoing the self-expressive eclecticism that Francis Grasso and the Loft's David Mancuso had liberated at the beginning of the decade.

Soon, Flash earned the title of "Grandmaster"—inspired by a hood named Joe Kidd who compared Flash's mixing ability to a form of chess genius—and an army of fans so eager to hype up his skills on the mic that he wound up with five of them sharing his stage. As a crew, Grand-master Flash and the Furious Five—Melle Mel, Cowboy, Kid Creole, Scorpio, and Raheim—had hit on something distinct. From DJ Holly-wood onward to Herc and younger up-and-comers like Lovebug Star-ski, DJs were often expected to provide their own crowd-participation stage banter, such as the classic "Throw your hands in the air / And wave 'em like you just don't care" and "When I say ho, *you* say ho!" call-and-response lines. Starski in particular coined the phrase "hip-hop" itself in a back-and-forth military march cadence with the Furious Five's Cow-boy, though it took a while to catch on as a descriptor of an entire sub-culture.

But having an ensemble cast of MCs who each brought something different to the table was key, and crowds grew accordingly. In Septem-ber of '76, their ability to rock discos, park jams, and crew battles against

the likes of the Treacherous Three and Cold Crush Brothers earned
them a surprising opportunity from promoter Ray Chandler: a gig at the
Audubon Ballroom, the nearly three-thousand-seat venue where Malcolm X had been shot and killed in 1965. Flash figured it was a risk, but
the fact that they packed the house with lines down the block was all the
proof they needed that this whole thing was going somewhere. By 1977,
Flash had earned himself a host of new gigs—including a weekly DJ set
in a South Bronx club called, of all things, Disco Fever.

1977 was New York's annus horribilis and a turning point all in
one. While the wider world was riveted by the chaos that the increasingly embattled city was going through that year—the contentious shit
talking from newly signed Yankees slugger Reggie Jackson, the unknow-
able horror of fame-seeking serial killer Son of Sam, the music press's
growing fascination with the iconoclastic punk sounds emerging from
CBGB in the Bowery—the hip-hop world was undergoing a moment of
flux. That summer, looting broke out during a citywide blackout, which
had a profound effect on the DJ scene in the Bronx: countless purloined
stereo systems and turntables found their way into the hands of aspiring pretenders to Herc's throne everywhere. That same summer, during
a gig at the Executive Playhouse, Herc found himself in the middle of a
wrong-place-wrong-time situation when three teenagers causing what
Herc called "a discrepancy" wound up stabbing the DJ three times—
twice in the side, once across the hands. Herc survived, but the incident
gave him enough pause that he felt compelled to go on hiatus.

1977 was also the year the New York–rooted disco scene went international, from the opening of the infamous celebrity magnet Studio
54 to the box office and Billboard chart phenomenon that was the
Brooklyn-set (and largely whitewashed) *Saturday Night Fever.* And if one
group out of New York could be considered the catalyst for disco's late-
decade emergence, it was Chic. A group of conceptual-minded jazz-funk
session musicians led by master songwriters Nile Rodgers and Bernard
Edwards—formerly known as the Big Apple Band until Walter Murphy
notched smash hit "A Fifth of Beethoven" with a backup band of the
same name—Chic aimed to capture the soul-jazz sound of Donald Byrd,
the stylish Euro-fashion allure of Roxy Music, and the disguised-in-
plain-sight alter-ego vibe of Kiss. And in a disco world where who your
band members were was less important than how the music they made

sounded on the dancefloor, Rodgers and Edwards took their session-chops anonymity to the ideal destination: their picture wasn't even on the front *or* back of their '77 debut LP.

As New York's long hot summer entered its final weeks, the band's debut single, "Dance, Dance, Dance (Yowsah, Yowsah, Yowsah)," ran wild in discos across the country. Its follow-up, "Everybody Dance," was a hit, too, but the band's anonymity had its drawbacks: Rodgers and Edwards weren't considered famous enough to make it past Studio 54's infamously elitist doormen, even though they'd been invited there by Grace Jones and their records were constant fixtures on the set list. They were so irritated by this development that they went home and vented their way through a spur-of-the-moment protest song. The refrain—"Ahhhh, *fuck off!*"—stuck with them, and not wanting to waste a catchy hook on a surefire FCC ban, they reworked it as "Freak out!" The ensuing song, "Le Freak," became the biggest-selling single in Atlantic Records history.

Chic's music was tailor-made for DJs, but music *by* DJs was still an unknown quantity, especially for a genre as young and in flux as hip-hop. At one point in late '78, a downtown art-scene figure and hip-hop enthusiast named Fred Brathwaite—aka Fab 5 Freddy—suggested to Melle Mel that Grandmaster Flash and the Furious Five should cut a record, and Mel was thoroughly confused by the idea. *A record of a record?* Flash turned down similar overtures, too: "I was asked before anybody. And I was like, 'Who would want to hear a record which I was spinning rerecorded with MCing over it?'"

There had been albums of disco mixes before. 1974's *Disco Par-r-r-ty,* released on NYC-based Polydor imprint Spring Records, was the first, and contained two sides' worth of continuous-mix music featuring many of the same tracks (James Brown's "Sex Machine," Mandrill's "Fence Walk," Lyn Collins's "Think [About It]") that formed the bedrock of Bronx hip-hop DJing. And some DJs followed in DJ Hollywood's footsteps by selling their own mixtapes.

But hip-hop was still a largely regional phenomenon best experienced live, and for DJs the live money was far more reliable. Who'd want to hear a recording of a DJ? What was the point of an MC if there wasn't a crowd to hype up, but rather just some kid listening in their bedroom or on a transistor radio? Clubs could make money off DJs and MCs because they tended to run cheaper than hosting traditional bands, but

how could a record label translate that success, even as a growing phenomenon, into actual sales?

This, fatefully, is where Chic and hip-hop intersected for the
first (and by no means last) time. Their 1979 single "Good Times" was
released right as June turned to July, and hit #1 on both the pop and
R&B charts in August. But it was their last big hit in the United States,
where a burgeoning cultural fatigue with disco spurred a popular backlash. At least a few Chic LPs and singles were doubtlessly blown up as
part of the conflagration that was Disco Demolition Night, the notorious record-destroying stunt at Chicago's Comiskey Park that has been
called the day disco died. (Irony of ironies, it happened between games
of a Major League Baseball doubleheader featuring teams from the two
cities, Detroit and Chicago, which would come to redefine post-disco
dance music in the 1980s.) When "Good Times" was knocked off the
top of the pop charts by the Knack's new wave / power pop horndog
rock anthem "My Sharona," the sly implications of doom in the second
verse of Chic's waning hit—"A rumor has it that it's getting late / Time
marches on, just can't wait / The clock keeps turning, why hesitate? / You
silly fool, you can't change your fate"—came across in instant hindsight
as disco's reckoning with its own cultural expiration date. Anything that
wasn't palatable to the straight white males in the eighteen-to-thirty-
four demographic had its radio days numbered.

And yet that Bernard Edwards bassline was a killer—one that held
down a groove so undeniable that it would find itself quickly capitalized
on for a historic first. In August 1979, producer, songwriter, and record
label founder Sylvia Robinson took out some studio time to cut the first
single for her brand-new hip-hop label, Sugar Hill. Robinson was one
of the label owners who'd approached Flash earlier and asked him if he
was interested in putting out a record, but when Flash and a host of others skeptically declined the offer she assembled a group of ringers from
Englewood, New Jersey, and had them cut a single.

Before 1979, there were more than a few albums that people now
point to as precursors of rap as we know it, from Pigmeat Markham's
comedic 1968 single "Here Comes the Judge" to the poetry-and-
percussion works of Gil Scott-Heron and the Last Poets. The 1973 proto-
rap album *Hustlers Convention*, recorded by Last Poets founding member
Jalal Mansur Nuriddin under the alias "Lightnin' Rod" even included a
track where he delivered a verse over the Chuck Rainey Coalition doing

an instrumental cover of Buddy Miles's "Them Changes"—a hip-hop prototype if there ever was one. And even Fatback Band, a New York funk group that had already built up a string of modestly successful dance hits starting with 1972's "Street Dance," dropped a single in March '79 titled "King Tim III (Personality Jock)" that's considered the first legit commercially released rap record.

But "Rapper's Delight," as credited to the Sugar Hill Gang, was the catalyst for rap as an emerging genre of recorded music, whether or not it was considered legit. The lyrics were largely aggregated or otherwise lifted from routines that Robinson and the MCs—Wonder Mike, Big Bank Hank, and Master Gee—had heard elsewhere. (One infamous instance involved Cold Crush Brothers member Grandmaster Caz offering to lend Hank any of his lines from a rhyme book, and Hank using one that actually wound up referring to *himself* by Caz's alias "Casanova Fly.") Nobody in any of the five boroughs had ever heard of the Sugar Hill Gang, and yet there they were in September with a single that would become the first Top 40 rap hit in history. And they weren't even using a DJ—the "break" was replayed live by a bunch of session musicians. The artists that had spent the last six years building the very structure of hip-hop music were confused at best, pissed at worst.

Chic were pissed, too. "Good Times" was at or near #1 when "Rapper's Delight" was recorded, had slipped out of the Top 10 when it was released, and was out of the charts entirely along with Chic's underperforming follow-up singles when "Rapper's Delight" peaked at #36 in January of 1980. That wasn't the best year for Nile Rodgers and Bernard Edwards. Their album *Real People* stiffed in a discophobic market. Their mix of Diana Ross's album *Diana* was rejected by Motown for being too uncharacteristic for the singer and was replaced by a watered-down (if commercially successful) version. And Queen—one of the rock bands so beloved by the disco-sucks demographic—notched a #1 of their own with "Another One Bites the Dust," a significant lift of Chic's signature heavy bottom-end bassline and chicken-scratch guitar sounds, which Chic were no longer entrusted with by the labels that once swore by them.

And now here was this weird novelty song that just flat-out *copied* them? Subsequently, the first commercially released single to position itself as a re-creation of hip-hop, flawed as it was, also became the first hip-hop single to result in a lawsuit for uncleared appropriation of a preexisting piece of music. Rodgers and Edwards eventually earned their publishing, but not before being intimidated by a mysterious foursome of goons at their Power Station studio who hinted that it would be "in their best interest" to leave Sugar Hill Records alone.

"Rapper's Delight" might have been the first spark, but it took a bit longer for something a bit more true to the origins of hip-hop to make it to mass market. Eventually Sugar Hill signed Grandmaster Flash and the Furious Five shortly after they cut a debut single, "Superrappin'," for rival Enjoy Records shortly after "Rapper's Delight" beat them to the punch. And after a couple early successes for the group based around their MC routines—"Freedom" and "The Birthday Party" both hit the R&B Top 10 in 1980—Flash finally got his spotlight. Released in 1981, "The Adventures of Grandmaster Flash on the Wheels of Steel" was a showcase of Flash displaying the turntable technique that, descending from the lessons of Kool Herc, became the first commercially released recording of hip-hop as it originally existed, a DJ-rooted form of music. Flash needed three turntables and a pair of mixers for the three-hour session, which required somewhere in the neighborhood of a dozen takes; every time he missed a cue or was otherwise unsatisfied, he started over from the beginning just to make sure the whole thing was an unedited performance.

Blondie's song "Rapture," the NYC punk icons' effort to meet rap on its own turf and a #1 hit in March of '81, included superstar singer Deborah Harry actually name-checking Flash—"Flash is fast / Flash is cool"—which Flash naturally cut into a sharp back-and-forth as if to say *that's me she's talking about on a chart topper.* Then he drops in "Good Times," old news by '81 but a savvy way to start his own Merry-Go-Round: *this* is how that break from "Rapper's Delight" was *supposed* to sound. He scratches through it, drops in a few bars from the unmistakable break to "Apache" for some of that '73 flavor, extends that break for a second go-round, then *immaculately* feints the drums-and-bass groove to "Another One Bites the Dust" before letting the break play out.

And then he scratches alongside it to the beat of the bassline, the scratch revealed not just as a showy maneuver but a piece of percussion in itself, recorded music remolded in real time. Then back to "Good Times"—*ay Queen, you know where your shit came from*—while he cuts in his own crew, from the previous Grandmaster Flash and the Furious Five single "Freedom" shouting "Grandmaster! Cut faster!" The parade-of-hits itinerary plays out medley-style through a couple other Sugar Hill cuts—their own "The Birthday Party" and Sugarhill Gang's "8th Wonder"—but "Good Times" is the glue that holds it all together, reemerging as the refrain that Flash uses to build increasingly elaborate segues and scratches.

"The Adventures of Grandmaster Flash on the Wheels of Steel" wasn't a hit outside the clubs, but it was something more important: a piece of history that doubled as a brilliant metacommentary on how hip-hop could alter the actual meanings of musical works. It was the kind of music criticism, sonic manipulation, and flat-out dance groove that only a DJ could make, and only a hip-hop DJ could conceive of. It didn't just open doors, it tore the roof off—and the future of music was wide open to anybody brave enough to reach out for it.

## 2 | *Change the Beat*
### Hip-Hop's First Crossover

**Hip-hop's reckoning with punk and new wave gives rise to early crossovers—and the makings of its own reinvention.**

IT's JULY 30, 1982, about a year and a half after Blondie's Grandmaster Flash nod in "Rapture" gave him his first crossover cosign. At the Roxy NYC, a Chelsea roller rink / nightclub and an epicenter of hip-hop culture, another person namechecked in the song is checking out a remarkable collision of worlds. He's Fab 5 Freddy, and he knows his way around. A graffiti writer who branched out as a scenester when he studied a book on pop art and noticed a resemblance to the subway-car tagging taking late '70s New York by storm, he'd soon become a major chronicler of and ambassador between the downtown gallery scene and old-school hip-hop. One moment, he might be catching a DJ battle in a Brooklyn armory; the next he'd be taking on both sides of the lens as both a cameraman and regular guest for *TV Party,* a cable access show hosted by Warhol associate and former *Interview* magazine editor Glenn O'Brien.

This particular night, he's catching a showing of Julien Temple's Sex Pistols pseudo-documentary *The Great Rock 'n' Roll Swindle,* which had been released back in 1980 but hadn't made its way to the States until this limited showing at the Roxy. The Sex Pistols had long since broken up, with John Lydon having formed Public Image Ltd and Sid Vicious having died of an overdose in the West Village before the '70s concluded. And the punk crowd that made the Bowery club CBGB famous had been mutating into something else entirely—post-punkers, no wavers, and other assorted art-scene types who still wanted to dance even though the disco scene had locked them out. When the film ends, Freddy notices what happens when the mostly white downtown punk rockers start to share the floor with the black and Latin hip-hoppers who came in from uptown. "I just anticipated kids from the Bronx beating the shit out of weird-looking punk rockers," he recalled. Instead, the dancefloor brought them together: "You had punk rock kids with mohawks, standing next to b-boys. It was the first time each other was seeing each other."

But the avant-garde of downtown Manhattan had already begun to warm to hip-hop, albeit gradually. If punk and disco were opposite poles of late '70s NYC club culture—a dichotomy established early on in an editorial in the inaugural of *Punk* magazine, January '76, headlined "Death to Disco Shit!"—the early '80s found a far more compatible culture in this new DJ-driven, MC-boosted, break-dancer- and graffiti-inspiring grassroots movement. It was dance culture without the doorman, from the streets instead of the boardrooms, and laced with a sense of an entirely new paradigm—and, as so often happens in majority-white subcultures dating back to before jazz, it incorporated a fascination with black culture that ranged from legit camaraderie to wide-eyed fetishism. Once something gets picked up by that subculture, there's a briefly thrilling and hopeful stretch where creativity flourishes, and then the money vultures swoop down, cash in, and leave a skeleton to be exhibited in a history museum as an example of What Was.

The punk world's run-up to this cross-cultural meeting began in earnest years before the Roxy scene described by Brathwaite, and even before the recording of Blondie's "Rapture"—all thanks to one of the most unexpected groups of hip-hop converts thinkable. British punk sensations the Clash were one of the most critically respected bands in the world as the '70s came to a close, especially when their double LP *London Calling* established them as masters of subgenre-uniting style that could incorporate rockabilly, reggae, New Orleans R&B, and disco under the same umbrella. The black-and-white cover photo of Paul Simonon about to smash his bass onstage like an executioner bringing down an axe was interpreted as a band closing the door on traditional mainstream rock and roll that Elvis Presley had opened—a point driven home by the *London Calling* sleeve art typography that mimicked Elvis's self-titled 1956 debut LP on RCA.

And its decade-straddling release dates, hitting UK shelves in December '79 and crossing the Atlantic to reach American stores in January 1980, stood as a year-zero statement in itself, if mostly in hindsight: *we've paid tribute to nearly every postwar pop music form we could get our hands on—so what's next?* One year later, *Sandinista!* was their answer: as sprawling a look into the future of pop music as *London Calling* was into its past, the overstuffed, overambitious, relentlessly adventurous triple LP steeped itself in dancehall, electro-dub, world music, indie pop, and every other genre forecast that *NME* and *Melody Maker* hadn't figured out a name for yet. And it opened with a rap track.

"The Magnificent Seven," recorded in NYC's Electric Lady Studios in April of 1980, didn't come from nowhere. The Clash had arrived in New York with little precise planning on just what they were going to write and record, but the ideas came to them anyways, fast and frantic and often difficult for the band themselves to even describe. (In a hand-written list of twenty songs that had been recorded during the album's sessions through the end of March, Joe Strummer denoted the style of two tracks as "funk," three as "Clashabilly," and six simply as "strange.") When they weren't in the studio, they were immersing themselves in New York's nightlife, a band that once sang that they were "so bored with the U.S.A." back in '77 finding out firsthand that there was a world of exciting cross-cultural creativity hidden beneath all the fast food and TV cop shows and imperialism.

Hip-hop proved impossible to miss, especially for a group of young left-leaning punks hungry for newness. At some point, various members of the band got in the habit of raiding record stores for every hip-hop 12-inch they could find, with Mick Jones in particular becoming so obsessed he'd started carrying a boom box around everywhere, blasting mixtapes. (The rest of the band gave him the tongue-in-cheek nickname "Whack Attack.") "The Magnificent Seven" was written and rapped by Strummer, who wasn't so much auditioning for a role as Melle Mel Mark II as he was revamping Dylanesque "Subterranean Homesick Blues"–style stream-of-consciousness sociopolitical absurdity ("Italian mobster shoots a lobster / Seafood restaurant gets out of hand / A car in the fridge, a fridge in the car / Like cowboys do in TV land"). But the bassline, provided by Ian Dury & the Blockheads' Norman Watt-Roy filling in for a film-shooting Paul Simonon, was impossible to deny. Frankie Crocker, WBLS's dance music tastemaker, made its dub version "The Magnificent Dance" a smash hit among black audiences. The crossover, it seemed, was primed to jump both ways.

By the time the Clash set up their now-legendary run of concerts at Bonds International Casino in May–June 1981—an eight-show stand they expanded to seventeen concerts when tickets were nearly double oversold—they had three hip-hop-style cuts in their setlist. Along with "The Magnificent Seven," there was another *Sandinista!* selection called "Lightning Strikes (Not Once but Twice)"—a cartoonish but affectionate outsider travelogue of New York—and the electro-funk-tinged single "This Is Radio Clash," whose sleeve art and video made for a figurative and literal backdrop for the work of graffiti artist turned European tourmate Futura 2000. But magnanimous punkers that they were, the Clash decided that if they were going to take their own stab at hip-hop, it'd be only right if one of the acts that fueled their newfound enthusiasm made their way onto the bill. And so Grandmaster Flash and the Furious Five, still a couple months prior to the release of "The Adventures of Grandmaster Flash on the Wheels of Steel," were given the honors of opening on the first two nights of the series: May 28–29, 1981.

It was, as recognized by nearly every musician involved, a complete disaster. The hostility of the Clash's audience toward Grandmaster Flash and the Furious Five seemed motivated by some nebulous sour mood; postmortem concert reviews cited technical difficulties, poor sound, and an overcrowded audience as possible motivators for the bad vibe. As the set progressed, the crowd grew increasingly unwelcoming—Melle Mel's call-and-response had his "Say hoooo!" was answered with "*Fuck you!*"—until a barrage of paper cups during the opening verses of "The Birthday Party" cut their set short. When the Clash finally hit the stage, Strummer made a point to shame the audience for their disrespect, a moment that seemed to haunt him for years after he saw the limits of his audience's tolerance for discovering new sounds. But it echoed an atmosphere of format-segregated rock backlash that had been brewing for a long time, from the debris of Disco Demolition Night in '79 to the infamous abuse Prince received from the audience when he opened for the Rolling Stones in Los Angeles later in '81. *We don't listen to your shit, so what the fuck are you even doing here?*

Maybe part of the problem was that hip-hop was party music. It was not, as yet, seen as *rebel* music—not by the standards of the aging rock establishment, anyways, compared to the transgression offered by punk. One potential reason for this was bluntly addressed in April 1979, when rock critic Lester Bangs wrote an article for the *Village Voice* titled "The White Noise Supremacists," a mortified look at racism, ironic or otherwise, in New York's early punk culture. "This was stuff even I had to recognize as utterly repellent. I first noticed it the first time I threw a party.

The staff of *Punk* magazine came, as well as members of several of the hottest CBGB's bands, and when I did what we always used to do at parties in Detroit—put on soul records so everybody could dance—I began to hear this: 'What're you playing all that nigger disco shit for, Lester?'"

But even the increasingly woke Bangs had his reservations about hip-hop. For the 1981 *Village Voice* Pazz & Jop Critics Poll ranking the most acclaimed albums and singles of the year—won by *Sandinista!* in the former category, with "The Adventures of Grandmaster Flash on the Wheels of Steel" coming in third in the latter—Bangs submitted a protest ballot lamenting what he saw as the sorry state of music that year. His entire perspective on hip-hop came down to six words: "Rap is nothing, or not enough."

• • •

"The Adventures of Grandmaster Flash on the Wheels of Steel" was definitive as a document of early DJing, a revolutionary piece of music to those in the know. What it wasn't was a hit. It peaked in the States at #55 on the Billboard R&B singles chart, some fifty-plus places lower than the Top 5 showings for "Good Times," "Rapper's Delight," and "Another One Bites the Dust." "Adventures" might have been doing well on New York radio, but it wasn't moving off shelves, at least nationwide, and Flash heard word from friends in the Sugar Hill offices that Sylvia Robinson wasn't thrilled. Flash and the Furious Five had to reconvene and consolidate some more ideas for potential hits.

One of Flash's inspirations came from another downtown crossover: Tom Tom Club, an offshoot of art-punk legends Talking Heads featuring husband-and-wife team Chris Frantz and Tina Weymouth, who cut a self-titled album and released it in October 1981. Key among the record's tracks were the lyrical stream-of-consciousness rhymefest "Wordy Rappinghood" and the joyous cartoon funk of "Genius of Love," the latter of which paid tribute to first major-label rapper Kurtis Blow alongside established musical legends like Smokey Robinson and Bob Marley. Both singles collectively hit #1 on the Billboard Dance chart in January 1982, making Tom Tom Club the second act to make pole position with a rap song (so to speak).

"It's Nasty (Genius of Love)" was Grandmaster Flash and the Furious Five's attempt to capitalize on it, though like other Sugar Hill projects outside the special scratch exhibition Flash agitated for, this cut replayed the "Genius of Love" riff using a live band instead of cutting and scratching it. The song peaked at #22 on Billboard's Hot Soul Singles chart in the last week of March '82, just a few notches behind their peak of #19 for "Freedom" in October 1980. It wound up being the last thing they'd release before they found themselves at a turning point that changed the mainstream perception of hip-hop forever.

Ed "Duke Bootee" Fletcher wasn't a part of the original, pre–Sugar Hill incarnation of Grandmaster Flash and the Furious Five. He was a writer, percussionist, and sometime rapper for the Sugar Hill house band with an adventurous ear developed through years of jazz gigs, and Robinson saw him as a go-to guy with hitmaking potential. One night, while hanging out with coproducer Jiggs Chase and smoking a joint, Duke noticed his leg was hanging off the edge of the couch he was lying on and wrangled that observation into a hook: "Don't push me, 'cause I'm close to the edge / I'm tryin' not to lose my head."

The rest came to him loud and clear, drawn from casual observation of the day-to-day drama going on in the park across the street from his house in Elizabeth, New Jersey—nicer digs than the South Bronx, but not immune to trouble. Soon, Duke had written another memorable refrain—"It's like a jungle sometimes it makes me wonder how I keep from goin' under"—and four verses' worth of social-struggle rhymes that invoked homeless women, porno theaters, piss-soaked stairwells, and the economic strife of early Reaganomics. (In one cruel twist, a memorable scenario in the first verse—"I tried to get away but I couldn't get far / 'Cause a man with a tow truck repossessed my car"—actually happened to Flash himself a few months before, only it was Sugar Hill who revoked the lease on the canary yellow Lincoln Continental they'd given him because he wasn't cranking hits out fast enough.)

If the lyrics to this new track, dubbed "The Message," were a shock, the music was its own kind of startling. Interpolating the Tom Tom Club might've been a good move for a party rap single, but Duke had immersed himself in the work of another Talking Heads side project: frontman David Byrne's incendiary, experimental album with futurist composer-producer Brian Eno, *My Life in the Bush of Ghosts*. If "The Adventures of Grandmaster Flash on the Wheels of Steel" was the breakthrough moment for hip-hop's cultural contributions to a musical language based around reinterpreting and deconstructing other artists' work, *My Life in the Bush of Ghosts* was avant-rock's moment, and it used a far more direct method of juxtaposing prerecorded pieces of existing music and sound. Following in the footsteps of cut-and-paste experiments by musicians like Holger Czukay and Cabaret Voltaire and picking up on the dance music world's possibilities brought up by dub and disco remixes, Eno and Byrne took pieces of singing, sermons, prayers, exorcisms, and radio call-in shows and manipulated them into "lead vocals" over their own compositions.

Duke hadn't capitalized on that idea just yet, preferring to focus more on the way the album's complex, asymmetric melodic elements were set around the bassline's more droning rhythmic simplicity. (In a case of a popular genre naming convention failing to catch on the first time, he liked to call this idea "trance music.") So while "The Message" still sounded compatible with the bouncy, roller-boogie jams put out by funk bands in the early '80s, it also had all the otherworldly electronic reverb and elasticity of an Eno/Byrne cut. Put it on a mix between a funk jam like Zapp's "More Bounce to the Ounce" and the *Bush of Ghosts* track "Regiment" if you want a powerful example of how it could all come together.

"The Message" wasn't the first explicitly sociopolitical hip-hop song; a B-side cut by an MC named Brother D, "How We Gonna Make the Black Nation Rise?" was dropping knowledge about racism, pollution, and economic inequality as early as 1980. (In the wake of "The Message," Island Records reissued it in 1982 as an A-side for the UK.) And the fifth and final verse of "The Message" that Melle Mel added to Duke's lyrics—"A child is born with no state of mind / Blind to the ways of mankind"—was repurposed by Mel from the group's 1979 pre–Sugar Hill single "Superrappin'." But to have an entire protest song on a similar level coming from a well-established group like Grandmaster Flash and the Furious Five at their peak was an even bigger deal. The catch was that most of the group was reluctant to even put their name on it. Flash and his crew were wary about dropping such a bleak-sounding track into their repertoire of party anthems, and Robinson took advantage of the group's reluctance to reduce the main MCs on the track down to just the two songwriters, Duke and Mel. The song was credited to Grandmaster Flash and the Furious Five, but in reality it was more the Furious One Plus One.

Still, Sylvia Robinson got the hit she and the rest of the world wanted. In a time before SoundScan made tracking record sales significantly more accurate, hitting only #62 on the Hot 100 seems like an accounting error, given how massive "The Message" was everywhere else—reported as a two-million shipper that went gold in less than three weeks, a dance club heavy-rotation pick, and a prominent #4 on the R&B chart that Billboard had recently (and bluntly) renamed "Hot Black Singles." Odds are it could've been even bigger if the recently launched MTV actually played the low-budget cinema verité video they shot for it—a New York street-scene overview that had the feeling of Martin Scorsese B-roll—but the network had been infamously leery of playing anything by black artists until Michael Jackson's *Thriller* sold all the copies in the world and forced their hand. Still, it became an anthem that dwarfed anything that had come before it in hip-hop; there's likely not a boombox that's been manufactured that never had "The Message" pumping through its dinner-plate-sized speakers.

In critical terms, "The Message" was the runaway singles winner of the 1982 *Village Voice* Pazz & Jop Critics Poll—earning fifty-two more votes than second-place finisher, Marvin Gaye's "Sexual Healing," and triple that of The Clash's "Rock the Casbah" at third. And its street-struggle themes won over critics who were skeptical about hip-hop's staying power. Melle Mel's closing verse is rightly hailed by rap scholars as an all-time great, even if it had been largely overlooked the first time around in '79, and Kurt Loder writing for *Rolling Stone* audaciously called it "the most detailed and devastating report from underclass America since Bob Dylan decried the lonesome death of Hattie Carroll." Its musical merits, meanwhile, were given the kind of attention that was usually reserved for a straight-up rock song. In a piece published on November 11, 1982, the *New York Times*' Robert Palmer focused on the Sugar Hill house band sound that Duke brought to the fore: "A searing protest from the ghetto and a brilliant funk record that boils funk down to a spare, mostly electronic dialogue of polyrhythms that is almost Zen in its emphasis on space and silence . . . it suggests that while technology is rapidly transforming the sound of black-oriented popular music, there is still no substitute for a first-rate rhythm section that stays together and plays together."

The man for whom that rhythm section substituted was optimistic, at least outwardly. "Until ['The Message'], rap had a limited audience, something that was either a novelty for kids or dance music just for the black audience," Flash explained to Robert Hilburn at the *Los*

*Angeles Times* for a feature piece on March 27, 1983. "We had always felt we could reach all people, regardless of age or color. That's what 'The Message' did for us." Something else "The Message" did for them was to push them further toward a repertoire of additional social-issue songs—including not just a follow-up in "New York, New York" but a literal sequel, "Message II (Survival)," the latter more accurately credited to Melle Mel & Duke Bootee. It seemed like an improvement over the scattershot identity the crew exhibited on their 1982 debut full-length LP, also titled *The Message*—"Dreamin'," "You Are," and "It's a Shame" all inexplicably sounded like they were aimed for an R&B cross-over market, as if the Furious Five were the Temptations of rap. But on that album and the singles they continued to put out into 1983, the actual presence of Flash—of the actual cut-and-scratch basis of hip-hop DJing—was greatly diminished. There were familiar breaks replayed by the house band, but good luck finding a *zuka-zuka* among them.

Instead, the next move for hip-hop was to climb all the way aboard a new sound that Grandmaster Flash and the Furious Five had found some promise in before "The Message" went massive. 1981's "Scorpio" was almost frightening in how robotic it sounded: take an antsy, subway-car-rhythm rattle of a beat, far closer to the contemporaneous electronic dance prototypes of Kraftwerk's *Computer Love* or Human League's *Dare* than the post-disco boogie funk they'd gotten audiences accustomed to. Then, drop a droning, monotone, yet intense hornet-buzz vocoder over it—a demon escaping from a *Tempest* arcade cabinet and demanding that you "shoooooow nooooooo shaaaaaaaaame, shake it baby!"

Hip-hop's relationship with this strain of electronic music had more than one historical offshoot to account for—"Sharevari," a 1981 single by Detroit's A Number of Names, featured faux-Eurotrash-accented rapping over a hypnotic analog synthesizer groove and anticipated a bumper crop of Motor City sounds that would soon coalesce under the name of techno. "Scorpio" and its New York–rooted, hip-hop-adjacent status as a new flavor of b-boy music christened it with a similar name: electro. If your crew didn't have a live band—or didn't want one—there was potential in investing in synths, sequencers, and drum machines, especially once they became more acceptable as a part of hip-hop.

Afrika Bambaataa was no stranger to the electronic sounds that disco and its '70s-ending offshoots were putting forth; the oft-bootlegged live

set sold as *Death Mix—Live!!!* in 1983 came from a circa-1979 set that featured such selections as "Firecracker" from Japanese synth-poppers Yellow Magic Orchestra and the choppy Eurodisco of Parisian-produced,
Chicago-rooted singer Queen Samantha. But the reason the potato-
fidelity *Death Mix—Live!!!* even saw a cash-in release was the runaway
success of 1982's "Planet Rock," credited to Afrika Bambaataa & Soulsonic Force and produced by a white disco remixer who'd just moved
to NYC from Boston by the name of Arthur Baker. Baker had worked
with Bambaataa before: after fatefully steering Bam away from doing a
rap over a "Genius of Love" beat, he suggested using Gwen McCrae's '81
single "Funky Sensation" as the basis for a backing track instead, and the
resulting "Jazzy Sensation" (credited to Afrika Bambaataa & the Jazzy
Five) was the first single ever released on Tommy Boy Records.

    But "Planet Rock" was a whole other world apart. An interpolation
of two different Kraftwerk songs—1977's "Trans-Europe Express" and
1981's "Numbers"—the unstoppable groove of "Planet Rock" was largely
created using beats sourced from a Roland TR-808 drum machine,
a deliberate effort to re-create the sound of the original Kraftwerk
records. (Baker had to stumble on a *Village Voice* classified ad reading
"Man with drum machine, 20 dollars a session" just to get access to one.)
Play the melody through a space-age polyphonic Prophet-5 synthesizer,
throw in a few explosion sounds and orchestra stabs that were stored in
a digital sampling synthesizer the studio just happened to have, and all
of a sudden you had the "substitute for a first-rate rhythm section" that
Palmer's *Times* piece hadn't anticipated.

    By the time Baker and Bambaataa had concocted a follow-up in Jan-
uary 1983, the hyperventilating arpeggiated sequencers and clean digital precision of "Looking for the Perfect Beat" had plenty of company.
The downtown scene took to electro with a feverish enthusiasm, finding its synthesized melodies and mechanical drumbeats readily compatible with new wave and synth-pop leading lights like New Order and
Depeche Mode. The fashion set caught on quick, though they had to
play catchup to one name in particular. Ruza Blue had hit New York as
a UK expat and former dance-mime troupe member, whose punk-world
bona fides included a job running a downtown boutique called World's
End 2, an offshoot of a famous London shop set up by former Pistols
manager Malcolm McLaren and fashion designer Vivienne Westwood.

    McLaren was also the manager of the new wave group Bow Wow

Wow, and when he booked them to play East Village club the Ritz in September of '81, he signed on Bambaataa and the b-boy Rock Steady Crew as openers. In the audience that night, Blue was an instant convert: "That was when my mouth dropped and hip-hop replaced punk for me in terms of main musical interests." Blue soon found an ideal guide in Fab 5 Freddy, who hung out with her at the Disco Fever and bestowed on her the hip-hop-style alias "Kool Lady Blue." And scenester-wise, what worked for London's Soho seemed to work for NYC's: when Blue established a hip-hop night in November '81 at Negril, a two-hundred-capacity basement club, both punks and b-boys gathered to watch the likes of Bambaataa and Jazzy Jay man the decks.

By June '82, she'd taken her club clout to the Roxy and established a "Wheels of Steel" dance night that drew from hip-hop and its components of funk and soul, while mixing in the latest cutting-edge post-punk, dub, and electro. An article in the April 1983 issue of *New York* magazine featuring Blue among the culturally influential Brits in NYC describes the scene as "that lively black youth culture that includes 'breaker dancing'—a complex form originating in the South Bronx—and the new music known as 'rap' and 'scratch.'" The vibe was thriving, even if the language hadn't entirely been finalized yet.

McLaren, meanwhile, had his own designs. While he was as fascinated by the deconstructive possibilities of hip-hop as any Guy Debord enthusiast could be, McLaren introduced the World's Famous Supreme Team in the liner notes of his 1983 LP *Duck Rock* with an almost deadpan *hey, have you heard about this crazy new thing* flatness: "The performance by the Supreme Team may require some explaining, but suffice to say they are DJs from New York City who have developed a technique using record players like instruments, replacing the power chord of the guitar with the needle of a gramophone, moving it manually backwards and forwards across the surface of a record. We call it scratching."

The 1982 single that preceded the *Duck Rock* LP, a cult hit called "Buffalo Gals," is preposterously weird in ways that simultaneously rely on musical innovation and outsider absurdity: a mixture of turntablism, minimalist drum machine beats, and square-dance calls based on the old blackface minstrel song of the same title, it was the most popular tribute to the art of scratching since "The Adventures of Grandmaster Flash on the Wheels of Steel." While Flash was reduced to a photo-op role in his own crew, only allowed to cut loose on the turntables during live shows,

the huckster who made and destroyed the Sex Pistols was hitting the
UK Top 10 with something far sillier—though it still proved irresistible
to old-school hip-hop fans anyways, since it still bumped hard at its core.

And it wasn't just the musical side of hip-hop that proved popular among the gallery set: another one of the *TV Party* crowd's big cultural coups was helping make graffiti an art-world sensation, as Glenn
O'Brien befriended a tagger turned expressionist pop artist named Jean-
Michel Basquiat. Basquiat's work was so remarkably striking and new
that he became immediately famed as a hip-hop cultural figure who'd
penetrated art society. By the end of 1981, Basquiat would go on to film a
starring role in an O'Brien-produced, belatedly released motion picture
titled *Downtown 81,* exhibit one-man shows of his art in Modena, Italy,
catch the interest of Andy Warhol, and stand in at the turntables for the
"Rapture" video when Flash couldn't make the shoot.

But his most lasting contribution to hip-hop came a couple years
later, in 1983, when he produced and designed the sleeve for a rap 12-inch
titled "Beat Bop." Already a member of his own noise-rock band called
Gray, Basquiat's musical contributions were wildly eccentric, more com-
parable to Lee "Scratch" Perry's dub engineering than anything heard in
traditional hip-hop. Multi-instrumentalist and Basquiat friend Al Diaz
provided the percussion and other elements, including a violin, but it
was filtered so drastically that it sounded mechanical, almost industrial.
Basquiat also wrote lyrics, intending to use the track to stage a lyrical
battle between himself and another hip-hop-rooted visual artist, Rammellzee, who had called Basquiat out. But the latter artist found Basquiat's verses laughably corny and subbed in a sixteen-year-old kid who
went by the name K-Rob to complete the track instead. "Beat Bop"
still stands as an avant-garde hip-hop classic, as well as a rare collector's
item—original mint copies have gone for as much as $3,000 or more, in
keeping with the astronomical prices collectors have paid for Basquiat's
own original artworks.

Even the omnipresent Fab 5 Freddy got on the mic, if briefly. More
of a TV personality, visual artist, and social gadfly than a dedicated MC,
Freddy still had his share of experience on the mic, including a rare 1981
novelty Christmas song with Blondie called "Yuletide Throw Down"
that was exclusively offered through UK magazine *Flexipop.* (It is, at
least one hopes, the only Christmas song to namedrop Son of Sam.) But
Freddy only needed one shot at immortality on wax, and it came with

1982's "Change the Beat," a bilingual French/English slice of new wave drum machine rap produced by Bill Laswell of art-funk group Material. For the B-side remix featuring French rapper Beside (pun intended?), Laswell added the touch of a hissing vocoder voice concluding the song with an exclamation—"Ahhh, this stuff is really fresh!"—supplied by Laswell's manager Roger Trilling as an in-joke imitation of Elektra exec Bruce Lundvall. That snippet, which already sounded like it held the dynamics of a slippery DJ scratch, became the single most sampled piece of musical work ever recorded. The first time it was sampled was in the Laswell-produced "Rockit," the 1983 hit single for jazz icon Herbie Hancock featuring a legendary DJ scratch performance by Grand-Mixer D.ST.—itself one of the biggest moments in the mainstreaming of turntablism.

But something was getting lost in the process. By the time "The Message" changed the game, hip-hop had ceased to center the DJ, with MCs graduating from their supporting roles as crowd-pumping hype-men. Now it was an art form largely dictated by rappers—the ones who could act as the charismatic frontmen or a tight ensemble cast, who could come up with all the memorable hooks, who didn't even need somebody else's old records providing breaks behind them when they could just get some state-of-the-art synthesizer technology to get the dancers moving. The hits still came, and many of them resonated as legitimately great classics of the form—but next to the origins of park jams, massive sound systems, and tooth-and-nail DJ battles, this new wave of hip-hop was almost unrecognizable. And soon it wouldn't even stand as the new wave: by 1984, artists like Grandmaster Flash and the Furious Five would find themselves stamped with the label of "old school."

• • •

There's a film that memorably captures Flash at his peak. It's the tail end of 1981 and he has his gear set up in the far-from-glamorous setting of a Bronx apartment's kitchen, manning his turntables with a gas range and some ugly wallpaper as a backdrop. Fab 5 Freddy watches calmly—though it could just be the sunglasses making him look nonchalant—as Flash turns his back to the mixer, showing off his name emblazoned on the back of his track jacket as he switches up the crossfader. It takes a moment to really get rolling, but it's for a purpose: cutting between extended drum breaks from "God Make Me Funky" by the Herbie

Hancock protégé band the Headhunters—just simple, almost muted grooves—is a lead-in to something more revelatory. And that revelation hits as Flash finally spools up the unmistakable bell-driven beat that opens smooth jazz keyboardist Bob James's 1975 cover of Paul Simon's "Take Me to the Mardi Gras." As he lets his technique unfold, the film cuts in to other scenes in a park: b-boy team the Rock Steady Crew, most of whom look like fresh-faced teenagers, unfurl low-slung James Brown–via–Bruce Lee contortions on a red parquet-pattern slab of linoleum, while Lee Quiñones works on spray-painting a colossal mural at the East River Park Amphitheater.

The movie is *Wild Style,* a low-budget, high-value docudrama featuring punk-funk musical cues composed by Blondie guitarist Chris Stein, centered around a graffiti writer known as Zoro (played by Quiñones) and his adventures in searching for his big break. By the time it premieres at the New York New Directors and New Films Festival in March 1983, idea man Freddy and producer-director Charlie Ahearn will become widely acclaimed for making the first feature-length motion picture document of hip-hop as an art movement, canonizing MCing, DJing, graffiti, and b-boying as its "four elements." That Ahearn also put it together as a corrective to mainstream cinema's portrayal of the Bronx as some hellish *Fort Apache* murderscape was something of a bonus, but there was reason to be optimistic. At least for a while. Hip-hop had its stars, its sounds, its visual signature, its own way of moving, its home. It would take something drastic to shake its foundation apart.

But March 1983 is a bad time for Flash. His name appears more often on the records than he does, the only money he's making comes from doing live shows, and he was learning too late that Sugar Hill's contract was screwing him out of publishing and royalties. Worst of all, his diminishing role in the group and his growing disillusionment has had a hand in steering the clean-cut gearhead kid he'd been toward an increasingly detrimental cocaine habit. The record industry, execs and performers alike, had been running on coke for a while, but Flash is in the worst possible time, place, and state of mind for it: in his autobiography, he pinpoints March '83 as the first time he tries crack after a regular snorted line of powder cocaine does nothing for him. As "The Message" becomes popular enough in Europe to send Grandmaster Flash and the Furious Five on a tour there, the DJ spends most of his time not onstage or sightseeing but in his hotel room getting high.

Two months later, backstage at a taping of *Soul Train,* Flash and Melle Mel get into a screaming match over who's making money off "The Message" and everything else with Flash's name attached. Even through the haze of the high he's been getting to try and take his mind off the business side of things, the gears won't stop turning in Flash's head. And considering how expendable he's felt as a contributing member of the crew, his decision to try and get out of his Sugar Hill Records contract seems like as much an act of self-preservation as it is a risk. In November, Flash is at a low: a lucrative touring opportunity with Rahiem and Kid Creole, two other Furious Five members who wanted out of Sugar Hill, was cut off when Sylvia Robinson threatened to sue them if they used their professional names. But there was an entirely different legal matter just over the horizon.

Liquid Liquid were a group of dance-punk pioneers who put out a string of well-received singles and EPs on Ed Bahlman's New York–based indie label 99 Records, alongside such underground favorites as the Scroggins sisters' funky post-punk band ESG and experimental modern-classical guitarist/composer Glenn Branca. Liquid Liquid were fated to find themselves at a turning point for sample culture and more than one corner of the New York music scene. An October 11, 1983, *Village Voice* piece by Michael Hill sets the scene of a show at the Roxy: Sal Principato, the group's vocalist, tossed copies of the band's *Optimo* EP into the crowd, shouting "You know where this came from!" This was in direct reference to the fact that the Sugar Hill house band lifted the unmistakable two-note bassline and bridge from "Cavern," one of the EP's songs, for a new Melle Mel single called "White Lines (Don't Don't Do It)." Even a line in the chorus to "Cavern"—"Slip in and out of phenomena"—was rewritten for "White Lines" as "Something like a phenomenon."

"Cavern" had been picking up a significant amount of steam on WBLS, as well as in clubs. And not just in New York—legends like Paradise Garage resident DJ Larry Levan and the Funhouse's future Madonna producer Jellybean Benitez were deep into it—but also in Chicago, where house music founding fathers like Frankie Knuckles and Ron Hardy spun it. Yet while having its sound picked up for a hip-hop hit by a group of the Furious Five's stature initially flattered at least some of the members of Liquid Liquid—"It was this amazing thing at first, and then it got complicated with all the legal stuff later," recalled bassist Richard McGuire—the fact of the matter was that its publishing situation wasn't as easily resolved as the one that would eventually give Nile Rodgers and Bernard Edwards a share of "Rapper's Delight."

In fact, the *Voice* reported that Bahlman had been approached by Sugar Hill for a split publishing deal for "White Lines," and he'd not only rejected them due to already owning 100 percent of publishing for "Cavern," he lawyered up in an effort to "protect the writers of the song." Sugar Hill put out the "White Lines" single anyways, and massively complicated the issue by issuing the record under the misleading billing "Grandmaster & Melle Mel." What ensued was a case of mutually assured destruction: 99 Records sued Sugar Hill Records, reps from Sugar Hill threatened Bahlman by sending machete-wielding goons to scare all the customers out of the 99 Records store, and Flash found his name misleadingly invoked for a song he had nothing to do with.

In the end, after more than fifteen months, nobody really won. Flash spent months in a protracted legal battle trying to get his career back in escaping from Sugar Hill, and failed to win the rights to royalties and ownership he'd been seeking; the only thing the courts granted him was the right to the name "Grandmaster Flash" in March 1984. And thanks to the legal costs of the whole situation, a frustrated Bahlman shut down 99 Records and retreated from the music industry entirely. Despite being awarded a $600,000 settlement and credit on "White Lines," Bahlman received none of it when Sugar Hill declared bankruptcy in November 1985 after an ill-advised, money-hemorrhaging distribution deal with MCA.

But the writing was on the wall for the first wave of hip-hop superstars well before then. Once you had Rodney Dangerfield cutting rap singles and b-boys poplocking intercut with Egg McMuffin footage in McDonald's commercials, the urgency for something new to come around felt more distinct than ever in the five years hip-hop had been on wax. By the end of 1983, the answer began to look clear after a single, "It's Like That" backed with "Sucker M.C.'s (Krush Groove 1)," began making major noise. Coproduced by Kurtis Blow collaborator Larry Smith and Blow's manager, an aspiring label owner named Russell Simmons, the debut single by Hollis, Queens, group Run-D.M.C. authoritatively switched up the predominant upbeat, colorful disco-party paradigm of hip-hop for something starker and harder-hitting.

Joseph "Run" Simmons (Russell's kid brother) and Darryl "D.M.C."

McDaniels rapped more deliberately than the smooth, up-tempo likes of Melle Mel, but what they lacked in slickness they made up for in impact. "It's Like That" might as well have been a 45 playing at 33 1/3 as far as pacing went, but it absolutely clobbered. And "Sucker M.C.'s" was even more of a shock: the backing track was scarcely more than a beat from an Oberheim DMX drum machine; the damn thing *didn't even have a bassline.* It did have scratching, at least, as memorably displayed during the first few lines of D.M.C.'s pugilistic fourth verse as an almost mechanical precision-timed interlude by the group's DJ, Jason "Jam Master Jay" Mizell. They were revolutionary, and they knew it: by January of 1985 they'd declared themselves the "King of Rock," belting knuckle-duster lines over the wailing guitar of Eddie Martinez and declaring themselves "all brand new, never ever old school."

It wouldn't take long to feel like a coup d'état had taken place. Shortly after "It's Like That" / "Sucker M.C.'s" dropped on Priority Records, Russell Simmons was introduced to a hip-hop-loving punk rocker NYU student named Rick Rubin, and the two partners would go on to establish Def Jam Recordings. By the end of 1984, the label had already put out three historic singles: T La Rock and Jazzy Jay's musically stripped-down but lyrically intricate "It's Yours" took the Run-D.M.C. precedent to a bass-heavy extreme, LL Cool J's "I Need a Beat" introduced the sixteen-year-old MC as a literal new-generation rapper, and the Beastie Boys' "Rock Hard" took the punk/hip-hop crossover moment to its wildest conclusion by recasting three Jewish hardcore scenesters as streetwise goons rapping over AC/DC's "Back in Black."

The latter single was withdrawn over the uncleared sample, but by the time the Beasties' debut LP *Licensed to Ill* dropped on Def Jam in November '86, they had the clout to get away with sampling Led Zeppelin, Black Sabbath, and the Steve Miller Band. Their only competition for rap group superstardom that year? Run-D.M.C.'s *Raising Hell,* which made the group the first hip-hop act to reach nearly every record-sales milestone available thanks to the runaway success of their Aerosmith cover/collaboration "Walk This Way." In 1976, punk had stood in opposition to the heavy metal and hard rock titans that filled arenas; in 1986, hip-hop gleefully flipped the script and made these titans their source material. Punk influence might have made hip-hop cool for critics and downtowners, but AOR crossover was where you backed up the Brink's truck.

Bambaataa would keep the downtown-sensibility punk-rap crossover simmering a little while longer with "World Destruction," a track released in 1984 under the name of his side project Time Zone, featuring Bam literally duetting with John Lydon about the doomed state of late Cold War world affairs over barbed-wire guitar riffs. And as the live-band era of hip-hop production receded, many of the old studio-band musicians would later go on to further success in alternative and experimental music: drummer Keith LeBlanc, guitarist Skip McDonald, and bassist Doug Wimbish would form the industrial-tinged funk-hop group Tackhead in 1987, with Wimbish also going on to further cult stardom as part of alt-rock greats Living Colour. But hip-hop had emerged from an underground movement into an increasingly mainstream context, and punk had started to turn further inward toward the tribalism and insularity of hardcore. Those two worlds might meet in unexpected ways later in the decade—in one instance, Brooklyn rapper Chubb Rock's 1988 song "Daddy's Home" sampled "Re-Ignition" by hardcore pioneers and CBGB regulars Bad Brains, a band the Beastie Boys looked up to in their early punk years—but all you have to do is listen to Sonic Youth's Thurston Moore trying to MC on Ciccone Youth's 1986 ironic forty-second goof "Tuff Titty Rap" to get the idea that the two worlds had grown far apart.

Flash managed to escape his brush with addiction after a harrowing near-death overdose in 1985, cleaning himself up as he started to engineer a post–Sugar Hill comeback. But he would spend much of the decade's remainder watching others on the come-up, wracked with a mixture of pride in the world he'd helped create and ambivalence over the thought that this world was far too big to keep him at the top. He still had his name, but the block parties were gone, the parks were getting unsafe, the Audubon was boarded up, the Disco Fever lost its license. Kids didn't need the booming sound systems of the park jams when they could get it through state-of-the-art boom boxes or custom-built speakers in their Jeeps. The Bronx of old-school Kool Herc–sparked legend may have burned out—but at least Flash's name could still draw a crowd downtown.

# 3 | *Funky Drummer*
## Sampling Reaches the People

**The dawn of the sampler turns the break
into a weapon with limitless potential.**

To CONTEND WITH WHAT HIP-HOP HAD BECOME as an art form by
the late 1980s, all you really have to do is acknowledge a term fans have
broadly agreed on to describe the time period it bookended: the Golden
Age. Its end date varies at some point or another in the early to mid-
'90s, but its beginning feels far more definitive. In a rough two-year
stretch from 1986 to 1987, two records sold millions—Run-D.M.C.'s
*Raising Hell* and the Beastie Boys' *Licensed to Ill*—while literally dozens of albums and singles, many if not most of them debuts from new
and up-and-coming artists, began to build a new pantheon of stars that
would carry hip-hop well into the next decade.

And yet this wave swept away the old school so thoroughly it set a
precedent for how quickly an established star could be rendered obsolete. Grandmaster Flash signed with Elektra in 1985, the potential for a
long-repressed artist to get a new, autonomous start wide open in front
of him. But the returns diminished almost immediately. Between his
addiction and his time in court with Sugar Hill, Flash had lost contact
with what was hot in the streets, and his time in the studio with his
rebranded crew was split with time making made-to-order mixtapes
that paid the rent but ground down his enthusiasm. "The phone would
ring and somebody would say, 'Flash, I want some "Dance to the Drummer's Beat" mixed with "Bongo Rock," then I wanna slow it down with
some "T Plays It Cool" by Marvin Gaye and [something by] Sade . . .
then throw down some Janet Jackson in the mix, and make it all fresh.'
It was like taking orders at a restaurant."

That sapped enthusiasm might explain the albums he released on
Elektra in the late '80s. 1985's *They Said It Couldn't Be Done* was a solid-

enough regrouping effort that actually made a point to showcase Flash's scratch technique on a few tracks, and there were a couple decent stabs at picking up some of the newer trends in hip-hop at the time; "Rock the House" in particular was a major nod at the hard rock crossover sounds that Run-D.M.C. had displayed that year with "King of Rock." But it was also overstuffed with the same misguided R&B crossover ballads as *The Message* LP was in '82, and the synthesized pop-rap take on old-school hip-hop couldn't compare to the far catchier likes of Whodini or U.T.F.O. (Flash even flatly admitted as much in the October 1986 issue of *Rock & Soul* magazine: "Last year's album was a mistake. We thought our fans were ready for more singing from us. We were wrong.")

1986's *The Source* was an improvement just on the basis of it easing up on the balladry, but its beats were already starting to sound like they were playing catchup two years after "Sucker M.C.'s" and "It's Yours" made art out of the drum machine. By 1987, *Ba-Dop-Boom-Bang* put Flash squarely in the critical doghouse despite the presence of Run-D.M.C. producer Larry Smith: Nelson George's April 7 review for the *Village Voice* called the not-yet-thirty crew "graybeards" and proclaimed that "[their] voices are thin and uncommanding; their raps about smelly underarms, designer jeans, and self-help are wack."

Flash's trade wasn't obsolete, however, and was still well represented in the new generation of hip-hop stars. Just about every new-school crew had a DJ that earned dedicated tributes: the song that catapulted Eric B. & Rakim into instant renown, "Eric B. Is President," was named in honor of the man behind the decks, though the new school's emphasis on the MC over the DJ confused first-time listeners into assuming that the Eric B. in question was actually the one rapping. Plenty of other showcase tracks by new-school MCs highlighted their turntablists' technique, too—from L.L. Cool J's "Go Cut Creator Go" to Run-D.M.C.'s "Jam-Master Jammin'."

Even with the stylistic changing of the guard, most of these groups— usually operating on hip-hop-dedicated labels like Def Jam, Cold Chillin', or B-Boy Records—still gave artists space to acknowledge the DJ's role in the now largely MC-driven genre. And a sound dedicated to classically defined breaks—looped, chopped, or otherwise manipulated components of recorded sound—would quickly come to legitimize a new mutation of the technique that DJs had established back in the 1970s, usurping the session bands and drum machine electro beats that had dominated the early '80s. There was just one new twist: most of these beats wouldn't come from turntables.

• • •

The first major hit to blatantly, prominently feature a recognizable portion of a preexisting recorded drum break wasn't a hip-hop track, or even a dance record, but a comeback single from a veteran English prog rock band reinventing themselves as a new wave–adjacent commercial rock juggernaut. Trevor Horn joined Yes in 1980 to fill in for departing founding member / singer Jon Anderson on *Drama,* but remained in the band's good graces as a producer once Anderson returned for 1983's *90125.* For the album's recording "Owner of a Lonely Heart," an AOR-style rocker written by South African singer/songwriter Trevor Rabin that Horn had to beg Yes to record, Horn decided to use his new production role to add an attention-getting flourish: a brief clip of the drum breakdown to Funk, Inc.'s 1971 cover of Kool & the Gang's "Kool Is Back," a recurring sample that dramatically opens the song and later returns to lead into Rabin's searing guitar solo. Along with the famous razor-slashing orchestra hit that punctuates the verses—a stock sound of the Fairlight CMI, and the same one that Arthur Baker used on "Planet Rock"— the "Kool Is Back" break was a historic instance of sample-based production trickery that sounded both distinctly weird and oddly feasible. (Though "Owner of a Lonely Heart" hitting #1 on the pop charts probably helped with the latter.)

Horn was hardly finished there. Around the same time he was working his Fairlight alchemy in the studio with Yes, his own avant-pop side project—fittingly called Art of Noise—was pushing sample-based music even further. Less than three weeks before "Owner of a Lonely Heart" dropped as a single on October 8, 1983, the first Art of Noise EP, *Into Battle with the Art of Noise,* inaugurated Horn's record label ZTT on September 26. And "Beat Box"—later remixed into countless "Diversions," with the 1984 12-inch remix "Diversion One" its most famous—was one of the most audacious compositions of the early sample era.

Like "Owner of a Lonely Heart," "Beat Box" drops in pieces of the "Kool Is Back" break—and also, in a bit of recursive humor, builds its main beat off sampled drums played by Yes drummer Alan White. 1984's

"Close (to the Edit)," originally the "Diversion Two" mix of "Beat Box," made the joke even clearer—sampling both "Owner of a Lonely Heart" and another *90125* cut from Yes, "Leave It," and then giving the track a title that alluded to the prog band's 1972 album *Close to the Edge*. Both Art of Noise tracks gleefully blurred the lines between musique concrète sound effects (a revving motor, screeching tires) and recorded sampled instruments, recognizable sounds of both music and nonmusic united in a heightened artificiality. Or, in simpler terms, they sounded like they were actually going through with what the "Close (to the Edit)" music video depicted them doing: cavorting in an abandoned rail depot, dicing a bunch of musical instruments to pieces with industrial power tools.

Yet sampling had to arrive in a different guise for hip-hop. Groups like Art of Noise were popular enough in clubland, and hip-hop artists were familiar with the sounds they were putting out. The question remained, however: in a genre built off the break, where do you get your funk from—and just where is it going to?

If "The Adventures of Grandmaster Flash on the Wheels of Steel" was the definitive record when it came to capturing the spirit of scratching on wax, hip-hop's reckoning with sampling is a bit blurrier and has more than a few precedents. But its most outlandish one came fairly early, left a striking impression, and cast a long shadow. Doug DiFranco and Steve Stein—a twenty-seven-year-old sound engineer and a thirty-one-year-old ad copy supervisor at Doyle Dane Bernbach, respectively—were hip-hop converts who followed the genre's development from its downtown crossover days.

Like many other New York bohos, Steve Stein got hipped to it through a Deborah Harry / Chris (no relation) Stein guest DJ set on an area radio station, and soon found himself hanging out with Di Franco at Kool Lady Blue's dance nights at the Roxy getting geeked over the likes of the Cold Crush Brothers and Afrika Bambaataa. The record-collecting Stein had a history of being a hobbyist DJ—first at a Park Slope Food Coop, then a dancehall upstairs from the neighboring Jamaican-owned bicycle repair shop—but his media-messenger brain gave him some additional turf to play on. "It's about making a message that will resonate with people," Stein is quoted as saying in relation to his music in Hua Hsu's liner notes for his compilation album *What Does It All Mean?* "You can do it for buying toilet paper, or you can do it as an artist, and unleash an idea into the world."

And the opportunity to unleash one particularly formative idea came in 1983. DiFranco and Stein, operating under the hip-hop alias Double Dee and Steinski, entered a contest held by Tommy Boy Records to remix G.L.O.B.E. and Whiz Kid's "Play That Beat Mr. D.J." Their submission, initially dubbed "The Payoff Mix" and retroactively appended with the title "Lesson 1," was assembled out of cut-and-paste tape recordings after fourteen hours of work. And it included so many different nods to old-school hip-hop, radio ad trickery, and free-floating pop culture debris that it felt halfway between a megamix and a page out of *Mad* magazine.

The original first verse, preserved in "The Payoff Mix," both highlighted the eclectic genre-crossing of the time and came across like a dare Double Dee and Steinski were ready to take; as the original "Play That Beat Mr. D.J." lyrics stated, "Punk rock, new wave and soul / Pop music, salsa, and rock and roll / Calypso, reggae, rhythm and blues / Mastermix those number one tunes." So they did: in just under five and a half minutes, the two remixers dropped in vocals from recent dance hits by artists including Herbie Hancock, Culture Club, and Indeep, but spliced in more abrupt and irreverent portions of pop culture audio, too: snippets of the Supremes' "Stop! In the Name of Love" and Little Richard's "Tutti Frutti," Humphrey Bogart dialogue from *Casablanca* ("You played it for her, you can play it for me . . . play it!"), and two important components of origin-point hip-hop—the Incredible Bongo Band's "Apache" and James Brown's "Soul Power." They won the contest handily, though the judges—including Bambaataa, Shep Pettibone, and Jellybean Benitez—didn't discover until later that Double Dee and Steinski were a couple white guys born in the '50s.

In 1985, "The Payoff Mix" would share space on a Tommy Boy 12-inch with two other "Lessons." "Lesson 2 (James Brown Mix)" slickly juxtaposed eleven late '60s and early '70s funk jams from the Godfather of Soul with a couple more hip-hop cuts (including Bambaataa's "Looking for the Perfect Beat" and the B-Boys' "Rock the House") and a few key funk breaks that would be sampled on record for the first of many times here—like Sly and the Family Stone's "Dance to the Music" and Rufus Thomas's "Itch and Scratch Pt. 2." And "Lesson 3 (History of Hip Hop Mix)" both told and rewrote its titular curriculum: whether or not they were regular fixtures in South Bronx DJ crates throughout the '70s, the breaks from songs like Led Zeppelin's "The Crunge," Dynamic

Corvettes' "Funky Music Is The Thing," and Herman Kelly and Life's "Dance to the Drummer's Beat" remained inescapable in hip-hop production long after.

The "Lessons" single was so riddled with copyright issues that it was never officially sold, though promos and bootlegs spread the word far enough. These mixes were startling in their composition: somewhere between medleys, DJ routines, and late-night channel-surfing sessions, the beats played out steadily but switched focus quickly, hopping from one moment to the next with absolutely no space for even the most attention-deficient listener to get comfortably familiarized, much less bored. Double Dee and Steinski would soon split to get back to their day jobs, though Stein would find the music-making bug hard to shake and continued to put out further cut-and-paste media-commentary hip-hop sound collages well into the twenty-first century.

Double Dee and Steinski had a specific advantage, however: access to a recording studio and a significant amount of experience in tape splicing. And while that was an efficient way to create a megamix, actually building a backing track based entirely on a break or two took something more time-consuming. Before the advent of the sampler, and even during its early days, making a track from breaks meant making "pause tapes": using a dual cassette deck to play a piece of music on the first deck, pause the recording on the second deck once the sample had finished, rewind the first deck back to the start of the sample portion, and record the sample again, repeating the process dozens if not hundreds of times in order to build a looping beat that would hopefully be seamless-sounding enough to work.

The practice is almost as old as hip-hop on wax: in 1980 one fly-by-night label, Bozo Meko Records, released a 12-inch bootleg of a Grandmaster Flash and the Furious Five performance and put an instrumental beat on the B-side, attributed after the fact to Bambaataa, Afrika Islam, and Jazzy Jay. "Fusion Beats (Vol. 2)" was a blend of decade-old songs: James Brown's "Get Up, Get Into It, Get Involved," the organ-driven break to the Mohawks' "The Champ," and early funk group Dyke and the Blazers' "Let a Woman Be a Woman—Let a Man Be a Man." It was a raw-sounding construction that didn't always fits its loops together perfectly. But it was the ancestral prototype of hip-hop production using breaks without a turntable, and it sold like it was free. "If you were a hip-hop DJ back then and you didn't have two copies of this record," producer Easy Mo Bee recalled on his Instagram, "there was something terribly wrong with you."

Pause tapes were how countless producers who would become major players in the late '80s and early '90s cut their teeth. But to finesse and control loops like a pro, you needed a sampler—and in 1984, samplers were prohibitively expensive unless you had access to a studio that had one. Workarounds could be found, though, if producers were resourceful and lucky enough. And Marley Marl was both. Born Marlon Williams and raised in a Queensbridge housing project, Marl's home-studio capabilities were already rolling in 1984 when he recorded fourteen-year-old Roxanne Shanté's smash hit "Roxanne's Revenge" in his apartment as a response track to U.T.F.O.'s "Roxanne, Roxanne." Shanté's track had the young battle rapper in rare form, and her riposte to U.T.F.O. started a whole wave of response tracks—the "Roxanne Wars"—that drastically boosted the profile of both the producer and the MC.

Marl's education was pivotal—he interned at Unique Recording Studios during the peak Arthur Baker electro years, studying early electronic dance music and experimenting with the studio's Fairlight. Bobby Nathan, who co-owned the studio with his wife, Joanne, was a head-over-heels evangelist for sampling, buying an E-mu Emulator and immediately filling thousands of 5 1/4-inch floppy disks with everything from movie clips to recordings of him banging on car parts in a junkyard. It was only a matter of time until Marl picked up on that infectious spirit of experimentation.

As Marl recalled to NPR in 2013, he was in the studio, working on Captain Rock's 1984 record "Cosmic Blast." In the process of recording a vocal sample from Cerrone's disco break anthem "Rocket in the Pocket," he accidentally picked up a piece of the snare drum from the track. And in the process of playing the loop back to edit it, he realized that the snare he'd recorded sounded better than the one already in the drum machine he was using. The epiphany hit Marl that if he could isolate a beat like that, he could do that for any drum sound he wanted—a kick, a hi-hat, a snare—and from any drummer he wanted. If he wanted to rebuild an entirely new drum pattern from an old funk single, he could do so, in a far more granular and individualistic style than just looping a beat could.

In other words, Marley Marl split the break atom: even with the split-second storage of the day's drum machine technology, he was able to create a workaround that could actually lead to identifiable hip-hop production styles. Better yet, with his own custom-built beats replacing the rigid, tinny, preprogrammed sounds of standard drum machines, he could free up rappers to let their vocal deliveries ride over trickier, more complex and energetic sounds, liberating MCs' flows and opening up the potential for nuance and technical wizardry in the verses as well as the beats.

By 1985, Marl was a well-regarded up-and-coming production wizard, with his MC Shan–featuring single "Marley Marl Scratch" showing off both his DJing mastery and his taut, hard-hitting drum machine programming. He'd become the on-air DJ for WBLS radio host Mr. Magic, who'd started his radio career in 1979 for pay-for-airtime station WHBI, becoming the first DJ to bring rappers like Kurtis Blow and Melle Mel on the air pre–"Rapper's Delight." Marley Marl caught Mr. Magic's attention with a remix of "Buffalo Gals," and once he became a regular on the *Rap Attack* show the two became so deeply associated with each other that they named Marley's collective of artists after an alias Mr. Magic sometimes used: from "Sir Juice" came the Juice Crew.

And it was the Juice Crew that inspired one of the most notorious hip-hop battles of the entire decade. Mr. Magic and Marley Marl's tastemaking was make-or-break for hip-hop artists all over the five boroughs, and countless up-and-comers hinged their future success on getting airtime on *Rap Attack*. That year, a crew out of the South Bronx called 12:41 showed up at Power Play Recording Studios to meet Magic and Marl with a copy of their new single "Success Is the Word." The MCs had promise—a couple graffiti artists turned rappers named Levi 167 and KRS-One—but the beat, a bouncy and frivolous sounding backing track that cheesily interpolated the theme from *Gilligan's Island*, was enough to make Mr. Magic write the whole thing off as wack. The ensuing grudge would pit two boroughs of New York against each other for hip-hop supremacy in 1986 —and inspire another young producer to put his own mark on the history of sampling.

Cedric Miller, aka Ced-Gee, was another Bronx native who grew up with Scott Sterling, better known as DJ Scott La Rock. Scott met KRS-One during his time as a social worker at Franklin Men's Shelter, where the homeless and often itinerant KRS lived. And once Scott and KRS formed a new crew called Boogie Down Productions with Derrick "D-Nice" Jones, Scott called on Ced-Gee to join up in a coproduction

role. The reason was obvious: Ced had an SP-12, and he knew how to
use it. The E-mu SP-12 was a sampling drum machine, and Ced, the only
hip-hop beatmaker in the Bronx to own one, exploited it to the fullest.
Whereas other producers might use it to make simple loops, Ced had
the same brainstorm as Marley Marl, building entirely new breaks from
pieced-together sampled beats and chopping it all up using techniques
even the manual didn't hint at. And his first masterpiece with Boogie
Down Productions was "The Bridge Is Over."

This 1987 single was the pivotal nuclear option deployed in the
"Bridge Wars," the back-and-forth beef on wax between the Juice Crew
in Queens and the Bronx-based BDP. And it was spurred by MC Shan
and Marley Marl's 1986 single "The Bridge"—a big-up of Queens's hip-
hop early days that KRS-One reframed in '86's "South Bronx" as a revi-
sionist attempt to claim Queens was where hip-hop actually originated.
KRS made pains to name-check all the '70s Bronx hip-hop legends in
his verses he deemed responsible for hip-hop's origins—including Kool
Herc, Bambaataa, and "a kid named Flash"—all while mockingly mim-
icking MC Shan's actual flow and rhyme patterns. When MC Shan's
"Kill That Noise" retaliated with veiled not-naming-names threats,
"The Bridge Is Over" called out everyone in the Juice Crew's orbit ("I
finally figured it out, Magic mouth is used for sucking / Roxanne Shanté
is only good for steady fucking") under the banner of Mr. Magic's rival
radio host DJ Red Alert.

But the dis went deeper than that: BDP's beats themselves featured
drums that sounded remarkably similar to the ones Marley Marl used.
Legend has it that this all went into motion thanks to Marl losing his
reel of signature drum sounds at Power Play Studios—a misplacement
(or theft) Marl traces right back to that fateful day Magic trashed "Success Is the Word." Six months after "The Bridge Is Over" dropped, Marl
found his reel again at Power Play—on the manager's desk—and was
told by one of the studio engineers that Ced-Gee had "found" his drum
reel there and used pitched-up versions of Marley Marl's drums to create
his own beat for "The Bridge Is Over."

Ced-Gee claims otherwise, stating that he simply used the same
sample source for "The Bridge Is Over"—the Honey Drippers' 1973 single "Impeach the President," a popular break in itself—that Marl did for
"The Bridge." If you believe Marl's side of the story, and you believe in
karma as a force of retribution, it might have bit Ced-Gee in the end:

thanks to label shenanigans, B-Boy Records diminished his coproduction role on BDP's debut *Criminal Minded* to a "special thanks," costing him a cut of the profits. But by then Ced was already moving on to another level with his own crew, Ultramagnetic MCs, and the Juice Crew just kept on growing as Marl's production technique was further refined. Alleged thefts and to-the-bone rivalries could sting, but at this point things were just moving too fast to hold anyone back.

•  •  •

In 1986, James Brown would face a strange two-pronged revival of his music. The pandering hyper-patriotism of 1985's *Rocky IV* soundtrack feature "Living in America" debuted in the Top 40 in January 1986 and eventually gave the Godfather of Soul his first U.S. Top 5 hit since "I Got You (I Feel Good)" hit #3 twenty years earlier. But it was a back-catalog release, one largely aimed at funk obsessives, that would wind up shaping his late '80s legacy even more definitively.

The album was called *In the Jungle Groove,* a double LP released on Polydor in August 1986 that culled from recordings Brown and his band made between September 1969 and July 1971. The album featured a thorough cross-section of his funkiest tracks, most of them backed with versions of the J.B.'s—the tightest band of their time, whether live or in the studio. The covered time period included that crucial stretch where the band included such names as bassist and future Parliament-Funkadelic superstar William "Bootsy" Collins; Bootsy's brother Phelps (aka "Catfish"), a guitarist famed for his staccato "chicken-scratch" technique; James Brown Revue regular Bobby Byrd on organ and backup vocals; and a joyously intense horn section that included trombonist / musical director Fred Wesley and sax maestro Maceo Parker.

The personnel rotated often—the Collins brothers in particular were with the J.B.'s less than a year before they found a less tyrannical bandleader in P-Funk's George Clinton—but the sound was consistent: extended grooves heavy on staying deep in the pocket, fusing nearly mechanical steadiness and accuracy with vivid flesh-and-blood liveliness. And the driving forces of this sound were a pair of drummers— Clyde Stubblefield and John "Jabo" Starks—who, along with conga player Johnny Griggs, made the idea of the hip-hop break such an effective one.

*In the Jungle Groove* is their master thesis. Assembled and coproduced by music researchers Cliff White and Tim Rogers, with a Greenwich Village–born DJ named Danny Krivit providing a couple of crucial edits, it's the collection that canonized the early prime of the J.B.'s at the absolute perfect time. Here were the tracks that not only built hip-hop at its earliest moments—there's a remix of "Give It Up or Turnit a Loose," that vital component of Kool Herc's Merry-Go-Round—but were about to become the sound of its immediate future. "Talkin' Loud and Sayin' Nothing," "Get Up, Get Into It, Get Involved," "Soul Power," "Hot Pants (She Got to Use What She Got to Get What She Wants)"— all of these were sampled dozens if not hundreds of times over the ensuing years.

The big get was a nine-minute-plus version of "Funky Drummer," the unexpurgated version of a track previously available only as a 7-inch single. 7-inch records, being significantly smaller than 12-inch singles and LPs and requiring a faster 45 RPM play speed as opposed to the long-playing 33 1/3, are notoriously difficult to use in quick-cutting DJ sets. But with "Funky Drummer" now on 12-inch, it was primed to find its way into many more crates—and, fatefully, the repertoires of nearly every producer who laid their hands on the album. Krivit made the savvy call of dropping a "Bonus Beat Reprise" of "Funky Drummer" at the end of the first LP's second side, creating a wide-open playground for mixers: aside from the occasional James Brown interjection ("Ain't it funky!") and brief hits of guitar chords, it's just the clean, unadorned Clyde Stubblefield drum break, as familiar and inseparable from hip-hop and dance music composition as the 3-2 clave rhythm that Bo Diddley turned into a signature beat of rock and roll.

There's at least one obscure usage of "Funky Drummer" that predates *In the Jungle Groove*—a self-released 1985 single by the Bay Ridge, Brooklyn–based MC Quick Quintin & M.C. Mello J. titled "The Classy M.C.'s"—but the way "Funky Drummer" truly affected hip-hop in 1986 is best heard in a flourishing producer's debut for an untested MC. Marley Marl jumped on "Funky Drummer" almost immediately, initially creating a beat based around it as a demo track for a Queens-based duo, Kool G Rap & DJ Polo. It already boasted all the signature elements that would define the break—the guitar, Brown's "Ungh!" a loop of Stubblefield's drum solo at its most resonant—but then Marl wrapped his own drum machine programming around it, doubling up the beat and giving it a slippery intricacy. "It's a Demo" blew up *Rap Attack* and made a legend out of the then-unheard Kool G Rap, an MC who would go on to pioneer hardcore gangsta rap in its East Coast form throughout the late '80s. If Marley Marl wasn't the absolute first producer to use the drum break from "Funky Drummer," he was definitely the first to popularize it.

Then there was Flash. Formidable DJs were still revered in '86, but the likes of Marley Marl and Ced-Gee had begun to thoroughly change what the other elements of hip-hop production sounded like, and *The Source* had none of that. The drum programming, provided by Flash and Rahiem, was still stuck with one foot in 1984 with its tinny snares and handclaps, and the production was riddled with R&B melodicism when listeners were increasingly flocking to percussion-first hardcore funk. The cruelest irony of *The Source* was found in "Fastest Man Alive," one of those tracks meant to highlight Flash's pioneering DJ technique.

And we hear "Funky Drummer"—brief moments of it—put to use cutting Brown's voice back and forth, counting up to four and back down to one, an endless tease of a beat that never actually arrives. Instead, Flash scratches vocal clips and sound effects over a version of "Apache" that sounds more like a backing track for Tiffany-grade teeny-bopper mall pop than the Incredible Bongo Band warpath from back in the day. The opportunity to do amazing things with Stubblefield's drums were right in Flash's fingers, and he let it slip away.

It would take a real group of firebrands to give those rhythms their due, and then build up hot-rodded versions of them that turned both funk and hip-hop into the sounds of intense musical warfare. A slow-burning '86 coalition that would explode into the public eye the following year changed everything thanks to "Funky Drummer" and the rest of the Stubblefield/Starks–driven James Brown canon—and it came from a crew that was hardly content to stop at just revolutionizing production. Spectrum City was a group out of Long Island fronted by Carlton Ridenhour, a DJ at Adelphi University's WBAU since 1982 who also MCed under the name Chuckie D—later shortening it to the more grown-man alias Chuck D. After dropping a 12-inch on Vanguard Records in 1984—a double A-side of "Lies" and "Check Out the Radio"—that didn't do much for the group's profile, Ridenhour was starting to harbor doubts about even rapping, as he'd been at it since his teen years in the late '70s. In 1986, at age twenty-six, he felt too old to be an up-and-comer.

But when former WBAU program director Bill Stephney landed a

job with Def Jam, he got Rick Rubin's ear, and before the end of the
year a reinvigorated Ridenhour and company had parlayed a four-song
demo into a record contract. And their identity would coalesce around
a new phase of college-educated, pro-black, hardcore political assertive-
ness. Chuck D. fine-tuned his booming voice into such a heavy-hitting
tool of authoritative revolutionary sermonizing that he felt compelled
to bring in a comedic foil known as Flavor Flav to ease the onslaught
and provide some balance. And in the wake of Bernhard Goetz's vigi-
lantism, the police-beating death of Michael Stewart, and the still-raw
nerves from that December's racist beating death of Michael Griffith in
the Queens neighborhood of Howard Beach, they'd found an identity:
if New York was going to treat young black men as public enemies, then
Public Enemy is what they'd be.

As important as Chuck and Flav were to the group's lyrical core—a
massive breakthrough for its emphasis on social justice, a revolutionary intelligence, and invocations of the Black Panthers and Malcolm
X—it was just as crucial that their producers completed the brain trust.
Instead of just one single Marley Marl–style beatmaker or a rotating
cast of drum machine mercenaries, Public Enemy relied on a production unit. The core of this group were brothers Hank and Keith Boxley,
whom Chuck rechristened with the surname "Shocklee" as an academic
dig at electrical engineer and Silicon Valley pioneer turned racist eugen-
icist William Shockley. Shockley's July 1945 report to the United States
Department of War on the necessity of killing upward of ten million
Japanese for the United States to win World War II was an influence
on America's decision to drop the atomic bombs on Hiroshima and
Nagasaki—which made the production crew's name, the Bomb Squad,
brutally ironic. Alongside looping wizard and multi-instrumentalist
coproducer Eric "Vietnam" Sadler and Terminator X, their exploding-
collage master of a DJ, they would build the kinds of dense, sample-
based, layers-upon-layers soundscapes that pushed the ideas of what
could constitute a musical hook.

"Public Enemy No. 1" was the first big salvo, and it was a daring riff
on one of James Brown's most notorious musical performances. When
Fred Wesley & the J.B.'s first cut "Blow Your Head" in November 1973,
Brown met Wesley in the studio to give it a listen, only to be distracted by
a Moog synthesizer that the J.B.'s were considering experimenting with
on later sessions. Brown turned it on, maniacally vamped on it, and added

the squirrelly, head-swimming solo as an overdub to the track, much to Fred's chagrin. Fortunately, what Wesley thought was the doomed work of mad science became a popular centerpiece of the J.B.'s 1974 album *Damn Right I Am Somebody*. And once the Bomb Squad got their hands on it a dozen years later, they took that whirring, wobbling, buzzing squall of electronic noise and turned it into an apocalyptic drone.

It shocked the unwary. While giving it a February 21, 1987, world premiere on rap attack, Marley Marl seemed baffled over how to cut it, and mixed in voice clips of someone wailing "I don't like it!" (Mr. Magic enjoyed the beat, but not the rhymes; "No more music from the suckers," he declared.) A largely complimentary Jon Pareles profile based around their debut album *Yo! Bum Rush the Show* in the May 10, 1987, *New York Times* described "Public Enemy No. 1" as one of the Bomb Squad's "measured doses of irritation." John Leland, who would soon become a frequent target of Chuck D's frustration against the critical masses, was less charitable in his April 21 *Village Voice* writeup: "There's this migraine tone that runs through the center . . . it's annoying, it's unmusical, and . . . it doesn't justify the paranoia it induces. It's a non-verbal fuck you."

The Village Voice might've been apprehensive about Public Enemy in '87, but skateboarding magazine *Thrasher* was all about them: "The lyrics are too radical for the radio and too black for any Washington wife," wrote critic Jill Cuniff, who'd go on to cofound the Beastie Boys–adjacent alt-rock band Luscious Jackson. "So if you want a record that's all concrete and no Stove Top, you're gonna have to BUY *Yo! Bum Rush the Show*." Soon enough, teenage Gen X skate punks everywhere did just that, and it wasn't uncommon to find PE sharing suburban-rebellion stereo time with the Dead Kennedys or Metallica. Downtown art-scene crossover was all well and good, but this was an even bigger territory to conquer: a frontier of noise, a reaction to a promising movement in music that was threatened with the complacency that came from platinum sales. If a hip-hop group could capture the same level of intensely alienated, restlessly agitated energy as the underground punk and metal acts were doing, it could define the reality of a crack-era, Reaganomics-damaged America through not just words, but the music itself.

*Yo! Bum Rush the Show* wasn't the most technologically cutting-edge production job, at least not compared to what Marl was laying down in Power Play. But the collective unit put so many hours into searching for just the right sounds and painstakingly assembling them that their imprint was as live as sample-based music had felt up to that point. Hank would always make sure the hand of the DJ was present, bringing Terminator X in to cut in an idea through a turntable to give it a more lifelike feel than just punching in a sample would. Hank's notion to juxtapose dissonant chords and lay down non- or even anti-musical elements to build tension came from an informal but observant self-taught education, one more about finding an intangible energy than leaning on musical theory. Still, he was in tune enough to recognize they were building beats around Chuck D's weighs-a-ton baritone and Flav's hyped-up tenor, and thanks to a household jazz upbringing, Hank recognized the strength of using specific counter-rhythms and melodies to support the MCs' vocals.

And since those vocals were some of the most powerfully forward-sounding to ever bust through a subwoofer, the Bomb Squad were free to run wild: dropping dissonant piano chord stings into the title track, bringing in Living Colour guitarist Vernon Reid to lay down serrated riffs over "Sophisticated Bitch," and treating Terminator X's gnarled yet agile scratch technique like a rock band would a guitar solo. The drums could still be familiar— Stubblefield and Starks are all over *Yo! Bum Rush the Show*—but the Bomb Squad multitracked so many different sampled fragments of snares, kicks, and hi-hats over one another that the actual drum sounds became something entirely new.

Later, post–*Bum Rush* productions kept their presence loudly felt through the end of '87. Summer single "Rebel without a Pause" found an even more hair-raising J.B.'s loop than "Blow Your Head": Maceo Parker's shrieking sax crescendo from 1970's "The Grunt" was mutated from an opening shot to an ongoing panic-attack scream, as though it was the wordless internal monologue driving the machinery that made Chuck and Flav go off. Along with pushing the tempo up about ten beats per minute past the rest of the hip-hop hits of the time, Hank made the conscious decision to stick with the cheaper, lower-storage Ensoniq Mirage he'd used to create the demo, despite gaining access to a more powerful AKAI S900, because Hank preferred the effect of the older sampler's limitations creating a delay in reloading the loop.

A little later on, *Less Than Zero* soundtrack selection "Bring the Noise" rode off an *In the Jungle Groove* itinerary ("Funky Drummer," "Get Up, Get Into It, Get Involved," and "Give It Up or Turnit a Loose" all got connected to the beat like pistons on a crankshaft), with the wailing guitar intro to Funkadelic's '75 funk-metal explosion "Get Off Your Ass and Jam" overlaid like the siren announcing their call to arms. It sounded abrasive enough that rerecording it with New York thrash metal icons Anthrax in '91 was pretty much a lateral move.

The February release of *Yo! Bum Rush the Show* started something of a holy trinity of hip-hop albums that spanned the first half of 1987 and set a standard for hip-hop through the early '90s. BDP's *Criminal Minded,* with its Bridge Wars artillery boosted by early examples of gangsta rap ("9mm Goes Bang"), crack-epidemic stories ("Remix for P Is Free"), and lyrical intricacy ("Poetry"), proved to be an instant-classic debut when it dropped in March. And when *Paid in Full,* the debut by Eric B. & Rakim, dropped in July, both Eric B.'s sample-rich production and Rakim's relaxed yet rhythmically intricate flow and writerly rhymes became the standard that all aspiring hip-hop artists would weigh themselves against.

All three albums spoke through the echoes of *In the Jungle Groove* and its peers, the late '60s / early '70s lexicon of funk and R&B that had first inspired hip-hop in its primordial, DJ-driven origins at 1520 Sedgwick. Back then, those J.B.'s and Funkadelic and Syl Johnson cuts were contemporary, or at least recent; but in 1987, they were old classics, memories from childhood or even nods to another generation—the past. And this new wave of producers would build that past into a future nobody saw coming: a sea change in the way music was recorded, reinterpreted, marketed, compensated, and canonized. The MCs were still the stars, but now the DJs were building sounds nobody else could—and ultimately, turning a party-rocking, club-gig profession into something far more historically profound than anyone could have anticipated.

•   •   •

Flash recalls his reactions to that wave of 1987 in his autobiography, impressions he seems more enthusiastic about examining than the actual music he was putting out back then. The time a kid from Adelphi came up to him at a record store and played him that same four-song demo that got Public Enemy signed to Def Jam, the feeling of pride Flash got when BDP repped the same Bronx that he grew up and made his name in, the way he heard his own musical taste in Eric B.'s James Brown appreciation while Rakim "was doing for rapping what I had done for DJing" by constantly testing the boundaries of what was possible in hip-hop.

But the following year was a watershed. 1987's holy trinity was surprisingly outdone by a trio of sophomore releases in '88 — Public Enemy's career-defining, perennial greatest-rap-album-ever candidate *It Takes a Nation of Millions to Hold Us Back,* Boogie Down Productions' turn toward consciousness with *By All Means Necessary* after the tragic murder of DJ Scott La Rock, and Eric B. & Rakim's immaculate refinement of crate-digging production and linguistic agility on *Follow the Leader.* And just counting the number of debut albums from artists out of NYC — Ultramagnetic MCs' abstract masterpiece *Critical Beatdown,* EPMD's party-starting *Strictly Business,* Biz Markie's comedic *Goin' Off,* the story-telling clinic of *The Great Adventures of Slick Rick,* and Marley Marl's Juice Crew–showcasing first full-length *In Control, Volume 1* — competition for the hip-hop consumer dollar had never been fiercer.

It was in this environment that Grandmaster Flash would reassemble the original Furious Five, no hard feelings, for Elektra's *On the Strength.* But even bringing Melle Mel, Cowboy, and Scorpio back into the fold couldn't recapture the magic: as enthused as Flash was about the sound of the new hip-hop golden age, the decidedly old-school MCs sounded uncomfortably anachronistic over beats that couldn't quite match what had emerged in the past five years, much less what was killing it on the radio at that very moment. The "Walk This Way"–style remake of "Magic Carpet Ride" featuring Steppenwolf's John Kay, the message track about chain-snatching called "Gold," the re-re-re-introductory scratch feature "This Is Where You Got It From" — it all felt more like a group of veterans trying to regain their bearings. And with the crack overdose death of Cowboy in September 1989, less than two weeks shy of his thirtieth birthday, the reunion was cruelly cut short, with Flash's recording career left somewhere between dormant and sporadic for much of the '90s.

But Flash had no reason to be bitter about it. He recognized that his pioneering role in popularizing hip-hop and mastering a whole new way of DJing was something nobody could take away from him, and he'd get reminded of it every time a new wave of hip-hop artists stoked his fannish enthusiasms again, or when a superstar like Notorious B.I.G. showed up at a gig just to hang out in his DJ booth. In 1976, Flash played in front of a few thousand people at the Audubon and felt like he'd finally made it; just over twenty years later, his audience numbered in the millions throughout cable TV as the in-house DJ for HBO's Emmy-winning talk show *The Chris Rock Show*. He'd crossed over from being an old-school memory to a respected legend, someone who Was There and Did That, an actual living breathing reason that countless people became who they were. For someone whose big achievements mostly boiled down to playing other peoples' records, Flash left an almost out-sized impact. But for Flash, playing other peoples' records meant chron-icling the sounds of history, of capturing just the right moment and doing everything he could to make it last.

And so were the countless DJs he influenced. In the heart of *Nation of Millions*, there's a track, "Terminator X to the Edge of Panic," featur-ing a live-recorded intro from their 1987 Hammersmith Odeon show in London where Chuck D and Flavor Flav briefly take the old MC role of hyping the crowd up for their DJ. What follows is a pyrotechnic acceler-ation of the techniques pioneered more than ten years previous, kicking off with a sly acknowledgment (and possible usurping) of the originator: a brief cut and scratch of Queen's theme to the 1980 motion picture *Flash Gordon,* with Freddie Mercury's famous cry of "Flash!" replaced with a cut-in of Chuck D shouting Terminator X's name. Whether the torch was passed or snatched, history was both acknowledged and added to, respected and mutated. And for a culture that skeptics assumed had an expiration date, what happened instead was the formation of a lineage without a projected conclusion. You can hear it at the outro of "Rebel without a Pause," the beat that "Terminator X to the Edge of Panic" literally inverted, when a portion of that same Hammersmith Odeon concert is cut in at the end to let the MCs' voices shout a demand that almost sounds like amazement:

> *Bring that beat back!*
> *Bring that beat back!*
> *Y'all wanna hear that beat, right?*
> *Bring that beat back!*
> *1! 2! 3! 4!*
> *Hit it!*

Cue "Funky Drummer."

# Part II
# The Prince

Gravediggaz, circa 1992. Photograph by David Corio / Michael Ochs Archives / Getty Images.

# 4 | *Synthetic Substitution*
A New Medium Finds Its Canon

**An emergent sample culture gives rise to a new way
of hearing (and rewriting) the music of the past.**

IN 1972, A CHICAGO-BORN SINGER named Melvin McClelland, better known by his harder-to-misspell stage name Melvin Bliss, was in
Queensbridge doing some networking. His career had been an unevent-
ful one by that point—Bliss was pushing thirty and hadn't so much as
cut a single, mostly sticking to live gigs in small jazz clubs—but a chance
encounter with the mother of Herb Rooney, a singer and songwriter
for a vocal R&B group called the Exciters, proved to be fateful. Rooney
was looking for a singer to cut a tune he'd written, a mid-tempo love
song titled "Reward." And since every single needs a B-side, the flip of
"Reward" was another number Rooney wrote called "Synthetic Substitution." Bliss later mused that neither he nor Rooney really knew what
the song was supposed to be about, but the message of the lyrics aren't
that opaque:

> *Lightbulbs substituting my moonlight*
> *Rays of the sun replaced by man*
> *You're the only thing that's real in my life*
> *Took the work from a horse*
> *Gave it an engine*
> *Copied the wings from a bird*
> *They just had to fly*
> *I wonder what's next, what's next*
> *Watch out my love, it could be you*

After its release in 1973, the song faded into obscurity almost immediately: despite some localized success in New York, the single failed to

chart nationally, and the label it was recorded for—the NYC-based Sun-burst Records—went bust less than two years later after putting out just over a dozen releases in total. But it's still a haunting, mournful performance. Bliss's voice is miked so that it sounds like it's calling through a parking garage, and the uncredited backing band plays a groove hovering somewhere between lounge jazz and gutbucket funk on an oddly tuned piano. It's a song too strange and fascinating to be entirely lost to history, but it might have been stranded as a long-lost artifact of a one-and-done music career if not for Ced-Gee.

When he wasn't using his SP-12 to create mortar shells for BDP's salvos in the Bridge Wars, Ced was building the beats that would make his group Ultramagnetic MCs into cult heroes—and acting as one of the few examples of an eventually common hip-hop title, the producer/MC. As 1986 saw sample-based production being built into something more concrete and complex than just a permutation of drum machine composition, Ced and his fellow MC Kool Keith, inspired by the break-driven production of Eric B. & Rakim's "Eric B. Is President," got the motivation to create their own track where they rapped over a bare drum loop. Ced had lucked into hearing "Synthetic Substitution" at a block party, and Keith was able to borrow a copy from a friend, so that provided the break they needed—in more ways than one.

The end result was a single called "Ego Trippin'," which blended James Brown vocal soundbites, Moe Love's on-point scratching, and a masterful cut-up of the drums from "Synthetic Substitution" that added in pieces of its piano riff for rhythmic emphasis. The rhyming sounded weirder than anything out that year, as Ced went abstract all over the place with rhyme-scheme-defying scientific and technical lingo, and Keith mutated traditional meter and flow as an up-yours to old-school simplicity. But the beat was so hard, so immediate and brisk and alive, that it all fit together and opened the door for MCs and producers to go even further out to distant reaches of style.

A little more than thirty years later, "Synthetic Substitution" has been sampled over seven hundred times. Hundreds upon hundreds of songs sprang up from just one, creating an entire legacy from the only commercially released single by an artist—and not even the A-side of the single, at that. It was a song warning of the perils of technological advancement, but instead of the feared logical conclusion of "replacing a woman with a love machine," the real synthetic substitution was to use this very song to replace session bands with an endlessly modular and mutable recording to manipulate as they wished. And Melvin Bliss was far from the only artist to be plucked from obscurity to find his work spreading far beyond his or anybody else's initial expectations. Short-lived and underheard bands like disco-funk group Banbarra ("Shack Up"), synthesized R&B instrumentalists Manzel ("Midnight Theme"), and Latin soulsters Herman Kelly & Life ("Dance to the Drummer's Beat") became exponentially more popular for their breaks ten or fifteen years later than they ever were the first time around, a reversal of fortune for bands that turned out to be nowhere near as ephemeral as their short discographies predicted they'd be.

And it was with this growing phase of sample culture that hip-hop started to find itself in a continuum between past and future: a recognition of what music meant and sounded like in previous eras that also built something which commented on and updated those traits. Early hip-hop wasn't especially distant from its source material when it came to time and memory; the hardcore funk breaks that Herc and Flash spun weren't always hot on that week's charts, but they were contemporaneous, or in recent memory at the very least. But "Synthetic Substitution" was over a dozen years old when Ced-Gee first sampled it, and by the end of the '80s a significant percentage of sample sources in hip-hop production were released somewhere between fifteen and twenty years previous. Compare a beat made in 1982 with a house band or in 1984 with a drum machine to a beat made six years later on a sampler, and it's the latter track that will sound more in keeping with what a DJ might have been spinning in the mid-'70s. For instance, more than five hundred songs across multiple genres of hip-hop and dance music have sampled or otherwise interpolated the Incredible Bongo Band's "Apache," a staple of block parties since its 1973 release—but maybe ten of those songs predate the beginning of sampling's golden age in 1986.

The timing for all this was fortuitous. The presumed triumph of the West's form of capitalist democracy that followed the 1989 fall of the Berlin Wall dovetailed with a late '80s surge of commercialized nostalgia. As aging baby boomers and their younger siblings and offspring in Generation X faced the waning years of the decade with a turn toward a fondly remembered past—Beatles albums reissued on the new must-have CD format, all your old favorite shows airing constantly on Nick at Nite, every movie you remember from your childhood available to rent on VHS—hip-hop's awareness of the past, and its creators' ability to reconstruct it, took on its own undercurrents of longing. If the end of history felt like a slow but sure turn toward the idea that an unwritten future had no real shape or form to it, this wave of music arose from the very idea that the past was all they really had to build the present with— the future would have to wait.

*In the Jungle Groove* might have done a lot to enable hip-hop's reconnection to its classic funk roots via James Brown, but Clyde and Jabo couldn't provide every drum break. And as samplers found more users from Queens to the Bronx to Manhattan throughout 1986, a new generation of beatmakers needed a leg up on source material. From the early days of hip-hop, DJs clung to the idea of never giving away their best breaks—a sleeve-hiding, label-removing, snitches-get-stitches code of protection that they maintained in order to preserve their status in the ranks. If you were going to find something as unlikely yet amazing as the B-side to Melvin Bliss's only single, or an LP of funky bluegrass led by session bassist Doug "Bad" Bascomb, or a decades-old Tom Jones single that never charted anywhere, you didn't share that shit with *anybody*.

But if there was money to be made in it somehow, you'd get the occasional attempt to capitalize on selling breaks to DJs when they couldn't find the original wax in stores. Paul Winley, a doo-wop mogul turned record dealer, caught on after finding out that some of the remaindered LPs and back stock he'd been selling back to Downtown Records and other stores was selling at a colossal markup thanks to demand from hip-hop DJs. So Winley started his own compilation series in 1979 with the double-*sic* title *Super Disco Brake's,* which Downtown sold under the counter. The series was well circulated but poorly assembled: the rights were sketchy at best, songs were frequently (and possibly deliberately) mislabeled, and the low-grade recordings were sourced from vinyl instead of masters—which is why, among other things, volume 1's inclusion of "Take Me to the Mardi Gras" by Bob James has a skip in it. The breakbeat market had been found and filled, at least with a stopgap, but it still needed refining.

Lenny Roberts and Lou Flores provided that refinement—and helped reshape the way old music was listened to, built around, revived, and canonized. As soon as there was such a thing as a hip-hop record market, record collector Roberts and DJ Flores—known today by aficionados as Breakbeat Lenny and Breakbeat Lou—were getting deeply acquainted with it. Lenny had been clued in to the Bronx's particular tastes by his son, who steered him toward the selection at Downtown Records and led Lenny to discover just how much some of these out-of-print records were going for—sometimes as much as $2,000. Naturally, Lenny caught on fast and began buying certain albums from the deep-discount remaindered or "cut-out" bins, snapping up hundreds of copies for pennies on the dollar until he held a local monopoly on in-demand break records like the Jimmy Castor Bunch's *It's Just Begun*.

Lou, a DJ since 1974, went from DJing with other peoples' wax to collecting records of his own in 1978, and met Lenny around 1980 as part of a record pool giving feedback to labels about a particular record's chance of success in different types of clubs. At some point, Lenny and Lou got to talking about how disappointing it was that the nascent hip-hop record industry was putting rappers into studios with session bands or drum machines instead of break-spinning DJs. Concerned about the foundations of hip-hop being lost, they decided to go in together on creating some bootlegs of their own—ones that would sound better and be given more curatorial care than *Super Disco Brake's*.

Their first shot at building what would eventually become a crucial foundation for sampling was largely anonymous, a series of 12-inch bootlegs that were untitled save volume numbers. They were only recognizable through the illustration on the label of a cheerful-looking octopus with its tentacles madly coordinating a pair of turntables. (A manufacturing credit to "Enterprise Music Incorp. Hollywood, FLA." was a red herring to obscure the bootlegs' NYC origins.) Lenny and Lou picked the selections for each volume, and Lou remixed them where appropriate, extending the breaks themselves to make it a bit easier for DJs without a Grandmaster Flash–level amount of coordination to mix them. None of the artists was credited, and many of the song titles were truncated, so the unlicensed nature and the DJ's code of silence went hand in hand.

When the mainstream record industry continued to push rap records with drum machine beats in the mid-'80s, the operation was briefly put on the back burner. But Marley Marl's use of sampled beats struck a nerve, particularly the drums from "Impeach the President" for tracks like "The Bridge." By 1986, five years after they'd begun the series, Lenny started hearing demand for the "Octopus Breaks" from record store owners again—particularly Stanley Platzer, who worked at the Music Factory in Times Square and kept immaculate, encyclopedic track of every trending record with a break in it. Lenny and Lou's mission was renewed, and this time it would be legit, using the best possible audio fidelity and vinyl quality available. They might look like bootlegs, complete with deliberately generic-looking text-only covers, but thanks to careful mastering they often sounded better than the originals.

The first volume of this new series was pressed in 1986, a revision of an Octopus Breaks record that featured full credits and licensing. Getting the rights for back-catalog material was comparatively inexpensive at the time; it wasn't uncommon to pay as little as five cents for the mechanical license to use a song for a compilation, the same approach that let K-Tel Records put together their famous *20 Original Hits! 20 Original Stars!* albums on the cheap. For Lenny and Lou, it could cost each new compilation as little as thirty cents to license per copy. Press up two thousand copies of a comp with six to eight songs on it and you could have yourself an entire pallet of records to sell to DJs for a fraction of the cost it might take to buy a single collectors-price copy of a song that appeared on it. At that rate, Lenny and Lou's label Street Beat Records could afford to include two copies of the 12-inch in each package, perfect for DJs. The sleeves still left off artists' names, but the songwriting credits were there for knowledgeable heads to puzzle out.

And from volume 1, *Ultimate Breaks & Beats* was a staggering success. Not necessarily one quantifiable in sales, but definitely in impact: among the first volume's selections was the Winstons' "Amen, Brother." This song, often shortened to just "Amen," was the source of a four-bar, six-second drum solo by G. C. Coleman that Flores deliberately slowed down from its original 45 RPM to 33 1/3 in the *UB&B* rendition to make its tempo easier to mix while still being danceable. As a front-to-back listening experience, it was jarring—*UB&B* deliberately included tracks in their entirety, so "Amen, Brother" played at its intended speed until the slowed-down break came in—but as a building block for DJs and sample-based producers, it was a godsend.

The "Amen break" started to appear in hip-hop songs like Steady B's "Stupid Fresh" and Salt-N-Pepa's "I Desire" in 1986, the same year *UB&B* was inaugurated. And by 1990 it had caught on in the UK music world once the rave scene started to integrate breakbeats into a new mutation of techno and acid house called breakbeat hardcore. An entire subgenre—eventually to spin off as jungle, then drum and bass—was built almost whole cloth off the specific energy of the Amen break flipped back to its original frantic 45 RPM speed and beyond, proof that the influence of hip-hop production was primed to bleed over into entirely different scenes spawned an entire ocean away. Less than twenty-five years after its appearance on the first volume of *Ultimate Breaks & Beats,* "Amen, Brother" has been sampled in the neighborhood of three thousand times, at least in acknowledged releases.

The *Ultimate Breaks & Beats* canon was a thorough and sprawling one, and it did more than any work of curation to date to reveal hip-hop's origins as a genre rooted in funk but not strictly beholden to it. The first three volumes included rock selections by the Monkees ("Mary Mary") and the Rolling Stones ("Honky Tonk Women"), disco cuts by D.C. LaRue ("Indiscreet") and Cheryl Lynn ("Got to Be Real"), and jazz-fusion works by Roy Ayers Ubiquity ("Boogie Back") and Upp ("Give It to You"). It reinforced the roots of the old-school—every piece of Herc's Merry-Go-Round, from "The Mexican" to "Give It Up or Tur-nit A Loose" to "Apache," are duly represented—and accounted for the more esoteric corners of the Zulu Nation repertoire, like Cerrone's Eurodisco "Rocket in the Pocket" or Dexter Wansel's prog-jazz "Theme from the Planets."

And no sooner would it reintroduce some track from the early DJ era of hip-hop than a producer would sample it for the first time—then the second, then the third, until the personal selections of long-retired DJs became hip-hop lingua franca long afterward. It didn't matter if you were a complete unknown like Dynamic Corvettes or a hitmaker like Bill Withers, whether you were as iconically cool as Funkadelic or as guilty-pleasure as KC and the Sunshine Band, a chitlin circuit veteran like Rufus Thomas or a new wave synth-popper like Gary Numan: your music provided at least a few bars that bumped, so this is where your music belonged. To collect and listen to all these tracks was to hear the history of music three times over—as the original article, as the source of a break, and then as a historical document to be reworked and ver-sioned and commented on.

But eventually *Ultimate Breaks & Beats* had to reckon with its own impact, and Lenny and Lou had to scramble to keep a step or two ahead of the producers who were wringing every last kick and snare from their selections. By the end of 1987, sixteen volumes of *UB&B* had been offi-cially released by Street Beat—not counting a phantom volume 8 that was quickly deleted and later replaced with a different entry under the same catalog number. Nearly every break anyone might have heard at some mobile DJ's park jam in 1977 had been given a second lease on life by producers ten years later. But *UB&B's* later releases—featuring spectacular, memorable illustrated covers by graffiti artist Kevin "Kev TM7" Harris starting with volume 12—were popular but increasingly sparsely released. Only three volumes dropped in 1988, and another three in 1989, right when sampling was starting to reach a watershed moment, before volume 25 closed out the series in 1991.

Lenny and Lou had initially planned to do twenty-five volumes and see where things went from there. But in deciding to close the door on *Ultimate Breaks & Beats* so definitively—the gray cover of volume 25 reflected the same plain cover style as the early volumes, and doubled as a tribute to the passing of Lou's production partner Chep Nuñez—they'd also given DJs and producers their own challenge. The training wheels were off, and it wouldn't be enough to just have deep crates anymore—you had to figure out new things to *do* with those breaks, where they'd merge and mesh, how they'd call and respond to each other, how they'd bring additional light to the personality of whoever was rhyming over it. The foundation of hip-hop had been rebuilt, but it was up to a new generation to cultivate it from there.

• • •

Here's a funny thing about the career of Paul Huston: a man considered one of the great auteurs of sampling got his big break with a hip-hop group famous for using live instruments. In 1984, Stetsasonic producer/MC Glenn "Daddy-O" Bolton had caught DJ Prince Paul doing a mix routine at a DJ battle in Brooklyn's Brevoort Projects that left a theatrical impression—as he recollected to *The Source* for their April '99 issue, "Paul was spinning Liquid Liquid's 'Cavern' . . . like he was mad at the turntables." Paul was still in high school, and had signed up for the DJ battle on a whim after a friend offered him a ride to the show. But he'd already been working the decks for years, having caught the itch after attending a series of block parties circa 1977 as a ten-year-old. By 1981, he'd earned a rep as the neighborhood DJ of Amityville, Long Island, sealing it thanks to a routine cutting up Trouble Funk's go-go classic "Pump Me Up." And by the time Stetsasonic approached him for a DJ role in the group, he'd already made friends with an aspiring MC and beatboxing wiz named Biz Markie. It might have taken a bit for the teenage Paul to let his new gig actually sink in, but it happened fast: he wound up recording some scratches for a demo that would become Stetsasonic's 1985 debut single "Just Say Stet," and before he knew it, he and the rest of the group had signed a record contract with Tommy Boy before he was even old enough to watch an R-rated movie without parental guidance.

Stetsasonic's 1986 debut album *On Fire* was a solid foot in the door, though it wasn't easy to get a cohesive sense of where the band was headed just yet. Having live musicians share space with a DJ on stage might have been noteworthy at live shows, especially with the stated purpose of being able to replicate on stage exactly what they did in the studio. But the band's sound on record didn't always differ significantly from recent old-school records that used session keyboardists and guitarists. Except that sometimes it was more of a mess — there are a couple stretches of one track, "Rock De La Stet," where a guitarist, a keyboard player, a drum beat, and a Prince Paul scratch routine of a beatboxer are all layered over one another in a massive pileup of sound. Still, Paul was able to learn on the job even when he didn't have the spotlight, and Stetsasonic were happy to give him a few shots there anyways: his scratch technique wasn't merely integrated into their band, but highlighted and boasted about on cuts like the twofer closers "Bust That Groove" / "Paul's Groove." And when it all came together, like it did on their club-banger single "Go Stetsa I," Stetsasonic's future as a genuine phenomenon seemed assured.

Thanks to their differences in age and experience, the MCs in the crew—Frukwan, Delite, and Daddy-O—also acted as mentors to Paul, despite the distance between the two parties: the Stetsasonic crew all lived in Brooklyn's East New York neighborhood, while Paul still lived in Long Island, more than an hour away. (Daddy-O actually had to send Paul rehearsal notes in the mail, since calling him would rack up long-distance charges.) While most of Paul's learning experience was just covering the basics of working in a musical group—collaborating with songwriting, pitching ideas, and participating in a band as a sort of democracy—he had already learned beforehand how to make beats of his own, even if he hadn't grown to consider it full-fledged production just yet. Working with anything more complicated than a drum machine still wasn't common at that point, especially for smaller independent acts that hadn't been blessed with a Rick Rubin budget, so the contributions of someone with Paul's skills were crucial. Just how crucial they were, however, still seemed a bit up in the air.

Paul had an off-kilter sense of humor to his work—one that would occasionally shine through on a track like "4 Ever My Mouth," which was literally nineteen seconds of a beatbox-laced rhythm with the MCs shouting "Boom boom boom boom!" over it. But as one-sixth of the group—one-seventh once drummer Bobby Simmons was factored in a little later—Paul's more outlandish ideas were typically outvoted. While his role in Stetsasonic was an important one, it didn't provide the sort of idiosyncratic expression that Paul was itching to show off. And the further that sampling developed as an art form, the more he wanted to try. All he'd need was the right people to try it with.

Paul became a big deal in Long Island's hip-hop community just on the basis of having a song on the radio. And in late 1986, Vincent "Maseo" Mason, who DJed for a rapper named Gangster "B" (complete with quotation marks), called on Paul to help out with programming a beat for a record. Paul wound up unhappy with what he'd come up with on his Sequential Circuits TOM drum machine: the producers wanted him to create a beat that sounded like the backwards loop of the Beastie Boys' "Paul Revere," and Paul only did it reluctantly after protesting that he wasn't into the wholesale lifting of another artist's ideas. Maseo was sympathetic to Paul's anti-biting stance, and offered him another gig that would fit his creative impulses better: Maseo was a DJ in another group with two mutual high school acquaintances of his and Paul's, namely rappers Kelvin "Posdnous" Mercer and David "Trugoy" Jolicoeur. They called themselves De La Soul, and they had a pause tape demo of a track called "Plug Tunin'" that Maseo was anxious for Paul to hear.

The beat was done on a shoestring, and the arrangement needed work, but Paul heard potential. More important, he heard adventurousness: as jankily as it was put together thanks to their limited resources, the loop they'd built was singularly weird, a loping sort of elephant-walk horn riff somewhere between oboe and baritone sax from the Invitations' 1965 B-side "Written on the Wall," with the singers' wordless doo-wop refrain thrown in for good measure. Picking up on a shared sensibility for the off-kilter, Paul enthusiastically set to work adding his own touches to the beat with a four-track recorder, including a little piano from Billy Joel's "Stiletto" and some beefier drum beats courtesy of Manzel's super-scarce *Ultimate Breaks & Beats* highlight "Midnight Theme." When De La came in to hear what Paul had done to the track, they were amazed: Posdnous, who'd gotten his copy of "Written on the Wall" from his father's formidable record collection and built the first-draft beat from there, later remarked that "right from there [Paul] made me feel at ease. He was a person who was thinking on the same level as us."

From there on out the creation of the next few De La Soul tracks arose from a strong formula that Paul described as "a deep record collection and a lot of laughing." De La and Prince Paul were emerging as a new strain of hip-hop creatives—artists who had grown up with hip-hop as a primary musical influence and were figuring out just how far they could push it to make it fit more esoteric tendencies. In short, they were nerds, more enthusiastic about turning weird in-jokes and preposterous ideas into true-to-self personal expression, rather than changing to fit some perceived popular movement.

And it worked: "Plug Tunin'" was a left-field hit when it was released in early 1988, and their follow-up was even stranger: an abstract-verse attack on rhyme biters called "Potholes in My Lawn" that featured a distinctly cartoon-country sound thanks in part to two unusual sample sources from 1970—the "sad trombone"–esque sax/harmonica harmonics from Eric Burdon and War B-side "Magic Mountain," and the twangy, yodel-and-jaw-harp hillbilly put-on "Little Old Country Boy" from Parliament's debut album *Osmium*. It's easy to picture both of those sampled songs residing on the same turn-of-the-seventies record shelf somewhere, maybe even played back-to-back on a fairly adventurous free-form radio show during Nixon's first term. (There's also a savvy drop of the then-instantly-recognizable piano riff from "Synthetic Substitution," almost commenting on its increasing popularity as a sample source.) But De La and Prince Paul built something with those old cuts that, through clever sonic juxtaposition and intricate next-level rhyme schemes, made the gap of musical development between '70 and '88 feel like an eyeblink.

When the success of these '88 singles promptly led to their 1989 debut album *3 Feet High and Rising*, it all came into deep focus. Paul's idea to use a game show bit on the record as a framing device to introduce the De La Soul members to record buyers helped give the album a colorful sense of eccentric humor, and the album featured no less than ten tracks that came across more like comedy bits than actual songs—an idea that would soon become Paul's oft (and oft-poorly) imitated trademark skits. Most of these came from spontaneous goof-off sessions—getting a bunch of people in the studio to chant against dated, conformist hip-hop fashion ("Take it *off!* / Take those fat laces off / Take it *off!* / Take that bomber off"), or turning Pos ad-libbing some horny moans as a joke into the Barry White–sampling sex farce "De La Orgee," or doing an entire track, "Can U Keep a Secret," consisting of whispered innuendo ("Paul has dandruff / Posdnous has a lot of dandruff / Mase has big fat dandruff / Trugoy has dandruff / Everybody in the world, you have dandruff"). Some gags were more elaborate: one striking highlight was a wild excursion into a sampling free-for-all, "Cool Breeze on the Rocks," which strung together some quick scratches and nearly two dozen snippets from song lyrics invoking the word "rock" in less than forty seconds.

And when they put the work in to do a full-fledged track, Paul gave them a wide-open roadmap, revolutionizing the way sample-based tracks were built by pitch-shifting different melodic elements into the same key and layering pieces together to create new harmonic and percussive dynamics. That resulted in some unpredictable source material that was ruthlessly honed into hip-hop shape. Two cuts, "Eye Know" and "Say No Go," flipped familiar hits by Steely Dan ("Peg") and Hall & Oates ("I Can't Go for That [No Can Do]"), respectively, and in ways that had De La's MCs using the titular vocal samples from the source material as ways to complete their own thoughts and ideas—a sort of metacommentary call-and-response. ("Eye Know" kept the "I know I love you better" line from "Peg" in the spirit of the original, but turned Hall & Oates' "You got the body now you want my soul . . . say no go" line from a romantic struggle into an anti-crack message.)

And "The Magic Number," the first track on the album after the intro, was a tour de force of *did I just hear that?* unlikely juxtapositions: a song that sampled and liberally interpolated Bob Dorough's *Schoolhouse Rock* edutainment song "Three Is a Magic Number," it also sourced the album's title from a 1959 Johnny Cash song ("Five Feet High and Rising"), nodded toward precedent through Double Dee & Steinski's proto-sampling mixes ("Lesson 3"), and threw in a line from Eddie Murphy's self-titled 1982 comedy album *Delirious* ("Anybody in the audience ever get hit by a car?") just for the hell of it. All this while Pos and Trugoy spun motormouthed internal rhymes through rhythm-sparring deliveries that jumped right into the fray. Here, sampling didn't just build loops—it formed conversations.

*3 Feet High and Rising* was almost entirely uncompromising as far as collective-effort hip-hop went. And even when De La came to a song reluctantly, they found a way to make it integral to their identity. Maseo and Paul were prodded by Tommy Boy to make a commercial "radio record," which the group thought might upend the everything-goes *Duck Amuck* vibe the rest of *3 Feet High and Rising* expressed so vividly. But the two DJs figured that if they were going to do something for the charts, they might as well make it fun, and they built a dizzyingly catchy beat off a loop of Funkadelic's "(Not Just) Knee Deep" that Pos and Trugoy wrote some of their most pointed lyrics to. "Me Myself and I" became a statement of identity that shrugged off the "hippie" reactions their early singles got tagged with and asserted that their style, as odd as it seemed in a genre loosely defined by gold-chain fashion and street-hewn toughness, wasn't an affectation or an intrusion. As a single, it was a smash. As an album track, they put it near the end of the record, like a QED.

The reaction was impressed, if often novelty-addled: *These guys are from the suburbs? What's with all the weird comedy? These beats don't sound like hardcore funk breaks!* In March of '89, some nine months before the album won the *Village Voice* critics poll, Robert Christgau called De La Soul "new wave to Public Enemy's punk" and referred to their style as "kiddie consciousness, junk-culture arcana, and suburban in-jokes"—a compliment, if a bewildered one, softened by the A-minus-earning upside that "you can dance to them." Michael Azerrad used more than one piece in *Rolling Stone* to describe *3 Feet High and Rising* as "psychedelic," despite the album's pointed lack of references to hallucinogenic drugs. Tommy Boy's marketing department even got the self-aware idea to advertise *3 Feet High and Rising* with an ad featuring a white suit-and-tie yuppie holding a copy of the album with the caption "I came in for U2, I came out with De La Soul," adding a paraphrased pull quote from Robert Hilburn at the *Los Angeles Times* calling it "the *Sgt. Pepper's* of the Eighties"—high praise, albeit on rock's terms.

As far as hip-hop's terms went, Paul was heating up. Even as his role in Stetsasonic was diminishing by 1988's *In Full Gear,* he was notching hits for a wide scope of artists. He brought De La Soul with him for Queen Latifah's lighthearted but empowering "Mama Gave Birth to the Soul Children," which blended familiar breaks like Dennis Coffey's fuzzed-out funk instrumental "Scorpio" and the arena rock drums of Billy Squier's "The Big Beat" into a quick-moving, manic pastiche of madcap horn riffs and beat-boxing samples. Hard-hitting lyrical don Big Daddy Kane got Paul for the leadoff title track to *It's a Big Daddy Thing,* which channel-surfed through clips from '85 horror flick *Re-Animator* ("Is Mr. Kane loose in this hospital?" "In the morgue, I think, Doctor") and the ITC Entertainment fanfare that used to herald the beginning of *The Muppet Show* before busting through the doors with a beat that turned the Memphis Horns from Otis Redding's "Swingin' on a String" into an up-tempo barrage. And 3rd Bass, whom Def Jam signed and positioned as the more street-cred version of the recently Capitol-bound Beastie Boys, immortalized themselves and a debuting young guest rapper named Zev Love X with the Paul-produced "The Gas Face," one of his subtler beats but no less intricate than his wild pastiches for De La. The way he balanced the piano from Aretha Franklin's "Think" with the bass and drums of the Emotions' "I Like It" was an Atlantic-meets-Stax master class in bringing southern soul to NYC. (It's a testament to Paul's ear that he messed up the drum pattern programming somewhere along the way, but still came up with a "mistake" of a shuffle beat that 3rd Bass still liked.)

Through all these modes, Paul's production was constantly shifting to accommodate his sprawling musical inspirations, a music-scholar approach that could fit just about any musical idea that struck him. The future seemed wide open—at least, it did when it looked like the future would arrive.

· · ·

As big an imprint as Prince Paul left, hip-hop production in 1989 could be defined as the stories of three different Pauls—the other two being a tragedy and a rebirth. Each of them took the idea of being an outsider in hip-hop and expressing it with the help of a sampler: refining production techniques, expanding the source material beyond the traditional *Ultimate Breaks & Beats* canon, and making their idiosyncrasies feel welcoming thanks to a broad-minded sense of what an expanding, postmodernism-savvy hip-hop audience could appreciate. All three of them had a role in predicting where hip-hop would go in the

'90s—predictions that would be fulfilled by protégés or dashed by the record industry, but ones that augured a creatively daring future nonetheless.

Paul McKasty, aka Paul C, was a white kid who'd picked up a bass guitar at an early age and used his wide-breadth knowledge of pop and soul history, musical theory, and engineering to prep himself for his burgeoning interest in hip-hop. By the time he was twenty, he was putting in time as a studio rat working behind the boards, and it wasn't long before he set up shop at 1212 Studio in Jamaica, Queens, cultivating a formidable set of skills with the SP-12 and its more advanced successor, E-mu's SP-1200. For one track with his group Mikey D & the L.A. Posse, "I Get Rough," he recruited a local teenage beatbox phenom named Rahzel to make some bass sounds, then arranged and pitch-tweaked those sounds until he'd recreated the bassline to the Commodores' "Brick House" with them.

This was the kind of technological sorcery that got the attention of Ced-Gee—right at the peak of the Bridge Wars, when the idea of a producer from the Bronx collaborating with one from Queens seemed like madness. But while MC Shan and Marley Marl traded shots on wax with Boogie Down Productions, Ced had more on his mind than just beef, and the Ultramagnetic MCs felt fine with inter-borough détente if it meant getting someone on board who knew how to make beats sound immaculate. The 1987 single "Give the Drummer Some" was that brain trust's big triumph, a fusion of the "Funky Drummer" break with fragmented, tight-timed pieces of the Dee Felice Trio's soul-jazz interpretation of James Brown's "There Was a Time." Most confounding was how Paul C was able to isolate portions of the Felice track like they were stems and boost them to the skies, isolating and enhancing the resonance of each drumbeat to create the kind of clean-yet-filthy percussion sounds that sent other producers into awestruck dazes.

Paul C's treatment of sample source material was influential, too. When he got a gig to mix and engineer *Crazy Noise,* the 1989 debut by EPMD affiliate Stezo, Paul lost it over a beat Stezo had picked out for "It's My Turn," a song from one-album wonder Skull Snaps titled "It's a New Day." The opening drum pattern was so sick, so easy to beatmatch with other samples, and so diabolically dense that Paul lobbied for it to open "It's My Turn" as a two-bar loop that gave it just enough time to breathe on its own before the other samples dropped in. That was the first of well over four hundred uses of the "It's a New Day" drums, every one after "It's My Turn" a shot at chasing that astounding initial high. (Many of them wound up sampling the Stezo record instead of the Skull Snaps original; Paul C's production upgrade was that thorough.)

Thanks to his growing profile, McKasty had his mind set on forming a whole production crew, consisting of himself, Stezo cohort Chris Lowe, and a producer/MC named Large Professor, who'd recently joined Toronto transplants K-Cut and Sir Scratch in a new group called Main Source. But Paul C was laying the groundwork for a future that would be forced to continue without him. On July 16, 1989, he spent the night at 1212 Studio engineering a session for a group out of Boston known as the Almighty RSO, a crew of hopefuls managed by David Mays—who had also founded a fledgling hip-hop newsletter called *The Source* the previous year. It turned out to be the last work he'd ever do: the next morning, his older brother Tim found Paul dead in his home from three gunshot wounds, all aimed at his head. He was just over two months away from turning twenty-four. No motive was ever truly figured out, and the only caught suspect was released for lack of evidence.

The ripple effect was devastating to rappers who associated with Paul. Super Lover Cee & Casanova Rud, who had a Paul-engineered smash with 1988's "Girls I Got 'Em Locked," were wrongfully implicated in the shooting by the NYPD and saw their reputations and careers suffer irreparable damage before they were cleared. The first Organized Konfusion album, which was slated to have significant input from Paul, was scrapped as fledgling MCs Prince Po and Pharoahe Monch had to deal with the anger that came from the loss of a mentor. And a devastated Stezo retreated from music for five years, releasing a scattered handful of singles in the mid-to-late '90s when all but the most hardcore heads had forgotten about him. But Paul's legacy would remain—in the liner-note acknowledgments of *Let the Rhythm Hit 'Em,* or a shoutout on Organized Konfusion's debut single "Fudge Pudge" ("Paul C to the organisms!"), or a student who became a master. Large Professor, who spent countless hours learning everything he knew about the SP-1200 from McKasty, would name his publishing company Paul Sea Productions in his honor.

Less than two weeks after McKasty's murder, on July 25, 1989, an ambitious sophomore album by a supposedly washed-up group hit store shelves. Michael "Mike D" Diamond, Adam "MCA" Yauch, and Adam "Ad Rock" Horovitz were, at one point, the biggest hip-hop act in the world—the most notorious, the best-selling, the most crossover-friendly. But despite the commercial success of 1986's *Licensed to Ill*, the Beastie Boys felt trapped. Their rowdy, frat-boy antics on wax, on stage, and just about anywhere else they had cameras on them, were starting to wear thin both for the press and themselves. The beer-guzzling brat façade that made the butt-rock/rap crossover "(You Gotta) Fight for Your Right (to Party!)" had started as an ironic goof that the once-and-future punks had considered a fun joke with a short shelf life. But the longer it went on, and the more stages they shared with firebrands like Public Enemy or time-tested world-beaters like Run-D.M.C. in '87, the more their commitment to the bit appeared to crack in the wake of hardcore hip-hop's ascendance.

Def Jam's control issues weren't doing them any favors, either. Rick Rubin, who'd helped mold them into the multiplatinum superstars they'd awkwardly grown into, had his mind set on Colonel Parker-ing them into a comedy movie, *Scared Stupid,* that was supposed to put them into an Abbott & Costello–style haunted house farce updated for the '80s. This, of course, would mean recording a bunch of new songs for a soundtrack. And if that fell through, they were still under contract for a second album.

Instead, the Beastie Boys came home from a beer-stained, cage-dancer-strewn, giant-hydraulic-penis-featuring 1987 headline tour thoroughly exhausted. They'd tried to live up to the role of being Mötley Crüe, Black Flag, and Run-D.M.C. all at once, earning the adoration of a massive teenage crossover audience and the scorn of everyone else from Dick Clark to Tipper Gore's censorious Parents Music Resource Center. The crowd ate it up, but the digestion process seemed rough. One nineteen-year-old who attended their concert in Syracuse, New York, on April 10, 1987, summed it up in terms that seemed simultaneously fanboyish and damning: "They're pulling the greatest scam on America. You put three idiots on a stage with a giant phallus and they make a million."

When the tour ended and the Beasties finally got some time to reconvene in New York, the pressure to get back in the studio remained. But between the fatigue and the money they were still owed, they seemed less than enthusiastic about giving Simmons and Rubin the *2 Licensed 2*

*Ill* they wanted. In response, Russell Simmons withheld $2 million in royalties from *Licensed to Ill* from the group, citing breach of contract and the costs of dealing with copyright infringement claims thanks to the album's samples. Not a year after going platinum, the Beastie Boys wanted out. Out of Def Jam, out of their self-parodying image, out of everything but the chance to fool around with some side projects and figure out how to enjoy making music again.

They found solace in Los Angeles. With *Scared Stupid* scrapped, Horovitz had signed on to play a role in a movie called *Lost Angels,* so Diamond and Yauch joined him in Hollywood, mostly to hang around and decompress while the lawyers worked out their separation from Def Jam. One evening, in February 1988, they wound up at the apartment of a club owner / DJ / indie label proprietor named Matt Dike, whose label Delicious Vinyl got off the ground the previous year with releases by West Coast rappers like Tone-Lōc and Mellow Man Ace. Not one to pass up an opportunity to pick up a group in transition, Dike added a little something to the party's soundtrack: an instrumental demo called "Full Clout," authored by two other party attendees named Mike "E.Z. Mike" Simpson and John "King Gizmo" King. The Dust Brothers, as they'd become known, had assembled a pastiche of mid-'70s funk jams so dense with drum breaks and seamless rapid-fire transitions that it was almost symphonic. Well over a dozen songs went into the making of "Full Clout," including riffs from Ronnie Laws's Rufus cover "Tell Me Something Good," machine-gun drum rolls off fusion drummer Alphonse Mouzon's "Funky Snakefoot," and a fistful of selections from Rose Royce's *Car Wash* soundtrack—a lot to fit into just over three minutes. But it was so streamlined and purpose-built for dancefloors that when Dike put it on during a DJ set, the crowd went nuts for it, actually applauding at the end.

As sales pitches went, "Full Clout" was an epiphany. The Beasties flew back to NYC the next day, and despite Simpson's difficulties in getting the Dust Brothers' two-track beat-tape demo FedExed to New York, he heard back from Mike D a little later letting him know the Beasties were game for doing a session in LA with those beats. After recording early-draft vocal tracks for "Full Clout" and the other beat, a slinky, almost narcotic-sounding down-tempo cut called "Dust Joint," another piece of the puzzle got filled in: Eric Carr, a Capitol Records A&R rep who had known their music back when they were sharing punk bills at

SYNTHETIC SUBSTITUTION 77

SoHo arts center the Kitchen with a noise band called Sonic Youth, got word from a lawyer acquaintance that the Beasties were looking for a new label. Carr's excitement over the "Full Clout" / "Dust Joint" demo butted up against Capitol's wariness over taking such notorious trouble-makers on board when they were still feuding with Def Jam, a label from which they hadn't yet officially broken free. (A headline on the cover of the April 2, 1988, *New Musical Express:* "'There'll never be another Beasties album'—RICK RUBIN.") But Carr's vision won out, especially after rumblings of interest from rival label MCA (no relation), and the Beastie Boys found a new lease on life.

Though the band's regular itinerary of wine, weed, and mushrooms didn't do wonders for their productivity, their partnership with Dike and the Dust Brothers was invigorating. The Beasties were infatuated with how the beats sounded, tightly packed collages of both famous and obscure sounds that touched on nearly every single famous popu-lar musician of the previous thirty years, letting them act as everything from foundational rhythms to ad-lib punchlines. If there was one unify-ing theme, it was an outlandish refraction of the '70s, hip-hop's origin point blown up to the size of a five-story mural and filled with so many musical details and asides and in-jokes that it felt like a concept album about record collecting.

The list of artists sampled and interpolated on *Paul's Boutique* has a remarkable crossover with the most beloved and successful groups to put out records between 1969 and 1979—James Brown, the Isley Brothers, Isaac Hayes, Curtis Mayfield, Jimi Hendrix, Sly and the Fam-ily Stone, Pink Floyd, the Band, the Jackson 5, Led Zeppelin, Kool & the Gang, the Eagles, Alice Cooper, AC/DC, the Ramones, Chic—all mingling freely with mid-tier cult favorites (the Fatback Band, Sweet) and cutout-bin obscurities (Ballin' Jack, Funk Factory). These sources were then mixed with more recent hip-hop source material—brief vocal clips and tweaked beats from Public Enemy, Boogie Down Produc-tions, Crash Crew, Lovebug Starski, Funky 4 + 1—and on "Johnny Ryall," a song about an old singer turned down-on-his-luck wino, themselves circa *Licensed to Ill*.

Along with "Full Clout" (renamed "Shake Your Rump") and "Dust Joint" (now "Car Thief"), the *Paul's Boutique* brain trust came up with recontextualizations so preposterous it's like they were daring their sample sources to object. The Beatles might have seemed untouchable in 1989 — Michael Jackson, who owned the rights to their songs at the time, had previously blocked the Beasties from interpolating "I'm Down" for a song cut from *Licensed to Ill*—but fuck that, why not put together a two-part suite called "The Sounds of Science" sampling songs from *Sgt. Pepper's* and *Abbey Road* and *The Beatles?* Why the hell not build a beat around a souped-up rework of Mayfield's theme to *Super Fly* to do a song about hucking eggs at people? "Those Shoes" is wasted on the Eagles, but you know what's really good? Using that scuzzy white-knuckle bassline for a song about a multistate crime spree called "High Plains Drifter." There are too many highlights to choose from—even singling out the best bit of the marathon nine-part, twelve-plus-minute "B-Boy Bouillabaisse" is a tough call—but if anyone wanted to hear just how far the Beastie Boys had come, they might lose their mind off a song like "Shadrach," a mic-trading, reference-dropping tour de force that swapped out boorish snottiness for pranksterish enthusiasm—"I once was lost, but now I'm found / The music washes over and you're one with the sound"—and masterfully chopped Sly and the Family Stone's "Loose Booty" like it was purpose-built for this very track.

The problem was that not nearly enough people actually wanted to hear just how far the Beastie Boys had come. The recording process was so protracted, the costs so outlandish, the change in style so supposedly uncharacteristic that Capitol had no idea what to do with the record, spending all of about a week promoting it before punting. The label hosted a big release party on its July '89 release date—more than half a year later than the Christmas '88 date they'd initially aimed for—and then, nothing. "I went to Tower Records," Ad-Rock recalled in a 2015 interview with Beats 1's Zane Lowe, "and they didn't even have it." Capitol Records president David Berman, who'd greenlit Carr's idea to sign the Beasties, had since been fired and replaced by Hale Milgram, who responded to the group's questions about getting further promotion with the news that Capitol would rather spend its time getting behind a new Donny Osmond record. *Paul's Boutique* sold half a million by late September, but compared to the in-every-home-a-copy success of *Licensed to Ill,* that was a massive failure—to paraphrase "Johnny Ryall," a platinum idea, but only a gold record. Still, the Beasties' shift into a cool-but-unserious squad of postmodern pop-culture tastemakers, emerging the same year as *Mystery Science Theater 3000* and *The Simpsons* brought similar comedic sensibilities onto nationwide TV, would leave a longer-lasting impression than their Budweiser-spraying party-dude debut ever did.

They weren't alone, of course. "Man, we was mad with you when you made *3 Feet High and Rising!*" Prince Paul recalls one of the Beastie Boys lamenting when they finally met him. "We were putting all these samples together and stuff! And we were like, awww, now we've got to go back to the drawing board!" In 1989, the frontier was still wide-open and uncharted enough that they could afford to do so, both creatively and financially. But it wouldn't take long for that window to close.

## 5 | *Talkin' All That Jazz*
### The Legitimization of an Art Form

**As copyright claims and clearance issues threaten sample culture, a new reconciliation between hip-hop and its musical predecessors emerges.**

BY THE END OF THE 1980S, sampling had become far more accessible in both monetary and technological terms. Whereas Marley Marl emerged in the middle of the decade after earning chops through access to state-of-the-art recording studios, many of the producers who'd begin to emerge as major New York players in the late '80s and early '90s—DJ Mark the 45 King, Large Professor, Lord Finesse, Pete Rock, DJ Premier, and countless others—were increasingly turning to more inexpensive home studio options based around equipment like the E-mu SP-1200, which was efficient, user-friendly, and could be had for $3,000 in 1987 (about $6,500 in current money). The more home studios sprung up, the more sample-based records emerged—and though this new wave of producers simply added to the riches of the golden age rather than oversaturating the market, the sheer prevalence of sample-based music started to gain notice in musical circles outside hip-hop and other forms of club music. The result was a generational rift that pitted hip-hop artists against their live-band forebears.

The total cost of licensing the samples on *Paul's Boutique* was in the neighborhood of $250,000—Beatles, Zeppelin, and all, everything on the level, at least for the foreseeable future. But there were still pitfalls and hazards when it came to the still largely untested world of sample-based music. A segment on *MTV News* from the fall of 1989, airing right around the same time as reports of the Berlin Wall's imminent collapse, laid out the controversy: on the one hand, UK production duo Coldcut's usage of "Im Nin'alu" for a remix of Eric B. & Rakim's "Paid in Full" was seen by Israeli singer Ofra Haza as a career boost; on the other, the whole practice was decried by bizzers like producer Bob Clearmountain, who complained that "any kid can do that with a . . . $300 sampler nowadays, and it just doesn't seem quite fair 'cause it really is stealing." Prince Paul and De La Soul figured prominently in the segment as well, but not just for their role in pushing the limits of sample-based music further: they had just become the target of a $1.7 million lawsuit by Mark Volman and Howard Kaylan, aka Flo & Eddie, the founding members of '60s pop-rock group the Turtles.

Despite De La Soul diligently clearing all the major samples in the high-profile songs on *3 Feet High and Rising,* their usage of the Turtles' single "You Showed Me" was overlooked for two reasons. First, because it was on a seventy-one-second interstitial skit, "Transmitting Live from Mars," that wasn't expected to get any airplay. And second, because the portion they'd used was so brief, altered, and juxtaposed with other samples that the group and their lawyer considered it a significant transformation of the source material. The Turtles' lawyer, Evan S. Cohen, disagreed: "They've made such insignificant changes to the sound of the recording that it is still infringement as far as we're concerned, and they have violated our exclusive rights in the sound recording," he told MTV reporters. His remarks in the November 1989 issue of *Spin* were even harsher: "This isn't just a financial objection . . . Flo and Eddie are genuinely upset with the way De La Soul chopped up and mutilated their song."

Never mind that the original song wasn't written by Volman and Kaylan—"You Showed Me" was actually written by Jim McGuinn and Gene Clark of the Byrds—or that the portion of the song De La sampled didn't feature any element of Flo & Eddie's singing whatsoever (the only vocals on "Transmitting Live from Mars" came from a French instructional record). The Turtles wanted to set an artistic precedent, and unlike Nile Rodgers's run-in with "Rappers Delight," this wasn't a cut-and-dry matter of another group of musicians quasi-covering an element of a song: this was an actual repurposed sound recording, reshaped to resemble something else entirely. The idea of a piece of music like a break becoming a sort of communal component for any DJ to use might have become its own tradition, tacitly approved by many of its source material creators like George Clinton and Hall & Oates as a way of keeping older back-catalog material in the public consciousness (albeit typically contingent on their getting fairly compensated for it). But Cohen rejected Tommy Boy's offer of $1,000 after the fact for the Turtles sample—the amount they would have spent to clear it beforehand—and continued with his lawsuit despite Tommy Boy lawyer Ken Anderson warning that the precedent might "seriously hurt, if not kill [hip hop] outright."

De La Soul settled out of court for an undisclosed sum, but others weren't as lucky. In a landmark case two years later, December 1991's *Grand Upright Music, Ltd. v. Warner Bros. Records Inc.,* the United States District Court for the Southern District of New York ruled that Biz Markie—the way-back friend of Prince Paul, early beneficiary of Marley Marl's production, and a rapper for whom Paul C helped engineer a Top 10 hit in "Just a Friend"—had infringed on the copyright of Gilbert O'Sullivan when he sampled the piano melody of the singer-songwriter's "Alone Again (Naturally)" for Biz's own "Alone Again" and put the record out without O'Sullivan's approval. (Biz had tried to pay the going rate for the sample, but was denied.) The result of the ruling dictated that all samples must not only be licensed, but cleared with the sampled works' creators before they could be allowed on a recording. Subsequently, mechanical rights holders could sometimes demand as much as 100 percent of all royalties for songs using samples of copyrighted works. While the ruling didn't immediately damage the creative potential that sample-based artists and producers were capable of, it went a long way in making the freedom of albums as sample-dense as *3 Feet High and Rising* and *Paul's Boutique* prohibitively expensive at best and logistically impossible at worst.

The worst thing about these legal and industry restrictions was that they were passed down without much knowledge of or respect for what sampling actually meant. In roughly ten years, from the late '70s DJ sets to the late '80s SP-1200 soundscapes, hip-hop had created a way of recognizing, acknowledging, renewing, and transforming a collective language of musical history that massively expanded the way music itself is listened to: as a mutable object, the calling up of fragmented memories that get the hook or the beat of a song stuck in your head and then make a new world out of that memory. It was the musical equivalent of restoring an old car to run faster or bounce on hydraulics or gleam with candy-colored paint; it was consolidating the sound of a lifetime's worth of record collections into a distillation of culture or place or time; it was a DIY end run around the rules of how music was made that drastically widened the possibilities for young musicians whose schools were increasingly underfunded in the arts. Most of all, it was en route to becoming the most pervasive, popular, and revolutionary black American art form since jazz—and its creators had to figure out, fast, just how to preserve this art form before corporate interference snuffed it out.

· · ·

Five years before his band's 1983 single "Juicy Fruit" formed the basis of Notorious B.I.G.'s hit single "Juicy," James Mtume appeared on a 1988 radio broadcast on Bob Slade's KISS-FM program *Week in Review* to discuss the pitfalls of sampling. And his objections weren't merely legal: they were aesthetic and moral. On this particular broadcast, Mtume called sample-based compositions evidence that "this is the first generation of African Americans not to be extending the range of the music," and claimed that sampling James Brown was like show guest Nelson George plagiarizing passages of James Baldwin's writing in his own book.

Mtume wasn't just some pop star: he'd long had ties to black political activism, coming up in the 1960s stumping for jazz as a link to the cultural identity of the African diaspora. And he had a part in some of the most revolutionary music ever recorded as a percussionist with Miles Davis's band, starting with 1972's incendiary free jazz / funk / rock fusion classic *On the Corner.* That lent his concerns the kind of weight that a bigshot AOR record producer or entertainment lawyer couldn't, and was provocative enough of a statement to send shockwaves through the musical community. By the time Mtume held forth at the 1989 New Music Seminar, his concerns were reaching a wider audience. "You cannot substitute technique for composition," he protested. "We're raising a generation of young black kids who don't know how to play music. It's like learning how to paint by numbers . . . that's based on someone else's thought and creative ability."

He'd also inspired some strong, well-thought-out retorts. Hank Shocklee, whose Bomb Squad had just helmed a masterpiece of sampling in Public Enemy's *It Takes a Nation of Millions to Hold Us Back,* echoed the sentiments that Chuck and Flav expressed in their track "Caught, Can We Get a Witness?" On record, PE had anticipated a future of creative copyright litigation that hadn't fully arrived in 1988—"Caught, now in court cause I stole a beat / This is a sampling sport / But I'm giving it a new name, what you hear is mine"—that producer Shocklee gave a technical and compositional dimension to. When challenged by an older black musician that "you spend 12 seconds sampling a record that a guy spent 15 years breaking his neck to get that sound . . . that's not creativity," Hank countered that "there is a difference between sampling and plagiarism . . . why should I spend eight days to get a snare drum sound like Phil Collins? He's done it for me. I can sample that in two seconds and get on to more important things." As a producer at the forefront of using sampled sounds to create entirely new drum patterns, melodic emphases, and built-up soundscapes, Shocklee's view of sample sources as a way to quickly juxtapose specific sonic details in order to do new things with them was the primary defense.

But it was Daddy-O, whose group Stetsasonic had refined their style during a tour with Public Enemy, who zeroed in on the deeper cultural implications. His appearance at the New Music Seminar, where he called sampling "musical collage" and compared it to the kind of iconography-repurposing pop art done by Andy Warhol, was the expansion of an ideological objection he first came up with as a direct response to Mtume's *Week in Review* appearance the year before. In its original form, this objection was titled "Talkin' All That Jazz," a single from Stetsasonic's 1988 sophomore album *In Full Gear* which made the pointed case that "Tell the truth, James Brown was old / 'Til Eric and Ra came out with 'I Got Soul' / Rap brings back old R&B / And if we would not, people could've forgot." The music video, one of the first directed by Fab 5 Freddy, added the framing device of the band going on trial—though Mtume, who was never directly mentioned in the lyrics, was swapped out for a couple of sneering, nerdy, establishment-type white lawyers as the group's video antagonists. "Of course we expect to win," scoffs one as they give an interview to the news on the steps of a courthouse. "Any self-respecting intelligent person knows that this so called 'band,' Stetsasonic, and the rest of this hip-hop music is just a passing fad . . . which one, is not creative, two, inspires violence and three, encourages thievery in the form of sampling."

Conflating Mtume's objections with those of a couple caricaturized copyright lawyers might have been somewhat disingenuous, but it was effective—and it helped highlight a connection that was growing more prominent in the hip-hop world as the '90s approached. Stetsasonic member Delite had previously brought up to Daddy-O the idea of doing a jazz-inflected hip-hop track, including the idea to sample the jittery

Cecil McBee stand-up bass from Lonnie Liston Smith's "Expansions" that held the rhythm down tight. That beat was laid down by Prince Paul when De La Soul was still an unknown quantity and Paul was still scrapping for input in the first group to hire him. (Paul was never credited.) The actual record didn't work as a sample, however, even when they slowed it down—so they brought in Don Newkirk, a producer/ musician whom Paul later recruited to do voice-over cameos on *3 Feet High and Rising*, to replicate it using a keyboard. When Tom Silverman got Daddy-O on the phone to talk to Lonnie Liston Smith himself for sample rights, Smith assented enthusiastically: "You can have that, man. That ain't 'Expansions' no more, you done made something new."

It was a prescient idea—one step ahead of the *Ultimate Breaks & Beats* canon (which didn't add "Expansions" until the series' penultimate volume in 1990), and two steps ahead of detractors who saw hip-hop production as strictly nonmusical. But it was more than just a simple aesthetic defense of the art of sampling by juxtaposing it and implicitly comparing itself to jazz. With hip-hop emerging as a dominant cultural force by and for black Americans, the need to keep it legitimized in the face of both detractors and corporate co-optation was key. With the commercial prospects of rap divided between multiple fronts of the genre in 1988—the increasingly political and militant hip-hop grabbing attention in New York, an insurgent wave of gangsta rap emerging out West, and a bass-driven, sexually explicit wave out of Miami—hip-hop seemed to land somewhere between a massive multi-scene expansion and an identity crisis. And while that meant new avenues of expression, it also meant more potential for get-rich-quick commercial fads to overwhelm more sustained movements and push them to the margins.

It's in an environment like this where the idea of hip-hop as a preservationist culture—not only of its musical predecessors, but of itself— began to take its strongest hold. Hip-hop in the late '80s was where the stakes in the long-standing arguments and divisions around musical integrity in a corporate system—deep niche interest versus wide commercial appeal; new risks versus what works; killing your idols versus revering them—felt higher than ever. And as the opposition to selling out and going pop took on an increasingly Afrocentric perspective, the artists that took the stance of staying true fueled some of the most uplifting music hip-hop had ever seen.

• • •

De La Soul contributed to a crucial perspective on hip-hop—that it could retain a fundamental connection to blackness while finding modes of expression that both defied and expanded the surface-level mainstream idea of what blackness actually was. But as often as their skeptics and detractors liked to position them as weird bohemian outliers, De La were far from alone, proof of which was displayed in an iconic, clique-establishing posse cut. "Buddy" was a track from *3 Feet High and Rising* that started out featuring a small group of De La's peers and, thanks to the recording sessions' open-door policy, was soon remixed into a veritable summit of like-minded rappers. And it was this gathering of MCs— Mike Gee and Afrika Baby Bam of the Jungle Brothers, Phife and Q-Tip of A Tribe Called Quest, and solo artists Queen Latifah and Monie Love—that would form the core of a crew that became synonymous with Afrocentric, jazz-inflected hip-hop. The name: Native Tongues.

The Jungle Brothers had already earned a rep as trailblazers with their debut album *Straight Out the Jungle,* a late 1988 release that proved profoundly influential on De La Soul during the recording of *3 Feet High and Rising.* (Pos and Trugoy admitted to lifting their flow for "Me Myself and I" from Mike and Bam's bouncy syllable-enunciating delivery on "Black Is Black.") *Straight Out* was an excursion into the idea of a new Afrocentrism, one that reenvisioned the motherland as a living cultural exchange partner rather than just an abstracted point of long-ago origin: Africa being where you were at, not just where you were from, a medallion you could always carry with you.

The production was suitably eclectic, running a funky gamut from classic James Brown and Sly and the Family Stone breaks to a pioneering effort at integrating contemporary dance music on the Todd Terry– assisted "I'll House You." But the album's been described, particularly retroactively, as an early effort of "jazz rap." It's not that there was a significant amount of traditional jazz actually sampled on the record, aside from some funkier soul-jazz crossovers by Eddie Harris, Grover Washington Jr., Ralph MacDonald, and Gil Scott-Heron woven into the production. It just *felt* right, though—their Afrocentric style was more utopian than militant, more lighthearted than stressed, and fully dedicated to eradicating the divide between mental reflection and bodily motion.

De La and the Jungle Brothers had clicked during a co-billed show in Boston, and when the former group invited the latter for a record-ing session, Bam called up another up-and-coming MC he knew since high school. This one was based in Queens—hence his recording name "Q-Tip"—and by the time the original mix of "Buddy" hit the airwaves, his group that the Jungle Brothers had dubbed A Tribe Called Quest had signed a deal with Geffen to produce a five-song demo tape. (The deal fell through, but the demo eventually got them a deal with Jive Records, an independent hip-hop powerhouse in the late '80s.) Q-Tip was imme-diately attention-getting as an MC, relaxed yet emphatic, with a nasal tone that somehow only added to his perceptive lyrical sharpness.

But he was also a secret weapon as a producer, crafting deeply jazz-influenced beats that made even his more frivolous lyrics sound sophisticated. His debut as both a rapper and a producer came through *Straight Out the Jungle:* whereas his guest spot on "Black Is Black" made his name in the former category, his skills as a beatmaker were on full display in "The Promo," a track that closed the CD version of the album and prominently sampled the five-note Malcolm Duncan tenor sax coda from Average White Band's "Would You Stay." Tip turned the conclud-ing moments of a slow blues number to the hook of something more substantial, a haunting refrain that hinted at far more than just loneli-ness or yearning—an intangible but immediate sense of *cool,* the kind of cool that had its first deep roots in the bebop era of the late '40s and was later passed down to Q-Tip through his jazz-enthusiast father.

It was an early reliance on the time-consuming practice of mak-ing his beats through pause tapes that infused Q-Tip's production style with a combination of painstaking craft and meditative focus, even after he graduated to more advanced technology. ("I must be, like, on some other shit, if I could sit here for hours and hours and do this with these records and get these little pieces and just continually loop it like that," he described it to rap journalist Jeff Mao in a 2013 interview.) From the earliest A Tribe Called Quest tracks, his beats had a distinct and wide-open sense of dynamics—when to let the beat breathe, when a conversa-tional tone sounds better than a straight-up rap verse, when the balance between deep resonance and calm quiet can nail a desired mood with uncanny precision. It was a philosophy Q-Tip attributed to reading an interview with Miles Davis on the intricacies and musicality of space—timing and juxtaposition and well-placed silence—that it really began to sink in.

The payoff came in 1990 with *People's Instinctive Travels and the Paths of Rhythm,* the first album to ever get the full five out of five mics on the famous rating scale used by *The Source.* "A completely original musical and spiritual approach to hip-hop," the review stated, "[with] sophisticated production invoking a jazz flavor." The influences weren't as far-flung as the Prince Paul beats on *3 Feet High and Rising,* but they were deeply rooted and boasted the kind of rarefied jazz knowledge that would soon prove absolutely necessary for New York producers at the turn of the '90s.

Opener "Push It Along" got its liquid-smooth but heavy-hitting drums from Billy Cobham and its cool-breeze-in-a-desert sax from Grover Washington Jr. Every portion of "Youthful Expression," from the cricket-chirp Hammond organ to the climbing/descending see-saw bass, was a slick rearrangement of Reuben Wilson's lively soul-jazz cover of Marvin Gaye's "Inner City Blues." And "Luck of Lucien" resurrected the backbone of "Fourty Days," a selection from Billy Brooks' 1974 *Windows of the Mind*—the only recording of a band led by the man who played trumpet in legendary vibraphonist Lionel Hampton's band back in the '50s. Just unearthing these underheard or forgotten records and reintroducing them to a younger audience was enough to shift the conversation deeper into jazz appreciation; that A Tribe Called Quest did so with such immediate flavor only made the connections that much more meaningful.

It felt like a culmination of ideas that had been kicking around for a while: behind nearly every great producer of the early sample era was a parent's formidable, jazz-filled record collection to influence them. But there are breaks sourced from jazz records, and then there are *jazz breaks*. The former had a presence from the get-go; the version of "Take Me to the Mardi Gras" that Bob James cut for his '75 album *Two* was an old-school favorite based on how hard its bell-rocking drum intro hit. But one would be hard-pressed to call Run-D.M.C.'s "Peter Piper" or T La Rock's "Breaking Bells" "jazzy," no matter if that's where James's records were filed. This new phase of production actually felt more musically and philosophically in tune with jazz, making their connection to the music synonymous with a greater sense of positive-minded purpose and knowledge of self. It all fit with the defense of sampling that Daddy-O put forth at the '89 New Music Seminar in the wake of the controversy that inspired "Talkin' All That Jazz" in the first place: "Sampling gives young blacks a sense of their musical heritage." And the Native Tongues proved that this heritage was being carried well into the future.

•  •  •

Despite the hassle that the Turtles sample lawsuit brought down on him, Prince Paul spent 1990 with plenty on his plate. A couple beats for Big Daddy Kane's *Taste of Chocolate* kept him on the radar for hardcore heads, while another gig contributing two cuts to *To Your Soul,* the second album by Brooklyn rapper the Jaz, resulted in a young up-and-comer named Jay-Z dropping one of his earliest hot verses on "It's That Simple" and giving him a high-praise name-check ("For a dope beat you seek the Prince Paul"). And he spent much of the year working on follow-ups to albums by artists he'd worked with before, from Stetsasonic (*Blood, Sweat, & No Tears*) to 3rd Bass (*Derelicts of Dialect*), that would hit stores the following year. It was steady work, even though these projects might not have given him the creative free rein that *3 Feet High and Rising* did.

But it was a record he hadn't been banking on having a major hand in, the second album by De La Soul, that pushed him to another level entirely. "At first, I didn't want to do the second album," Paul told *Complex.* "[The] guys from De La came up to me and said, 'Yo, we're going to work on the second album.' I replied, 'Word. Good luck!' But they were like, 'Yo, we want you to be down. You're part of the team.'" Paul came on board, though he initially intended to help make the album as a sort of instructional moment; De La were filled with ideas and Paul felt that showing them how to run the production equipment would give them more independence. But it was still a free exchange of inspiration between Paul and De La, and it had come at a time when the latter were visibly chafing at the residual effects of their debut's reputation.

Going from being unknown quantities to occupying a choice spot under the record industry's microscope might have had a lot to do with it; being stepped to on tour by goons who thought the colorful clothes and peace-sign iconography made De La Soul easy to pick fights with didn't help much, either. The crew were still wiseasses who dedicated themselves to their own notions of nonconformity, but the happy-go-lucky vibe of their debut was impossible to sustain now that they had expectations to clash with.

They went from rising to dead in one album. The D.A.I.S.Y. Age was over; it couldn't be Da Inner Sound, Y'all when the inner was pulled

outside. And *De La Soul Is Dead* marked a deliberate shift toward cyn-
icism starting with the cover—an illustration of an overturned, broken
flowerpot spilling three wilted daisies and dirt all over a stark, empty
white backdrop. Instead of skits introducing the group as a bunch of
affable weirdos, the album was framed by a series of bits where a group
of kids find a De La Soul tape in the garbage (*De La Soul Is Dead* itself, a
sly bit of recursive humor), which finds its way into the hands of a scowling bully and his two toadying friends. They pop in every few tracks to
deride the music like a hip-hop prototype of *Beavis and Butt-Head*, and
come to a damning conclusion during the outro: "What happened to
the pimps? What happened to the guns? What happened to the curse
words? That's what rap music is all about, right?" They toss the De La
tape back into the trash where it was discovered and head off to listen
to MC Hammer instead.

It was a deliberately self-aware irony, of course; De La were still
proud of the songs they cut for *De La Soul Is Dead,* and they had justi-
fiable reasons to be. It was cynical and dark at times: there are tracks
about all the fights they got provoked into ("Pease Porridge"), all the
rappers haranguing them for a quick cosign ("Ring Ring Ring [Ha Ha
Hey]"), the travails of a crack-addicted sibling ("My Brother's a Baseh-
ead"), even a bleak storytelling cut about the revenge of a girl on the
father who molested her ("Millie Pulled a Pistol on Santa"). But it was
also wickedly funny, featured even more outlandish lyrical excursions
than the original, and came together as a sprawling but characteristically true-to-self suite of music and comedy that felt like it had room for
almost everything. Paul and the group pulled together some wild pastiches that stood as some of the era's finest.

"Oodles of O's" pulled a creative coup by melding the springy walk-
ing bass line from Tom Waits' cabaret-beatnik cut "Diamonds on My
Windshield" to the snap-tight drums from Lafayette Afro Rock Band's
"Hihache," a vibe that crossed up white singer-songwriter bohemian-
ism and funk geared toward the African diaspora in Paris. Young-love
anthem "A Roller Skating Jam Named 'Saturdays'" was a masterful update
of early '80s disco-rap for the sample-rich era that melded '70s cuts from
Chicago, Instant Funk, Mighty Ryeders, Tower of Power, and a snatched
vocal snippet from Chic's "Good Times" together, then brought in
young singer Vinia Mojica to give it one of the most joyous sung hooks
of the golden era. "Shwingalokate" emerged as an even wilder P-Funk

homage than "Me Myself and I" did, all exclamation-point horn sections and Bernie Worrell synth squiggles over a booty-motivating bassline. And "Pease Porridge" was diabolically weird, building itself around an old-timey tap-dance number sourced from the B-side of a Harlem Globetrotters tie-in single "Sweet Georgia Brown."

Throw in genre goofs like hip-house parody "Kicked Out the House," the dozens-battle-of-the-sexes exhibition "Bitties in the BK Lounge," and bizarre interludes making fun of tough-guy hood narratives like "Who Do U Worship?" and it was as much a great comedy record as it was a great hip-hop record. *De La Soul Is Dead* might have sounded like a bitter self-rebuke of a title, but the group largely picked it because they thought it was funny. As much as its attitude diverged from the chill lightheartedness of *3 Feet High and Rising, De La Soul Is Dead* still felt like a lot of fun, especially since it was also a major step ahead for sample-based compositions. How the most far-flung ideas could all come together to create such a distinct record felt like some kind of minor miracle of production.

But it also came at a time when it seemed like a rift in Native Tongues was already starting to form, and it sounded like it. Prince Paul and De La Soul were thrown into this bohemian jazz-based group by association, and they typically meshed well with their Native Tongues cohorts, but *De La Soul Is Dead* felt a bit stylistically at odds. Paul rarely gravitated toward jazz breaks, and this album in particular was notable by its almost complete absence of them, even if the beats still sounded slippery and esoteric at times. Meanwhile, *The Low End Theory*, the sophomore album that A Tribe Called Quest released just over four months later and the one that fully established Phife Dawg as Q-Tip's legendary partner on the mic, was an entire exegesis of jazz's role in hip-hop—starting with Q-Tip's very first verse ("Back in the days when I was a teenager / Before I had status and before I had a pager / You could find the Abstract listenin' to hip-hop / My pops used to say it reminded him of bebop") and continuing through references laced in the lyrics and beats sourced from the a who's who of connoisseur jazz. Trace the origins of the beats on *The Low End Theory* and you would be connected to the worlds of Art Blakey and the Jazz Messengers, Grover Washington Jr., Jimmy McGriff, Brother Jack McDuff, Jack DeJohnette, Dr. Lonnie Smith, Joe Farrell, Eric Dolphy, Cannonball Adderley, and Ron Carter—the latter of whom actually appeared live playing stand-up bass on

"Verses from the Abstract." By the time "Jazz (We've Got)" popped up in the album's latter half, the associations were permanent and indelible.

That divergence of styles between De La and their peers might not have been the largest rift—both '91 releases earned five-mic raves from *The Source*—but Q-Tip caused a bigger one when he made the decision to change his management. Kool DJ Red Alert, the Zulu Nation–affiliated radio DJ who had held down the Bronx during the Bridge Wars and mentored the Native Tongues in their formative years, had managed A Tribe Called Quest in their early days. But during the *Low End Theory* recording sessions, Tip jumped to Rush Management, headed by Def Jam impresario (and "A Roller Skating Jam Named 'Saturdays'" guest announcer) Russell Simmons. ("We thought [they] had done good by De La Soul, and we wanted to explore that," Tip told *Vibe* in a Native Tongues retrospective for their February 2007 issue.) The Jungle Brothers were already in the midst of a rough stretch: after releasing their second album, *Done by the Forces of Nature*, in November 1989, an album that received even more rapturous critical and fan praise than their pioneering debut, they'd started work on a record, the wildly experimental and psychedelic *Crazy Wisdom Masters,* that would get them caught up in a years-long struggle with their label, Warner Bros.

Now, already feeling underrated and rejected by both their label and the mainstream hip-hop world, the Jungle Brothers saw this management change as a direct, and in part personal affront, as Red Alert was Mike G's uncle. Feelings got caught, and friendships were tested to the point of breaking. "Success ruined a lot of Native Tongues," Mase recollected in the same *Vibe* article. "Things were happening too fast for some people, and things were not happening fast enough for others. Money was destroying the relationships." Afrika Baby Bam put it more bluntly: "They have been trying to erase the Jungle Brothers out of the books, when I was the one that started the whole thing . . . Maseo has always been good people and a real dude. But Q-Tip and Pos, I don't know." During what should have been the creative peak of the Native Tongues' core, the future looked shaky.

•  •  •

The *Ultimate Breaks and Beats* compilations capitalized on a just-ahead-of-the-curve ability to catalog classic DJ breaks dating back to the '70s and reintroduce them to a new generation of producers, ones who'd grown up watching DJs spin them and came of age with the ability to directly sample them. But by the early '90s, finding and staking claim to all but the most obscure breaks had become remarkably difficult, while record labels actually directly courted hip-hop fans with promises of pulling back the curtain on prized source material. "You Gotta Hear Blue Note to Dig Def Jam!!!" shouted the cover tagline to the first volume of *Blue Break Beats,* a compilation series the venerable label began putting out in 1992 to emphasize jazz music's continued influence on golden age producers. But the word had been out for a while: when the '90s arrived, there was no shortage of emerging hip-hop producers who had tapped into the deeper veins of jazz music to create their own styles.

After the murder of Paul C, Large Professor was brought in to complete the work his mentor had started on his tracks for Eric B. & Rakim's 1990 album *Let the Rhythm Hit 'Em.* Though neither Large Professor nor Paul C were given specific producer credits (save a memorial dedication to the latter), Eric B. and Rakim were suitably impressed by the work Large Professor had done completing Paul C's unfinished portions, including the first single "In the Ghetto," that Eric got Large Professor another gig making beats incognito for Kool G Rap & DJ Polo's *Wanted: Dead or Alive.* But ghost-producing these beats didn't reveal the intricacies of his style quite like the work Large Professor did with the group Main Source.

Along with K-Cut and Sir Scratch, Large Professor was a major creative force in the group, acting as producer/MC/DJ triple threat and contributing significantly to its heavy jazz inflection on beats. Not every track on their 1991 debut *Breaking Atoms* was as steeped in it as the Donald Byrd–sampling frustrated romance song "Looking at the Front Door" or the killer-cop national pastime metaphor "Just a Friendly Game of Baseball" and its ruminative rework of a track by alto sax player Lou Donaldson. But Large Professor put a certain multilayered musicality into his tracks that treated its source material like carefully malleable components of a bigger compositional whole. He built as much around melody as he did around the beat, and had the tendency to incorporate different segments for the verse, the chorus, and the bridge to give a track a more dynamic feel. He could make everything he extracted sound like it came from a jazz record, even when it didn't—an evocative resonance that defined a whole image of New York for a good stretch of the '90s.

At the same time, just north of the Bronx in Mount Vernon, another DJ was launching his own career. Pete Philips—aka Pete Rock—had been energized by the first wave of late '80s sample-flipping producers, including the underrated, ahead-of-its-time production work of the Bronx's Mark "The 45 King" James. The 45 King liked to source his beats from overlooked 7-inch records, and built distinctly horn-centered cuts like his 1987 instrumental "The 900 Number" (a dancefloor-exploding flip of the baritone sax from Marva Whitney's "Unwind Yourself") or a number of tracks on the classic '89 Queen Latifah album *All Hail the Queen* (the sax on "Ladies First" alone is an ideal early blueprint for how to use brass in a hip-hop beat). And with the 45 King as a precedent, Pete recognized that the ear for horns he was developing himself could evolve into something even more transformative. Pete had grown up in a record-collector household and grew to value the thrill of finding breaks nobody else had discovered—at one point, spending so many hours digging through dusty stacks of LPs that he got sick from it, and started bringing gloves and a facemask on successive trips as though he was working in a hospital.

Pete came up with something special once he combined that level of cratedigger dedication with his efforts to introduce sounds that other producers had only hinted at—chopped and layered into intensely soulful meditations on recursive fragments of melody, with grimy drums and intricately filtered, clean yet heavy bass lines that proved nigh-impossible for anyone else to credibly imitate. Pete Rock's beats blurred the borders between a weathered past and an in-the-moment present, archeology and architecture all at once. By 1991, he'd both created one of the greatest remixes of all time—his transformation of Public Enemy's "Shut 'Em Down" into a richly dense *boom bap* bass-snare rhythm with a Tom Scott sax riff droning like an alarm call—and a stunning debut EP with his rap partner C.L. Smooth, *All Souled Out,* that put them both on the map as future stars. A year later, their debut *Mecca and the Soul Brother*—featuring their single "They Reminisce Over You (T.R.O.Y.)," a dedication to late friend and Heavy D. & the Boyz dancer Trouble T Roy—became one of the most retrospectively beloved hip-hop records of its time, a slow seller that made up for in long-term reverence what it lacked in initial buzz.

And if Pete Rock and C.L. Smooth had any direct peers, it was Gang Starr—another group featuring a laidback but wordy MC and a producer/DJ with an almost supernatural sense of musical reinterpretation. The beatmaker in question, DJ Premier, took the early innovations of hip-hop as sound collage to new levels. His technique surpassed the virtuosity of Grandmaster Flash on the turntables, his ability to build entirely new vocal hooks and phrases from pieces of other rappers' lyrics was the sharpest example of music as metacommentary since Double Dee & Steinski's "Lessons," and he arguably did more than anyone to establish the sound of classic early '90s hip-hop as the sound of jazz reincarnate. It was established early with 1989's "Manifest," later rereleased and remixed as "Words I Manifest," which went as far back as it could to the source of bebop—Charlie Parker, as represented in the piano riff from a 1946 recording of "A Night in Tunisia"—and brought it back through soul, funk, and Preemo's own inimitable scratching. And with     Guru as the MC laying out his surgically precise verses with a focus that was calm to the point of deadpan, Gang Starr earned an identity as a group capable of invoking the same kind of sophisticated artfulness as the classic jazz artists they sampled.

1990's "Jazz Thing," a Branford Marsalis–cowritten cut from the soundtrack to Spike Lee's *Mo' Better Blues,* built a whole constellation around a thorough history lesson laced with references to Charlie Parker, Dizzy Gillespie, John Coltrane, and Ornette Coleman to go with samples of Louis Armstrong, Duke Ellington, Thelonious Monk, Charles Mingus, Kool & the Gang, and Gang Starr themselves. Guru's concluding line: "And more and more people, yes, they will be knowin' / Jazz ain't the past, this music's gonna last / And as the facts unfold, remember who foretold / The 90's will be the decade of a jazz thing." Their third album, 1992's *Daily Operation,* was packed with beats that expanded on the ideas of classic jazz riffs: the string-drenched soul crossover of Ahmad Jamal covering Foster Sylvers's "Misdemeanor" turned into non-stop unresolved tension on "Soliloquy of Chaos"; "2 Deep" building a whole cage-pacing tiger walk out of a horn section riff from Eddie Harris' "Lovely Is Today"; constructing an entire beat from the precision thunderstorm of a Buddy Rich drum break on "The Place Where We Dwell." There were so many possibilities that Premier got away with using a granite-melting suspense-flick horn fanfare from Johnny Hammond's "Big Sur Suite" as a twenty-four-second instrumental interlude. He called it "24-7 / 365"—a warning of the work ethic you were dealing with if you ever wanted to try and top it.

There were plenty of other groups and producers who created hip-hop records under the influence of jazz, enough to fill out an already-packed early '90s record release schedule: just for starters, there were the sociopolitical conscious-rap crew Brand Nubian, bohemian Grammy-winners Digable Planets, and the massive Bronx-based collective Diggin' in the Crates Crew (D.I.T.C. for short), featuring three top-tier producers in Lord Finesse, Diamond D, and Buckwild. They ranged in tone from idealistic positivity to maniacal boasting to true-crime bleakness, but they all made clear the connections between hip-hop and jazz. What started as a defensive bulwark against accusations of overly simplistic ideas and a deliberate effort to find a new style that built off more than just heavy funk drum breaks had emerged as something definitive and characteristic, a previous generation's sound passing its genes down to a youth movement it raised to carry its tradition in new forms.

And no album captured that collective moment quite like *Illmatic*. Nasty Nas debuted on record in 1991 with an opening guest verse on Main Source's *Breaking Atoms* track "Live at the Barbeque." He was immediately quotable, with a flow that rivaled Rakim's straight out of the gate and a lyricism that portrayed him midway between genius and sociopath: "Verbal assassin, my architect pleases / When I was twelve, I went to hell for snuffin' Jesus." That verse, his appearance on MC Serch's "Back to the Grill" in August '92, and his Large Professor–produced solo debut single "Halftime" less than three months later were all listeners had to go by for nearly three years, but those three years were enough to build a massive groundswell of anticipation and hype best expressed by a *Vibe* article from their April '94 issue: "[A] genuine lyrical B-boy by the name of Nas . . . has emerged from behind the intellectual clouds left by weak artists, faked funk, and wasted radio airtime. . . . Real hip hop lovers know the genesis of Nas is to be witnessed, for his lyrical style and innovation will play an important role in the evolution of modern hip hop."

*Illmatic*, released that same month, had called on the skills of a who's who of producers to bring Nas's already vivid scene-setting lyrics into emotive soundscapes. If there was an observation and an emotional connection for a young black man hustling in Queens, Nas embodied it on the mic—the triumphs and frustrations, the euphoria and the despair. And the ensemble cast of beatmakers, one of the first examples of a hip-hop production classic by committee, assembled an album that was the most cinematic work the genre had ever seen.

DJ Premier used his ear for tension to create fever-dream anxiety out of Joe Chambers piano riffs ("N.Y. State of Mind") and gave Nas's post-traumatic survival stories an ironically upbeat counterpoint through the Hammond B-3 of Reuben Wilson ("Memory Lane [Sittin' in da Park]"). The handful of beats Large Professor contributed included the simultaneously euphoric and sinister "It Ain't Hard to Tell," turning a fragment of a sax solo from a Kool & the Gang song into a recurring exclamation of the divine. Pete Rock's "The World Is Yours" traded in his usual horn-section recursion for a slyly rearranged Ahmad Jamal piano loop; he also used a different piece of the same song by session drummer Jim Gordon that Large Professor sampled for "One Time 4 Your Mind," and pieced it into his beat it so subtly it might as well have been an inside joke. And the thumb piano / upright bass–driven Heath Brothers loop that Q-Tip built the prison-correspondence narrative "One Love" from created such a deep atmosphere of longing, mournful and hopeful all at once, that even the savvier heads who knew Tip was the production master-mind of A Tribe Called Quest's greatest beats could have been thrown by how emotionally nuanced it was.

The most telling (and surprising) musical moment on *Illmatic*, though, came from L.E.S., a cohort of Nas's from the Queensbridge housing projects who earned his first-ever production credit with "Life's a Bitch." A sleek rework of the Gap Band's smooth 1980 R&B ballad "Yearning for Your Love," it flawlessly captured the album's push and pull between fatalism and gratitude, underscoring Nas and his debuting colleague AZ's existential live-for-today lyrics with a sound that tugged at the line between romantic and nihilist. And then, after the last repetition of the hook ("Life's a bitch and then you die, that's why we puff lye / 'Cause you never know when you're gonna go"), the sound of a cornet that bordered on the anguished pierces through the beat and renders heat-hazed day into snowbound night. The man playing it is Olu Dara, who had spent the '70s and '80s gigging with avant-garde and free jazz musicians like James Blood Ulmer, Henry Threadgill, and David Murray. He is also Nas's father.

• • •

Still, the question remained: was sample-based hip-hop, a form of music dependent more on careful engineering and painstaking repetition and refinement than off-the-cuff spontaneity, particularly compatible with the improvisational and constantly mutating structure of jazz? There were technological breakthroughs on the horizon that would soon at least allow for compromises in that department, but the SP-1200 remained the weapon of choice for producers like Large Professor and Pete Rock until later in their careers. Hip-hop as a live-band proposition, even hybridized like Stetsasonic were, seemed like a weird gimmick.

That could be why Guru's *Jazzmatazz* spent so much of its liner note space justifying itself. Even after *Hard to Earn*—and *Mecca and the Soul Brother* and *Breaking Atoms* and *The Low End Theory* and all that—it seemed risky that Guru concocted the idea to build a rap album around the live-band contributions of the same jazz legends that hip-hop producers were regularly sampling. In the liner notes to *Jazzmatazz,* renowned hip-hop journalist Bill Adler made a point of highlighting some of the live-band jazz/hip-hop crossovers that had led to this moment, from Quincy Jones's 1989 *Back on the Block*—its Grammy-winning title track featured verses by Ice-T, Melle Mel, Kool Moe Dee, and Big Daddy Kane—to Miles Davis's final album, 1992's *Doo-Bop,* produced by hip-hop beatmaker Easy Mo Bee. (That latter album was critically panned, but no matter: one year later, he created the jazzy, Johnny Hammond–sampling beat for the Notorious B.I.G.'s debut single "Party and Bullshit.") And he also made a point of highlighting both the detractors and the ambassadors of the jazz world in terms of receptiveness to hip-hop, even ones from the same family: both the rap-hating Delfeayo Marsalis and his Gang Starr–collaborating brother Branford get shoutouts.

Branford appeared again on *Jazzmatazz,* along with a host of other handpicked musicians who Guru felt represented the best of the soul-jazz stars he grew up on in the '70s and started rapping over in the '80s. Keyboardist Lonnie Liston Smith, trumpeter Donald Byrd, and vibraphonist Roy Ayers were three of the leading lights in both those eras, with indelible R&B crossover classics that eventually made their way into DJ crates from the Bronx on out. The Stetsasonic-sampled "Expansions" ("Talkin' All That Jazz"), the Main Source–sampled "Think Twice" ("Looking at the Front Door"), and the A Tribe Called Quest–sampled "Daylight" ("Bonita Applebum") were some of the most instantly recognizable cuts in their respective original artists' repertoires even before they became often-used breaks. Guru remained cautiously reverent in his efforts to bring these artists into his project, confessing in the notes that "I was leery. It had to be done right. . . . My main concern was to maintain my street credibility and to represent the hardcore rap crowd because they've got me to where I am now." But it was pulled off better than anyone could have hoped. Once the working method was established—Guru started with a rhythm track, then brought in the jazz musician to play for a while as he wrote lyrics with their solos as inspiration—the songs that came out of it felt as true to the spirit of hip-hop as anything a strictly sample-based beat could provide.

A handful of high-profile rap albums followed *Jazzmatazz* in its efforts to further establish hip-hop and live-band music as integral partners in '93. The Roots' *Organix*—parts of which were recorded literally a day after *Jazzmatazz* was released—was an independent release that established the Philadelphia band as a powerful successor to Stetsasonic. An entire live band's worth of musicians—including drummer Ahmir "Questlove" Thompson, keyboardist Scott Storch, and bassist Leonard "Hub" Hubbard—the Roots would occasionally interpolate portions of other songs into their own, but more often than not just composed their own rhythms and melodies for their MCs, Black Thought and Malik B., to run roughshod over. (More than twenty-five years later, they've released a dozen studio albums, collaborated with John Legend and Elvis Costello, won three Grammys, and become the house band for *The Tonight Show*—making them arguably the most resiliently successful hip-hop group to debut during the golden age.) The Blue Note label got into the act as well, with the UK-based group Us3 building an entire album, 1993's *Hand on the Torch,* out of a combination of session musicians and samples taken entirely from the Blue Note catalog. Lead single "Cantaloop (Flip Fantasia)," an up-tempo track based around a piano loop from Herbie Hancock's "Cantaloupe Island," hit #9 on the Billboard Hot 100 and helped *Hand on the Torch* notch a place in history as the first Blue Note album to sell a million copies.

• • •

*Buhloone Mindstate,* De La Soul's third album, was never intended to be a turning point—a reboot, maybe, a consolidation of all their ideas into something less absurdist and more focused on the mic virtuosity that many critics and fans saw as secondary to their comedic strangeness. But it was also a necessary expression of—and a release valve for—the group's biz-machine burnout. If *De La Soul Is Dead* shifted between bitter and goofy, its follow-up had a wit inseparable from how acerbic it was, if artfully so. It was defiant in the face of fleeting bandwagon fans, dissolving friendships, and industry expectations (the titular mindstate is underscored by the phrase "We might blow up but we won't go pop"), but still not disillusioned enough to forget why making music brought them joy in the first place. They ran wild with ideas that made them seem as diametrically opposed to both frothy pop-rap and hardcore gangsta postures as possible. A sequel to Ultramagnetic MCs' breakthrough '86 single "Ego Trippin'," "Ego Trippin', Part Two" skewered rap braggadocio using as many references to other rappers' (and their own) lyrics that they could get away with, voices taking on a meta-critical means of reference that took the juxtapositions of sampling one step further. And in keeping with the times, the production saw De La and Prince Paul finally fully immersing themselves in the jazz-rap vibe of '93 with tracks saturated in electric piano and skating hi-hats and an entire horn section—a live one, consisting of James Brown alumni Fred Wesley, Maceo Parker, and Pee Wee Ellis in deep jazz-funk mode. (That they lucked out into clearing a Michael Jackson sample from *Off the Wall*'s "I Can't Help It" for "Breakadawn" was a powerful bonus, too.)

It was the kind of remarkably strange album that only expanded the *ways* De La and Prince Paul were capable of strangeness, not so much a concession to the ideas that were churning through the minds of the jazz-inflected producers who emerged as '80s flipped to '90s as it was a recognition that it was one of the few places they felt at home. But *Buhloone Mindstate* proved to be the last moment where Prince Paul felt like an actual part of De La Soul. Paul was still leaning toward his odd sense of humor and the eccentricities that came with it—one of the album's few skits, "Paul's Revenge," features him seething about not getting due credit from *The Source* for an unreleased version of a Slick Rick song he produced—while De La seemed intent on maturing into something more autonomous. It was a possibility that Paul had anticipated this and even helped it along; after all, he wasn't even sure if he was going to have a major hand in *De La Soul Is Dead* at first. But growing apart from a group he considered major freewheeling creative collaborators would mark a significant moment for Paul: with De La Soul accomplishing everything they could with Paul on board, and with Stetsasonic on hiatus after the 1991 release of *Blood, Sweat, & No Tears,* Paul's production schedule looked uncomfortably empty.

# 6 | **Constant Elevation**
## Hip-Hop's Rising Underground

**As hip-hop approaches a mid-'90s commercial plateau,
it threatens to splinter into factionalism—and finds a
place for hardcore iconoclasts underground.**

EAST COAST HIP-HOP'S GOLDEN AGE was reaching a fever pitch all throughout late 1993 and much of 1994, with a who's who of artists releasing essential debut albums. It wasn't just Nas with *Illmatic:* the future of New York rap looked bright thanks to the likes of D.I.T.C. affiliates and street-rap cult heroes Black Moon (*Enta da Stage*) and O.C. (*Word . . . Life),* the hell-raising boom-bap practitioners the Beatnuts (*Street Level*), hardcore hip-hop icons M.O.P. (*To the Death*), the DJ Premier–produced metaphysical lyricist Jeru tha Damaja (*The Sun Rises in the East*), Jersey-based underground duo the Artifacts (*Between a Rock and a Hard Place*), and—most fatefully—*Ready to Die,* which introduced the Notorious B.I.G. as the most compelling crime-rap storyteller out of NYC since Kool G Rap. Factor in some of the classics released by acts like KRS-One (*Return of the Boom Bap*), Organized Konfusion (*Stress: The Extinction Agenda*), Digable Planets (*Blowout Comb*), Salt-N-Pepa (*Very Necessary*), Redman (*Dare Iz a Darkside*), Queen Latifah (*Black Reign*), Leaders of the New School (*T.I.M.E. [The Inner Mind's Eye]*), Gang Starr (*Hard to Earn*), Beastie Boys (*Ill Communication*), and Main Source (*Fuck What You Think*), and you could easily peg the stretch from the September '93 release of *Buhloone Mindstate* to the end of '94 as a bona fide East Coast hip-hop renaissance.

But the catch to experiencing a golden age is that it might not be clear one just happened until it ends. And even then, the wealth might not have spread far enough to keep you rolling through the down times. Eric B. & Rakim released their final album together, *Don't Sweat the Technique,* in 1992, then broke up over money problems stoked by their label; Rakim wouldn't release another album until 1997. Shortly after releasing their sophomore album *The Main Ingredient,* Pete Rock & C.L. Smooth split over creative differences, and two albums Rock produced for up-and-comers in 1995—InI's *Center of Attention* and Deda's *The Original Baby Pa*—were shelved when Elektra Records' distribution deal for his label Soul Brother Records fell through. And Public Enemy, who took nearly three years to follow up their well-received fourth album *Apocalypse 91 . . . The Enemy Strikes Black,* received a lukewarm reception for 1994's *Muse Sick-n-Hour Mess Age,* an album that quickly fell off the charts. In *Rolling Stone,* writer Touré opened his two-out-of-five-star review with the stinging line "I guess by now we should be used to watching black heroes die in public," and lamented the aging group's irrelevance in their efforts to pit PE's political agitation against the increasing popularity and success of gangsta rap. Like many of their generational hip-hop peers—Brand Nubian, Big Daddy Kane, Jungle Brothers—their diminishing returns were followed by an extended silence that lasted into the later years of the decade, as though their creativity had been entirely spent.

The dismay over the state of hip-hop, even in one of its most creatively rich moments, was literally personified in a track by Common Sense, an emerging rapper whose Chicago roots belied a distinctly NYC-rooted approach, aided by the jazz-laced beats of producer No I.D. In "I Used to Love H.E.R.," the breakout single from his '94 sophomore release *Resurrection,* Common compares hip-hop to a woman he grew up smitten with, only to see her corrupted by trend-hopping gangsta commercialism: "Stressin' how hardcore and real she is / She was really the realest before she got into showbiz." The metaphor might have felt overly purist or even alarmist in the wake of so many classic hip-hop records that preceded it in the year, but it turned out to be more prescient than anything. For the rest of the decade, hip-hop would be defined by the battles for its soul—between tradition-bound New York and the gangsta upstarts out in Cali, then the Dirty South; between musical integrity and flashy materialism; between underground cred and mainstream crossover. These forces weren't inherently *meant* to be oppositional, and could easily coexist in the right musical contexts. But that right musical context wasn't easy to find when so many things were at stake, not the least of which was pride.

A microcosm of this uncertainty, hip-hop's recent but endangered past colliding with its defiant, visionary future, arrived on a single day in autumn. It was the release date—November 9, 1993—of two albums considered by hip-hop aficionados to be unimpeachable classics, seemingly divergent in their sounds and their outlook but tied closer together than first listens might reveal. One was *Midnight Marauders,* the third and arguably greatest album by A Tribe Called Quest, a raw, funky, hook-filled refinement of the conscious-minded, good-natured jazz vibes that permeated *The Low End Theory.* It was created in a relaxed environment where ideas came quickly to Q-Tip and Phife, with the pressure of following up a classic eased by the enthusiasm of making another one. It followed Jungle Brothers' *J Beez wit the Remedy* and De La's *Buhloone Mindstate* in a sort of trilogy for the last wave of original Native Tongues albums; along with affiliate Queen Latifah's *Black Reign,* these records wouldn't be followed up for at least two and a half years, and only then by records that marked striking departures from their predecessors as they reemerged in a hip-hop world that had changed drastically.

The other album to come out that day was the debut from a group out of Staten Island that had spent nearly a year building buzz off a late '92 single that took the underground by storm. The crew was an unprecedentedly massive ensemble cast of innovative MCs, each with their own distinct lyrical style and personality formed through years of rap battles. And when this group was signed to a contract, the crew's de facto leader made sure to demand a clause that would give each individual rapper in the crew the opportunity to negotiate with any label they felt like working with when they were ready to put out solo albums. It took a while to find a label willing to accommodate this unconventional clause, but once they did, the gambit paid off. The record they put out was a radical change from the norm, grimier and more lo-fi than anything else on shelves that fall. But not only was it a critical success and a fast favorite of hardcore hip-hop fans, it laid the foundation for a movement that would transform the entire idea of what both underground and commercial hip-hop could actually mean. And it might not have happened without Prince Paul.

• • •

Prince Paul's 1992 wasn't his lowest point, but it might have been close. Two years prior, after the success of *3 Feet High and Rising,* Def Jam had entrusted Paul with his own imprint label—which Paul, possessing the sense of humor he did, proceeded to name Dew Doo Man Records. (His business card featured a cartoon illustration of a cheerfully smiling pile of shit, decades before the poop emoji became iconic.) Despite his already-impressive production portfolio, Paul had difficulty keeping the endeavor going: he was only able to cut a record with one group, a trio of immigrants from the West Indies who called themselves Resident Alien. In a self-aware nod to the whole situation, Paul featured himself in a promotional video for the song "Ooh the Dew Doo Man," one of three songs featured on Resident Alien's only release, 1991's *Mr. Boops* EP. He's depicted in a suit, sitting at a desk placed in the middle of an otherwise-featureless white void of a room, an oversized, unsigned contract hanging behind him, and letting off a frustrated tirade to a pacing secretary: "Great, great. Here I am, producer Prince Paul, my own record label, Dew Doo Man Records, and I don't even have any rap acts. What kind of [shit] is this?"

The punchline of the video is that Resident Alien and another MC named Mic Teluxe are signed to the label. The punchline in the real world is that Def Jam considered the album, christened with the Public Enemy–lampooning immigration-joke title *It Takes a Nation of Suckas to Let Us In,* to be far too weird to put their promotional weight behind. Paul's goofball sense of humor was on total overload: the album opens with a skit featuring Paul crashing his car into a cesspool truck, and the truck's workers, played by the members of Resident Alien, refusing to give him mouth-to-mouth because "he got shit on his lips." But his production was even more far-flung than it was on *3 Feet High and Rising:* multiple tracks that flipped dancehall, reggae, and rocksteady to play up the crew's Caribbean roots, a song that switched beats montage-style in the middle of the track with miniature skits acting as interludes ("Oxtail, the Burger, and One Chicken Wing"), a new jack swing pastiche that took the already fading style just seriously enough to feel a little off ("It's the Resident Alien"), and a throwback to up-tempo b-boy cuts like Arthur Baker's "Breakers Revenge" before enough time had passed to make it sound nostalgic instead of dated ("Are You Ready?"). Never mind that Paul went all-out on the beats—the drums on *Nation of Suckas* are some of the hardest anyone had put on record at that point—Def Jam opted to shelve the album, and before '92 was halfway through, Dew Doo Man was defunct.

The rest of Paul's production slate that year was nearly nonexistent: aside from a remix of Cypress Hill's single "Latin Lingo," his output in '92 was a trio of beats for Boogie Down Productions' album *Sex and Violence*—all of which wound up on the record in a state Paul considered unfinished and not up to the standards of an MC Paul admired. KRS-One later apologized to Paul years later, but the damage had been done; Paul's beats on the record sound like solid first drafts with unfulfilled potential. Ironically, one of the beats was for a track, "How Not to Get Jerked," that featured KRS rapping about all the steps a performer needed to take to avoid being rejected or otherwise screwed by the record industry. None of those lines mentioned the possibility that being too forward-thinking might be a problem.

And since Paul's unconventional tastes were far enough outside of the mainstream to make him a liability if his weird ideas didn't sell as many records as *3 Feet High and Rising* did, he found himself written off by his former champions in the industry. A year after Russell Simmons had lent his voice to De La Soul's "A Roller Skating Jam Named 'Saturdays,'" Paul heard from MC Serch, who'd wanted him to contribute some beats for the former 3rd Bass member's solo debut for Def Jam. Serch relayed what Simmons told him: "Why you trying to get Prince Paul, man? He's played out. He's wack." De La still believed in Paul enough to bring him on one last time for *Buhloone Mindstate,* but not even having a hand in the group's third rule-rewriting classic album in a row was enough to keep the shine on.

At this low point, Paul started making a set of beats for no particular purpose; if he was going to have his actual submitted work rejected or sat on by labels, he could still create something on his own terms. And since his terms at the time involved feeling frustrated, angry, and depressed, that's how the beats turned out. Even considering how embittered De La could sound on *De La Soul Is Dead,* the stuff Paul was putting together in '92 was unusually gloomy: minor-key piano rattling like a trapped hornet, basslines falling into the abyss, Stax soul reanimated into a zombie lurch, and early '70s psychedelic funk melted down into corrosive, flesh-stripping chemicals. Sooner or later, Paul decided that the beats were too good just to keep to himself, and he picked a few of them for a demo tape before setting out looking for some MCs to complete his misanthropic vision.

He found them all in the ranks of disillusioned artists who had dealt with failure on the same label, Tommy Boy, that had given Paul his first success. Poetic was the MC of the one-rapper-two-DJ crew Too Poetic, a Long Island group with one 12-inch to their name in 1989 (the Paul C.–mixed "Poetical Terror" / "God Made Me Funky") and an in-the-works full-length album, *Droppin' Signal,* that Tommy Boy scrapped. Despite his early potential as an agile-flowing, party-rocking MC, Poetic hadn't had any success getting a new deal once Tommy Boy dropped him, and by the time Paul sought him out, he was working a factory job and living with his sister. Frukwan, an old friend Paul had known since his earliest days in Stetsasonic, had left the group before their '91 swan song *Blood, Sweat, & No Tears;* Paul found him making clothes out of his house as a side gig and brought him on to the project, giving him a chance after feeling as though he'd been overshadowed in Stetsasonic by Daddy-O.

Then there was Robert Diggs—or "Prince Rakeem," as his sole Tommy Boy single credited him. 1991's "Ooh I Love You Rakeem" was a track as goofy as its boardwalk-caricature cover, a raw-sounding MC trying to pass himself off as Biz Markie comedic. It was a weird fit: his out-of-tune crooning on the hook ("I've got *tooooo many lad-ees, IIIIIIIIIII've* got to learn to *saaaaay no*") sounded so awkward it felt like a deliberate parody, and his verses about womanizing were relayed with the kind of delivery that sounded like he'd be better off making elaborate threats. Rakeem did the beat, too, an Otis Redding–sourced riff on horn-heavy southern soul that sounded lighthearted but still had some oomph on the drums.

The single stiffed, along with the B-sides—an Easy Mo Bee–produced cut called "Sexcapades" and a battle-rap throw-in titled "Deadly Venoms (Vocals Up)," the latter of which showed the most promise—but Rakeem wasn't easily discouraged. Paul had known him since 1989, and had made some beats for him in a demo session; now he was brought on as a combination MC/producer. As Paul recalled in a profile piece for the second issue of *Wax Poetics* in 2002, "[Rakeem] recorded stuff really rough—kind of like how I did in the beginning with De La—not really knowing what he was doing. At that point, I was becoming a technical-head, working with sequencers on the computer, trying to get stuff to sound a certain way. Watching [him] really brought me back to the raw guts of the music and not the technology behind it. I owe a lot to him for bringing me back to that."

Once Paul had them all assembled, the crew brainstormed on just how they'd best express this industry-rejected, convention-attacking attitude they all shared. Paul doesn't remember who came up with the name Gravediggaz, but the concept fell into place quickly: if gangsta rappers made street crime their identity, then this new group would take things to the next level and go for all-out horror, with Paul's dark beats as inspiration. Frukwan became the Gatekeeper, Poetic renamed himself the Grym Reaper, Prince Paul briefly considered the wordplay-style Pall Bearer before deciding on the Undertaker, and Rakeem called himself the RZArector—a name that would later be shortened to the RZA, his onetime graffiti tag "Razor" transformed into a piece of musical onomatopoeia. Paul trusted the MCs to have free rein with the concept, and left to their own devices, they riffed off one another battle-style to hone their ideas, steel sharpening steel.

By late '92, their six-track demo was complete, a diabolical string of morbid scenarios (including "Pass the Shovel," "2 Cups of Blood," and "1-800 Suicide") that became the closest hip-hop had ever gotten to the atmospheric, morbid, doom-laden heaviness of Black Sabbath. But an album built around the work of four artists who had grown disillusioned to the point of hostility toward industry norms would, unfairly but unsurprisingly, be a hard sell. Prince Paul shopped the demo around for a year, and got more of the "old and washed up" feedback that brought Gravediggaz into existence in the first place. But eventually, by summer '93, they caught the interest of Jon Baker. Baker was the cofounder of Gee Street Records, who handled the UK releases of Jungle Brothers and Queen Latifah records in the late '80s and had signed psychedelic rap group P.M. Dawn in the early '90s. Whether or not it was a strange-bedfellows situation to add Gravediggaz to the roster of a label that had its biggest success with the Spandau Ballet–sampling neo-hippie #1 hit "Set Adrift on Memory Bliss," at least the former rejects had someone who believed in them.

Baker had picked up Gravediggaz largely on the merit of Prince Paul's track record, but as the group went into the studio that fall to pick up where they'd left off a year previous, another member of the group was gaining a significant amount of attention for a project he'd been working on after the Gravediggaz demo was completed. Before Tommy Boy dropped RZA from their roster, they briefly humored an idea he pitched to them of a rap crew he'd been developing with a few of his friends, and one ad in *The Source* actually listed the name of this crew at the bottom of the label's roster of artists: *Wu-Tang Clan*. But Tommy

Boy decided to sign the Irish American–styled House of Pain instead—
"Damn, they chose a bunch of whiteboy shit over me," RZA recalls
thinking in his book *The Wu-Tang Manual*—and disillusionment set in.
It didn't help that his cousin Gary Grice, who rapped as the Genius and
released an album in 1991 for Cold Chillin', had become fed up with the
lack of promotion from the label and asked for his release. RZA had a
couple other aspiring rappers in his crew that were similarly frustrated
by their lack of prospects—another cousin named Russell Jones, who
had joined RZA and the Genius in a group called All in Together Now,
and a roommate of RZA's, Dennis Coles.

At their lowest point, they moved from New York to set up shop
dealing drugs out in Steubenville, Ohio, where some members of RZA's
family lived. But their criminal enterprise was short-lived thanks to a
rare stroke of luck. When an enraged street hustler went after RZA over
a girl Dennis had been seeing, RZA wound up in a gunfight—a case of
self-defense with zero casualties, but an incident that saw RZA charged
with attempted murder. When he was found not guilty and spared the
eight-year sentence the prosecutor called for, the RZA, who had been
struggling between an Islam-rooted spirituality and his own desperate-
measures situation, hit a moment of clarity: if he had to hustle, he'd put
that effort back toward music. By 1992, RZA was back in New York,
the Genius was renamed GZA, cousin Russell called himself Ol' Dirty
Bastard, and Dennis became Ghostface Killah. The rest of the Wu-Tang
Clan came from the ranks of RZA's childhood friends—Method Man,
Raekwon, Inspectah Deck, and U-God joined that year, with Masta
Killa finalizing the crew's original lineup for '93—and RZA gave them
a promise: he had a five-year plan that would culminate in the crew hitting #1.

RZA was still billed as Prince Rakeem on the sleeve of the independently released 1992 single "Protect Ya Neck," but there was no sign
of the clownish ladies' man to be found on the mic or the beats. Instead,
he's a fuming, snarling, thoroughly commanding presence belting New
Testament phraseology with Old Testament fury ("Turn the other cheek
and I'll break your fuckin' chin"). The other members' lyrics promised
nothing short of an absolute war on a crumbling rap establishment, from
Inspectah Deck's emergence "deep in the dark with the art to rip the
charts apart" to GZA's damnation of his previous "Cold Killin'" label:
"That's what you get when you misuse what I invent / Your empire falls

and you lose every cent." And the beat sounds unholy: it lifts the same sax squeal from the J.B.'s "The Grunt" that Public Enemy so brilliantly exploited, only winnowing it down to a faint wail that sounded more like a theremin than a horn; juxtaposed with a truncated Philadelphia soul string section (the Intruders' 1968 "Cowboys to Girls") smeared like a bloodstain across the tape, and a piano sting from the score to an obscure 1978 Jackie Chan kung-fu film (*Snake & Crane Arts of Shaolin*), RZA built a fragmented melody that added a sense of unreal suspense to the track's ruthlessly hard drums.

When the debut album *Enter the Wu-Tang (36 Chambers)* dropped in November '93, that was it: the idea that a hip-hop act needed polished state-of-the-art sounds and crossover-accessible themes to succeed had been not only challenged but brutally toppled. The album's mixture of crime narratives, philosophical musings, and punchline-driven boasts of lyrical supremacy were taken even further than most MCs who specialized in just one of those categories had even tried. In many ways, it was a funhouse mirror reflection of *3 Feet High and Rising*, with the middle-class Long Island swapped for the rougher parts of Staten Island—redubbed "Shaolin" in a nod to the UHF-station-aired martial arts movies that informed much of the group's personality—and a light-hearted absurdity exchanged for a disenfranchised frustration. But the pop culture polyglot language was still there, from its Buddhism–via–Five-Percent Nation religious outlook (referred to in RZA's *Wu-Tang Manual* as a "Grand Spiritual Megamix," theology as a DJ set) to the pastiche of film, TV, comic book, and especially musical touchstones that drew on shared experience to build a recognizable world that was nevertheless far bigger than any one individual could speak to.

And while the ensemble-cast collection of MCs was one of the bigger draws of the Wu-Tang Clan, RZA's production was every bit as crucial. RZA cites Prince Paul as "the only person I knew doing the kind of bugged-out sampling I was into" in the *Manual:* "I never thought about imitating his style, but he did show everybody that you could take anything with a sampler—cartoons, children's records, French lessons—and make it musical." As long as it fit the narrative and the mood RZA was building, it could work, whether or not the context was radically transformed. "Wu-Tang Clan Ain't Nuthing ta Fuck Wit" is proof of that, and not only from the way it manages to wring a sense of unhinged menace out of a vocal hook from the theme to '60s superhero cartoon parody *Underdog*. Deep in the beat, there's a piece of sampling meta-commentary, lifting some of its percussive sounds from Marley Marl's beat to Biz Markie's 1987 single "Nobody Beats the Biz"—a sample of a sample, a faded second-generation mutation of an already-juxtaposed fusion of the drums to Lafayette Afro Rock Band's "Hihache" and the Hammond B-3 organ sound from Steve Miller Band's "Fly Like an Eagle." It was common knowledge (and common courtesy) among hip-hop producers that using a drum sample from another producer's hip-hop record instead of the actual record the producer sampled was a cheap tactic. But this wasn't RZA taking advantage of someone else's access to a choice beat, it was him throwing down a conceptual gauntlet: the previous decade's production greats were just as much a malleable piece of hip-hop history as the old break records were, and their lineage was shifting from contemporaneous to historic, a style to be recontextualized even as a new wave of producers saw to it that it was becoming outmoded.

But the metacommentary wasn't the real strength of the RZA's style—or, as he'd display over the years, his "style as no style," a way of moving through forms that seemed simpatico with Bruce Lee's *jeet kune do* approach to martial arts as a versatile, reactive mode bent on doing away with rigid sequential styles of fighting. For RZA, a combination of three previously under-exploited musical ideas was the key. First off was his own early fascination with a jazz legend who, despite being a titan of the genre, was only sporadically sampled thanks to his nonintuitive sense of timing. "Early on, I saw that movie *Straight, No Chaser*—a documentary about Thelonious Monk," RZA recalled in the *Manual*. "I watched it and saw how this guy was playing and it was just . . . *crazy*. I mean, he'd play a note or two. Smoke a cigarette. Smack the piano. Walk away from it, come back. And it was like, 'You can do anything! There's no rules to it!'"

Monk had been sampled sporadically before RZA—Gang Starr's "Jazz Thing" being the most notable instance—but RZA took to that style enthusiastically. It wasn't just that he sampled Monk's vertigo-chord piano notes from a performance of Duke Ellington's "Black and Tan Fantasy" for "Shame on a Nigga" and Monk's own "Ba-Lue Bolivar Ba-Lues-Are" for "Clan in da Front"—it was the detuned piano riff played through "Wu-Tang: 7th Chamber" and the zither sounds in "Da Mystery of Chessboxin'" that RZA composed himself. A technological limitation created another characteristic: "The piano is detuned because I sampled the note that I was playing. It couldn't be in tune because they didn't have time stretching then. Back then, if you sampled a note and played it on another key of the keyboard, you couldn't keep the same BPMs . . . but I just thought it sounded dope that way."

Second, there was one vital element in RZA's early choice of source material: as often as he relied on classic breakbeats like "Synthetic Substitution" and the soul jazz standbys of early '90s East Coast hip-hop like Roy Ayers and Lonnie Smith, the more characteristic elements of his sound would come from Southern soul. RZA had spent a brief period of his childhood living in the South, raised Baptist in the early '70s before moving back to New York at age seven; it's highly plausible that some of the earliest music he'd remember hearing would be from artists on Memphis-based labels like Hi Records, home of the legendary Al Green, or Stax, where Isaac Hayes had become a superstar. In the March/April 2006 issue of *Scratch* magazine, RZA brought up Eric B. & Rakim's 1990 album *Let the Rhythm Hit 'Em,* and one track in particular, the love song "Mahogany," that sampled Al Green's "I'm Glad You're Mine." Not only did Eric B. use the rhythm of Al Green's "I'm Glad You're Mine," he preserved its relaxed tempo and actually incorporated the strings and horns from the original. That gave the hip-hop love song a sense of suave, leisurely seduction that, in its time, felt like a change of pace. And it changed RZA's outlook on how hip-hop production could sound: "I was like, 'why didn't they make the whole album like this?'"

And so he found his own routes through that sound—grimier, more foreboding routes, but evocative ones. The B-side of "Protect Ya Neck" was "After the Laughter Comes Tears"—later shortened to just "Tearz"—and it was the first officially released Wu-Tang track to call its beat up from Memphis, sampling Wendy Rene's 1964 Stax single "After Laughter (Comes Tears)." It built off the song's heartbreak and longing to create a more deliberately constrained but still severely tense and anxious beat from the recurring organ riff, and made a refrain out of Rene's titular chorus. Turning that sweet soul into corroded hardcore hip-hop was a savvy move, a juxtaposition that found even further expression in "C.R.E.A.M.," the love-conquers-all romance of the Charmels' 1967 Volt single "As Long As I've Got You" reduced to a cell-pacing piano and organ loop made to reflect the original lyrics' desperation in the Wu's scraping for money. There was an air of intergenerational commentary in this kind of sampling: not only did RZA want to maintain certain sonic allusions in the composition of his beats, he brought back the underlying social framework of '60s and '70s soul—and then twisted it into modern shape as a deliberate contrast between the ambivalence of the post-civil rights era and the crack-poisoned, HIV-infected reality of '90s inner-city life. And since the Wu-Tang were known not just for their tone of East Coast street-level aggression but for their ability to translate it into scenes of real human tragedy, the tone of the old R&B ballads of the '60s and '70s fit their narrative perfectly.

Finally, there's the actual *feel* of his beats, the technological limitations of the aging sampling hardware that RZA was eager to transform into a new method of conveying rawness. Like the detuning issue, it was a contradiction turned strength: the sampler could create countless limit-breaking opportunities to create more intricate, more deeply layered samples, but at the cost of audio fidelity. RZA caught on to an early, low-budget version of this trick in the late '80s, when all he could afford was a consumer-grade Casio toy keyboard that could only sample two seconds' worth of sound. RZA bypassed this limit by speeding the turntable playing the sample source as fast as possible, then slowing the playback all the way down on the Casio, losing a bit in fidelity but still getting as much of a break's length as he could.

He kept that approach as he worked out the intricacies of the SP-1200, and then the Ensoniq EPS, which he preferred for being a keyboard-based sampler that let him play samples like melodies. As the *Manual* put it, "I started chopping things down to notes and chords, not knowing which chords they were but knowing them as sounds." And in making *36 Chambers* primarily on the EPS, he used a similar workaround he did on the Casio, exploiting as much of the keyboard's time-stretching abilities as he could. By lowering the sample rate, he could increase the amount of time he could dedicate to a sample, while losing something in the resolution of the sound: what it lost in frequency, it gained in griminess, the actual "lossiness" that came with the sound's digital decay making the beat sound rawer, harsher, heavier.

That's what RZA brought to the table with Gravediggaz as well as Wu-Tang Clan, and why his beats felt like a continuation and advancement of what Prince Paul had sparked in both good times and bad. By the time *6 Feet Deep* dropped in August 1994, it had undergone a bit of tumultuous revising—its original title *Niggamortis* and a track called

"Pass the Shovel" didn't make it to American pressings—but its RZA associations had helped its delayed emergence for the better, and not just on some coattail-riding business. "6 Feet Deep" and "Graveyard Chamber" showed off RZA's bizarre fusion of Shaolin monk and Thelonious Monk to perfection.

Meanwhile "Diary of a Madman," the album's lead single, was a tour-de-force collaboration between RZA, Paul, and RZA cohort RNS that played out like a sordid true-crime B movie in miniature. "Okay, I understand you guys are pleading insanity, claiming demonic spirits possessed you to do these hideous murders," mutters a judge in the skit that opens the track. "Can you please explain to the court how these so called spirits made you into these raving madmen?" The grisly answers came over operatic backup vocals from '50s Johnny Mathis easy listening love ballads, brilliantly turned into the wails of agonized spirits. Despite the fact that all the gruesome imagery in the lyrics was only implied in the visuals, the art house–quality video, created by an emerging director named Hype Williams, was repeatedly rejected by MTV for being too morbid. No matter—Gravediggaz reached their audience anyways, sharing bills not only with hip-hop acts like Ice Cube and (ironically enough) House of Pain, but rock and metal crossover acts Korn and Biohazard. And naturally, they wound up touring with Wu-Tang Clan, all sharing the same bus, RZA performing double duty with both crews.

RZA fulfilled his promise to make the Wu-Tang Clan's individual members just as creatively and commercially undeniable as their collective effort. Instead of "buying a car or whatever rap stars were supposed to do," he put the money he'd steadily started to earn into turning the basement of his Staten Island townhouse into a full-fledged studio. Then he went to work, putting in overtime hours every day making beats for the Wu-Tang solo members, until he'd filled over 150 floppy disks' worth of candidates. And soon, a stretch of outstanding solo albums—Method Man's rugged prizefighter bout *Tical,* Ol' Dirty Bastard's deliriously unhinged party record *Return to the 36 Chambers: The Dirty Version,* Raekwon and Ghostface's hard-boiled pulp-crime narrative *Only Built 4 Cuban Linx . . . ,* and GZA's lyrically scientific wordplay masterwork *Liquid Swords*—all dropped in a twelve-month span starting in November 1994. RZA's Staten Island townhouse basement studio had become a hit factory with all the efficiency of an assembly line, except instead of turning out identical mass-market product he made bespoke works that highlighted each MC's characteristic traits. In the process, RZA went from a producer working on intuition to an auteur behind the boards, handling not just the beats but the mixing, arranging, and engineering. At one point he even made the decision to get eight different audio compressors—"one for each voice in the Wu-Tang Clan. That way, once I found the way I wanted someone to sound, I never had to touch it again."

But then disaster struck: shortly after wrapping up *Liquid Swords,* a massive rainstorm hit and the drainage system that the townhouses were connected to wasn't enough to stave off the downpour. Somewhere between three to four feet of water flooded RZA's studio, and an estimated five hundred beats were lost, including the bulk of work for the upcoming Ghostface and Inspectah Deck albums. The former's *Iron-man* was rebuilt back up into another bona fide solo Wu classic for '96, but RZA stated in retrospect that "Ghost's voice doesn't sound as good as it did on *Cuban Linx,* because we had to go to someone else's studio to do it—we had to leave Shaolin." As for Deck, his *Uncontrolled Substance* remains one of hip-hop's great what-ifs; it came out three years later than the pre-flood plans originally called for and only featured two beats from RZA himself. The album's respectable enough, but it stalled the momentum of one of the Wu-Tang's sharpest MCs and was one less chance for RZA's musical vision to manifest at its finest.

After the second Wu-Tang album dropped, losing all those beats would prove the least of RZA's worries. In August 1997, while touring with Rage Against the Machine off the five-year-plan-culminating multi-platinum success of #1 sophomore album *Wu-Tang Forever,* the crew had started to fracture. At some points on the tour, tens of thousands of fans in the audience would be throwing up the Wu-Tang "W" hand signal to a stage where only three or four members were present. It got to the point where RZA felt that "money, fame, and ego" was enough to doom the Wu-Tang, and he canceled the remainder of the tour. Reflecting on that time he'd spent working his fingers to the bone for a musical project that was on the verge of self-destructing, RZA wrote, "I'd spent two years living in a basement, and that time changed me . . . I wasn't that same Polo-wearing cool motherfucker my friends grew up with. Now, I was this Afro-nappy, fang-mouthed Gravedigga-type kid—this monster."

It took an epiphany to snap him out of it during one of his lowest moments: drunk and high on "all kinds of drugs," locked out of his own house by a wife who'd been cheating on him, and lying on the lawn with Kinetic 9, a friend whose Wu-affiliated group Killarmy had just released the cult classic *Silent Weapons for Quiet Wars.* Kinetic pointed out a flower that RZA had laid down on, "like it grew under me during the night," and RZA plucked it to study it for an hour, "just zoned out, with my spirit doing weird shit, like I was seeing Heaven." At some point, RZA had an ego-death epiphany: the flower had lived, and it had died, an example of the inevitability of the beginning and end of all physical things. And so a producer who'd spent upwards of five years resurrecting old beats from long-gone decades found closure. By 1998, the RZA had developed a new keyboard-driven "digital orchestra" sound for his solo debut *Bobby Digital in Stereo* that, with rare exceptions, bypassed samples completely.

As for Paul's place in hip-hop's future, that still seemed yet to be determined. His own productions and collaborative efforts on *6 Feet Deep* covered all kinds of ground, from the nascent Wu-Tang revolution to the darker, stranger ideas catching on in beat-driven music out of the UK. (In one of the era's most fitting exchanges of transatlantic musical trends, trip-hop standard-bearers Portishead and Tricky both collaborated with Gravediggaz: the former added an additional layer of grit and murk over "Nowhere to Run" in '94, and the latter created two bleaker-than-bleak co-productions with RZA for 1995's *The Hell E.P.*) And according to Paul himself, the beats he made for *6 Feet Deep* are still some of his favorites, even considering their frustrated origins. But as he'd soon find out, the establishment of a successful hip-hop underground meant that there needed to be a mainstream to battle against— and by 1996, the mainstream was no place to fuck around.

• • •

Notorious B.I.G.'s *Ready to Die,* Mobb Deep's *The Infamous,* Raekwon's *Cuban Linx,* and Jay-Z's *Reasonable Doubt* all emerged over a two-year stretch starting in 1994 that refined and escalated the ability of New York hip-hop to stand astride the worlds of both the mainstream and the underground. These albums also reinforced New York's identity as a stronghold of a rap lifestyle that went hand-in-hand with the culture of crime—drug trafficking in particular—which bolstered an image of the hip-hop hustler as a hybrid of '70s blaxploitation antihero and Scorsese/ Coppola mafioso.

All these albums were phenomenal, featuring compelling lyricism and storytelling from emergent MCs and production that rivaled the best hip-hop records of the peak golden age just a few years prior. But they also made purists nervous, and some rap veterans worried that the success of a handful of unusually good crime-rap records would overwhelm and crowd out other styles of hip-hop. And those fears were most starkly personified in the sophomore album by an MC many had considered a standard-bearer of hip-hop classicism. When Nas followed up *Illmatic* with *It Was Written,* the feedback among hardcore fans was somewhere between skeptical and horrified: instead of the likes of Pete Rock, Q-Tip, and Large Professor, Nas had farmed most of the record's production duties to Jean-Claud "Poke" Olivier and Samuel "Tone" Barnes, a duo collectively known as Trackmasters.

Poke's contributions to *Ready to Die* put them on the map — especially "Juicy," a coproduction with Bad Boy Records mogul-artist Sean "Puffy" Combs that made a surprise hit out of a beat lifted from Mtume's frothy, catchy 1983 R&B hit "Juicy Fruit." (Incidentally, Pete Rock claims that Puffy overheard him making the original version of the beat when Puffy visited Pete's home studio, and reproduced it without giving Pete credit.) And Trackmasters' contributions to *It Was Written* were in a similar mode, the grimy atmosphere and haunting soul-jazz beats of *Illmatic* swapped out for glossier production techniques and familiar '80s and '90s pop hits: Sting's "Shape of My Heart" for "The Message"; Eurythmics' "Sweet Dreams (Are Made of This)" for "Street Dreams"; Whodini's "Friends" for "If I Ruled the World (Imagine That)." When writer kris ex reviewed *It Was Written* in the September 1996 issue of *Vibe,* his issue was with "its consistently aggressive attempts at pop music . . . Nas requires a sonic tapestry as multihued and breathtaking as his rhymes — and then the pop success he obviously desires will occur, organically." But the apparently inorganic pop success of *It Was Written* shot to #1 on the album charts and went double platinum two months after its release, selling four times as many copies as *Illmatic*'s five hundred thousand shipped.

The very same day *It Was Written* came out — July 2, 1996 — De La Soul released *Stakes Is High,* their first album without Prince Paul on the boards. The title track laid out one of the core messages of the album, featuring an embittered verse by Trugoy, totally fatigued with the state of rap:

*I'm sick of bitches shakin' asses*
*I'm sick of talkin' 'bout blunts, sick of Versace glasses*
*Sick of slang, sick of half-ass awards shows*
*Sick of name brand clothes*
*Sick of R&B bitches over bullshit tracks*
*Cocaine and crack, which brings sickness to blacks*
*Sick of swoll' head rappers with their sicker-than raps*
*Clappers of gats, makin' the whole sick world collapse*
*The facts are gettin' sick, even sicker perhaps*
*Stickabush to make a bundle to escape this synapse.*

They sounded borderline burned out, but that was still better than all-the-way exhausted, which Prince Paul absolutely was by 1996. Despite the cult-classic success of *6 Feet Deep,* Gravediggaz hadn't been enough to give him the same level of production clout he'd earned at the turn of the '90s: an effort to get an Amityville group called Horror City off the ground failed when the demo he produced for them was ignored. Odds are that the "horrorcore" rep Gravediggaz were tagged with had become considered so gimmicky that labels didn't want to go for another Prince Paul group whose name—a tongue-in-cheek reference to the paranormal book and film series *The Amityville Horror*—promised a shock-rap itinerary that the group weren't actually intending to deliver. A second Gravediggaz album, *The Pick, the Sickle, and the Shovel,* came and went, just a thing Paul minimally worked on primarily as a favor to Frukwan and Poetic to help keep their careers going. And when an opportunity arose for an actual solo album—a verbal commitment to Serath "Skiz" Fernando to cut an album for Skiz's experimental indie label WordSound—Paul decided that the best usage of this opportunity would be a deliberate effort at career suicide.

"I was fed up with the whole music business," Paul stated in the 2002 *Wax Poetics* profile, "and had been thinking of just moving down South, opening up a Jiffy Lube or Dunkin' Donuts, just getting out entirely." So his final farewell would be *Psychoanalysis: What Is It?*—a series of inside jokes, absurd style parodies, and moments of willful stupidity that would take his sardonic sense of humor to the narrowest ends possible. In his words, "it's not meant for people to like." "Beautiful Night (Manic Psychopath)" hit a twisted nerve with its morbid hook ("It's just a beautiful night for a date rape /A beautiful night for a kill") and Paul's confessions, delivered to a crackly old LP of a quasi-Freud shrink, of murder and mayhem that deliberately one-upped and rendered grotesque the kinds of sex boasts and gun-clap violence that mainstream rap was starting to make ordinary. There were parodic goofs on rap-reggae on "Vexual Healing (Vacillation)," old-school '80s drum machine hip-hop à la Schoolly D on "J.O.B. (Das What Dey Is!)," literally dick-waving Miami bass on "Booty Clap," and all kinds of deranged gross-out routines and comedy sketches that lurched belligerently across some of the most nauseated, unsettled beats Paul had ever put together.

This time, Paul's instincts were wrong for the better. As it turned out, plenty of hip-hop fans shared Paul's disillusionment with the industry—but instead of giving up on the potential of rap to be a countercultural movement again, they helped establish underground hip-hop as a far stranger and more oppositional force than it had been at any point prior to the mid-'90s.

Fondle 'Em Records, a vinyl-only label founded by Robert "Bobbito" Garcia of the legendary hip-hop radio program *The Stretch Armstrong and Bobbito Show,* took advantage of Bobbito's tastemaker instincts to put out projects by artists that the mainstream industry had become too conservative and bottom-line-obsessed to touch. The Ultramagnetic MCs' Kool Keith and the group's affiliated producer/MC Godfather Don teamed up as the Cenobites for the first Fondle 'Em release, and it showed them both in rare form, posting up gory, scatological diatribes against the record biz and wackness in all its forms.

Other subterranean crews like the Juggaknots and the Arsonists offered up esoteric yet still hard-bumping tracks that sounded like master classes in how to make golden age boom-bap beats sound like the art-damaged future. Despite its ability to reach a largely untapped blend of preservationist rap heads and avant-garde futurists, Fondle 'Em was far from the only label pushing the limits of what hip-hop could be, and by 1997 labels like Rawkus, Stones Throw, Solesides, Rhymesayers, and Hieroglyphics Imperium had joined in to create a network of like-minded hip-hop iconoclasts from one coast to the other.

WordSound, which had also signed Jungle Brothers cohort Sensational and would later release the lost tracks from their aborted 1993 avant-garde effort *Crazy Wisdom Masters,* fit right in that off-kilter space. And the label helped make *Psychoanalysis* a sleeper hit, a hip-hop comedy cult classic with the kind of inside jokes that played well outside, too. One avowed fan was Chris Rock, who'd emerged as a superstar after the 1996 HBO special *Chris Rock: Bring the Pain* started earning the once-struggling *Saturday Night Live* alumnus comparisons to Richard Pryor. Rock brought Paul on for his 1997 album *Roll with the New,* hiring him to make a handful of in-studio sketches to be interspersed with the live stand-up bits. And it took off with the help of Paul's cutting sense of parody—including a brutal mockery of Puffy and Faith Hill called "Champagne," which turned the instrumental from Run-- D.M.C.'s "Rock Box" into a takedown of R&B's late '90s trend of what Rock called "a bunch of people singin' over rap beats." Instead of managing a donut shop, Prince Paul wound up winning a Grammy for Best Spoken Comedy Album in 1998—his first of three with Rock.

If that wasn't vindication enough, Tommy Boy—the label that had both nurtured and frustrated him since the mid-'80s—got in touch with him to reissue *Psychoanalysis* and sign Paul on to give him a bit more free rein. In 1999, Paul put out two albums on the label that finally made it clear just how integral his influence was to hip-hop's strange nether realm between mainstream success and underground cultishness. *A Prince Among Thieves* was his magnum opus, a full-length concept record / "rap opera" featuring the Juggaknots' Breezly Brewin in the role of an up-and-comer named Tariq who turns to the drug trade in an attempt to fund the recording of a demo tape. The album featured nearly every MC Paul ever worked with and a few that he hadn't— Horror City, Kool Keith, Big Daddy Kane, Chubb Rock, Biz Markie, De La Soul, Everlast from House of Pain, Brand Nubian's Sadat X, and RZA in a cameo as himself.

And later that year, Paul teamed up with Dan "the Automator" Nakamura, a producer out of San Francisco whose psychedelic beats on 1996's *Dr. Octagonecologyst* gave Kool Keith a massive crossover that both hardcore hip-hop heads and new jack indie kids could appreciate. Paul and Automator hit it off after the former remixed the Dr. Octagon track "Blue Flowers," and after they both realized they shared a mutual appreciation for the obscure, surrealist one-season Chris Elliott sitcom *Get a Life,* they joked about starting a group named after one of its episode's premises: Handsome Boy Modeling School. Somehow Automator convinced Tommy Boy that this joke of an idea was an actual thing, and so the two worked together to create *So . . . How's Your Girl?*—an all-star project that alternately sounded like trip-hop, acid rock, noise techno, indie pop, and good old-fashioned East-meets-West Coast boom-bap. If nothing else—and the album did plenty—*So . . . How's Your Girl?* at least got the Beastie Boys' Mike D, John Lennon's son Sean, hardcore techno-punk Alec Empire, Company Flow / future Run the Jewels rapper-producer El-P, and sketch comedy hipster priest Father Guido Sarducci on the same record.

Paul's career since then has been the kind of unpredictable that he'd spent decades getting used to: get a bright idea, see that idea shrugged at, ricochet from one label to the next, put together an album as a high-concept fuck-you, see that fuck-you either unexpectedly rewarded or predictably shot down, and on to the next idea. At one point, he put together an album, 2003's *Politics of the Business,* that was an intentional effort to parody the very idea of selling out, inspired by Tommy Boy's reaction when *A Prince among Thieves* stiffed on the charts (no thanks to the half-hearted support of the label). "I tried to make it sonically as close to a Jay-Z record as possible. It may be my best record, but my least favorite, 'cause it doesn't embody me as much," he told *Wax Poetics* before it came out. Years later, in 2011, he told *Complex* that it was an intentional effort to answer Tom Silverman's demand for hot singles and crossover potential with blatantly transparent sarcasm—but nobody got the joke, least of all Tommy Boy, who'd folded as a record label by the time the album was complete. So, in 2017, he redid all the backing tracks and created a grip of beats that made the whole thing, repackaged as *The Redux,* sound less like a parody and more like himself. It was a sound hard-earned.

# Part III
# The Doctor

Dr. Dre during the "Straight Outta Compton" tour, Milwaukee, 1989. Photograph by Raymond Boyd / Michael Ochs Archives / Getty Images.

## 7 | *Funky Enough*
### How the West Was Made

**A whole coast away from its New York roots, hip-hop finds a new sound in the hands of a young producer still finding himself.**

NO REGIONAL CLASH BETWEEN TWO POINTS in the United States captures the American popular imagination quite like the contrast between New York and Los Angeles. The two cities have been pitted against each other in pop culture for decades: the nineteenth-century America built vertically versus the twentieth-century America sprawling horizontally, four seasons versus one, hardworking grittiness versus entertainment-world glamour. The binaries are largely false and often shallow, but they're followed regardless, whether it's by each locale's respective media or the residents who refuse to believe they've picked the nation's second-best city to live in.

To say that hip-hop was no exception to this trend is putting it mildly. In the ten-year span from 1987 to 1997, the rap scene out of Los Angeles would find a new sonic identity, help define the personality of the city, break nationwide, create superstars to rival any out of New York, sell millions of records, inspire numerous motion pictures, spur countless moral panics, get tangled up in organized crime, and give the hip-hop world its biggest icon and martyr. This didn't completely discourage crossover between the stars of both cities, whether it involved in-person collaboration or just shared notions of how to put together beats. But provincialism is an easy thing to rally around, especially for perceived outsiders. And in America, you couldn't get that much further outside the original epicenter of hip-hop than Los Angeles.

Rap in LA had a rapid development time for a scene so literally distant from its origins, though it still took a couple years for things to really click. "The Gigolo Rapp," a single credited to Disco Daddy & Captain Rapp, came out in 1981 and became what's generally agreed to be the first legit, non-comedy rap record out of Los Angeles. (In keeping with the East Coast's tendency to use contemporary funk and R&B hits as a basis, its beat was a live-band re-creation of Rick James's fresh-off-the-charts "Give It to Me Baby.") But the LA hip-hop sound was made even more deeply distinct in 1982 with Ronnie Hudson and the Street People's "West Coast Poplock." The song celebrated the very idea of a Cali-originated dance style—in this case, popping, a herky-jerky yet distinctly rhythmic series of motions that resembled anything from robotic movements to stop-motion animation—with the interpolated music of Roger Troutman and Zapp. Troutman, whose signature synthesized voice-distorting "talk box" and unreal ear for a hard-bouncing hook gave Zapp a long string of R&B hits in the '80s, was just one of many distinct practitioners of the heavily synthesized funk style known as "boogie" that would usurp disco in the early '80s, along with contemporaries ranging from relative newcomers like Rick James and Prince to well-adapting veterans like George Clinton and Earth, Wind & Fire.

Soon, more stars began to emerge, including Tracy Marrow—aka Ice-T—whose careers of both DJing and robbing jewelry stores were both soon eclipsed by his charisma as an MC. His early single "The Coldest Rap" was a regional success in 1983 based largely on club play and word of mouth—the radio wouldn't touch it thanks to its Iceberg Slim–informed hustler/pimp lyrics—and staked a further claim on LA's unique sound by riding off an intricate synthesized track that sounded like it owed just as much to Kraftwerk as it did to Troutman. Ice-T couldn't have asked for better musicians: Daniel Sofer, a wiz on the Oberheim OBX8 synthesizer, had a place in beatmaking history for recording all the drum samples Oberheim used for the DMX drum machine, while the group's other keyboardist and bassist were none other than Jimmy Jam and Terry Lewis, who would emerge as superstar writer-producers that same year when SOS Band's "Just Be Good to Me" became a big R&B and club hit.

But few examples of California's nascent sense of its own hip-hop scene were as powerful as Uncle Jamm's Army. A crew whose very name was inspired by the P-Funk mothership, Uncle Jamm's Army was a party promotion team that ruled Los Angeles's club scene like no other. The collective began when DJ Rodger Clayton joined up with the mobile sound system–owning Martin brothers—Gid, Greg, and Tony—in December 1978. Clayton, later known during his peak years with the

Army as Mr. Prinze, had already spent five years DJing; like Herc, he spun his first set during his high school years in '73, though since it was Cali he held his fifty-cent-admission party in his dad's garage instead of a housing project's rec room. The Army developed much like the hip-hop mobile DJs out of New York, running dance parties that started out in clubs and schools, with Torrance's Alpine Village being their adopted home base. Other DJs and crews would battle them for turf and cred— sometimes through sheer perseverance in self-promotion, sometimes through more underhanded means like covering up UJA's posters with their own—and some would maintain enough of a foothold to hold off the Army's advance.

But the Army had tapped into something that a younger audience of black and Latinx heads would push to the forefront of West Coast R&B: boogie was still hot, but the kids wanted something faster, something more futuristic, something that hadn't been played out. That something was electro, the style of dance music that fused funk and boogie with synth-pop and electronic music and saw its earliest hip-hop crossover success with Grandmaster Flash and the Furious Five's "Scorpio" in '81. The smash success of Afrika Bambaataa and Arthur Baker's work on "Planet Rock" in '82 reverberated even more loudly and enduringly in LA than it had in New York, and cuts like Twilight 22's "Electric Kingdom," Cybotron's "Clear," and Hashim's "Al-Naafiysh (The Soul)" became cult sensations in '83 off their up-tempo staccato drum machine grooves and poplock-frenzy rhythms. Those latter three artists originated out of the San Francisco Bay Area, Detroit, and the Bronx, respectively, but Uncle Jamm's Army made them the sound of Los Angeles.

By then, with the Army's colossal booming system earning awe-struck word of mouth and Clayton's crates getting a boost on early exclusives and promos thanks to his job running the DJ Booth record store, the Army had come to dominate the city. Crowds of more than ten thousand freak dancers, funkateers, new wavers, and every other corner of early '80s R&B fandom would show up to venues as big as the sixteen-thousand-seat Los Angeles Memorial Sports Arena—the NBA Los Angeles Clippers' home court—just to dance to a DJ. And it wasn't just Clayton stunning them. Another star emerged in the crew, Greg "Egyptian Lover" Broussard, a spectacular showman on the decks who'd sometimes play records upside-down and backwards by turning the needle facing upwards and placing it on the wax from underneath.

And when he brought a Roland TR-808 drum machine into the fold, he'd add a sort of real-time remixing and multi-mixing to the Army's repertoire, blurring the lines between hip-hop DJing and electro programming. It was machines all the way down, from the 808 to the decks to the synthesizer-dominated jams being spun in the first place. When Clayton called his '73 garage party "Industrial Shop," he had no idea how prescient that name would sound ten years later.

From there, the clout started to hit like an avalanche. Clayton marshaled his promotional savvy to bring the superstars of East Coast hip-hop to California, including class-of-'84 hitmakers from Run-D.M.C. to Whodini to U.T.F.O. And soon the Army were putting out their own records: 1983 single "Dial-a-Freak" b/w "Yes, Yes, Yes," a Clayton/Egyptian Lover co-production, was so big in LA that it became as omnipresent as the latest hits from *1999*-era Prince and Michael Jackson circa *Thriller*. When Egyptian Lover put out a solo joint the following year, a 12-inch called "Egypt, Egypt," it blew up even further, making him one of the biggest stars in the city and a permanent icon of electro. From where they stood, Uncle Jamm's Army had no rival.

But from where Alonzo Williams stood, the Army's monopoly was far from assured. Williams had not only known Clayton when the latter had started DJing, the two actually worked together in a crew called Disco Construction. And after they went their separate ways, Lonzo formed his own group of challengers to the DJ throne. In 1979, Williams became the owner and Friday night DJ of Compton Eve's After Dark club, and used his position to put on an auxiliary squad of other DJs that he eventually dubbed the World Class Wreckin' Cru. By 1983, he had a set lineup: rapper Cli-N-Tel, DJ Unknown, Antoine "DJ Yella" Carraby, and Andre "Dr. Dre" Young. (Despite the "surgeon" gimmick and get-up that he'd be saddled with in the crew's early years, Dr. Dre's alias was actually a takeoff of basketball great Julius "Dr. J" Erving—a curious inspiration for an early '80s Angeleno when Dr. J's Philadelphia 76ers were perennial rivals of the Los Angeles Lakers.)

As the electro scene took off, it was Dre and Yella that started garnering the most attention: the two DJs had become inseparable since just after graduating high school, and were quick to establish themselves as the most talented members. According to Yella, they were drawn to hip-hop after watching Run-D.M.C. do a short but impressive set performing their first single during their 1983 Los Angeles debut. Ten minutes was all it took for Yella and Dre to decide that they could work that same angle, too. That wasn't New York hip-hop's only firsthand inspiration for the duo: Davy DMX, who was DJing for Kurtis Blow at the time, had spent a couple days teaching Yella the ins and outs of scratching and mixing. Yella then passed his knowledge on to Dre shortly after Dre, then seventeen, battled his way into the Cru with a bizarre but effective (and perfectly beatmatched) blend of Jive Rhythm Trax's 1982 electro DJ beat "122 B.P.M." and the Marvelettes' 1961 Motown oldie "Please Mr. Postman."

Enter KDAY, the AM outlet that just-hired music director Greg Mack was about to turn into the first radio station to play hip-hop 24/7. Mack, who'd been brought on in July of '83 to boost the station's flailing relevancy among young black and Latinx listeners, had initially caught on to the same notion as everyone else: that Uncle Jamm's Army were the biggest party starters in LA. When Mack caught one of their sets at the Sports Arena, he was so stunned at the crew's ability to draw such a massive crowd and keep them dancing all night long that he offered them a regular mix-show gig on KDAY. But Clayton was reluctant—according to Mack, Clayton stated that the Army didn't need radio to be successful, and the part-timer pay didn't seem to compensate for Mack's notion of "free advertising." The Army still earned themselves a gig contributing mixes to the station's coveted Saturday night slot, *Saturday Night Fresh*, in the fall of 1983. But the Army and Mack fell out when KDAY, for some never-entirely-clear reason, failed to play a series of commercials the Army had bought advertising an upcoming party. According to Egyptian Lover, "Greg blamed it on another person. Another person blamed it on Greg. Roger went up there and started choking Greg Mack out . . . it was like, 'OK, now we can't drop mix shows on KDAY no more.'"

Uncle Jamm's Army jumped ship to a better-paying gig at rival station KGFJ, which left a major opening for an actual hand-picked crew to take up the mantle. It just so happened that Lonzo had convinced Mack to hire Yella and Dre, who were still making names for themselves and were more amenable to being paid in exposure. The two DJs would put together mixtapes of hip-hop and R&B at Lonzo's garage-based home studio—mixes that would be known as "Traffic Jams"—and their status as the station's in-house "Mix Masters" boosted their profiles considerably. Almost too considerably: within barely a year, their side gig selling tape copies of the mixes at the Roadium Swap Meet made them more than enough money to make up for their not getting paid for their creation and radio play. Mack remembers Dre's skills in particular: "I had never heard anything like it before—it was multi-tracking. He would lay down a beat and then he would overlap it with an accapella and overlap that with a harmony, basically making a song out of the mix."

Increasing commitments to the World Class Wreckin' Cru's recording career cut into Dre's spare time and ended his days as a KDAY regular after about a year, but he continued to create mixes long afterward, raking in swap meet dollars with tapes like *'85 Live!* and *'86 in the Mix!* It's fascinating to listen to these mixes now, with the knowledge of what Dre would get up to just a couple short years later: both tapes consisted of two half-hour mixes, one for each side of a sixty-minute cassette, that pushed up-tempo electro, funk, and hip-hop to startling levels of rapid-fire free-association, aided by Dre's uncanny dexterity on the decks and a sense that anything that could rock a party would work, genre be damned.

On the first side of *'85 Live,* Ready for the World's Prince-alike "Oh Sheila" would segue into Kraftwerk's epochal synthpop classic "Numbers" via clips from Paul Hardcastle's dancefloor Vietnam lesson "19," before moving on to other up-tempo synth-heavy hits by Prince ("Erotic City"), Sheila E. ("The Glamorous Life"), Lisa Lisa & Cult Jam ("Can You Feel the Beat"), and Egyptian Lover ("Computer Power"). The other side was slower and more hip-hop oriented—Whodini ("Friends"), the Real Roxanne ("Romeo"), the Fat Boys ("Jailhouse Rap"), and LL Cool J ("Dear Yvette")—but no less intricately mixed or hard-hitting.

*'86 in the Mix!* had a similar format, but with a twist. The up-tempo first side established its electro-rap emphasis early on—including more cuts that drew from electro-compatible forms of hip-hop like the Miami bass scene (2 Live Crew's "We Want Some Pussy") and an inspired blend of "Planet Rock" with the Beastie Boys' "Brass Monkey." But just before the halfway point, the mix was interrupted by a jet airliner *whoosh,* the pitched-up voice of LA rapper (and Dre's cousin) Sir Jinx arrived to announce that "we goin' back to the *old school,*" and the remainder of the side was dedicated to a block of classic late '70s and early '80s funk from Zapp and Parliament-Funkadelic.

It wasn't just nostalgia at work. Gang culture was a major fixture of LA in the 1980s, and when members of the Bloods and Crips started causing commotions at parties, DJs had learned to placate them by playing the old-school funk jams they preferred—George Clinton's "Atomic Dog," Zapp's "More Bounce to the Ounce," Parliament's "Aqua Boogie," and other less frenetic but seriously bass-heavy mid-tempo jams. "In the back of every crate, there was an emergency song," Egyptian Lover recollected in a brief mini-documentary on the scene put out by Red Bull Music Academy. "We put on [Parliament's] 'Flash Light,' gangstas would stop fighting and [go] 'that's my jam,' and start throwing up their gang signs and crip-walkin' and just having fun." But as gang culture became even higher-stakes during the Reaganomics-era influx of crack cocaine and heavy weaponry, where fistfights gave way to handguns and then to submachine guns, those emergency records just weren't enough. "When we first started doing dances," recalls Alonzo Williams in the same documentary, "the gang factor was maybe 5 or 10 percent of the overall clientele. As time moved on to the late '80s, 50/50. By the '90s? It was 90 percent gangstas, 10 percent civilians."

That development came to national attention in an ugly way in the summer of '86. On August 17, 1986, a Run-D.M.C. concert in Long Beach was shut down after gang violence broke out in the crowd. It was a trend that had followed the group during their *Raising Hell* tour that year, from New York to Pittsburgh to Atlanta, but this event was the worst: according to Clayton, who'd attended the show, "The Long Beach Insanes had stole a Mexican girl's purse and some Mexican dudes went upstairs, broke in the broom closet, and went down and hit up the Long Beach Insanes . . . with brooms and mops and sticks with sharp edges on 'em. Then all the black gangs got together . . . and they just start whupping every Mexican boy, every white boy, throwing 'em off the second level." Greg Mack was on stage about to announce opening act Whodini when one of those thrown victims landed on the stage just feet away.

The show was cancelled, but the damage was done, with one fatality and at least forty-one acknowledged injuries resulting from the melee. Afterwards a frustrated Run, who noted the lack of such violence at the Sports Arena the previous year, stated that "these gangs stand for everything that rap music is against . . . we don't want nothing to do with this rampaging stuff." Some people, mostly hip-hop fans, believed him. Other, more powerful people believed Tipper Gore, head of the Parents Music Resource Center, when she claimed that "angry, disillusioned, unloved kids unite behind heavy metal or rap music, and the music says it's okay to beat people up." KDAY did their part to organize and pro-

mote an October 9 "Day of Peace"—a two-hour call-in show featuring
Run-D.M.C., R&B legend Barry White, and '84 Los Angeles Summer
Olympics boxing gold medalist Paul Gonzales hearing pleas for nonvi-
olence from frustrated members of the community and gang-bangers
looking for a way out. But promoters and other authority figures took
the moralists' side: "I think it's going to be a while before we see another
big rap show in this town," stated one LA-based concert promoter, Ava-
lon Attractions majordomo Brian Murphy. "We need to give it some
time to cool off."

• • •

That same year, Dre and Yella were creatively languishing in the Wreckin'
Cru. Their album *Rapped in Romance* was poised to follow up the local
success of their '85 debut EP *World Class* with major-label distribution
on CBS/Epic and all the money that came with it. Most of that money,
however, went to Lonzo, who bought a new BMW with part of the pro-
ceedings and subsequently freed up his old Mazda RX-7 to sell to Dre.
Unfortunately for both men, said RX-7 was sporty enough to provoke
Dre's tendency to accumulate speeding tickets, which Dre would then
miss his court date for, resulting in overnight jail time and Lonzo having to spend significant amounts of money for bail. And when *Rapped
in Romance* bricked, the record deal didn't last either, which meant that
Lonzo was increasingly reluctant to add to the thousands of dollars'
worth of investment in keeping his lead-footed DJ out of lockup. When
one of Dre's stints in jail fell on a night the Wreckin' Cru didn't need
him for a gig, Lonzo left Dre hanging, ostensibly as a lesson to get his
shit together. So without his early mentor to bail him out, Dre wound up
calling another guy he knew who was always good for money.

Eric Wright was a diminutive but larger-than-life hustler who was
known for an intense work ethic and an ability to win fistfights against
much larger adversaries. After dropping out of high school, he'd started
making money off the crack trade that drug trafficking kingpin "Free-
way" Rick Ross had brought to South Central LA, but a focused,
business-minded approach to his illegal activities meant that Eric was
often on the lookout for more legitimate means of making money. Early
'80s South Central wasn't the easiest place to do so: federal job programs
had been slashed by Reagan's budget cuts, and the drug trade—later

linked to Reagan's funding of anti-communist military forces in Central America—was the closest thing there was to a boom economy. The lingering effects of discrimination and police brutality that led to the 1965 Watts riots had left multiple generations of black Los Angeles residents disillusioned, especially since many of them had migrated to LA from the South to escape the discrimination and poverty that they instead found in potent new forms.

But Eric knew he had an escape route. He'd saved up enough money, about $250,000, to set him up for an enterprise that wouldn't be so close to a guarantee of being shot dead or rotting in jail. And since the drive of being an all-day hustler translated pretty well into the straight business world, he figured he could do just as well—better, even—if he shifted his focus to the entertainment world. Eric was one of thousands of young South Central heads who had snapped up Dre's swap meet mixtapes every time they dropped. But for him it was different: one of the first times Dre had ever done a DJ set for an audience was in Eric's backyard after a block party, and Dre called this gig one of the big opportunities for him to build that mixtape-buying audience in the first place.

Before long, Eric started up a rapport with Steve Yano, who co-owned the booth at the Roadium with his wife, Susan, where all those Dre mixes were sold. It was a gray-market sort of thing—the Yanos' record business hadn't exactly *cleared* the songs on those mixes, and they were doing brisk business in prerelease and white-label exclusives, too—but it still appealed to Eric. And since Dre was doing such good business for the Yanos, Eric wheedled Dre's phone number from Steve, which eventually led to Eric giving Dre a new gig as their own mobile DJ unit, High-Powered Productions.

Their nascent working relationship was starting to pay off enough to give Dre a potential alternative to working with the Wrecking Cru, and by the time Dre called Eric for bail money, Eric had found another angle to his enterprise. Steve had dissuaded Eric from the idea of setting up his own record shop, and suggested that a record label might be a better business instead. So while Eric was more than willing to bail Dre out, it was under one condition: Dre would make him a beat for his new label, Ruthless Records, as soon as they could figure out who they could get to rap on it. It was like Dre flipped his tape over: now that the electro phase of his career was winding down—along with the scene

itself—he could cultivate a new side of himself that didn't involve making loverman raps or dressing in glittery quasi-Prince costumes. And in
1986, that side had plenty of inspiration to draw from.

The year before, a Compton MC named Toddy Tee had seen his
homemade tape of a track called "Batterram" get so popular—first on
the streets, then with an assist from KDAY—that it was rereleased
on Epic with new production by LA funk hitmaker Leon Haywood.
Originally a rework of a goofy John Wayne parody rap called "Rappin'
Duke," Toddy wrote his own new lyrics about the massive military-grade
machines that the LAPD would use to bust down doors to suspected
crack houses, with Haywood's minimalist synth-funk sound hovering
somewhere between gliding cool and late-night menace. And a ways
north, up in Oakland's East Bay, another rapper named Too $hort was
making bank off spitting X-rated rhymes about sex and drug dealers
over LinnDrum machine beats and selling tapes of them out of his car, a
savvy meeting of street hustle and DIY art.

But it was another hit by the still-emerging Ice-T that put the sound
of Los Angeles gangsta rap into its sharpest relief. Three years after cutting his electro-rap debut, Ice-T had enlisted Wreckin' Cru alumni the
Unknown DJ to create something that had the vibe of "P.S.K. What
Does It Mean?"—a 1985 single from Philadelphia MC Schoolly D, who
rapped about sex, drugs, and threats of violence over the starkest, most
echo-soaked scratch–and–drum machine production available. The
answer to the titular question—P.S.K. stood for Park Side Killas, a West
Philadelphia set—canonized Schoolly D as the first MC to make a reputation specifically as a "gangsta rapper." If Dre taking an alias inspired
by a Philadelphia 76er was a weird move, Ice-T reaching the next level
of fame inspired by a Philadelphia PSK'er was a crucial one, as "6 'n the
Mornin'" became a go-to gangsta anthem at a moment where hip-hop
was just starting to come to terms with what gangsta actually was. The
boom-bap drum machine programming wasn't entirely regionally distinct from what producers like Mantronix and Rick Rubin were doing
with 808s out East, but in a city far more used to synthetic drums
than old-school breaks it came to characterize a West Coast style that
sounded best booming out of subwoofers in slow-moving cars.

So Dre was inspired and more than ready to create his own answer
to that stark, drum machine–driven sound. At first, the idea was to bring
in an aspiring group from Brooklyn called Home Boys Only, or H.B.O.

for short, who had moved to Orange County by '86. H.B.O. didn't have a track of their own to record yet, but Dre and Eric had brought another artist into the mix to take care of that. O'Shea Jackson, better known as Ice Cube, had known Dre for a while: they'd cowritten a track called "She's a Skag" as Stereo Crew, and he was also a member of a Wreckin' Cru–affiliated group called C.I.A. with Sir Jinx and a third rapper named K-Dee. The group had evolved from making Blowfly-style filthy parodies of the day's rap hits (Run-D.M.C.'s "My Adidas" reworked as "My Penis," for instance) to cutting a few original tracks for Lonzo's Kru-Cut Records. They sounded like a diabolical blend of the Beastie Boys and Run-D.M.C., all emphatic, booming voices treating every syllable like an exclamation point, and Dre's minimalist drum machine beats for their '87 EP *Cru' in Action!* fit that style to a T.

Cube in particular had a vivid lyrical credibility that outpaced his actual day-to-day life. A tough-minded but more-or-less clean-cut teenager who studied to be an architectural draftsman in case the whole rap thing didn't work out, he was able to flip his perceptive observations on Compton's street life into stories so detailed, gang-bangers who met him were shocked to learn Cube wasn't part of a set himself. The track Dre and Eric arranged Cube to write was called "Boyz-n-the-Hood," its lyrics deep in regional slang and lifestyle that called up imagery from lowrider car culture, Uzi-spraying crime stories, and crack-casualty petty thievery. But when Dre presented Cube's lyrics to H.B.O., the New York transplants were both confused by the South Central lingo ("six-four" Chevy Impalas weren't status symbols out East) and turned off by the violence. They ditched the session and left Dre and Eric hanging.

Now they had all this studio time but no rappers to use it. Cube wasn't available to record the lyrics he'd just written, either—he was still considered part of C.I.A. and Lonzo's whole stable. Same with Dre—the Wreckin' Cru wasn't his only gig, much less his preferred gig, but it was still a gig, and he hadn't earned the leverage yet to jump ship completely. But Dre figured, hell, Eric's even closer to the lifestyle outlined in "Boyz-n-the-Hood" than Cube was—why not have Eric do the track? Eric offered plenty of reasons why not, chief among them that he wasn't actually an MC and didn't know how to rap.

But Dre refused to waste this opportunity, or the beat he'd made for it. Dre had created a stripped-down but subwoofer-rattling banger of a rhythm offset by a deceptively chirpy-sounding synthesizer melody, punctuated between verses by scratches that incorporated everything from recent rap cuts like LL Cool J's "Three the Hard Way" to old R&B jams on the order of Jean Knight's 1971 smash hit "Mr. Big Stuff." It nodded to classic DJ tradition and contemporary bicoastal 808-driven hardcore hip-hop, while still drawing from Dre's background in electro and funk to pinpoint something a bit more regionally distinct. He had a hit, and he knew it. So after some coaching and direction, Dre finally convinced Eric to give it a shot, one line at a time. It took take after take, punch-in after punch-in, and everything Dre could do to ease Eric's frustration and reluctance. But after hours and hours spent making sure each of the track's five verses were on point, and that Eric's high-pitched, drawling taunt of a delivery was shaped into a raw-power expression of merciless cool, Dre had actually helped create an MC where one hadn't existed before. Right there, Eric Wright became Eazy-E.

They pressed up five thousand 12-inch singles at a cost of $7,000 in anticipation of the single's success and sold it through the Yanos' record stall. And sold it and sold it and sold it. Eazy had brought on a bunch of friends and acquaintances to shop the single around—a prototype for the now-common rap industry "street team"—which eventually culminated in a meeting with Greg Mack. Once they created a radio-friendly version that edited out the curses, Dre and Eazy were able to get some spins on KDAY. Spins on KDAY meant more demand, and somewhere between its March '87 release and the end of the year, "Boyz-n-the-Hood" had ridden its request-line ubiquity to a sales number, post–national distribution, rumored to be as high as five hundred thousand. The complementary nucleus of writer Ice Cube, producer Dr. Dre, and rapper Eazy-E had hit on something with the potential to be not just successful but transformative. They needed to capitalize on this, ASAP.

In August 1987, five months after the release of "Boyz-n-the-Hood," it all came together under the banner of N.W.A—a supergroup collective of artists who were meant to embody everything that Los Angeles was prepared to bring to their version of gangsta rap. N.W.A, or Niggaz Wit Attitudes, had formed around the Cube/Dre/Eazy trifecta, with Yella rejoining the group after a three-month stint working as a parking valet. An MC named Krazy Dee and electro producer/rapper Arabian Prince rounded out their earliest incarnation. Debut single "Panic Zone" was a showcase for the latter artist, who'd already put out a couple of singles—1984's "Strange Life" and 1985's "It Ain't Tough"—that reign as gems of the electro movement today. With Dre on the boards, Arabian Prince rapping, and Egyptian Lover pulling a feature spot contributing a vocoder hook, the waning era of electro was given a powerful send-off from three of its key practitioners.

Yet it was the other two tracks on the single that were the real portents. "8 Ball," a tribute to the power of malt liquor, was another Eazy showcase where his gradually improving delivery was boosted by Dre's bass-over-everything production. But while its drunk-and-disorderly gunplay felt like a solid-enough continuation of the storytelling raps of "Boyz-n-the-Hood"—this one, cowritten by Cube and a friend of Eazy's named Lorenzo "MC Ren" Patterson—it was "Dope Man" that nailed down N.W.A. as the group to watch out for as L.A. rap standard-bearers. For one thing, it was the track where Ice Cube became the Ice Cube people know today—a storyteller whose authoritatively cutting, permanently scowling voice relayed tales of street crime with a barely concealed disgust bordering on nihilism.

And as Cube spit his lyrics about baseheads and the dealers that served them, Dre's beat—a machine-gun fusillade of drum machine kicks and snares among the hardest and most immediately throat-grabbing to ever come out of an 808—was laced by an exotic sound familiar to students of classic funk. It was a keening, whining ARP synthesizer line, lifted from Junie Morrison's solo on the Ohio Players' 1973 #1 R&B hit "Funky Worm"—a skewed, quasi-Arabian melody that added a sense of vertiginous menace to the track, like a police siren warped and melted under the influence of hallucinogens. This, more than anything beforehand, made one thing distinctly clear: the sound of synthesized '70s funk was going to be a part of West Coast hip-hop's DNA for a long time to come.

If there was one notable catch to Dre's production, it's that he was never as beholden to the idea of the traditional break as most East Coast producers and DJs were. Even as hip-hop beats continued to transition from the do-it-yourself rhythm programming of drum machines to sampled loops, Dre was uninterested in relying heavily on samples. "Me and Dre personally were really into not sampling," Arabian Prince stated in a 2008 interview with *L.A. Record.* "We'd throw in effects or scratches or sirens or whatever, but if it came to a guitar sound or something, we'd rather play it. So we'd get someone to come in—try to recreate it before we ripped it. That's why N.W.A. sonically sounded better than a lot of other records."

It was more a matter of fidelity than anything; Dre was the kind of studio-bound gearhead who'd rather have a crisp-sounding live-band interpolation than a grimy-sounding sample. But given the way the sound of hip-hop was developing through 1987 and early 1988, any emerging producer worth their SP-1200 would ignore the work of Marley Marl or the Bomb Squad at their peril. For N.W.A's debut album, 1988's *Straight Outta Compton,* Dre would do his part to show that the West could put up production every bit as complex, dense, and referential of classic funk as anything out of New York. And hot on the heels of Public Enemy's release of *It Takes a Nation of Millions*—which dropped less than two months before *Straight Outta Compton*—Dre passed a formidable test.

The first three cuts on *Compton* were electrifying, a drastic shift from the 808/ARP-sample sparseness that drove "Dope Man"—a necessary move not just out of keeping pace with the sound of '88, but out of a need to bring something even heavier to accompany the group's more relentless lyrical assault. The opening title track built its drums off a slowed-down loop from the Winstons' "Amen, Brother" back when only a handful of producers had capitalized off its dense, on-point, funky-to-death drum break, and none with the impact that "Straight Outta Compton" did (though thousands of songs' worth of "Amen" break samples followed). Not content to just loop it, Dre and Yella punched in heavier bass kicks and between-verse barrages of scratch-collage hooks to ramp up its impact. (It's in those hooks that they slickly juxtapose the more Cali-rooted nods—including vocal clips from "West Coast Poplock" and Dezo Daz's '87 Compton-shoutout single "It's My Turn"—like they're local color.)

Sample-wise, "Fuck tha Police" was a bit more concerned with sounding like what was hot in '88 than what was distinct from New York—most of its percussive elements came from the James Brown catalog, and its melodic through line came from a guitar riff lifted from an early '70s Roy Ayers record—but even its passing resemblance to the Bomb Squad's DNA was overwhelmed by Dre's ear for turning the bass up in the mix. And "Gangsta Gangsta" was a veritable symphony of samples: super-boosted bass and guitar from Steve Arrington's '83 boogie-funk jam "Weak at the Knees," call-and-response vocal clips from rap contemporaries Slick Rick, BDP, and the Beastie Boys, and one of the heaviest 808 beats put together to date.

The catch is that N.W.A's fame and success, while impossible without Dre, was only sporadically credited to his production by journalists. Never mind those first three cuts' flag-planting declarations of Dre as a standard-bearer of the West Coast's new hip-hop stronghold, or the crossover success of later Cube-written, Dre-rapped single "Express Yourself"—a more radio-friendly and upbeat yet no less defiant homage to the same-titled Charles Wright & the Watts 103rd Street Rhythm Band's post–civil rights era ode to free expression. It was Eazy, Cube, and Ren getting the lion's share of the attention, and while their personalities made N.W.A stand out, it was the controversial nature of their lyrics that overwhelmed the discourse about them on all sides.

It wasn't just that *Straight Outta Compton* became one of the hottest-selling albums of the late '80s off the strengths of its musical content—it was the rebel image, the controversially confrontational nature of it all, that captured the popular imagination. Instead of just observing and describing the effects of economic blight and the crime and police brutality that followed it, N.W.A credibly presented themselves as the inevitable end result of those conditions: the monsters that a racist America made. Conservatives loathed the anti-authoritarian overtones, liberals recoiled from the all-too-casual misogyny, and everybody wrung their hands over the violent imagery. The group became a musical symptom that threatened to eclipse the actual sociological cause.

In May of 1989, coinciding with an infamous tour that would eventually result in riots and the group's arrest after a show in Detroit, *LA Weekly* ran a Jonathan Gold profile of N.W.A that tracked their ascent from the recording of "Gangsta Gangsta" ("The white people look shocked, the black people embarrassed. A drive-time jock rubs his temple hard. One promotion guy cackles in the corner, muttering, 'I love to work dirty records . . .'") to a photoshoot where Eazy hauls out "an arsenal bigger than Sergeant Samuel K. Doe needed to overthrow Liberia." What Gold called "hard rap"—though the term "gangster-rap" was also used in the article—was portrayed primarily as having "brought together a self-selected community of kids by becoming an image of what their parents feared most."

Concerning "Boyz-n-the-Hood," "A lot of people hated the record,

because while the urban-gangster life had been romanticized since
Capone, nobody had ever made it sound quite so much fun before."
(Eazy's retort: "It *is* fun.") Cube made credible claims of non-advocacy
for a lifestyle he was more dedicated in chronicling than endorsing:
"We're just telling them what the gangbanger shit is like. And what
would happen. At the end of the song, you might end up in jail or dead.
If you get away every time, you'd be a super hero." But in the end, it
didn't matter to MTV, who refused to play the video for "Straight Outta
Compton," or to the FBI, where a rogue agent sent Ruthless Records a
letter condemning "Fuck tha Police" for encouraging violence against
police officers. N.W.A were *dangerous*.

Meanwhile, what else could Dr. Dre do but keep making beats? His
successes from 1988 and '89 were not only widespread, but eclectic: in
just a two-year span, he contributed production to Eazy-E's gleefully
vulgar solo joint *Eazy-Duz-It*, J.J. Fad's pop-rap party-starter *Supersonic*,
the self-titled smash R&B debut album by Wreckin' Cru alumni (and
Dre's girlfriend) Michel'le, and, most promisingly, the first album by
Dre's cohort and sometime ghostwriter the D.O.C.

If *Straight Outta Compton* was the world finding out what Dr. Dre's
sound was in '88, 1989's *No One Can Do It Better* was Dre finding out how
far his sound could go. Leadoff cut "It's Funky Enough" and later single "The Formula" were canny blends of West Coast 808 rhythms and
familiar '70s R&B interpolations (the Sylvers' "Misdemeanor" and Marvin Gaye's "Inner City Blues," respectively). The up-tempo rhythms that
had once driven Dre's electro tracks returned as funky hip-hop breaks
for high-BPM cuts like "Lend Me an Ear," "Whirlwind Pyramid," and
"Portrait of a Master Piece." And "Beautiful but Deadly" nodded toward
rap-rock while still sourcing its heavy guitar riff (replayed by Stan "the
Guitar Man" Jones) from Funkadelic's "Cosmic Slop." There was even
an interlude, "Comm. Blues," that was basically a short but soulful (if
tongue-in-cheek) old-school slow blues with Michel'le vamping on lead
vocals. It was a more-than-promising debut for an MC who had all of
the sound of the West Coast without any of the controversial baggage—-
D.O.C. was more of a Rakim-style MC who focused on wordplay and
moving a crowd than repping gangsta culture—and with its mixture of
well-curated samples, feverish scratching, and live-band interpolation,
it drew off everything Dre had wanted to accomplish as a producer at
that point.

It was also one of the last production jobs Dre would do before everything started to fall apart. On June 25, 1989, just over a month before the release date of *No One Can Do It Better,* a touring Dre heard the news from his mother that his little brother Tyree, who had grown up idolizing Dre, had been killed in an altercation. The man who murdered Tyree was a gang member who accosted Tyree and three of his friends while they were cruising down Crenshaw Boulevard, and he threw Dre's brother so hard against the concrete that he broke Tyree's neck. The news devastated Dre, and left him with pangs of personal guilt: Tyree had wanted to hang out with N.W.A during their tour, but Dre had brushed him off, promising that maybe he'd fly him in to one of the later tour stops sometime. After the tour, people close to Dre started noticing that he started to drink heavily for the first time in his life.

• • •

By 1990, hip-hop as a genre was finding itself in an increasingly bizarre relationship with mainstream attention. Two of the most successful crossover singles of the year—and, up to that point, *the* most commercially successful singles in rap history—came from flashy pop-friendly phenoms who seemingly appeared out of nowhere, even as the controversy around hip-hop hit a boiling point. MC Hammer, a former Oakland A's batboy turned rapper/dancer who had built a small following in the late '80s through diligent street marketing and word of mouth, gradually cultivated a video-friendly, image-based style that emphasized accessible and dance-friendly themes. His 1990 album *Please, Hammer, Don't Hurt 'Em,* which dropped that February, eventually spent twenty-one weeks at #1 on the Billboard charts and would become the first rap album in history to sell ten million copies—thanks largely to the success of single "U Can't Touch This" and its catchy if rudimentary sampled loop of Rick James's 1981 hit "Super Freak."

Hammer's rep as the squeaky-clean genie-pants-clad rap superstar you could market to Middle American churchgoers was still on the rise in March when *Newsweek* posted a cover feature, "Rap Rage" (*Yo! Street rhyme has gone big time—but are those sounds out of bounds?*), that featured a shot of bewildered-looking PG rapper Tone LĐc peering over his shades as if to ask the reader, "Can you *believe* this shit?" Writer Jerry Adler, who had no previous experience listening to hip-hop, wrote an alarmist four-page article titled "The Rap Attitude" that focused almost exclusively on the more incendiary themes of two groups—Public Enemy and N.W.A—and attempted to tie it into the class-based griev-ances of "the millions of American youths who forgot to go to business school in the 1980s."

The article came to the conclusion that rap was "bombastic, self-aggrandizing and yet as scary as sudden footsteps in the dark," scatter-ing adjectives like "repulsive," "nihilistic," and "savage" along the way. For a form of music to be portrayed this way by a periodical read by millions of Americans as one of their primary news sources was signifi-cantly damaging: at its mid–golden age creative peak, with a conscious rapper for every gangsta and a party-rocker for every revolutionary, boil-ing down more than a decade's worth of culture to its most contentious moments was the kind of ignorant media scare that nonetheless left a significant, lasting impression on the American pop-culture psyche. The window for hip-hop to be taken seriously by mainstream America was rapidly narrowing.

And then one man threatened to shut it completely. A dirt bike enthusiast turned rapper named Robert Van Winkle—better known as Vanilla Ice—picked up where Hammer left off with the runaway success of his single "Ice Ice Baby" and the album it originated from—originally released in 1989 as *Hooked,* but reissued the following September with the none-more-nineties title *To the Extreme.* Like Hammer, the Dallas-born, Miami-based Ice rode flashy, photogenic cartoon fashion and a sample from a familiar 1981 pop hit to a four-month chart-topping run and the ten million mark for record sales. Unlike Hammer, Vanilla Ice was white. And not the comedic, Catskills-Jewish white-passing of the Beastie Boys or the Brooklyn/Queens Def Jam bona fides of 3rd Bass, but an almost obliviously sincere turbo-WASP who overcompensated by playing up his questionable street cred wherever possible.

This eventually backfired in almost every way possible when it was revealed just how many people "Ice Ice Baby" ripped off on its way to becoming rap's first #1 on Billboard's Hot 100. The titular hook was lifted from black fraternity Alpha Phi Alpha, a point that 3rd Bass mocked on their 1991 *Derelicts of Dialect* track "Ace in the Hole" en route to completely dismantling him on "Pop Goes the Weasel." And when Mario "Chocolate" Johnson, a rapper out of California, claimed that he'd assisted in writing "Ice Ice Baby" without receiving credit or roy-alties, he called on a friend of his to set the matter straight. That friend turned out to be Marion "Suge" Knight, a celebrity bodyguard and aspiring music mogul, who implicitly threatened to throw Vanilla Ice off a fifteenth-floor hotel balcony if he didn't sign the song's rights to Suge right then and there.

Most damning of all, when Ice was caught out for failing to clear the pivotal sample of Queen and David Bowie's "Under Pressure," he claimed that he'd significantly changed the bassline the sample lifted from: "It's not the same bassline . . . *Ding ding ding digga-ding-ding, ding ding ding,* that's the way *theirs* goes. *Ours* goes *ding ding ding digga-ding ding, tch-*DING *ding ding ding digga-ding-ding,* that little-bitty change. It's not the same!" The man who fronted the biggest hit rap single to date couldn't even own up to its sample-based origins.

N.W.A's popularity was skyrocketing in an America that was poorly prepared to deal with them; for millions of young hip-hop heads, that only strengthened N.W.A's credentials: they scared Tipper Gore and *Newsweek,* they were realer than MC Hammer and Vanilla Ice, and *they actually pissed off the FBI.* But that turned out to be the kind of reputation that makes even the most promising groups burn bright but fast.

The first tragedy came just before the decade turned: in November 1989, the D.O.C. was critically injured in a drunk-driving accident, sent flying through the rear window of his Honda Prelude after hitting a tree head-on. (He had actually been stopped by a police officer shortly before after a brief, aborted chase, but in a case of a stroke of good luck leading to bad, the cops let D.O.C. go with a ticket after posing for some friendly photos with him and the platinum record plaques he was carrying in the back seat.) When the paramedics arrived and tried to attend to him, he struggled so much that the breathing tube they inserted into his throat damaged his larynx, injuries that were further exacerbated when a surgeon removed an excess amount of scar tissue and permanently left D.O.C.'s once-sharp, booming voice with a gritty rasp. Eazy paid for his hospital bills, but it was a generosity mitigated by D.O.C.'s too-late realization that he'd signed away in the neighborhood of a million dollars' worth of royalty rights to Eazy in a trade for $5,000 worth of jewelry. "I was happy to be involved," he recollected. "I didn't think of money. I was just a team player willing to do whatever it took to make the team win because I figured if I gave all I could to those guys, sooner or later they'd give all they could to me."

He wasn't alone. In December 1989 Ice Cube, frustrated at how little he was making in royalties considering his double role as both a rapper and one of the primary lyricists for the group, left N.W.A for his own solo career. Cube pinned the blame on Eazy-E and the group's manager Jerry Heller, whose financial partnership kept N.W.A in the spotlight while also shorting the financials of every non-Eazy member in the group. But while the eventual dis track war between N.W.A and Cube would become one of the bitterest to date—Cube's 1991 track "No Vaseline" is still considered one of the harshest barrages of invective ever aimed at one rapper from another (and over a Cube / Sir Jinx-co-produced beat based off Brick's good-natured disco-jazz-funk hit "Dazz," no less)—an equally significant salvo was fired at Dre's identity as a producer, if primarily by proxy. Cube initially harbored no ill will against Dre upon leaving N.W.A, and had in fact wanted to use Dre as the producer for his first solo album. But since Dre's contract with Ruthless didn't allow for it, Cube turned to another crew—one that N.W.A was often compared to in the press when it came to the dangerous, corrupting influence of rap on the minds of helpless young Americans.

Chuck D and Cube had struck up a rapport before when the latter needed some advice on whether or not to leave N.W.A. (Chuck advised against it, Cube recollected, "because the group was so meaningful to so many people.") So the confrontational sound and cultural impact of Public Enemy weren't far from Cube's mind when he flew to Def Jam's New York offices in January of 1990 to meet the Chuck-recommended producer Sam Sever, who handled beats for 3rd Bass. As it turned out, Sever was a no-show, but Chuck D met with Cube instead, bringing him to a recording session for Public Enemy's *Fear of a Black Planet* and snaring him for an eleventh-hour guest verse on their track "Burn Hollywood Burn." (Later that year, Cube would actually go to Hollywood, no burning necessary, and shoot his first film role in John Singleton's South Central gang drama, named after the song Cube wrote for Eazy—*Boyz n the Hood*.) Cube and PE clicked immediately, though Chuck remembers Cube telling Hank Shocklee that Dre and Eazy had laughed off the idea of an N.W.A member working with a bunch of East Coast producers. Supposedly Dre himself warned that if this partnership went down, "then you'll barely go gold."

*AmeriKKKa's Most Wanted* did go gold—though less than three months after its May '90 release is a pretty tight timeframe to be called "barely." More than that, it directly challenged Dr. Dre and everyone else on the West Coast as to whether one city actually had a monopoly on the sonic foundations of gangsta rap: the Bomb Squad's beats on Cube's solo debut were as true to Cube's vision of LA as anything he'd recorded while actually in Los Angeles. Cube and Sir Jinx's fingerprints were all over the influences, of course—Cube made a point of imparting his enthusiasm for deep-dive funk-aficionado favorites like Steve Arrington, Slave, Con Funk Shun, and Betty Davis to Shocklee, and he recalls that "with Bomb Squad it was like, 'We can't go to the real studio until we fill these two crates up with records that *you* like.'" Cube and Eric "Vietnam" Sadler winnowed upwards of seventy different loop ideas and drafts into a repertoire tailor-made to sound like the best of both coasts, with tracks like "The Nigga You Love to Hate" and "Once upon a Time in the Projects" sounding like they were recorded somewhere far west from chilly late-winter Manhattan, music tailor-made for drop-top Impalas created in a city where everyone took the train.

The lyrical animosity would come later; Cube doesn't so much as hint at his falling out with N.W.A until *Death Certificate* a year after. And his old group had fired the first shot that spurred "No Vaseline" in the first place, with Dre himself calling Cube "Benedict Arnold" on the 1990 *100 Miles and Runnin'* EP closer (and D.O.C. / MC Ren cowrite) "Real Niggaz." But N.W.A's troubles would only accelerate from there. 1991's *Niggaz4Life,* their second and final album, benefited from the newly instituted computerized SoundScan album-sales tracking system to debut at #2 on the Billboard 200, jumping up a slot to #1 a week later. But it was an even more contentious and lyrically grotesque album than *Straight Outta Compton:* for every hip-hop specialist magazine like *The Source* that called it 1991's best record, there was a *Rolling Stone* to give it a two-star pan and call it "hateful," "pathetic," "sleazy," and "tiresome." It didn't help that the second half of the album was loaded with troll-caliber misogyny, and without Cube's lyrical influence, the subject matter had a less nuanced and perceptive focus to its rage—shock value became a cause rather than the effect.

But under all that, you can hear something deeper emerging. The lead single from *Niggaz4Life,* "Alwayz into Somethin'," was its first glimmer—a mid-tempo cut that felt like a slow crawl, where its samples were traceable but otherwise seamless and indistinguishable from the efforts of a live musician; the bassline was actually played in studio by a session man named Mike "Crazy Neck" Sims. And you could hear the voice of

James Brown, an "ooh" from *The Payback*'s "Stone to the Bone," intermittently in the background, sure. But it wasn't nearly as prominent as
the Moog that Colin Wolfe played—a simple but resonant melody that
turned an old-school synthesizer sound into something simultaneously
threatening and euphoric. The West Coast had found its instrument.

# *G Thang*
## *The Producer as Superstar*

**Classic synthesized funk fuels the West Coast's signature sound—and hip-hop's biggest blockbusters.**

IT's 1991, and Bev Smith, host of BET call-in current-affairs TV program *Our Voices,* is giving a warm welcome to three colorfully dressed older gentlemen—ones who, in her words, "defined, shaped, and expanded funk music throughout the '70s and have found themselves in the midst of a funk rebirth in the '90s." The men introduce themselves like the larger-than-life artists turned cartoon heroes they've developed into over the past twenty-plus years: singer/songwriter/bandleader George Clinton, bass god Bootsy Collins, and classically trained synthesizer wizard Bernie Worrell, the three musicians most indelibly associated with the Parliament-Funkadelic collective. The conversation inevitably steers towards their contemporary legacy, and there's naturally a lot to discuss; after something of a mild fallow period in the mid-'80s, P-Funk has been massively amplified by hip-hop and given them a new generation's worth of audience.

When a caller from Louisiana asks about groups sampling P-Funk and whether there's an issue with appropriating Clinton's sound, George is quick to clarify that his main issue is with the record labels dropping the ball on getting the P-Funk musicians paid. "We're not upset at the groups at all! I think that it's taken away from them discovering their own new music if they sample it *too* much, but believe me, I'm happy that they sample it." Smith presses Clinton a bit on that: "You just talked about yourselves being professionals, being trained. Do you think sampling hinders these musicians?" "A little bit," Clinton concedes, "but like all things, it'll start something new. That's as artsy as anything else now."

Clinton knew all about how hip-hop could provide, of course. In 1989, he had released a comeback effort on Prince's Paisley Park label, *The Cinderella Theory,* that reckoned with his impact on hip-hop by integrating samples and scratching into the mix and included a guest spot by Public Enemy on the Prince Paul / Don Newkirk coproduced single "Tweakin'." It was fortuitous timing: between De La Soul's "Me Myself and I," EPMD's "One Nation under a Groove"–sampling "So What Cha Sayin'," and the overwhelmingly P-Funky early singles "Doowutchyalike" and "The Humpty Dance" by an emerging Oakland group called Digital Underground, 1989's a formative year for giving hip-hop a ride on the Mothership.

By this time, Clinton's taken to his hip-hop elder statesman status with a natural ease, providing a natural culmination of Digital Underground's tributes by appearing on their album *Sons of the P.* And he often had to play defense on hip-hop's behalf. When *Terminator X & the Valley of the Jeep Beets* came out in May, the Public Enemy DJ was slapped with a $3 million lawsuit for using a sample of the Parliament song "Body Language" on his track "Wanna Be Dancin'." Armen Boladian, whose Bridgeport Music controlled all the copyrights to recordings by George Clinton and music he made with P-Funk, filed the suit without Clinton's go-ahead, despite claims made by Boladian's executive assistant in an *MTV News* clip that it was a suit filed on Clinton's behalf. Clinton had to clarify the situation with his own MTV appearance—his "Tweakin'" guests Chuck and Flav alongside him. The suit was dropped.

There's a certain understandable self-interest at work behind Clinton's enthusiasm: a combination of dicey publishing rights issues and copyright-holder whack-a-mole, combined with pop radio and early MTV's reluctance to get behind the music of older black artists, had threatened to diminish his formidable musical legacy throughout the '80s. But hip-hop had reinvigorated demand for it, and it was the record labels, not the sample-flipping producers, that had kept Clinton's fair share of the profits out of reach. Clinton wrote in his autobiography that artists going after other artists was a waste of time: "Artists aren't allowed the luxury of fighting with each other. The lawyers and record executives fight over you and around you, for their own reasons. Those people went to school to beat you for your shit." For all of the musical ideas hip-hop artists had learned from Clinton, it was this experience with the business in which they'd find a real commonality.

• • •

The first half of Dr. Dre's 1991 was a relentless string of PR night-
mares. Not only were the innovative beats on *Niggaz4Life* continuously
overshadowed in the press by the controversy over the album's lyrical
obscenity, even hearing any of it in the first place could prove tricky
since radio stations and retailers were reluctant at best to promote the
album. And while Dre was working with Eazy-E on new material for a
planned double CD, tentatively dubbed *Temporary Insanity,* Eazy's self-
promotion was starting to get a bit out of hand, as if driven entirely by
the escalating moral panic around the group itself.

Eazy's most bewildering stunt came on March 18, 1991. After making a $25,000 donation to Los Angeles's City of Hope cancer treatment
charity, Eazy wound up on a Republican Party mailing list that attempted
to solicit further donations from him—including an opportunity to pay
just short of $2,500 for two seats to a "Salute to the Commander-in-
Chief" luncheon. Eazy was fine with dropping a couple grand in the
GOP's pockets just for the potential hilarity of America's most infamous rapper hanging out in George H. W. Bush's White House—a non-
partisan move dedicated solely to ginning up attention. "I don't give a
fuck," Eazy stated when asked whether he supported Bush's party. "I
don't even vote." At a time when Ice Cube's Nation of Islam–inspired
outlook was infusing West Coast hip-hop with firebrand politics, his old
bandmate slipping money into right-wing pockets for a laugh felt like a
direct insult to rap's activist movement, almost as much a fuck-you to
Cube as any Benedict Arnold comparisons were. "I never have dinner
with the president," Cube shot back in "No Vaseline"—a statement so
defiant he spat it three times in a row.

But N.W.A's beef with Cube would also wind up fueling one of the
most infamous and cruel moments in Dre's career. Dee Barnes was a
rapper, former KDAY radio personality, and host of a hip-hop show
called *Pump It Up!* on the still-young Fox network. She'd had a working relationship with Dre before, as her group Body & Soul were one
of several hip-hop acts who contributed to "We're All in the Same
Gang," the 1990 Grammy-nominated anti–gang violence single that he
produced. Despite her necessary breadth of knowledge, Barnes would
often wind up arguing with the producers of *Pump It Up!*—at one point,
as recounted in a December 1992 *Source* profile, she recalls getting into
an argument with them when the producers let slip they didn't know

who Slick Rick was—and was often waylaid by their questionable editing choices. In October 1990, in the midst of Barnes attempting to get a story together about N.W.A, cameras caught Ice Cube approaching her on the set of *Boys-n-the-Hood*. Cube, still bitter over the circumstances that made him leave the group, made a remark to the camera mocking N.W.A's then-current EP—"I got all you suckas a hundred miles and runnin'"—and threw in a "shoutout" to the D.O.C. that unflatteringly imitated his raspy post-accident voice. Jeff Shore, the show's producer, saw the clip as good fodder for the N.W.A story, and dropped it in—over Barnes's strenuous objections.

The following January 27, at a Hollywood record release party for Ruthless group Bytches With Problems, Dre found Barnes. By Dre's recollection, he was drunk. By Barnes's (and witnesses') recollection, their exchange of words was cut off by Dre grabbing Barnes by the shirt, then smashing her headfirst against a brick wall. N.W.A's promoter at the time, Doug Young, tried to intervene, but Dre's bodyguard pistol-whipped Young in the mouth and knocked out two of his teeth. Nobody else attempted to stop the assault. Dre, who was nearly a foot taller than the five-foot-three Barnes, subsequently tried and failed to throw her down a flight of stairs, kicked her in the ribs and stomped on her fingers when she was down, then followed her into the women's bathroom when she attempted to flee and punched her in the back of the head. Barnes filed a civil suit against the group for $22.7 million in damages for the assault and ensuing defamation after the fact. Dre pleaded no contest to misdemeanor battery and walked away with a $2,500 fine, community service, and an eventual out-of-court six-figure settlement.

The members of N.W.A glibly justified the incident in an August *Rolling Stone* profile: Ren and Eazy both agreed that Barnes "deserved it" and "had it coming," while Dre shrugged it off as the inevitable result of what happens when "somebody fucks with me." "Besides, it ain't no big thing," he remarked. "I just threw her through a door." Barnes countered with the perspective of someone who felt deeply betrayed by a person she used to trust: "They've started believing this whole fantasy, getting caught up in their press, and they think they're invincible. They think they're living their songs." The misogynist lyrics on *Niggaz4Life*—the ones that MC Ren told *Rolling Stone* were there to "[make] you laugh"—became harder to write off as mere edgy posturing.

Journalist dream hampton penned a righteously angry piece for the

*Village Voice* in July 1991 that confronted this intersection between the appeal of the music and the poison leaking from its messages: "Eazy-E, MC Ren, Dr. Dre, and DJ Yella are four punk ass mothafuckas who are due an ultra critical beatdown; Dre for (allegedly) stompin' *Pump It Up!* host Dee Barnes at a Hollywood party this January, the other three cowards for endorsing it." And yet she spent a significant portion of the article remarking, with an undercurrent of borderline-helpless frustration, that the West Coast's standard-bearers were winning a war for the minds of young hip-hop heads: "Blame who you will, but know that in the midst of Afrocentric showdowns N.W.A discovered irony and cashed in on the confusion. 'Positive' rap has thoroughly convinced the niggaz from Compton that they want no part of it: record sales and jeep rotation suggest that they've got allies, perhaps even some converts." The siren call of that funk-drenched production might have had a significant say in that success, but it wasn't working as justification: "The bass is smooth, seductive even, but there's not enough . . . aesthetics, distance, or devotion in the world to sever the drum from the brutal lyrics."

But countermeasures came nonetheless. Earlier that spring, one man out of New York tried to pull N.W.A's punk card: "Dre, beating on Dee from *Pump it Up!?* / Step to the Dog and get fucked up!" When the Ultramagnetic MCs affiliate Tim Dog dropped his single "Fuck Compton" in March of 1991, it was another in a long line of Ced Gee–produced assaults on outsiders attempting to eclipse hip-hop tradition, BDP's "South Bronx" on a five-year steroid regimen aiming its target roughly 2,800 miles west. The motive was simple enough: like the Ultramagnetics, Tim held a grudge over record companies bypassing his music and that of his underground New York peers in favor of the more headline-grabbing new movement coming out of California.

And the lyrics did as much as possible to emphasize not only the characteristics of the N.W.A members he had beef with, but the West Coast's entire fashion sense ("Take your Jheri curls, take your black hats / Take your wack lyrics and your bullshit tracks") and history of gang warfare ("Fighting over colors? / All that gang shit is for dumb muthafuckas"). All that was left to deconstruct was the West Coast style of production, and the beat spoke for itself: a revamp of the Ultramagnetics' 1989 single "A Chorus Line," it rallied around a litany of familiar, well-established *Ultimate Breaks and Beats* selections and let Tim's two-ton voice hit hard like a secondary bassline. No smooth, repurposed funk or Minimoog synths—just a murky bassline and a sharp busted-siren refrain sampled from ESG's '81 garage-funk classic "UFO."

More explicit jabs at Dre's production style would follow on Tim's November '91 full-length *Penicillin on Wax:* the intro was a direct lift of the beat from *Niggaz4Life* opener "Prelude," albeit with subtly heavier kicks and snares in the Rufus Thomas–sourced drums. Tim loudly proclaimed to N.W.A that he "stole'd your motherfuckin' beat and made it better to show the whole world that y'all ain't nothin' but a bunch of *pussies!*" N.W.A soon sued Tim Dog over the track, marking the first time one hip-hop act threatened another hip-hop act with legal action over a sample dispute. It was settled out of court, but Tim continued to shit-talk N.W.A to an almost hilarious extent. "If [N.W.A] were offended, they coulda stepped to me," Tim remarked in a statement to the press covered by *The Source.* "I even did a song called 'Step to Me' and they didn't."

But even Tim might not have anticipated the impact that this dividing line of a statement would make. Pride and defensiveness over ownership of hip-hop had long been a steady presence alongside the genre's growth—first between crews, then neighborhoods, then boroughs. But something about the brewing war between the coasts gave "Fuck Compton" and the follow-ups that appeared on *Penicillin on Wax* all a retroactive effect of someone putting a bullet in Archduke Ferdinand. All the moral and artistic battles played out in hip-hop's history to that point—creative freedom and crass commercialism, adventurous collaborations and resentful entrenchments, regional expansion and cold-blooded turf battles, good fortune and squandered potential—would be drastically amplified throughout the ensuing East Coast–West Coast wars. Fires would be stoked by businessmen who acted like gangstas and gangstas who acted like businessmen, all of whom played up hip-hop's increasing emphasis on a street cred increasingly indistinguishable from big-money criminal enterprise. It was a game of one-upsmanship that let record sales take precedent over everything, including the artists' actual lives. And before it all fell in on itself, it sounded spectacular.

• • •

By the dawn of the '90s, Dre had become just one member of a growing movement of West Coast hip-hop producers—maybe the most famous, but by no means the sole engineer of the region's whole sound. He wasn't even the only producer/MC to rep Compton at the time. If Dre had an artistic rival, it was David Blake, who took the name DJ Quik thanks to his rapid turnaround time when it came to making tracks. There was a craft in Quik's efficiency that came from a childhood immersed in music; he'd learned to play multiple instruments by middle school and began to make homemade mixtapes after being given a turntable as an eighth-grade graduation present. Profile, the label on which Run-D.M.C. became megastars, won a bidding war for Quik when his 1987 demo *The Red Tape* became an underground sensation and signed him to the label's first six-figure contract. Quik shared the same affinity for classic funk artists like Zapp and Parliament-Funkadelic that Dre did, but boasted even more of a preternatural ability to pick the most space-age-sounding elements of '70s and '80s R&B to turn into beats that personified Cali-flavored hip-hop.

The big payoff came with *Quik Is the Name,* which dropped in January '91—just about equidistant between the releases of *100 Miles and Runnin'* and *Niggaz4Life.* Quik's debut album connected the sonic vocabulary of LA hip-hop production even more explicitly to a smooth-rolling, synthesizer-driven, heavy-bouncing funk lineage in keeping with the early years of Uncle Jamm's Army. "Tonight," the 1984 single by New York boogie-funk group Kleeer, became "Tonite," a tribute to downing forties with his friends that ended with a third verse lamenting a pray-to-God hangover. (The album dropped three days before Quik, a self-admitted lightweight at the time, turned twenty-one—old enough to legally drink.) The title cut's up-tempo bass groove came from Cameo's pungently dank '79 jam "I Just Want to Be," pushing the pace of gangsta rap back up to BPMs that demanded dancefloor motion instead of just head nods. And "Loked Out Hood" was a masterful blend of two different 1974 cuts by Brooklyn proto-disco group B.T. Express and a swath of the P-Funk All Stars' 1983 single "Pumpin' It Up"—different strains of funk separated by a decade, but streamlined into something so redolent of 1991 Los Angeles that it should've come with a pair of James Worthy goggles.

Just as impressive was the fact that nearly everything Quik touched that year turned to funk—close-harmony R&B by the Emotions ("I Got That Feelin'"), the frictionless, satiny soul-jazz of Patti Austin ("Skanless"), the Stax-band blues of Albert King (2nd II None's Quik-produced "Just Ain't Me"). He'd run the gamut of the genre from its late '60s ori-

gins to its popular peak in the '70s and early '80s, simultaneously cod-
ifying funk as an integral element of his sound and expanding the very
idea of what that category could encompass. '69 James Brown or '82 Gap
Band, it all had its place, it all fit right in, just so long as it could bump. In
a way, Quik was building from and continuing a family lineage—"Born &
Raised in Compton" rode off a sample of "Hyperbolicsyllabicsesqueda-
lymistic," an Isaac Hayes song Quik remembered hearing his mother
play—but he was also going by the old standby of just sampling whatever
he and his friends thought sounded cool, regardless of where or when
it was from and whether it had any shot of commercial success. It all
just came together, fell into place, all thanks to Quik's eclectic attention
to musical detail.

On another point in a continuum between smooth and grimy—
decidedly closer to the latter—stood DJ Muggs. And if there was one
producer who embodied the qualities of both coasts in his work, it
was the Queens-born Lawrence Muggerud, who moved to Los Angeles at age sixteen in 1984. He'd grown up in New York infatuated with
the music his family played—his uncle in particular, who was maybe
nine years older than Muggs and shared a room with him, thus expos-
ing the youngster to a world of head-shop chic and vintage heavy metal
like Black Sabbath and Led Zeppelin that proved endlessly fascinating.
That world intersected with his late '70s discovery of and dedication to
hip-hop, and by the time he headed out west that particular mixture of
interests—a reflection of the big-family upbringing and cross-cultural
sprawl of his old Queens neighborhood—inspired lots of weed-fueled
music-listening hangout sessions with his friends that eventually led
him to try his hand at DJing.

His first major gig was spent manning the turntables as part of a
group called the 7A3, whose MCs—brothers Brett and Sean Bouldin—
were also NYC transplants, albeit from Brooklyn. Despite their sole
album being titled *Coolin' in Cali,* the 1988 release exclusively featured
beats by producers from back east—including the Bomb Squad on
the title cut (which drew heavily from Sly and the Family Stone's cir-
ca-'69 catalog) and a couple of beats by Stetsasonic's Daddy-O. The rest
were put together by Joe "the Butcher" Nicolo, a Philadelphia-based
producer—though Muggs has implied that Nicolo got sole credit for
beat ideas that Muggs came up with himself. Nicolo's big impact came
elsewhere, though; he'd go on to cofound Ruffhouse Records with part-

ner Chris Schwartz in '89. The same year Ruffhouse was founded, Muggs joined up with a couple other MCs from South Gate, a city in Los Angeles County that bordered Watts and had shifted over the course of a generation from a segregated white stronghold in the '50s to majority-Latinx in the '70s. Senen "Sen Dog" Reyes and Louis "B-Real" Freese had originally teamed up with Senen's brother Ulpiano in a group called DVX (Devastating Vocal Excellence), but when Ulpiano left for a solo career as Mellow Man Ace, DVX renamed themselves after a street in their part of town: Cypress Avenue led to Cypress Hill.

A 1989 demo got the group a deal with Ruffhouse, and their self-titled debut album turned out to be a slow-burning fuse. Their first single, 1991's "The Phuncky Feel One," was a decent-enough distillation of old funk standbys—the Meters, James Brown, Kool & the Gang, Rufus Thomas—with B-Real's piercing nasal whir of a voice and Sen Dog's smooth but latently powerful flow leading the way. But it didn't garner much notice until DJs in New York flipped the 12-inch over and caught on to what lurked on the B-side. "How I Could Just Kill a Man" was harder from the title on down, with both MCs channeling their brief experiences gangbanging with the Neighborhood Family Bloods into a pulpy, dark-humored look at the life they'd left in the abstract. The lyrics were slippery and held together with a stoned stream of consciousness, the hook was a monster dunk—B-Real the alley ("Here is something you can't under-staaaand"), Sen Dog the oop ("How I could just *killaman*")—and Muggs's beat was a thoroughly bizarre fusion of the recognizable and the exotic.

The familiar proto-funk lope of Lowell Fulson's 1966 soul-blues hit "Tramp" was run through on the chorus with a pitched-up squeal of Jimi Hendrix's backwards guitar from "Are You Experienced?" with the organ from the Music Machine's '66 garage rocker "Come on In" dropping in for the first few lines of the third verse. One last flourish—a borderline non-sequitur clip at the end of Suicidal Tendencies frontman Mike Muir scowling "All I wanted was a Pepsi!" from their iconic '83 punk/metal crossover thrash single "Institutionalized"—completed the picture. From Fulson's LA to Jimi's Seattle, and the early dawn of Cali punk to one of its most memorable statements, Muggs's beat pulled in a whole galaxy of West Coast music history into a collage of his adopted city's sonic heritage. The track first blew up in New York, and thanks to the timing of Cypress Hill's touring and shooting schedule, that's where the video was filmed—on the subway, in Times Square, outside the Apollo, with cameos by Ice Cube and Q-Tip emphasizing the bicoastal summit vibe of the whole thing.

*Cypress Hill* was one of the first albums to ride a West Coast buzz and a press fascination with Cali hip-hop culture to a platinum plaque despite its supposedly unbankable underground sound; the group admitted themselves they expected to do the kinds of not-quite-gold numbers that their hardcore East Coast hip-hop favorites like BDP and Ultramagnetic MCs did. And now those favorites were into their shit: Muggs emerged from a club in New York one night, overheard "How I Could Just Kill a Man" bumping from a car, and noticed that it was EPMD's funk-doctor producer/MC Erick Sermon behind the wheel. He must have been studying hard; the following year New Jersey rapper Redman's Sermon-produced "Time 4 Sum Askhon" sampled its titular hook from B-Real's voice on Cypress Hill's first hit. (It also swiped the "Tramp" break back and made it wilder; EPMD's 1990 track "Rampage" was the Fulson song's most familiar and successful sample usage until Muggs put his beat out.) As bicoastally appealing as *Cypress Hill* was, though, it was the group's sense of place and self—from the prominent nods to their Latinx heritage to the then-unprecedented amount of references to Cali-style weed culture—that let them extend a wider notion of what West Coast hip-hop actually was. And the contact high was potent.

·  ·  ·

If Quik's vision of funk was smooth eclecticism and Muggs's was psychedelic mutation, the version that Dre spent his 1992 concocting and refining was based in something a bit more conflicted. Conflict was the mode he'd been operating in since at least 1988, when N.W.A's regional-minded street music caught on in enough majority-white suburbs to get moral arbiters to lose their shit. He'd been operating from a defensive position ever since, if more as an MC than a producer. And with life-or-death struggles in Los Angeles taking a national spotlight at its brightest since Watts burned in '67, Dre's world was extending far beyond his own circle. A city that provoked its most famous hip-hop group to write "Fuck tha Police" was in search of a way to rebuild its identity after the conflagration that tore it apart when four of its police officers were acquitted for the brutal, caught-on-video beating of motorist Rodney

King. N.W.A had already written the warnings. Dre needed to create a coda.

Once again, Dre found his inspiration in a retrofitted vision of funk's past. That went as deep as his new label: to plan his escape from Ruthless, Dre had been working with a record producer named Dick Griffey, a major figure in the '70s and '80s as a music promoter, booker, and talent coordinator for syndicated R&B dance show *Soul Train*. In the record biz itself, Griffey's biggest success to that point had been a label that literally called itself the Sound of Los Angeles Records—or SOLAR. SOLAR emerged in the late '70s and became synonymous with the kind of funk that Dre and his LA peers had grown up under the spell of, boogie and R&B groups like Dynasty, Lakeside, Klymaxx, Midnight Star, and Shalamar. The label had hit a decline in the late '80s when the latter group, SOLAR's marquee act, began to lose star members. But Griffey had some connections.

Marion "Suge" Knight's omnipresence in the Los Angeles music world meant that the bodyguard-turned-mogul made himself a fixture around N.W.A when mutual friend and Ruthless session keyboardist Andre "LA Dre" Bolton introduced him to the D.O.C. in the late '80s. The two raised hell out on the town together, with D.O.C. as the hard-drinking fight instigator and Suge as the man who'd step in and clean house when D.O.C. got boxed into a corner. And after D.O.C.'s car wreck, Suge stayed by his bedside almost constantly, acting as both a friend and manager who made a point of giving him detailed info on just how much his Ruthless contract was screwing him. When Chocolate called on Suge to get him his "Ice Ice Baby" money in '91, it was Griffey that gave Suge the contact info for a New York attorney who could help settle the matter. When all was said and done—no balcony-dangling necessary—Suge pocketed $4 million in royalties, and his reputation as a hard-nosed businessman with intimidating presence was sealed.

Dre soon figured that if D.O.C.'s Ruthless contract was fucked up, so was his. And after Suge somehow got his hands on it—he reportedly visited the offices of Ruthless' lawyer, though the details on how he actually got the well-protected documentation are fuzzy—Suge proved his suspicions right. As Griffey later put it, "They had the worst contracts I had ever seen in the history of the record business . . . if I said draconian, that would be a kind word." The man who Dre had called "Benedict Arnold" turned out to be justified in leaving; between all the cold-blooded insults on "No Vaseline," the reason Ice Cube ditched N.W.A. would be the same catalyst for the crew's dissolution.

Eazy objected to Suge's efforts to get Dre paid—Eazy saw it as a betrayal of Jerry Heller—but when Dre refused to deal with Heller's bullshit and got the gears moving to jump ship, his Ruthless contract still held him back. Dre and Eazy wound up scheduling a meeting at SOLAR's headquarters in April 1991 to negotiate their terms, but Dre never showed. In his place, Suge and a couple of weapon-toting cohorts—accounts differ as to whether they had guns or just stuck to baseball bats—were there to give Eazy the Vanilla Ice treatment. Threats involving grievous bodily harm first to Heller and then Eazy's mother were thrown around. Eazy saw no choice but to sign the paperwork that released Dre, D.O.C., and Michel'le from their contracts at Ruthless. After *Niggaz4Life,* N.W.A was done.

What happened next in the formation of Dre's new label could hardly be heavier with metaphor if you fictionalized it. At first, the label was called Future Shock, a '70s-vintage appellation lifted from Curtis Mayfield's discography. But a more gangsta-leaning name soon emerged—Death Row Records. The initial game plan was artist-friendly: while Griffey maneuvered through major label distro and Suge handled paperwork and business operations, they'd each get a 15 percent cut, while A&R/songwriter D.O.C. and producer/MC/creative catalyst Dre would get 35 percent apiece. At the time, almost all the artists involved were scraping for money, and this made for both an all-out creative hunger and a hope that it would all pay off handsomely. Dre's solo debut *The Chronic* should've been a big payday for everyone.

But Death Row needed distribution, and labels like Sony were reluctant to provide for such an unknown quantity, especially considering the fallout of Dre's contract dispute with Ruthless. When Death Row finally inked a $10 million deal with veteran record producer Jimmy Iovine's up-and-coming label Interscope, Griffey and D.O.C. weren't a part of it: they were both frozen out of their collective 50 percent share, even as the former housed the Death Row studios and the latter was a major contributor to Dre's creative process. D.O.C. was hit especially hard by his old friend's betrayal, later stating that "the words don't exist to explain how demoralizing it felt"—but he still stuck to his job of finding words that existed to explain how Dre felt. "I still took my ass to work every day to make that record as good as I could because it represented me just as much as anybody else," D.O.C. explained. Yet even though it was an open secret that D.O.C. was one of Dre's main ghostwriters, he never got his financial due.

But Eazy did. Ruthless still had Dre on the contractual hook for four more albums, and in order to get *The Chronic* released, Iovine had to offer Ruthless a percentage of royalties from everything Dre produced. Eazy earned somewhere between 25 to 50 cents from each copy *The Chronic* sold, and was known to brag about making more money from the album than Dre did.

The air around Death Row was different, too. Initial recording sessions for *The Chronic* felt like parties, cutting sessions where wave after wave of young borderline-unknowns would find themselves in the recording booth scrapping for a choice position on the record. The biggest breakthrough star was Snoop Doggy Dogg, a Long Beach native whose frictionless, next-gen Slick Rick sing-song flow on Dre's first solo joint "Deep Cover" made him a phenom almost overnight. Meanwhile, the MCs and singers who shared his promise—Nate Dogg, Warren G, the Lady of Rage, Kurupt, Daz Dillinger, and RBX—formed a foundation for the label's future almost immediately.

But Suge was always there, and with him came a sense of tension that constantly felt on the verge of boiling over into violence. One infamous instance came in July 1992 during the *Chronic* recording sessions when two aspiring rappers, George and Lynwood Stanley, were visiting the studio on Dre's invitation. When Suge found out Dre had let them make a phone call from the studio, Suge lost his shit: he beat both brothers up, fired a shot through an office wall to intimidate them, made them strip to their underwear, stole Lynwood's wallet, and threatened their families. Dre had brushes with violence all throughout 1992: he'd been accused of breaking producer Damon Thomas's jaw that May, was involved in a New Orleans hotel lobby melee that same month, would be shot four times in the leg at a South Central party in July ("shot *at*," Dre maintained), and, upon returning to New Orleans in October, assaulted a police officer. But having violence intrude on the studio, the one place where Dre could work in a context that could at least feel peaceful, was a new kind of pressure.

Now imagine the kind of music to come out of all this turmoil. It was that legacy of the fight-defusing house party funk jam, the vintage synthesizers and the deeper-than-deep low end, that sustained Dre's sound: low and lean and mean, defiant and prepared to throw down even in celebration. This was the sound of g-funk—a genre descriptor coined by Ruthless alumni group Above the Law, whose 1990 single "Murder Rap" used booming bass and the panic-attack siren synths from Quincy Jones' *Ironside* TV theme to intimidating effect. Dre is credited as a coproducer on that track, but ATL's in-house producer/MC Cold 187um maintains otherwise. A second-generation funk scholar whose father (Richard Hutch) and uncle (Willie Hutch) both left memorable imprints on '70s Motown, Cold 187um had to concede coproducer credits to Dre on "Murder Rap" thanks to a clause in Sony's contract as Ruthless's parent company.

Dre did actually coproduce three other songs on Above the Law's debut *Livin' Like Hustlers,* including the N.W.A/ATL free-for-all "The Last Song," and the two producers got along well, with Cold187um applying his already extant familiarity with traditional songwriting and composition to the knowledge of hip-hop production he learned from Dre. As a DJ, Dre was fluent in the idea of synthesizing and consolidating portions of other people's music into his own performance, and the style that Cold 187um was laying down was a regularly acknowledged parallel to Dre's. Both beatmakers transitioned from late '60s/early '70s soul breaks on their groups' debuts to slicker, more synthesized late '70s/early '80s funk within a couple releases. They should've been able to share the wealth, both critically and commercially.

The catch was that Above the Law's *Black Mafia Life,* a formidable g-funk achievement in itself, never got a chance to beat *The Chronic* to store shelves despite being completed far earlier. *Black Mafia Life* was in development concurrently at Ruthless with *Niggaz4Life,* and was actually finished before the end of 1991, at which point Cold187um recollects playing portions of ATL's new album to Dre on the set of N.W.A's "Appetite for Destruction" video shoot. By that point, Dre had started to see Cold 187um as a mentee turned emerging success, but what happened next got the narrative twisted: when Dre left Ruthless and Sony realized *Black Mafia Life* was actually being produced by Cold187um, the label considered it a breach of contract and the album was tangled up in legal red tape until finally being released in February 1993.

So here was an album in *Black Mafia Life* featuring some new ideas from a largely under-the-radar producer—a usage of late '70s funk, especially Parliament-Funkadelic, that relied just as heavily on the music's

melodies and harmonies as it did the rhythm—getting beat to stores by
*The Chronic,* an album it directly inspired. "I was a young producer who
was trying to find his rhythm, trying to get his face in the game," Cold
187um told *Complex.* "But because I'm so young, I don't take it as being,
oh, I influenced him to do something great, he was highly influenced by
what I done. When you're young, you're not thinking . . . that you influenced one of the greatest producers in the modern era, so what does
that make *me?*"

Eventually Cold 187um got his frustration on record when he
addressed the situation in a guest verse on Kokane's 1994 track "Don't
Bite the Phunk." But whatever bad blood there might have been left
between Dre and Cold 187um was eventually mitigated by the latter's
lingering appreciation for the former's guidance in the first place, and
once the whole "who did it first" question is shelved, it's easier to appreciate both albums for what they represented. *Black Mafia Life* is dense
to the point of almost being claustrophobic, sharing a minor-key tension
and intensity with side one of *Niggaz4Life* and pushing melodies to the
point of vertigo. *The Chronic* is smoother, has more spacious-sounding
production, and balances out its tense moments with more triumphant-
sounding melodies.

But they both live through an odd paradox of g-funk: this is a style
of hip-hop that takes classic synthesized, melodic funk—music that's
celebratory, almost utopian in its optimism, and overall good-natured—
and brings it forward into a world that's significantly less joyful. *The
Chronic* is a triumph, earned arrogance and untethered creativity pushed
through a state-of-the-art SSL mixing console until the music itself
sounded chrome-plated. It's consistently deep, a master class in engineering and mixing velvety bass frequencies with nuanced treble, and
the ultimate culmination of the house party DJ tradition of throwing
on a classic synth-funk jam to diffuse gang-fight tensions. But the mood
feels tense from just the right angle, and it doesn't take a lot of straining
to hear the optimism of one generation's past run up against the tension
of their children's violent present.

"Fuck wit Dre Day (and Everybody's Celebratin')," the first track
after the intro, rides on a megamix of no less than five P-Funk and
George Clinton songs recorded between 1977 and 1982, a stretch of time
in which South Central's flourishing civil rights and black arts movements began to run up against the harsh realities of a postindustrial

economy and the eventual rise of Reaganomics. The music is deeply funky, but run through with a synthesizer melody that's flattened into something more sinister and taunting than anything Bernie Worrell or Junie Morrison put out on any P-Funk album.

Dre and Snoop's idea of a celebration is to call out all their enemies: Dre states that Eazy "used to be my homie, used to be my ace / Now I wanna slap the taste out ya mouth," Snoop finds a few different ways to demand that Tim Dog suck his dick, and they both team up to target 2 Live Crew's Luke Campbell—who earned their animosity with his 1992 track "Fakin Like Gangstas"—threatening to "rob you in Compton and blast you in Miami." P-Funk liked to goof on their musical rivals, too— Funkadelic's 1975 track "Let's Take It to the Stage" comedically called out Rufus ("Hey Sloofus! Tell us something good!"), Sly Stone ("Slick Brick! How's your loose booty?"), and James Brown ("The Godfather . . . Godmother . . . Grandfather!")—but it was never this personal.

In building a sonic world where the euphoria of funk was fused to gangsta lyricism, Dre brought out another side to hip-hop that rang heavy with a compelling paradox—smooth, slow-riding, blunt-smoking soundtracks that had all the upbeat components of boogie funk but still put on an air of defiant, finger-on-the-trigger tension. Lead single and #2 pop hit "Nuthin' but a 'G' Thang" reflected Leon Haywood's "Batterram"-producing role in early gangsta rap back at him with a rede-finitive loop of his 1975 satin-sheets slow jam "I Wanna Do Something Freaky to You." The Minimoog melody in the track is the logical con-clusion to the keening synthesizer he dropped from the Ohio Players' "Funky Worm" into N.W.A.'s "Dope Man" five years earlier, and its chart position and pop-culture omnipresence enshrined it as g-funk's most notable sonic flourish. But even the breezy contentment inher-ent in the original sample was undercut by dissatisfaction always lurking around the corner—getting burned by VD, having to stay strapped with a 9-millimeter, threatening smackdowns for shit-talk.

"Let Me Ride," another hit that built off P-Funk's catalog, is an even more telling juxtaposition. "Mothership Connection (Star Child)" was the '75 hit that kicked off Parliament's sci-fi ambitions, riffing off the era's *Chariots of the Gods*-spurred theory that the Egyptians were vis-ited by ancient astronauts ("We have returned to claim the pyramids / Partying on the mothership"). The song slyly incorporated Sun Ra–style Afrofuturism in a parallel with both abolitionist and civil rights–era calls for freedom, recasting the Underground Railroad spiritual "Swing Low Sweet Chariot" as the chorus of a spaceway trip to escape the pressure of a recession-damaged inner-city America. Dre's ride is more earthbound (the requisite '64 Impala), he's more concerned with causing strife than escaping it, and he wants nothing to do with activism: "No medallions, dreadlocks, or black fists / It's just that gangsta glare / With gangsta raps / That gangsta shit / Makes a gangs of snaps." In other words, why bother to preach Afrocentrism when being a g makes all the money?

Yet there are still some flashes of deeper insight between all the defiantly glowering hits. "The Day the Niggaz Took Over" is the unavoidable reckoning with the riots and rebellion that ensued in April 1992 after the Rodney King verdict. Some of it's based on the MCs' direct experience in the fracas—when Dre raps about scoring "A VCR in the back of my car / That I ganked from the Slauson Swap Meet," it's a nod to Snoop actually ducking out during the recording sessions and coming back with merch he looted during the chaos—but it also had its roots in a more focused protest.

The lyrics were a slight rewrite of an anti–police brutality track, "Mr. Officer," that finished its titular hook with the line "I wanna see you layin' in a coffin, sir" and included insults to LAPD chief Daryl Gates. It was kyboshed by Interscope in the wake of parent company Time Warner's blowback against Ice-T's "Cop Killer," a protest song the rapper recorded with his band Body Count. ("Cop Killer" and the Body Count album were Ice-T's foray into crossover thrash metal, but the media controversy lumped it all in with gangsta rap anyways.) But the real sentiment beneath "The Day the Niggaz Took Over" is still there when you account for the instances of nebulous lyrical threats against "motherfuckers" previously being aimed at the police.

All that was left was to swap out a Keith David cop-threatening monologue from the 1990 film *Dirty Work* for the frustrated tirade of a subject in Matthew McDaniel's documentary *Birth of a Nation 4\*29\*1992*: "If you ain't down for the Africans here in the United States—period point-blank, if you ain't down for the ones that suffered in South Africa from apartheid and shit, dammit, you need to step your punk ass to the side and let us brothers, and us Africans, step in and start puttin' some foot in that ass!"

That same documentary gives a voice to the most deliberately activist-leaning track on *The Chronic,* where a clip of a man demanding black financial autonomy ("Save your money, start your own business, and you true Africans will have put hundreds to work") segues into lyrics that lay out the dead-end side of gangsta life: Snoop witnessing the brutality of prison life as a teenager, Dre getting shot trying to rob a younger man he underestimated, and another Snoop verse witnessing the life and death of a young crew whose youthful complacency got them killed. The beat, a masterful revamp of Donny Hathaway's 1972 yearning, mournful namesake "Little Ghetto Boy," had all the thumping weight of Dre's bassline finesse, but it was where the floodgates broke and the album's overarching sense of cocky toughness receded into a vulnerability and anxiety over the future of the next generation of young black men.

The political angle wasn't a significant portion of *The Chronic,* but gangsta rap was never incompatible with examinations of its root causes and personal tragedies. The strength of street knowledge was built on those foundations, of that outward expression of invincibility in an inhumane world and the undercurrents of a longing for the world that should've been. South Central wasn't a paradise when Donny Hathaway and Parliament were crafting their first masterworks in the '70s, but there's a youthful nostalgia in those beats somewhere, an effort to carry some innocence or optimism forward even as it's shaped into a thematic maturity somewhere between cynical and fatalist.

The composition and creation of the music on *The Chronic* is generally regarded today as an auteurist work, with Dre as the mastermind controlling every single sound on the record. (One scene in the 2015 biopic *Straight Outta Compton* even depicts Dre spontaneously composing the Minimoog melody for "'G' Thang," even though it's a straight interpolation of the strings from "Something Freaky.") But Dre was something of a bandleader even as he excelled in more hip-hop-rooted technological methods of recording. As sampling became more cost-prohibitive and interpolation provided a less-expensive loophole, the presence of studio musicians like sax player/flutist Katisse Buckingham, guitarists Chris Clairmont and Eric "the Drunk" Borders, and keyboardists Justin Reinhardt and Colin Wolfe became central to the creation of *The Chronic.*

Wolfe in particular went back with Dre to the *100 Miles and Runnin'* EP—he composed a new melody for "Just Don't Bite It" when Herbie Hancock decided he didn't want "Watermelon Man" sampled for a song about fellatio—and they collaborated on some off-kilter musical ideas for *Muzical Madness,* a 1991 album by multi-instrumentalist Jimmy Z.

that let Dre expand his production ideas further than just pure hip-hop into acid jazz and fusion. And it was Wolfe who came up with the diabolical tritone bassline that held down "Deep Cover," inspiration that came from the jazz-tinged beats A Tribe Called Quest were laying down on *The Low End Theory*.

Wolfe remembered the concurrent *Chronic* sessions as similarly composition-heavy in *Wax Poetics:* "With 'Dre Day,' I was again thinking P-Funk when I came up with the bass line. . . . Once that comes in then you can hear the other stuff around it. I think Daz [Dillinger] did something with the melody line. I added the guitar, Rhodes, and the strings to the record." This was the musicality that older artists were concerned sampling was taking away from hip-hop—and in the process, it opened a new route of creation that had all the stylistic reinterpretation used by sampling but with a more original bent, style-homage bolstering or sometimes even replacing direct reference. You could still make beats with samples alone, and plenty of producers still did. But just as the Roots' *Organix* and Guru's *Jazzmatazz* erased the lines between sample-based beats and live-band performance from an East Coast boom-bap stance, Dre's g-funk embodied a form of hip-hop that didn't live on samples alone. And from there came the sense that there was only so far that other people's music could take you.

●   ●   ●

*The Chronic* was a smash, and so was just about everything else Dre put his mark on for the next couple years. Snoop Dogg's solo debut *Doggystyle* sold over eight hundred thousand copies in its first week, making it the fastest-selling hip-hop album ever to that point. Its production was proof that g-funk wasn't a gimmick but a now-characteristic defining sound of West Coast hip-hop, and since Snoop's personality and delivery was famously smooth and laidback he was able to unify Dre's broad palette of g-funk, which ranged from Bernie Worrell–via–Bernard Herrmann suspense ("Serial Killa"; "Pump Pump") to carefree weekend barbecue celebrations ("Gin and Juice"; "Who Am I (What's My Name)?") and all the shades in between ("Tha Shiznit"; "For All My Niggaz & Bitches"). Snoop even sounded suave rapping about his own death on the *Twilight Zone*–esque "Murder Was the Case," the remix of which was the peak of Dre's aspirations to make music sound even more cinematic than the movies.

But one of Dre's most notable brushes with influence didn't come as a producer. In 1993, George Clinton released a song titled "Paint the White House Black" that featured Chuck D, Flavor Flav, Ice Cube, and a host of other MCs—including Dr. Dre, who made an appearance on both the full-length album version and in the video for the single edit. He didn't so much rap as he riffed off the idea that the wrong Clinton occupied the Oval Office ("He don't inhale? Well I know I got the wrong motherfuckin' house!"), and recognized George as his ideal smoking partner ("I'll be droppin' some straight chronic at his front door").

This wouldn't be the last time Clinton collaborated with Ice Cube: *Lethal Injection*'s "Bop Gun (One Nation)" was an eleven-minute riff on the P-Funk catalog featuring Clinton himself reprising his vocals from Funkadelic's 1978 hit "One Nation under a Groove" interspersed with deeply referential lyrics from Cube, a cover version and a new song all at once. (On another cross-generational note, the song was coproduced by West Coast producer QD III—or, as it says on his birth certificate, Quincy Jones III.) But "Paint the White House Black" was the first time that Dr. Dre and Ice Cube had appeared on the same track since *Straight Outta Compton,* and even if it wasn't an official reunion, it was a clear reminder of what could be.

As Dre built an empire on g-funk, Cube had maintained his own popularity, peaking with 1992's best-selling *The Predator*—an album that featured eclectic but decidedly Cali-bound production from Sir Jinx, DJ Muggs, and a producer named DJ Pooh who'd previously made beats for LL Cool J and Ultramagnetic MCs. Along with his work on *I Wish My Brother George Was Here,* the eccentric but funky 1991 debut from Ice Cube's decidedly more abstract cousin Del tha Funkee Homosapien, Pooh's biggest contribution to West Coast hip-hop production was his beat for Cube's hit "It Was a Good Day."

A laidback, almost bucolic down-tempo cut chronicling an ideal day where everything goes Ice Cube's way, it's one of the slyest examples of a sample surreptitiously highlighting the underlying messages of a hip-hop song's lyrics: just as the good day in question seems like an unattainable dream, the beat is sourced from the Isley Brothers' 1977 single "Footsteps in the Dark," a slow jam about anxiety bordering on paranoia threatening to intrude on an otherwise loving relationship. The same groove where Ron Isley sang "Who feels really sure? / Can that feelin' guarantee your happiness shall endure?" is one where Cube keeps waiting for the other shoe to drop: "Hooked it up for later as I hit the door / Thinking will I live another twenty-four?" In the context of *The Predator,* an album otherwise bristling with the post-traumatic disillusionment of the LA riots, it's almost a moment of delusion, one cut off on the album by Cube scowling "Wait a minute, Pooh, stop this shit, what the fuck I'm thinkin' about?"

The record doesn't show whether Cube had a similar snap realization when it came to his feud with Dre, but by 1994 it was becoming apparent that the Ruthless rift that split them in 1990 was no longer the point of contention it previously was. Cube had went so far as to cameo in the "Let Me Ride" video in late '93, shortly before the two former N.W.A bandmates shared time on Clinton's track. So when it came time to turn Snoop's "Murder Was the Case" remix into the hook for a new Death Row compilation, Dre and coproducer Sam Sneed came up with a track to put on the record that Dre felt would benefit from an Ice Cube verse. That eventually led to the reunion track "Natural Born Killaz," an over-the-top Grand Guignol mockery of America's obsession with celebrity death that sounded like a g-funk haunted house. Cube and Dre clicked just as easily out of the booth as they did on the record, a beef squashed when their musical commonalities eclipsed their financial differences.

But as the two planned the possibility of a team-up album, initially to be given the Charles Manson nod title *Helter Skelter,* the complications of their legacy began to catch up with them. Ruthless and Eazy-E had made the borderline-spiteful decision to release the *5150: Home 4 tha Sick* EP, Eazy's first solo album since 1988's *Eazy-Duz-It,* the exact same week as *The Chronic.* (Despite beats contributed by Cold 187um and *Death Certificate* coproducer Bobcat, the EP was critically and commercially shrugged at, going gold but not much further than that.) If that release-date clash wasn't enough, Eazy's direct answer to the disses thrown his way throughout *The Chronic* was to call his next EP *It's on (Dr. Dre) 187um Killa,* the strikethrough in Dre's name denoting, gangtag style, that he was marked for death. Despite being a record dedicated to shitting on Dre at almost every opportunity, the beats to tracks like "Real Muthaphuckkin G's" and "It's On," produced by Rhythm D, traded off the same kind of Moog synth melodies that laced *The Chronic* and *Doggystyle.* Even the tracks dissing him were made in a style that held to Dre's terms.

That kind of hostility seemed like it would preclude any goodwill between Eazy and the other ex-members of N.W.A. Even MC Ren, one of Eazy's most ardent defenders and closest friends, had stated to multiple publications that they'd grown apart: "He went kinda way out and started acting crazy," he told *Rap Pages* in February 1994, "and I don't have time for that man. I don't need to be around anybody who is self-destructing." Yet when Eazy took a trip to New York to promote new Ruthless signees Bone Thugs-N-Harmony and visited the tastemaking hip-hop club the Tunnel with Krayzie Bone in tow, they spotted Cube—and proceeded to have a conversation that Bone characterized as "all smiles and love," as if "No Vaseline" had never happened. The idea of an N.W.A reunion album was brought up, and Cube seemed amenable, though it all hinged on the beef with Dre being settled and Jerry Heller staying hands-off.

Maybe it could've happened. We'll never know, because on March 26, 1995—less than three weeks after Dre released his Top 10 hit "Keep Their Heads Ringin'" for the Ice Cube–starring, DJ Pooh–cowritten comedy film *Friday*—Eric Wright died at age thirty of complications from AIDS. Eazy's passing left hip-hop with a sense of incompleteness, a lack of closure that might have otherwise have given the rap world vital proof that beef was nothing in the bigger picture when there was plenty of money and music to be made together. The rest of the '90s would be spent learning that lesson the tragic way.

# 9 | *Aftermath*
## Auteurism in a Post-Gangsta World

**A war between the coasts leaves two hip-hop legends
dead and one of its biggest producers adrift.**

ERNEST R. DICKERSON's 1992 *JUICE* is a fantastic hip-hop film hiding in a pretty good crime drama. Given its time and its setting—early '90s New York, particularly Harlem, during the full flush of hip-hop's golden age—it's impossible to miss how central the music is to the movie's structure, from Omar Epps's lead role as an aspiring club DJ to the intensely driving Eric B. & Rakim track that serves as the title theme, not to mention the rest of the film's snapshot of a soundtrack. One of those soundtrack selections pops up in a funny sort of reflection of how the film's place in rap history would stand in time, a series of strange accidental metacommentaries unfolding in the film's last five minutes.

As Epps's character Q flees an assailant, he wanders his way into a party and tries to shake his pursuer in the crowd. He's already been shot in the arm, and he weaves through the labyrinth of joint-passing partygoers uneasily, trying to play it off like there isn't a bloody wound staining the sleeve of his jacket. And the music blasting through the speakers isn't Naughty by Nature or Big Daddy Kane or EPMD or any of the other East Coast icons that are sprawled across the movie's running time—it's "How I Could Just Kill A Man," Cypress Hill's LA-made, New York-adored hit.

It's not long before Q spots his assailant: his former friend Bishop, whose eagerness to live the nihilist role of a stick-up kid has led to a handful of avoidable deaths, including one of their closest mutual friends. Bishop flees the party through a window, ascends the fire escape to the roof, and is there to ambush Q when he follows. After some brawling, Bishop's knocked over the ledge of the roof and is left holding on to Q for his life, pleading "Don't let me go" as though he's just realized everything he's jeopardized. But Q's grip fails him, and Bishop falls screaming into the pitch-black void several stories below. We don't see him land— he's just consumed.

The role of Bishop is played, in his first major starring film role, by Tupac Shakur. So after seeing a Harlem party soundtracked by a Los Angeles hip-hop group, for a film directed by Spike Lee's New York–educated cinematographer, shot in NYC and released through Hollywood's own Paramount Pictures, we see the fictionalized death of a man who was born in New York and eventually lost his life for real after antagonizing the city on behalf of his transplanted home of LA. And it's not the original ending, either. In the director's vision, Bishop's still hanging on to Q when he hears police sirens approaching. In a callback to the movie's early establishment of Bishop's father as a catatonic former inmate, Bishop tells Q that he doesn't want to go through the same trauma in prison. So he lets go willingly. His fall is silent.

•   •   •

No West Coast rapper burned as bright as 2Pac. In just over half a decade, he went from a backup member of P-Funk homage-payers Digital Underground to an intensely complex, endlessly charismatic knot of contradictions. Tupac was born the son of two New York–area Black Panthers: his mother, Afeni Shakur, was eight months' pregnant with him when she, her husband, and nineteen others were acquitted of bombing conspiracy charges in 1971's Panther 21 trials. He was raised in an environment of belief in revolution behind the barrel of a gun, as his stepfather Mutulu Shakur took part in an infamous 1981 Brink's truck robbery that left two cops dead. Out of that familial unrest came a cross-country move—first to Baltimore in '86 during Tupac's teen years, where he studied acting, music, and poetry at the Baltimore School of the Arts, and then to the San Francisco Bay Area in '88—that gave his experiences new means of expression.

Outlaw activism would inform 2Pac's career until the end, starting with his 1991 solo debut *2Pacalypse Now,* an album implicated as a motivating influence for the murder of a Texas state trooper in April 1992. At the time he was pulled over by the police officer he would shortly kill, eighteen-year-old Ronald Ray Howard was reportedly listening to "Soulja's Story," a down-tempo cut that relayed the story of a doomed criminal in the first person. There was a deliberately mournful cast to the song—production crew the Underground Railroad built it largely around an interpolation of Bill Withers's sorrowful soul hit "Ain't No Sunshine"—and the lyrical storytelling featured an inevitably grim conclusion of the narrator dying of a bullet to the head during an attempted jailbreak.

But Howard and his defense attorneys claimed that it and other 2Pac tracks like "Crooked Ass Nigga" and "Violent" encouraged and even motivated Howard's murderous tendencies. "The music was up as loud as it could go with gunshots and siren noises on it and my heart was pounding hard," Howard recalled weeks before his July 1993 sentencing gave him the death penalty. "I watched [the trooper] get out of his car in my side view mirror, and I was so hyped up, I just snapped." The trooper's widow, Linda Davidson, subsequently filed a civil suit against Interscope and its parent company, Time Warner. And even though the suit would eventually be dismissed on First Amendment grounds, Time Warner quickly dropped "Cop Killer" performer Ice-T and Oakland-based Black Panther–namedropping rapper Paris, while pressuring 2Pac and Dr. Dre to ease up on any further lyrical content that might be considered anti-police.

Shakur had his reasons to translate his own experiences with the police into outlaw invective—initially political, but quickly personal. In October 1991, a month before the release of *2Pacalypse Now,* he was accosted by police for jaywalking, and an escalation of words led to the cops beating him senseless and putting him in a chokehold. He'd go on to sue the Oakland PD for $10 million, with the intent to use the money to establish a foundation to build a boys' home and an organization to stop police brutality. But by 1993, when Shakur actually wound up exchanging nonlethal gunfire with two off-duty Atlanta cops in October, even the fact that he was released on bail and the charges were dropped couldn't stop the long shadow being cast over hip-hop's reputation.

While this wasn't the end of gangsta rap's political undertones, it was easy to notice that a rap movement as steeped in the ideas of "Fuck tha Police" as it was in "Dopeman" and "Gangsta Gangsta" was starting to lean more explicitly toward the latter. Before the Howard trial had concluded, 2Pac released his second album, *Strictly 4 My N.I.G.G.A.Z.,* in February 1993, and distinguished himself further with lyrics that put him in the revolutionary-gangsta company of Ice Cube and Ice-T ("Last Wordz"), and made a case for himself as more of a true-crime reporting scholar/activist than a criminal-goading punk ("Souljah's Revenge"). He also established genuine pop-hit potential with the Digital Underground reunion party classic "I Get Around" and the anti-misogyny anthem "Keep Ya Head Up." But the next year and a half would rewrite his future into something far bleaker.

Tupac's various scraps, altercations, and legal entanglements over the years were sometimes questionable, but usually just bolstered his rebel image. A rape case was something entirely different. According to his accuser Ayanna Jackson's 2018 account for VladTV, she had a previous consensual encounter with Shakur, but the rape happened when a later hookup with him involved members of Tupac's entourage joining in without her consent. (Tupac's explanation at the time: "These are my boys. I like you so much I decided to share you with them.") Tupac denied the charges to the end; his appearance on the *Arsenio Hall Show* on March 8, 1994, had him protesting that being raised almost entirely by women meant he would never consider "taking something from" one that way. Nevertheless, a jury convicted him of first-degree sexual abuse.

The day before the sentencing that would send him to jail for up to four and a half years, another incident happened that compounded Shakur's sense of self-conscious defensiveness until he was pushed to the point of paranoia. Before November 30, 1994, Tupac never had any particular beef with the East Coast in general or Bad Boy Records in particular. But that was the day he was shot and seriously wounded by three unknown assailants in the lobby of Manhattan's Quad Recording Studios. Though the gunmen were ostensibly there to rob him, Pac would question their motives; in an April 1995 *Vibe* profile recounting the incident, he suspected that "they knew me, or else they would never check for my gun. It was like they were mad at me." The robbers took tens of thousands of dollars' worth of jewelry, but left Pac with his diamond-studded Rolex—either an oversight in the midst of a chaotic stick-up or, as Pac suspected, an intentional message.

Despite gunshot wounds to his leg, his groin, his hand, and a pair that grazed the side of his head—the result of Pac's struggle that may have kept him from being killed—Shakur still opted to get in the studio building's elevator, ostensibly to duck the police that were starting to gather outside. Once he arrived in the studio—he'd gone there to do a $7,000 guest verse for Junior M.A.F.I.A. member and Bad Boy recording artist associate Lil' Cease—he saw dozens of men, around forty by his account, with Sean "Puffy" Combs and the Notorious B.I.G. among them. Pac was running on adrenaline, not having realized he'd been given two head wounds to go with the shots to his lower body, but he distinctly recollected that nobody would look at him.

From the unlikely survival of a barrage of bullets one night to a guilty verdict the next, the timing was enough to put a massive weight on Shakur's mind. He had a long time to ruminate over his circumstances in prison, but it was the material he recorded before his time inside that spoke for him the loudest. *Me against the World* was released in March 1995, a month after he began serving his sentence at Dannemora, New York's Clinton Correctional Facility—the same prison that housed New York State's death row for male inmates. (He was later transferred to Rikers Island.) It hit #1 on the charts—a first for an artist who was incarcerated at the time—and stayed there for a month, hitting double-platinum sales by the end of the year.

In the collection of his writings *Tupac: Resurrection, 1971–1996,* Pac called *Me against the World* a "blues record," driven by "all my fears, all the things I just couldn't sleep about." There are turns toward more gratitude-driven sentiments—to his "poor single mother on welfare, tell me how you did it" on "Dear Mama"; to an unnamed domestic violence victim (speculated to be TLC singer Lisa "Left Eye" Lopes) for whom he acts as a compassionate confidant ("Can U Get Away"); to hip-hop itself on "Old School," where he shouts out all the New York boroughs he would later declare war on. But the vast majority of the album was a reckoning with death, anxiety, mistrust, sorrow, regret, and paranoia that permanently established Tupac as rap's poet laureate of doomed alienation.

And that sense only got its hooks in deeper the longer he spent in prison. After spending eleven months in jail from his trial onward, time spent voraciously reading—he especially gravitated towards Niccolò Machiavelli's works, which famously declared that it was better to be widely feared than greatly loved—the vengeful Tupac took form once again. "I knew I could trust nobody. Trust No-Bo-Dy," he wrote in *Resurrection.* "Straight up, my closest friends did me in . . . my homies, people I would have took care of their whole family . . . [they] turned on me. Fear is stronger than love. Remember that. . . . All the love I gave did me nothing when it came to fear."

• • •

Pac's stardom and status as one of the world's biggest gangsta-rap icons meant he'd have to cross paths with the primary architects of the g-funk era somehow. Pac's actually credited with debuting the phrase itself ("I'm bumpin' g-funk, but you can call it what you want") on Above the Law's *Black Mafia Life* track "Call It What U Want" after Cold 187um used it to describe the group's style to him. But it was never a dominant strain of his sound. And no other rapper did so much to center hip-hop around the MC at the expense of a trademark production style. The kind of beats 2Pac rapped over were memorable, but rarely felt like the main reason the tracks hit so hard; it was up to Pac to hold each track's character in his hands, and he did it with a dramatically intense, technically agile yet emotionally stark flow that eclipsed everything else.

The production on *Me Against the World* took a major step toward changing that: it was a both-coast committee effort that ranged from down-tempo boom-bap moodiness to carefree lowrider glides. And it leaned toward Cali-friendly sensibilities with its well-deployed nods to classic funk and R&B jams by Cameo ("She's Strange" on "Young Niggaz," coproduced by Moe Z.M.D.), Zapp ("Computer Love" in Easy Mo Bee's "Temptations"), Quincy Jones and Stevie Wonder ("The Dude" and "That Girl," respectively, on Shock G's "So Many Tears"), and Maze featuring Frankie Beverly ("Happy Feelin's" on Mike Mosley's "Can U Get Away"). But Pac's voice was still front and center. With his charisma, it didn't even bear inspection that the Isaac Hayes–sampling, Moog-melody Dre-alike g-funk of the title track came from Soulshock & Karlin, two R&B producers from Denmark.

Few of the producers he used were household names on the level of Dre, or even hardcore hip-hop listeners' favorites like the Diggin' in the Crates crew. With a notable exception in Easy Mo Bee—who would also produce some of Notorious B.I.G.'s hottest tracks—Pac tended to stick with friends from way back in his Digital Underground days, producers like Shock G and Stretch of the group Live Squad. But his affiliation with the latter crew had changed by the recording of *Me against the World,* as there was a falling out between Tupac and Live Squad after Pac started to blame Stretch, who was present at the Quad Studios shooting, for not doing enough to protect him, and later collaborating with people Pac considered his enemies.

Pac loved that word "enemies." Notorious B.I.G. and Puffy became two of them when they put out the single "Who Shot Ya?" as the B-side

to Biggie's '95 single "Big Poppa" in February 1995. It didn't matter that
the track was recorded three months before the shooting, that it didn't
mention anybody by name, that the borough mentioned as the theoretical setting for Biggie's murderous exploits was Brooklyn, not Quad Studios' Manhattan. It didn't matter that every eyewitness in Quad Studios
from B.I.G. to Puffy to Uptown Records founder Andre Harrell remembers the group in the studio as more concerned and sympathetic than
the guilty-faced conspirators Pac depicted them as. And it really didn't
matter that Tupac and Biggie had gotten along remarkably well after
meeting on the set of John Singleton's Tupac-featuring film *Poetic Justice*
in 1993. After the release of "Who Shot Ya?" all bets were off: somehow,
nonspecific lyrics about gunplay became admissions of evidence that
Biggie and Puffy knew Pac would be set up.

During the interview he gave to *Vibe*'s Kevin Powell for that April
'95 cover story, Tupac claimed that "the vengeful Tupac is dead," and any
implications that Bad Boy knew about the shooting beforehand were
barely inferred, as though he was still trying to piece things together
without coming right out to point fingers. But that interview was conducted in January, a month before "Who Shot Ya?" dropped and sent
Tupac into a rage. And after spending so many months in prison rumi-
nating over it, he knew that the moment he was sprung from jail, he'd
have to address it. It was *who* sprung him from jail that sealed his fate.

• • •

The 1995 Source Awards were held on August 3 in the Paramount Theater at New York's Madison Square Garden, the second edition of the
hip-hop magazine's award ceremony dedicated to celebrating and showcasing the best hip-hop had to offer. As the only major awards show
to do so, it had already grown into a big-ticket event in its sophomore
year, with the ceremony being broadcast on television for the first time.
The mood was both raucous and subtly tense: the crowd had parceled
itself off in different regional and borough-based groups, with all the
New York artists flanking both sides and the LA contingent that Suge
had flown in—including representatives of both the Crips and Bloods—
filling out the middle.

And in the heart of NYC, the opening performance slot wasn't
dedicated to region-defying artists like B.I.G. or Wu-Tang Clan—it
was given to Death Row, with Dre literally bursting through the door

of a $100,000-plus Suge-provided prison-style stage to kick things off. From every crowd reaction during the following medley, it seemed like they were appreciated—the Lady of Rage and DJ Quik got good crowd pops, and when Snoop emerged on a lethal injection gurney to perform "Murder Was the Case," it was like Bernie Williams had just hit a walk-off homer for the Yankees. But the medley that Bad Boy staged was even better-received—and despite  the presence of Craig Mack performing his white-hot hit "Flava in Ya Ear" and great performances by R&B diva Faith Evans and B.I.G. (who'd just been given the award for Lyricist of the Year), the long-term takeaway came from Puffy's prayer-style mono-logue at the beginning, which concluded with the phrase "I live in the East, and I'm gonna die in the East."

What happened later in the show, when Suge Knight took the stage to accept an award on Death Row's behalf for *Above the Rim* winning Best Soundtrack, is hazy in its motivations. After shouting out Tupac—"Keep his guards up, we ride wit' 'im"—he declared, stumbling over his words slightly, that "any artist out there that wanna be an artist, stay a star, and won't have to worry about the executive producer trying to be all in the videos, all on the records, dancing . . . come to Death Row!"

It was like someone just dropped a sheet of glass on a concrete floor. Stunned silence was quickly followed by a whirlwind of booing, and the rest of the night would be driven by a tension that had barely been lurking beneath the surface. Puffy in particular was shocked by Suge's remark, recollecting that he and Suge had been cordial for a while, at least in a business sense: "I really couldn't believe it because homeboy me and him were friends . . . he would pick me up from the airport, show me a lot of love. I really had thought we were cool. Cool acquain-tances, being respectful of other people coming from other cities." His response, given while presenting an award later in the show, was care-fully stated to be as diplomatic as possible: "I'm the executive producer a comment was made about a little bit earlier. But, check this out: con-trary to what other people may feel, I would like to say that I'm very proud of Dr. Dre, of Death Row, and Suge Knight for their accomplish-ments. And all this East and West? That needs to stop." His statement was cut from the broadcast.

When he confronted Suge later that night at the Tunnel, Suge just brushed off Puffy's concerns: Suge claimed that the target of his remarks was actually meant to be Jermaine Dupri, the Atlanta-based executive

and producer whose label So So Def had recently emerged as a platinum player off records by R&B group Xscape and rapper Da Brat. And
Jermaine Dupri *is* all over the video for Da Brat's "Funkdafied"—even
if he had every right to be, having produced the song in the first place.
But Dupri also recalled being on good terms with Suge at the time. "Me
and Snoop was like [crosses fingers]," he told the hosts of *Drink Champs*
in 2017, the same YouTube show Puffy had made his claim to the year
before. "That's how [Snoop protégé] Bow Wow came [to So So Def]. Me
having beef with Death Row? Never. Suge was in my office, coming to
Atlanta, kicking it."

But nobody told the audience, who instantly saw the remarks as a
direct insult to the East. And nobody told Snoop and Dre, who came to
the podium together to accept Dre's Producer of the Year award immediately following Suge's remarks. Before the award was given out, director John Singleton stepped up to the mic, accompanied by Houston
Rockets point guard Sam Cassell (much to the chagrin of the Knicks
fans in the audience), and preemptively tried to defuse any further beef:
"We gotta kill all this East Coast, West Coast, South, Midwest dissen-
sion in rap. . . . There's a lotta devils out there that would be damned
if they could ban it, and we wouldn't be havin' no show and a lotta y'all
wouldn't be makin' no money." But the audience still responded coldly
when Dre was announced as a nominee alongside the likes of resound-
ingly cheered NYC heavies like DJ Premier and Pete Rock. When Dre
won out over Primo, Rock, and "Flava in Ya Ear" producer Easy Mo Bee,
Singleton cracked, "Uh-oh, we're gonna have some trouble here," and
only the presence of a sizeable West Coast contingent in the audience
kept Dre from being booed out of the building.

Snoop was memorably aghast, and his response was a Molotov
cocktail dropped in a puddle of gasoline. "The East Coast don't love Dr.
Dre and Snoop Dogg? The East Coast ain't got no love for Dr. Dre and
Snoop Dogg and Death Row? Y'all don't love us? *Y'all don't love us?* Well,
let it be known then! We know y'all East Coast! We know where the fuck
we at! East Coast in the muthafucking house!" It was an incendiary reaction that Dre's follow-up remark, while diplomatic, couldn't mitigate:
"We tryin' to make music for *everybody* to enjoy," he protested, before
giving the requisite shoutouts to Suge and Death Row and leaving the
stage in ashes. The war that Tim Dog's "Fuck Compton" anticipated had
completely engulfed hip-hop.

Two months later, Pac was out of jail. He had served nine months of his sentence along with another two months in jail awaiting trial when Suge Knight and Jimmy Iovine posted his $1.4 million bail, under the condition that 2Pac sign a three-album deal with Death Row. If Suge's enmity wasn't directed toward a clear, specific target during the Source Awards, he made sure everybody knew where he stood when he picked up the volatile MC and his anti–Bad Boy vendetta to add to his West Coast dynasty. *Me against the World* had made him one of the biggest stars in hip-hop, and putting him under the same roof as Dre and Snoop would assure that Death Row was *the* label for West Coast hip-hop. The prospect of pairing a rapper with the undeniable charisma of 2Pac with a producer as deeply creative and hitmaking as Dre was practically a money-printing formula.

But Dre had hit a dry spell. In August '94 he was sentenced to six months in jail after leading police on a high-speed chase down LA's Wilshire Boulevard in his white '87 Ferrari Testarossa and blowing twice the legal blood-alcohol limit. (Police clocked him doing 90 m.p.h.; Dre claims he topped 140.) Shortly after he got out, he learned of Eazy's illness, and never got a chance to talk with him before his former bandmate and adversary lapsed into a coma. Dre still saw him in the hospital and spoke a few words to him, but he couldn't know if Eazy heard him, and an official reconciliation was never registered. Thanks to his prison time, he helmed only a handful of tracks in late '94 and all of 1995—the "Murder Was the Case" remix, his Ice Cube team-up "Natural Born Killaz," and his *Friday* hit "Keep Their Heads Ringin'" chief among them—and depending on who you ask, either slightly or significantly ceded the production work on Tha Dogg Pound's late '95 release *Dogg Food* to Daz Dillinger.

The irony was that Dre and Pac had crossed paths more than a few times, just at weird angles. Dre made beats for tracks on the soundtracks to Tupac-starring vehicles *Poetic Justice* and *Above the Rim,* but neither of them—Tha Dogg Pound's "Niggas Don't Give a Fuck" and Lady of Rage's "Afro Puffs," respectively—featured Pac in any capacity. Pac's "If I Die 2Nite" lifted a Dre line from "Deep Cover" to complete its chorus, Pac's "Fuck it, if I die tonight" answered by Dre's "Tonight's the night I get in some shit." And while Pac wasn't officially affiliated with Death Row in 1994, he did have a cameo in the final shot of the "Natural Born

Killaz" video as a SWAT sniper who has his scope trained on Ice Cube, one gangsta revolutionary taking aim at another.

But *All Eyez on Me* wasn't an easy undertaking—even if it was a quick one, written and recorded almost immediately following Pac's release from jail in a cathartic span of two weeks. Pac would eventually record enough material to fill the first double CD in hip-hop history, the whole set stretching well over two hours (and counting as the first two albums in his three-album commitment). In many of his prison-era interviews, including the one he conducted for *Vibe* in early '95, he'd either hinted or outright stated that his old "thug life" persona was over and done with. But in an August 1996 interview with Rob Marriott that *Vibe* printed two months later, Pac cited a letter Puffy wrote in response to that '95 piece that got under his skin. "He said you can't be a thug for a second or a minute and get in and out of it, you gotta be in it forever. He didn't mean it as advice at the time, he said it to dampen things. So now, when I'm whoopin' his muthafuckin' ass, and it hurts, and all these people talkin' about 'stop, now,' remember what he told me."

And if the album's title wasn't enough to make him seem paranoid, his lyrics removed all doubt: no less than ten of the album's twenty-seven songs practically seethed with thoughts of betrayal and vengeance, from opener "Ambitionz az a Ridah" ("Spittin' at adversaries, envious and after me / I'd rather die before they capture me, watch me bleed") to "Holla at Me" (clapping back at a friend's betrayal, unnamed but likely Stretch), all the way through to the surveillance-state pressure of the title track ("The feds is watchin', niggas plottin' to get me / Will I survive? Will I die? Come on, let's picture the possibility"). And while much of the album's remainder was taken up by a series of love songs and/or fuck boasts, one track—the nice-guy-goes-slut-shaming "Wonder Why They Call U Bitch"—went above and beyond by featuring Faith Evans on the hook. At the time she was a Bad Boy artist—and Biggie's wife.

Most of the beats were handled by Daz Dillinger or Johnny Lee Jackson, aka Johnny "J," and the style was distinctly late-era g-funk, classic funk crates merged with live retro-boogie and modern R&B instrumentation. It sounded every ounce like a West Coast record, with Snoop duet "2 of Amerikaz Most Wanted" and SoCal/NorCal summit "Ain't Hard 2 Find" (featuring such Bay Area stars as the Click, C-Bo, and Richie Rich). DJ Pooh contributed the haunting thump of "When

We Ride"; DJ Quik laid out the bouncy bassline, icy melody, and Fred-and-Maceo horn hook of "Heartz of Men"; and QDIII closed the whole thing out with the "Heaven Ain't Hard 2 Find," another Left Eye tribute set to a gleaming interpolation of Bobby Caldwell's "What You Won't Do For Love."

So where was Dre in all this? Only drafting up the lead single and arguably Pac's most well-known song. "California Love" might be the ne plus ultra of g-funk, or at least its last great triumph: given all the promise and the budget and the freedom he'd ever want, Dre brought in Zapp's own talk-box maestro Roger Troutman to provide the immortal "West Coast Poplock"–referencing hook ("Cal-i-*forn*-ia / Knows how to *par-ty*"), fused it to a diabolically tight interpolation of Joe Cocker's 1972 single "Woman to Woman" (previously sampled directly by Ultramagnetic MCs for "Funky" in '87 — there's Ced-Gee again), and gave Pac a party anthem for the ages. There's something sort of what-if about it, really, as a celebration of West Coast hip-hop without malice or spite: it's one of the few moments of Pac's post-prison career where he sounds like he'd never been shot, the culmination of a version of him which remained that P-Funk-enamored Digital Underground disciple with a tough-love presence that radiated nothing but pure enthusiasm. "I don't want it to be about violence," he told *Vibe* at the time. "I want it to be about money."

A remixed form of "California Love" made *All Eyez on Me* in lieu of the original, even though it had peaked at #1 on the Hot 100. The remix, based around an interpolation of Kleeer's 1984 Eumir Deodato–produced song "Intimate Connection," was far less euphoric than the original, despite preserving all the original lyrics and Troutman's vocals: even at the same tempo, it felt like it crept, all shifty basslines and the kind of melodies that stir up dread just from their minor-key emphases. Maybe it better fit the album's sour mood.

Dre's other contribution to *All Eyez on Me* is a return to the George Clinton / P-Funk sphere of influence on "Can't C Me," which opened the album's second disc after passing through a few pairs of hands. Clinton himself, who provided the chorus, told *Genius* that he'd originally done this appearance for a Dre/Snoop collaboration, while other rumors placed it as the first draft for a planned Dre/Cube collaboration, until it eventually surfaced sometime in the early '00s as an outtake from *Dogg Food*. Whatever the case, it seems like something Dre had in the cham-

ber for a while, and handed off to Pac in an effort to get another foot in
the door of an assured blockbuster album. The lyrics were more paranoid vengeance writ large: "Must see my enemies defeated / I catch 'em
while they coked up and weeded / Open fire, now them niggas bleedin'."

Pac was increasingly losing control, blurring the boundaries
between dis tracks and genuine threats, and stabbing at his rivals with
undisguised contempt. "I have no mercy in war," he told Marriott. "I
said in the beginning I was gonna take these niggas out the game, and
sure enough I will. Already people can't look at Biggie and not laugh. I
took every piece of his power. Anybody who tries to help them, I will
destroy. Anyone who wanna side with them or do a record with them,
whatever, try to unify with them, I'm'a destroy. I swear to God."

This came two months after the release of "Hit 'Em Up," a track
that Pac had planned as his equivalent of "No Vaseline": a dis record so
to-the-bone and driven by unfiltered hatred that nobody could answer
it. It started with direct lifts from multiple Biggie-featuring Junior
M.A.F.I.A. tracks—hooks from "Player's Anthem" and "Get Money,"
and the Dennis Edwards "Don't Look Any Further"–sampling beat from
"Gettin' Money (the Get Money Remix)"—and went straight for the
nuclear option lyrically: "I ain't got no motherfuckin' friends," Pac snarls
on the intro. "That's why I fucked yo' bitch, you fat motherfucker!" It's a
point he restates in the first verse ("You claim to be a player, but I fucked
your wife"), before going on to threaten the entire Bad Boy empire from
Lil' Kim to Lil' Cease, and throwing in a low-blow sickle-cell joke at
Mobb Deep's expense.

But Dre was increasingly ill at ease with what was happening at
Death Row. He didn't find any enthusiasm for the whole coast-beef
situation, especially after shots were fired at the Dogg Pound's trailer
when they were in NYC to film the video for "New York, New York"
in December 1995. Both the song and the video, which featured giant-
sized Snoop, Daz, and Kurupt tromping through the streets of Manhattan and knocking over skyscrapers, infuriated the East Coast. And it
got a Capone-N-Noreaga response, "LA, LA," the video for which featured the Queens rappers and their fellow borough-reppers Mobb Deep
and Tragedy Khadafi tossing bagged-up Dogg Pound lookalikes off the
Queensboro Bridge. After getting into a highly visible and vicious feud
with Eazy, only to have him die before they could truly reconcile, what
was in it for Dre when this kind of shit kept escalating?

Dre's unease frustrated Pac, made him impatient. In that same interview with Marriott, Pac talked about his efforts to get Dre ousted from Death Row: "My decision was based on Dre not being there for Snoop during his trial," he claimed, referring to the three-year legal battle around Snoop's bodyguard shooting a rival gang member for which Snoop was eventually acquitted. But there were artistic differences, too: "Other niggas was producing beats, and Dre was getting the credit. And I got tired of that. He was owning the company too and he chillin' in his house. I'm out here in the streets, whoopin' niggas' asses, startin' wars and shit, droppin' albums, doin' my shit, and this nigga takin' three years to do one song! I couldn't have that. But it was not my decision. Suge was comin' to me. Death Row can never be weak, no matter what."

To Dre, Death Row felt like a cult, a gang, and a cutthroat business all at once—conditions he had been chafing against since *The Chronic.* "[Death Row's] whole business is gangsta rap. That was a conflict right there," stated rapper RBX in an October 1996 *Vibe* profile of Dr. Dre. "Dre told me, 'I'm sick of drive-bys and all that shit.' Then Tupac coming to Death Row was the straw that broke the camel's back." In the same piece, Dre summed up his departure from Death Row in the simplest terms possible: he told Jimmy Iovine "I'm ready to bounce. Make me a deal, and I'll make you some hit records. That was that. Very simple. I ain't got nothing to say to nobody. I'm just out. Period. I don't like it no more."

*All Eyez on Me* had been out for just about a month when Dre left Death Row, an event that seemed to not only spoil Pac's #1 victory lap but left him feeling betrayed and hostile in a way that felt like Suge was getting in his ear. One of the last songs Pac recorded during his lifetime was "Toss It Up," the first single from *The Don Killuminati: The 7 Day Theory,* which he recorded under the name Makaveli. Originally a mockery of the beat to Blackstreet's Dr. Dre–featuring R&B hit "No Diggity" until Blackstreet sent a cease-and-desist, it's a typical post-*Chronic* g-funk hanger-on of a beat that builds off Dre's ideas while at the same time insulting him: "Quick to jump ship, punk trick, what a dumb move / Cross Death Row, now who you gonna run to?"

The question didn't need an answer: Dre was back to finding work on his own terms, and he was being dissed by a ghost. "Toss It Up" and the rest of the Makaveli album were released posthumously, two months after Tupac Shakur was fatally shot after leaving a Las Vegas Mike Tyson fight as a passenger in Suge's BMW. A self-proclaimed thug with the potential to be a genuine activist in music had lost a battle with forces outside his control, no matter how much his growing anxiety had driven him to seek his own control over just about everything and everyone he saw as an obstacle.

And jumping ship from Death Row soon proved to be the right decision for Dre: Snoop Dogg's second album *Tha Doggfather* critically suffered from a lack of A-list beats despite his upbeat charisma, and it was the last Death Row album of any note before Suge Knight's probation was revoked in late November 1996 — a ruling contingent on his role in a melee that Tupac participated in hours before he was murdered. And there was one cruel postscript: while Pac never let go of his grudge against Bad Boy, his friend Greg Nice of NYC crew Nice & Smooth revealed in 2016 that Pac wanted to eventually put together an album featuring MCs from both coasts as well as the South, something that aspired to bring some unity back to hip-hop's scattered, divided regions. The working title was *One Nation.*

• • •

For someone who had played such a major role in defining the sounds of gangsta rap, Dre's reluctance to adhere to it was understandable — not just because of the fallout from Pac's bridge-burnings, but because crossing the age-thirty threshold nearly ten years after "Boyz-n-the-Hood" seemed like the right time to start a new phase. Dre the swaggering gangsta was never entirely himself on the mic, especially given how much of his lyrics were ghostwritten. Dre the studio wiz, meticulously obsessed with sound and possessing a DJ's instinct for finding the new and unheard, was who he seemed more comfortable being. But as an artist who became the first hip-hop megastar to make his rep both behind and in front of the decks, he had a long road ahead to reconcile what it meant to maintain his musical identity.

He called his new label Aftermath Entertainment, and it would be his route to finding himself in something bigger than just California g-funk. The label's first release, *Dr. Dre Presents the Aftermath,* featured a remedy against the coast wars in "East Coast / West Coast Killas," credited to Group Therapy, a super-posse consisting of RBX, B-Real, KRS-One, and Nas. The beat used the same Quincy Jones "Ironside" sirens that Above the Law's "Murder Rap" deployed to devastating effect six years prior, as though it was a deliberate door-closing bookend to Cold 187um's g-funk prototype.

And then there was "Been There Done That," a coproduction with a producer named Bud'da. It wasn't just a lyrical detour from gangsta subjects, it was a repudiation, depicted in the video as just a few unseemly hood scenes he observes impassively from the back of a limo en route to a lavish ballroom dance. (One of them, featuring a young black man being handcuffed on the hood of a white Testarossa, hints at his own recent past.) Gangsta shit was small-time: Dre was a "young black Rockefeller" with "a palace in the Hills overlookin' the sea / It's worth eight, but I only paid five point three." It was mafioso meets super-capitalist, punctuated by a jarring late-song shift from lavishly smooth, thick-bouncing synth-funk to a quasi-Tchaikovsky orchestra—one he lets play out for startling effect until he brings his familiar loping funk chords back in.

But the rest of the compilation wasn't up to snuff. Aside from the Group Therapy one-off and an appearance from West Coast cult favorite King Tee, most of the tracks came from artists whose careers stayed low-key at best, bottoming out with a thoroughly joyless cover of David Bowie's "Fame" featuring rap-singer RC that sounded like a hokey Halloween soundtrack. The comp got lukewarm, sometimes disappointed reviews—though none was more scathing than the one Dre himself gave in the 2017 documentary *The Defiant Ones:* "There's nothing more humbling than putting out a fucking flop."

And it was only the first of two. The Firm—a New York supergroup consisting of Nas, Foxy Brown, Nature, and AZ—was breathlessly hyped in the wake of Dre's *It Was Written* collab "Nas Is Coming," with more of that track's chilly crime-drama futurism just what fans were hoping for. Instead, *The Album* was a shameless, cliché-riddled pop move that reveled in awful pulp-crime skits and underachieving lyrics that focused on materialistic opulence at the expense of compelling ideas. And in splitting production duties with Trackmasters, Dre seemed lost: his beats on cuts like "Phone Tap," "Firm Family," and "Fuck Somebody Else" sounded like sleepier versions of the smooth jazz and suit-and-tie R&B cuts he sampled (or, more frequently, interpolated).

It all felt tied into the increasingly excessive mansions-and-yachts largess that hip-hop was finding itself reveling in during the peak-CD era of the late '90s. Called "the jiggy era," often with disdain by purists, the luxury-rap phase that followed in the wake of the receding coast wars felt like a bubble on par with the dot-com frenzy. The East Coast strain of "mafioso rap"—popularized and perfected by Wu-Tang Clan member Raekwon with 1995's *Only Built 4 Cuban Linx* . . . —became a Bad Boy–driven juggernaut, and after the Notorious B.I.G. was murdered on March 9, 1997, in an apparent retaliation for the death of Tupac, the grimier edges were increasingly sanded off to focus more on the *Lifestyles of the Rich and Famous* cash-flossing aspects of the music than the consequences that came with it.

And high-cost songs with stratospheric sample-clearance fees were the most opulent status symbols of all. Puff Daddy steered hip-hop production toward a revamp of the old formula that made blockbuster hits out of old pop songs for Vanilla Ice and Hammer: on 1997's *No Way Out* alone, he and his production crew the Hitmen made second-gen hits out of David Bowie's "Let's Dance" ("Been around the World"), the Police's "Every Breath You Take" (Biggie tribute "I'll Be Missing You"), and Matthew Wilder's "Break My Stride" ("Can't Nobody Hold Me Down"), as though he'd hit a wellspring of inspiration from a compilation of Top 5 hits from 1983.

It got weirder. Jay-Z, who had turned heads as a potential heir to Biggie with 1996's *Reasonable Doubt,* found himself rapping over samples and interpolations of Glenn Frey's cheeseball "You Belong to the City" (the Teddy Riley–produced "The City Is Mine") and the Waitresses' new-wave goof "I Know What Boys Like" (Puffy joint "I Know What Girls Like"), bizarre moments on 1997's otherwise immaculate *In My Lifetime, Vol. 1.* And in 1998, Bad Boy supergroup the Lox cut a single called "If You Think I'm Jiggy" based on Rod Stewart's "Do Ya Think I'm Sexy?" a disco-bandwagon punchline which had already lifted its melodies from Brazilian singer-songwriter Jorge Ben and R&B icon Bobby Womack.

But in some ways, the sample era's days seemed numbered in mainstream hip-hop. One more echo of the '95 Source Awards reverberated through the rest of the decade: when OutKast's award for New Artist of the Year was greeted with more boos from the audience, it was another Dre—André 3000, half of the Atlanta duo's lyrical brain trust alongside Big Boi—who had to assert himself. "I'm tired of folks—you know what I'm sayin'—closed-minded folks. It's like we got a demo tape and don't nobody wanna hear it. But it's like this. The South got somethin' to say."

And while Dr. Dre tried to find his footing, the hip-hop auteurs of the South—the ones who came from families that never made the Great

Migration trek to California—absolutely ate his lunch. Organized Noize, the production unit that helped OutKast notch that award thanks to their sleek, organic-sounding, gospel-inflected 808-and-live-band soul on their 1994 debut *Southernplayalisticadillacmuzik,* would build an Atlanta empire that defined the city's sound; between their production for TLC's R&B classic "Waterfalls" and Goodie Mob's debut *Soul Food,* they'd become untouchable by the end of 1995. The following year, over in Virginia, a producer named Timbaland would forge an unlikely but unstoppable hit out of off-kilter herky-jerky rhythms, synthesizer belches, and cartoon sound effects that made Ginuwine's "Pony" one of the most striking production breakthroughs of the decade. Literally one week after "Pony" dropped as a single, Aaliyah's sophomore album *One in a Million* let Timbaland's eclectic funk surrealism run wild, giving the young R&B singer a critical and commercial breakthrough and introducing the raucously talented MC Missy Elliott to the world in the process. And in 1998, a couple Virginia Beach friends of Timbaland's— Pharrell Williams and Chad Hugo, producing as the Neptunes—kicked off a long string of production hits when they laced Noreaga's "Super-thug" with a choppy, serrated keyboard riff that immediately established a lucrative signature style. These three production units would hold sway not only over hip-hop but the pop charts in general for much of the late '90s and early '00s. And none of them relied on sampling.

This was a part of the world Dre made, but he'd find a way to remake it soon enough, and fate struck with a trio of discoveries that would finally establish Aftermath as his empire. At the label's creative nadir, Jimmy Iovine gave Dre a tape by a motor-mouthed battle-rap wiseass out of Detroit named Eminem, and the two clicked immediately, with Dre creating some of his most uncharacteristically irreverent beats for Em's 1999 debut *The Marshall Mathers LP.* And a couple years later, Dre finally struck gold with a New York rapper—50 Cent, a headline-grabbing former crack dealer who seamlessly toed the line between hardcore street thug and crossover pop sensation in a way unseen since Tupac. Dre's tense digital strings and handclap beats pushed "In da Club" to a #1 spot on the Billboard charts in 2003, though it sounded more like a suspense-film score than the party anthem it became anyways.

But even as he reestablished his hitmaking bona fides, something about Dre seemed obsessed with legacy. His 1999 album *2001,* his first solo album since *The Chronic* in '91, was a widescreen expansion of what g-funk could mean. It was also a simultaneous look into the past and the future that often hinged on the fact that he had a rep to maintain. Not for nothing were two of the album's biggest hits titled "Forgot About Dre" and "Still D.R.E." And when Aftermath signed Compton-born rapper the Game, it was seen as Dre resuscitating the dormant West Coast scene through the vessel of an MC who had grown up on Dre's music. *The Documentary* was a smash, and an entertaining one, but it was hard not to hear it as a throwback.

The thing is, Dre's problem wasn't whether his music was still good; from '99 onward, it was clear he'd finally regained the creative juices that his later years on Death Row had drained from him. The problem was that he wasn't making *enough* music, and the culprit could be considered a direct side effect of sampling's diminished role in hip-hop. Dre had developed from a DJ into a producer who could balance the strengths of a sampler with the ability to compose his own rhythms and melodies, whether it was on an 808 or with a whole bank of synthesizers. But the best, hungriest work he made, from N.W.A to *The Chronic,* shone because the tools of traditional hip-hop production had technological and budgetary constraints, and was driven by a desire to show the world what hip-hop would sound like coming from a place it had scarcely been heard before. And in the heart of the 2000s, it soon became clear that Dre had difficulty handling the paired problems of perfectionism and unlimited means. Eminem and 50 Cent and the Game made him gigantic stacks of money, and that money could buy him any studio setup and session band and piece of equipment he wanted. What it couldn't buy was time.

Collaborative efforts came and went: he was supposed to make albums with Rakim, with Raekwon, with King Tee. All of them evaporated. In 2004, the same year he wrapped up his work on *The Documentary,* Dre announced that *Detox* would be the long-awaited follow-up to *2001*—a follow-up that became a punchline with each year that passed without it hitting shelves. His production work slowed down: in 2006, he'd contribute a few beats to Snoop Dogg's *Tha Blue Carpet Treatment,* another handful to Jay-Z's *Kingdom Come,* and several to Busta Rhymes's *The Big Bang,* but by 2008, he was sparsely doling out tracks to the likes of Bishop Lamont and Trick-Trick.

When *GQ*'s Alex Pappademas interviewed him in late 2007, he seemed uninspired by his surroundings: "A lot of rappers today are rapping the way they were in the Sugar Hill days. It's weird. It's just jewels and cars and clubs. I'm not knocking anybody for their hustle, but as a creator, there's nothing there for me to feed off or to make me say, 'Damn, I wish I woulda done that.'" It took a major comeback effort from one of his tightest collaborators to shake him out of it: 2009's *Relapse* might have been intended as a comeback for Eminem after a four-year struggle with writer's block and prescription drug addiction, but as Dre's first major effort providing a significant majority of an album's beats in ten years, it was a necessary sign of life for him, too.

Still, he kept moving up in the world. In November 2011, he declared that he was finally going to take a break from making music to focus more on the business side of his career—overseeing his own line of audio equipment called Beats by Dre and focusing on more behind-the-scenes work at Aftermath. Sometime a few months later, *Detox* was quietly scrapped for parts, though it was never made publicly official until 2015. And for a while, with his focus so deeply on making business deals and refining his Beats brand, it seemed like Dre was a living ghost, hiding in plain sight.

Still, he continued to make for a powerful cosign. When Compton-raised Aftermath signee Kendrick Lamar released his major-label debut *good kid, m.A.A.d city* in the fall of 2012, it was received as a next-generation expansion of all the themes Dre's early productions addressed—poverty, gang warfare, substance abuse, police brutality, black disenfranchisement—but with a tone that was more ambivalent and focused on his doubts and internal conflicts, vulnerable where *Straight Outta Compton* and *The Chronic* felt bulletproof.

And while the beats bore more of a resemblance to the synthesized gospel-soul soundscapes that Organized Noize and the rest of Dungeon Family contributed to mid-to-late '90s albums by OutKast and Goodie Mob than they did to Death Row g-funk, it established its roots firmly in Los Angeles, a logical progression that Kendrick's narrative vision held together despite an ensemble-cast production squad. Dre's voice appeared on the album—his feature "Compton," slotted in as the last song on the album, was the first track Kendrick cut for it—but his beats didn't. No matter, his brand was still strong: shortly before he turned fifty, Apple bought Beats—headphones, streaming service, and all—for $3 billion, pushing Dre's net worth to nearly $800 million.

If there was anything resembling closure on Dre's music career, it finally came in 2015, concurrent with the release of the N.W.A biopic *Straight Outta Compton*. What remained of *Detox* had been reworked into something more legacy-minded: an album simply titled *Compton* and released a week before the film hit theaters, inspired by his time spent on the set of the movie. It was as though he was reenergized by witnessing the reenactment of his life, and the album that he oversaw was alive with both reminiscence and possibility: veteran peers like Ice Cube, Snoop Dogg, the Game, Eminem, Xzibit, and Cold 187um shared space with current and future stars like Kendrick, Anderson .Paak, Justus, King Mez, and BJ the Chicago Kid. It was like a family reunion and a portfolio all at once, a collective sound that extended far past anything he'd done before, both as an MC channeling his collaborators and a producer uplifting them.

Even in embodying literally everything it's possible to do in hip-hop, from rapping and DJing and making beats to becoming a bandleader, A&R, label owner, and music bizzer, Dre never came across as someone *bigger* than hip-hop, no matter how rich and famous he became. He embodied a city, then a coast, then an empire—but he always had other voices to speak through, even when he increasingly veered away from feeding those voices into a sampler. He had conflicts, but his urge to share himself with others won out in the end—reconciling with Cube and Eazy, publicly apologizing to the women he'd hurt over the years, and finding himself incapable of half-assing anything he did because he wanted his collaborations to reflect well on everyone. And he did this as he'd established himself as a figure who'd changed how music was heard because he knew how to sell records, who knew how to sell records because he knew how to make them, who knew how to make them because he knew how to hear the music other people made. LA, New York, the world—Dre was always home.

# Part IV
# The Beat Konducta

Madlib crate digging, circa 2003. Photograph courtesy of B+ for Mochilla.com.

# 10 | *The Loop Digga*
### Sampling Preserves History (and Itself)

**As sampling becomes an endangered practice,
an underground movement turns it into a
limitless, time-warping act of preservation.**

IF SAMPLE-BASED HIP-HOP HAS ONE PARTICULAR IRONY, it's that it often relies on manipulating the music of the past, and in ways that could only be accomplished by the state-of-the-art technology of the present. A theoretical beat made in 1993 built around a song recorded in 1973 exists in both moments at once—the latter era's fidelity and technology and style altered just enough to mechanically reproduce a truncated, transformed, but still recognizable version of itself. And with each new development in hip-hop production, another mode of manipulation was added to an already exhaustive world of possibility.

Herc set the parameters with the extended, looped break. Flash turned the art of cutting and scratching into the main attraction. Marley Marl opened the door for the transition from DJ-spun breaks to sample-based ones. The Bomb Squad expanded the possibilities of sampled sound to make funk from sheer noise and vice versa. Prince Paul used his sampling knowledge and beat curation to open hip-hop up so it could seemingly come from anywhere. Dr. Dre turned hip-hop into a hi-fidelity hybrid of DJ-rooted breaks and electro/funk composition. And the RZA found insight in grimy, aged-sounding beats that felt lived-in with the passage of time.

That's twenty years' worth of knowledge spread across two tightly adjacent generations of artists. And in a genre that's so dependent on the acquisition and reinterpretation of source material, the idea of sample culture started to drastically shape the idea of a musical canon in a way that radio, record sales, and journalists never anticipated. The old media saw how many copies *Dark Side of the Moon* or *Thriller* or

*Nevermind* sold and decided that the ubiquity of the familiar product was what was important. Hip-hop artists saw what transformations could be done with a drum break or a riff from a record maybe a hundred people had ever bought, and elevated that once-forgotten music into renown for its ability to be reshaped. Importance versus obscurity, fame versus ephemerality, mainstream popularity versus underground influence—the boundaries didn't matter so much if you could get some head nods out of it.

So with hip-hop as a generations-long tradition grappling with changing times, shifting forms, and ensuing movements fighting between preservation and iconoclasm, what would it mean to make music that put artistic integrity first? Because in terms of hip-hop as a musical and cultural movement, especially in the face of the mid-'90s commercial explosion and the controversy over gangsta rap, the movement meant to uphold its traditions had to be innovative and conservationist at the same time. You can't get stuck in place doing the same shit people did five years before, but you don't want to disregard all the history made and the lessons learned, either—striking everything before your time from the record, like punk rock did in its mid-'70s efforts to establish its rise as a "Year Zero," would open an artist up to accusations of ignorance and disrespect.

And yet as the internet started to emerge from its college-bound utilitarianism in the early-'90s into a mass-cultural form of communicative and commercial media, some things just couldn't stay hidden. Whereas clearance fees and mandatory liner-note attributions had already started to take a lot of the mystery out of sampling and cratedigger culture, the existence of online markets—from the generalist auction site eBay to the specialist record dealer hub Discogs—and the growing prominence of sample-spotter sites like the 2003-established The-Breaks.com made some of sampling's more arcane origins that much more accessible to neophytes and outsiders.

This is about where sample culture really started to become self-aware: not just as an integral part of hip-hop production, but as a bulwark against forgetting and an exercise in discovery (or rediscovery, as it were). While some hip-hop icons were on their way to becoming media moguls in the late '90s, another segment of artists had their sights on becoming a different kind of tastemaker: the curator, the archivist, the antiquarian. And if the internet era did its share to foreground the cultural status of the geek—the fan so enthusiastic about their choice of hobby that it became an almost monomaniacal fascination—it did so with the side effect of enabling the kind of obsessive enthusiast that would set the stage for an entire renewal of an ethos that had been considered in danger of being lost completely.

• • •

Otis Jackson Jr. grew up in a household destined to make him a musician, and with the perfect timing to steer him toward the dustier corners of hip-hop. Born in October 1973, just over two months after Kool Herc's back-to-school DJ set, the Oxnard, California, native was raised by two parents with a musical background. His father, Otis Jackson, played session gigs with Tina Turner, Johnnie Taylor, and Bobby "Blue" Bland, and had a handful of commercially released 45s to his name, including a 1974 single—the smooth soul of "Beggin' for a Broken Heart" b/w the harder-edged antidrug funk "Message to the Ghetto"—produced and arranged by H. B. Barnum. (Other artists who worked with Barnum that year include Buddy Miles, Boz Scaggs, Gladys Knight & the Pips, and Johnny Mathis.) His mother, Dora Sinesca Faddis-Jackson, wrote songs and played piano. And his uncle was trumpeter Jon Faddis, a jazz director at Carnegie Hall and an omnipresent sideman in the '70s and '80s who played on albums by Charles Mingus, George Benson, Grover Washington Jr., Roy Ayers, Lou Reed, and Chic. Every so often he'd bring his mentor and friend Dizzy Gillespie over for dinner.

This is the kind of environment that gave Otis Jr. a head start on crate digging bordering on the absurd. Both his parents and his uncle had formidable record collections, and just by poring through the back catalog of albums Faddis played on he'd find himself hearing a litany of soul-jazz, fusion, and R&B records a decade before producers like Q-Tip and Pete Rock made them essential hip-hop components. His younger brother Michael, who also makes beats under the alias Oh No, recalled to *LA Weekly* that when they stayed at Faddis's house in Oakland, they never needed to worry about getting in each others' space: "We were supposed to share a room, but he'd constantly be in the room with the records, listening to Count Basie." Otis Sr. also had recording studio access, and Otis Jr. would tag along, learning by observing and finding endless fascination in the workings of music-making. "My pops had me at the studio since I was born," he told Red Bull Music Academy in 2016.

"That's why I got into music. He always let me go up on the controls and just mess with stuff."

By the time he was in junior high in the mid-'80s, Otis Jr. had a crew he hung around with that liked to breakdance and listen to hip-hop records—tracks with beats by Marley Marl, Paul C, Dr. Dre, and DJ Pooh. One friend, Romeo "DJ Romes" Jimenez, loaned him a Casio keyboard with modest sampling capabilities, and Otis Jr. would make beat tapes with it, little experiments that he'd spend an entire day working on. Being a hip-hop head sixty miles from downtown LA meant he and his friends were seen as the weird kids by other teenagers who spent most of their time getting caught up in gang warfare. But that just motivated Otis Jr. to spend more time inside the studio, with the blessing of his parents, and he and his crew were still close enough to the epicenter of West Coast hip-hop that they could find a way to network with other artists.

That's how their demo made its way to King Tee. By 1990, the crew were calling themselves Lootpack—and along with DJ Romes and rapper Jack "Wildchild" Brown, Otis Jr., now calling himself Madlib, was getting accustomed to the life of a hip-hop artist. And like Dre, he took the path of DJ turned producer turned MC. By 1993, Lootpack's affiliation with King Tee's Likwit Crew landed them a couple guest spots on the debut album by beer-and-weed party rappers Tha Alkaholiks, providing the only two beats on the album that weren't produced by Tee or in-house producer E-Swift. They stood out for their complexity on an album heavy with an East–meets–West Coast jazz-funk sound. "Turn Tha Party Out" jumbled up the already-familiar piano chords of "Synthetic Substitution" with slippery but hard-hitting drums from Little Richard's 1970 comeback cut "The Rill Thing" and doused the whole thing in half-subliminal jazz horns. And the wall-of-haze "Mary Jane" pushed the levels on its bassline to absurd levels of density, until each note felt more like a kick drum than a string being popped.

It was a good fit. Both Lootpack and Tha Alkaholiks were more about getting wasted than wasting people, a party where gangsta rap's firearms were all checked at the door. Madlib even handled the leadoff spot on the second Alkaholiks album, with "WLIX," featuring Lootpack and affiliated rapper Dudley "Declaime" Perkins, showing off Madlib's ability to wring a melodic hook out of just about anywhere. Any beatmaker with even the slightest inclination toward jazz could get a good break out of trumpet great Freddie Hubbard's '70s recordings, but it took a certain level of willful surrealism to build it from *Sing Me a Song of Songmy (A Fantasy for Electromagnetic Tape)*, Hubbard's 1970 experimental musique concrète collaboration with Turkish avant-garde composer İlhan Mimaroğlu. Madlib was centered enough to make sure the drums knocked hard—they came from Solomon Burke's 1968 Memphis-recorded version of Lee Dorsey's "Get Out of My Life, Woman," as previously used on Dr. Dre's *The Chronic* and Ice Cube's *The Predator*—but using that break as an excuse to layer all kinds of disorienting tones from an experimental work of early electronic music was one of the first signs that Madlib wasn't content to stick to anybody's script.

It wasn't until 1996 that Lootpack got to release anything under their own billing, however. 1996's single "Psyche Move" was released on a label Otis Sr. set up for his son called Crate Diggas Palace—the same name Madlib gave to both his studio and his extended crew. That single and the contemporaneous cuts released later on the archival 2004 comp *The Lost Tapes* show the burden of influence: "Psyche Move" itself is a choppy, lo-fi assemblage of chords that attempts to merge early Marley Marl rhythm-first minimalism with deliberate nods to DJ Premier's sense of jazz-rooted funk, "Innersoul" and "Attack of the Tupperware Puppets" were attempts to figure out what made Large Professor's beats sound so smooth yet bump so hard, and "Why Do We Go Out Like That?" made a point to push its Bennie Maupin jazz fusion loop through a g-funk-adjacent bounce to give its anti-gang lyrics regional flavor. Between *The Lost Tapes* and the early cuts Madlib mixed and reworked on 2010's *Madlib Medicine Show #5: The History of the Loop Digga, 1990–2000,* you can hear an already talented young producer figuring out his identity—or the first identity of many.

• • •

There was already a groundswell of underground hip-hop running up and down the West Coast by the mid-'90s, a movement that would span from Los Angeles to the Bay Area and radiate further from there. One epicenter was the Good Life Cafe, a South Central LA health food store / restaurant that established a weekly open mic night in December 1989. The scene took off almost immediately, and the rules of the open mic—one song only, no cursing, and cede the stage if the audience called out "Please pass the mic!" during your performance—created an atmosphere of youthful, good-natured strength through competition. It quickly became the premier place for developing MCs and poets to refine their style and test their ideas in front of a receptive if discerning crowd. The clientele gave it all a progressive, bohemian air that nurtured experimentation and complex rap technique, and by 1991 the scene had created its first stars, a crew called Freestyle Fellowship.

Their underheard 1991 debut *To Whom It May Concern* . . . stood out on its own terms, a clear West Coast analogue to New York's Native Tongues movement that still distinguished itself with its own scene's battle-rap agility. It wasn't just that the beats were jazzy; they flipped everything from late '50s Miles Davis to '70s fusion favorites like Billy Cobham, George Duke, and Weather Report, plus built a loop around the Turtles' "You Showed Me" just as an in-the-know fuck-you against anti-sampling sentiment. It was the vocals, provided by Myka 9, Aceyalone, P.E.A.C.E., Self Jupiter, and J. Sumbi, that pushed the boundaries of lyrical delivery past simple beat-riding rhyme schemes into flows that went deep into improvisation-honed, structure-defying contortions. By 1993's follow-up *Innercity Griots* they were broadening their audience thanks to an Island distribution deal and an ability to wow listeners from both lyrical content and sheer delivery alike. "Those standard sing-song raps are too easy and no challenge at all," Myka 9 told the *Los Angeles Times* in a June 1993 profile. "We do double-time passages and runs and riffs. We improvise and play off of each other's words and sounds — like jazz musicians do."

They weren't alone. Half a year before *Innercity Griots* dropped, another jazz-inflected album came out of the Los Angeles underground: the Pharcyde's debut *Bizarre Ride II the Pharcyde,* which became regionally noteworthy and spawned a nationwide cult hit single, the unrequited young-love lament "Passin' Me By." Producer J-Swift built that track around an instantly appealing hook from Quincy Jones's soul-jazz rendition of the Lovin' Spoonful's "Summer in the City," an organ riff that reflected J-Swift's own ear for keyboard hooks as a songwriter and piano prodigy. The rest of the album followed suit, a light-footed, bouncy concoction of peak '60s and '70s soul (James Brown, the Meters, Sly and the Family Stone) and jazz (Donald Byrd, Roy Ayers, Herbie Mann) that amplified the irreverence, self-effacing vulnerability, and goofy-but-agile deliveries of MCs Imani, Slimkid3, Bootie Brown, and Fatlip — a personality that posited them as South Central analogues to De La Soul and A Tribe Called Quest, with whom they soon began to tour.

This whole scene was largely considered by music journalists to be oppositional to gangsta rap, though a more honest assessment would be that it was fairly parallel to it. Just as A Tribe Called Quest could exist in the same orbit as Kool G Rap, a group like Freestyle Fellowship could operate from the same turf as Good Life attendee Ice Cube—better to have innovators breaking the mold than biters riding a bandwagon. In any case, LA in the early-to-mid-'90s was a fertile environment for a West Coast alt-rap movement that could expand nationally to college radio and indie-minded listeners. By 1994, Freestyle Fellowship's Aceyalone and Good Life alumni Abstract Rude had established a spinoff open mic called Project Blowed, and released a compilation of the scene's early champions that was distributed by the Beastie Boys' imprint Grand Royal in 1995. More than twenty years later, it would continue to motivate and launch the careers of wordy and incisive rappers like Busdriver, Pigeon John, and Open Mike Eagle.

About 375 miles up the coast, the Bay Area's contributions to indie rap were going just as strong. While Too $hort and E-40 were calling the shots with a string of underground gangsta classics, Cube's cousin Del tha Funkee Homosapien had assembled a supercrew of sorts that came off like an Oakland version of Native Tongues: Souls of Mischief, a group that notched an iconic album with 1993's jazz-laced *93 'til Infinity,* were joined by battle rappers Casual and Pep Love, DJ Toure, and jazz-funk encyclopedia producer Domino to form the crew Hieroglyphics. The political agitation of Paris, whose anti–police brutality and Black Power lyrics drew controversy during the major-label purge that ostracized Ice-T, found another set of comrades in the Coup, a group whose g-funk was an abbreviation of "guerilla" and featured the leftist lyricism of openly Communist rapper (and future *Sorry to Bother You* filmmaker) Boots Riley.

And the DJ scene was preposterous. By the early '90s, a lineage from Flash to DJ Premier had redefined the DJ's role in hip-hop from the beat-extending rhythm section to a freewheeling soloist. It was a group out of San Francisco, with the deliberately absurdist name Invisibl Skratch Piklz, that pushed DJing to its next phase—a battle-hewn focus on experimental technique and spectacular, lightning-cut virtuosity. The Skratch Piklz were a primarily Latino and Filipino American crew that among their massive and often-shifting numbers included Luis "DJ Disk" Quintanilla, Richard "DJ Qbert" Quitevis, Apollo "DJ Apollo" Novicio, Jonathan "Shortkut" Cruz, and future Beastie Boys DJ Michael "Mix Master Mike" Schwartz.

The Skratch Piklz constantly revolutionized a number of outlandish techniques that've since become standard elements in modern DJs' repertoires. Qbert's "crab scratch" is a crossfader technique using quick-moving three- or four-finger sequences to flip the fader switch back and forth at a dizzying rate. Mike's "Uzi scratch" is a short but extremely rapid-fire motion on a split-second portion of the record that gives the scratch a quivering, vibrating tone. And Disk's "orbit scratch" was a repeating three-tone back-and-forth rhythmic sequence punctuated with a multi-tap push of the fader. Each of these musical manipulations took the idea of cutting and scratching a break and refined it to such a degree that the scratching itself could often completely outshine the break. These DJs were so innovative and intricate that the Disco Mix Club had to dissuade them from entering their annual DMC World DJ Championships in 1993 after a multiyear run of domination because they were considered by awestruck, dispirited rivals to be completely unbeatable.

This resurgence in scratch-and-cut DJ culture, which hit a peak of popularity unseen since the early '80s, needed an entirely new term to describe it, and it was DJ Disk who coined it: they weren't just disk jockeys, they were *turntablists*. Between the Skratch Piklz and a crew called the World Famous Beat Junkies out of Orange County, the West Coast was a flourishing epicenter of DJ culture, and both crews' battles with New York's X-Men—later known as the X-Ecutioners when Marvel Comics lawyers got antsy—became the stuff of legend, a nonviolent version of the Coast Wars driven and judged entirely on turntable technique.

But the parallel developments in MCing and DJing on the West Coast, whether it was the Good Life's rhyme showcases or the Invisibl Skratch Piklz's reinvention of scratching, would also be accompanied by a new revolution in sampling, and you could find it emerging on one San Francisco label in particular. Solesides was founded in Davis, California, from the efforts of UC Davis college radio DJ Jeff "DJ Zen" Chang. In his recollections on the label's history for the liner notes to the best-of compilation *Solesides Greatest Bumps,* he took some good-natured jabs at the local hip-hop producers who made a habit of visiting the studio to plunder the station's record collection: "I was like, look man, you fools come up to my show every week, and spend more time skulking around the record stacks, pulling obscure jazz records, then hiding out in the listening booths, than you do hanging out with me and listening to my show. . . . I said, you should all stop fucking around and just make that record you always wanted to make, using each other's money. Or something like that."

The "something like that" would emerge in 1993 with a 12-inch featuring two of the artists who would come to define the label. One of them, a producer/MC named Tom Shimura—then known as Asia Born, later as Lyrics Born—contributed "Send Them," a hard-knocking exhibition of motormouthed mic skills over a loop of one of the biggest beats rock/soul drummer Buddy Miles ever hammered out. That was the radio-friendly party jam side of the single. The other producer, just a couple years into a still-young career making beats and remixes for MCs ranging from Paris to the New Jersey prison-inmate rap crew Lifers Group, had other ideas. He constructed a nearly eighteen-minute beat suite that took the idea of the hip-hop mix into borderline-prog turf, or as it said on the label, "hip hop reconstruction from the ground up."

It was, among other things, an editorial: early in the track, there's a clip of a newscaster introducing a segment on "rap music . . . much of the fascination: guns, drugs, violence, sex, is that all *rap* is about?" Less than a minute later, after a quick-cutting and soundbite-layering self-intro using the same pieced-together scratched and sampled phrasing made famous by DJ Premier, there's another familiar soundbite: it's that MTV News clip of Turtles lawyer Evan S. Cohen weighing in on Prince Paul's "You Showed Me" sample for De La Soul. "They've made such insignificant changes to the sound of the recording that it is still infringement as far as we're concerned, and they have violated our exclusive rights in the sound recording." By its very presence, this statement is included solely to be mocked.

The track, titled "Entropy," would sample at least forty-five acknowledged audio clips and songs—everything from obscurities like "Bad" Bascomb and Simtec & Wylie to funk legends like the Meters and the Bar-Kays—and integrate them into a sort of sweeping statement on the very nature of making beats in a genre that was building a future its detractors couldn't imagine. It was an early metacommentary on the role of DJing, sampling, and repurposing that seamlessly blended contemporaneous rap and its generation-old source material, highlighting the lineage from funk to hip-hop with the deep-dive knowledge of a connoisseur and the fearlessness of an artist who hadn't considered the possibility of having limitations. Even the classic repertoire came in for some scrutiny: at one point, a Solesides crew member chimes in with "A'ight now I don't wanna hear *Ultimate Breaks* Volumes 1–99, no Blue Note breaks, no Bulldog Breaks. Just pull somethin' outta the crate, man." If "Entropy" was the only thing DJ Shadow would contribute to the world of hip-hop, he'd leave it with a certifiable masterpiece.

There would, thankfully, be more. DJ Shadow, birth name Josh Davis, had already distinguished himself as a producer when he created 1991's "Lesson 4" on the Hollywood Basic label, a massive, sample-stuffed megamix sequel to Double Dee & Steinski's "Lesson" records. And he was still a couple months away from turning twenty-one when "Entropy" dropped in February '93. Not only that, but he'd have another genre-redefining track under his belt before the year was out. James Lavelle, a teenage wunderkind from England who cofounded the label Mo' Wax with British DJ/producer Tim Goldsworthy in 1992, was quick to catch on to Shadow's talents and signed him to the label. And Shadow's first Mo' Wax release, the "In/Flux"/"Hindsight" 12-inch, was epochally definitive. The A-side's down-tempo, twelve-plus-minute voyage through meditative soul-jazz, black revolutionary poetry, and elaborate scratching was so different from anything going on in either mainstream or underground hip-hop production that in the June 1994 issue of *Mixmag,* writer Andy Pemberton had to coin the genre "trip-hop" just to describe it.

Shadow was a highly skilled and adventurous DJ, but his success was also largely thanks to a recent development in sampling and recording technology. Akai's MPC series had started to catch on with hip-hop producers in the early '90s, and the machine's ability to make any sample playable as a percussive instrument on its touch-sensitive pads was beginning to reshape sampling beyond just the construction and layering of loops. It was more versatile and easier to use than the SP1200, allowing for real-time editing and on-the-fly juxtapositions of sounds that could be played the same way a keyboard could. Plug it in to a stereo system with an attached turntable or two and you could create tracks in your bedroom or your basement; take it out with you and you could play it live in front of a crowd as you reconstructed and remixed your own beats in real time. The big knock against sampling, and the pivotal misunderstanding of it by its detractors, is that it was supposedly a substitute for musicianship when in reality it was simply a replication (and, later, escalation) of DJ techniques. With the MPC alongside the era's new scratch techniques, the transition from DJing to sampling finally crossed the threshold into its own unique form of musicianship.

By the time the MPC3000 hit the market in '93, making the unit affordable for producers on a budget, Shadow had already spent a year or so cutting his teeth on its predecessor, the MPC60 II. And that's the model he'd stick with all the way through 1996, when he used it to create his first magnum opus. His debut full-length album *Endtroducing*..... is considered the first all-instrumental hip-hop album where every piece of music—each loop, scratch, and (occasional) dropped-in voice—was sourced through sampling. And even a couple decades later, the technique on display is remarkable: like his contemporary Pete Rock, Shadow gave his tracks a sense of restless, live-sounding momentum, making sure that while the drum patterns were all on-point, they never actually leaned on repetition, switching up patterns with subtle but dynamic variations. The drum fills alone were enough to make *Endtroducing*..... a tour de force: the breaks could play out for a few bars, only to shift shape and unfurl into elaborate MPC-programmed solos that sounded more like Max Roach or Elvin Jones than Clyde Stubblefield, the improvisational modes of jazz beats making their way into the steady-metered world of hip-hop.

Shadow's obsessive crate digging went hand in hand with his quest to find his own niche in that world. His upbringing in hip-hop as a white kid from the suburbs predated the commercialized fad years of rap and stood in opposition to the idea of a casual, surface-level appropriator's idea of the genre. But he was still an entire country's width away from New York, same as every other '80s Cali hip-hop head, and he wound up having to piece together the essentials through osmosis, study, and just plain luck. College radio filled him in to an extent, but as he told *Westword* in 2013, "In the '80s, what I didn't realize was that the music I heard was really being decided by people that may or may not have understood hip-hop . . . the hip-hop and rap that reached my ears was a lot more diverse than probably what a lot of New York took in because in New York you have the epicenter, the home of it all. But what was interesting was that I was getting Seattle's take on rap, I was getting Houston's take on rap, I was getting Detroit's take on rap, the Bay Area, Arizona, LA—all these records that never made it to the East Coast."

That was a lot to take in, and it left him with a wide-angle lens on beatmaking that always left him wanting more. His work on *Endtroducing. . . . .* coincided and also became a reaction to the ideas that Dre and others were putting forward of more live-band-based compositions in hip-hop that put sampling on the back burner. "Why are we all abandoning this artform?" he recalls thinking in the *Westword* interview. "What everybody else is doing is great, but I feel like there's a lot of work left to be done in this discipline." Along with that defense of an art he considered a still-developing form, Shadow instituted a personal rule that he wouldn't sample familiar breaks or prepackaged breakbeat collections, and that all his source material had to come from original releases instead of reissues—that's how DJ Premier and Large Professor did it, after all. But it still left him plenty of space to play: for "Swan Lake," a track he coproduced for Blackalicious with their own producer Chief Xcel in 1994, they assembled a beat using, among other components, three completely different early '70s soul-jazz covers of the Stylistics' "People Make the World Go Round" and made it sound seamless.

*Endtroducing. . . . .* was also a tribute to cratedigging, right down to the album art, featuring a blurry photo of Chief Xcel and a bewigged Lyrics Born rifling through the vinyl stacks of Sacramento's Rare Records. In a clip from the 2001 documentary *Scratch,* Shadow sits in the store's basement where he found most of the albums he sampled for *Endtroducing. . . . . ,* discussing all the music he unearthed that might not have ever been heard again if he hadn't stumbled across something lying on the top of one of the nearly head-high stacks of remaindered and abandoned LPs. Sometimes he'd find a long-dead bat that had mummified with age, and sometime he'd find a record that would join one of the dozens of others he'd build his first album around. And it kept him grounded: "Just being in here is a humbling experience to me because you're looking through all these records, and it's sorta like a big pile of broken dreams in a way. Almost none of these artists still have a career, really. So you have to kinda respect that in a way. If you're making records . . . you're sorta adding to this pile, whether you wanna admit it or not. Ten years down the line, you'll be in here."

When he came up from the basement and put it all together, the ensuing album was even more unfamiliar than anyone was prepared for. If there was any recognizable source material on the record, it came from somewhere far outside the boundaries of hip-hop, like a sample of the grinding guitars from Metallica's *Master of Puppets* dirge "Orion," or the gleaming electric piano from Björk's "Possibly Maybe," a track released on her album *Post* just the previous year. The rest of it was primarily filled out by artists who had long been forgotten to the mainstream, if they'd ever been known at all.

The piano from "The Human Abstract," a 1969 orchestral-psychedelic instrumental written by Capitol Records producer-arranger David Axelrod, fused with electric piano from Finnish prog-fusion keyboardist Pekka Pohjola's 1974 track "Sekoilu Seestyy" and the vocals from private-press hippie band Baraka's "Sower of Seeds" to create the haunting boom-bap soul of "Midnight in a Perfect World." "Changeling," a slowly mutating work of cosmic jazz-funk, got most of its melodic character from a feminist folk record by flautist Kay Gardner and a late '70s LP put out by the jazz ensemble of Rancho Cucamonga's Chaffey College, where Frank Zappa attended for a single semester in 1959. And "Napalm Brain / Scatter Brain," a track where Shadow brilliantly transitions from skulking funk-based hip-hop into frantic drum and bass before receding into meditative quiet, incorporated everything from the bassline to one of the only singles by a hopelessly obscure late '60s Chicago R&B band called the Fantastic Epic's to an Australian jazz-funk ensemble, the Daly-Wilson Big Band, performing a rendition of Richard Strauss's *Also sprach Zarathustra* à la Deodato. (The meditative bit came from the score to the 1976 Burt Reynolds film *Gator.*)

The album was rapturously received by a wide crossover array of music journalists and publications, which was something of a problem. For one thing, Shadow had gone into it intent on making it the last chapter of the sound he'd been establishing for himself since the beginning of the decade, hence the title *Endtroducing. . . . .*—emphasis on *end.* For another, its crossover success outside the hip-hop world into the general music-buying populace led to the misconception that Shadow was doing something *other than* hip-hop; record store customers often found the album filed under "Electronic" alongside the likes of Aphex Twin and Goldie. And he found himself sick of answering questions about the forty-three-second interlude joke track "Why Hip-Hop Sucks in '96" (the answer, as relayed by Lyrics Born: "It's the money"), as though he was some outside agitator talking shit about a genre where he didn't belong.

His ensuing work over the next couple decades was proof that he did, even if some of his efforts were pilloried for not sounding enough like *Endtroducing.....*—like the eclectic, star-studded, but critically and commercially ill-fated 1998 team-up with James Lavelle for UNKLE's *Psyence Fiction,* or the handful of tracks he did for 2006's *The Outsider* that dipped into the Bay Area's hyphy strain of rap. Still, even with fol-low-up studio albums that felt uneven at worst and almost-but-not-quite-transcendent at best, Shadow maintained and still commands a strong live presence as a DJ. And some of his best post-*Endtroducing.....* work came when he and Jurassic 5 DJ Cut Chemist united the Bay and LA strains of underground instrumental hip-hop for a series of shows and mixtapes—1999's *Brainfreeze,* 2001's *Product Placement,* and 2007's *The Hard Sell*—that showed off both turntablists' collector instincts and ear for breaks. Of course they had to differentiate themselves: by their own rules, everything they cut, scratched, and mixed had to be on 7-inch 45 RPM records, which DJs almost never used because they were harder to spin with. There'd always be untapped sounds somewhere.

•  •  •

"Peanut Butter Wolf" sounds more like a name for a cereal mascot than a hip-hop DJ. But Chris Manak had a way of getting ideas like that to make perfect sense. His family's roving state-to-state residencies even-tually landed him in San Jose at age six, which is where he found music as a way to connect with others once he finally put down roots. By the early '80s he'd grown immersed in the golden age of post-disco R&B dominated by the likes of Michael Jackson and Prince and Marvin Gaye, then supplemented that with a high school interest in new wave and synthpop contemporaries like the Cure and New Order as well as an interest in old psych and funk records from before his time. A clique-diplomat generalist, Manak's gregarious down-for-whatever tastes inev-itably drew him into hip-hop, and in 1989 at the age of nineteen he met Charles Hicks Jr., a rapper three years his junior who went by the name Charizma. It was Charizma who heard the little brother of Manak's then-girlfriend come up with a kid-logic goof-off character he called "The Peanut Butter Wolf," and Charizma dared Manak to officially take on the name. The dare was accepted.

Wolf and Charizma became close friends, put together a number of home recordings and demo tapes, and eventually broke on college radio en route to signing with Hollywood Basic with the help of DJ Shadow's then-manager Matt Brown. For a brief moment, they were labelmates with Shadow, as well as 2Pac-collaborating Digital Underground side project Raw Fusion and Paul C protégés Organized Konfusion. And they promisingly came across on their 1993 promo-only single "Red Light, Green Light" as a new-generation West Coast version of MC Shan and Marley Marl, a young visionary MC/DJ team who split the difference between LA Good Life skill-showcase rap and the Bay's cratedigger deep dives.

But that's not what Hollywood turned out to want from them. The label kept turning down Wolf's beats and even suggested bringing in outside production work, a blasphemous notion for a duo that saw themselves as a self-contained unit à la Gang Starr or Pete Rock & C.L. Smooth. That only hardened their resolve, and it would have likely primed them for next-level underground-sensation status if it weren't for a tragic turn of events. On December 16, 1993, Charizma was at a stop light in the run-down neighborhood of East Palo Alto when a carjacker tried to hold him up a gunpoint. When Charizma resisted, the robber shot and killed him. Just like that, one of the most promising hip-hop groups of the West Coast underground was extinguished, and a devastated Wolf couldn't bring himself to even touch his keyboard and sampler again for several months.

For a year or so afterward, just what Wolf wanted to do with his career seemed tenuous and up in the air. He eventually self-released a solo album, the instrumental beat record *Peanut Butter Breaks,* under the quasi-label Heyday Records in 1994. (It was the only release under that imprint; Wolf would discover later that the name for the label was already taken.) But while moving on and making new music was an important part of the process, there was still the idea in the back of Wolf's mind that the music he'd made with Charizma still needed a wider outlet. He shopped around their old demo to labels who were even more unreceptive to their idea of hip-hop than Hollywood Basic was. And soon enough, the frustrations and aspirations scraped up against each other enough that Wolf saw no other choice but to keep going DIY. In 1996, he put out the first commercial release of Charizma & Peanut Butter Wolf's recordings. Fitting to the title of the 12-inch single's A-side, the vinyl-only "My World Premiere" was the first catalog entry in his new label: Stones Throw Records.

Stones Throw slowly began to emerge over the next year as a label focused mostly on Wolf's indie-head vision of hip-hop: singles by Milpitas, California two-man MC crew Homeliss Derilex and solo rapper Encore, and instrumental full-lengths by Bay Area producer Fanatik (*Phanatik Beats*) and Beat Junkies DJ Babu working incognito as the Turntablist (*Super Duck Breaks . . . The Saga Begins*). In a disaster-courting twist, the *Super Duck Breaks* comp became an early (and accidental) financial boon for Stones Throw when Wolf's first choice for a pressing plant, Canoga Park's Rainbo Records, turned out subpar-quality vinyl that wore out quickly. This meant that unbeknownst to Wolf, the hyperspeed-scratching battle DJs would render their copies unusable after a few sessions, but since the collection was such a formidable scratch-battle tool, the DJs would keep buying fresh copies anyways.

*Rob Swift Presents Soulful Fruit,* a solo scratch showcase from one of the X-Men crew, showed a willingness to support foundational DJs out of New York alongside the Cali contingent. And San Mateo rapper Rasco, who'd built a following in the Bay as part of a group called Various Blends, emerged on the label as a solo artist with a string of singles and an album, 1998's *Time Waits for No Man,* that earned critical respect outside the usual cratedigger quarters—even if contemporaneous reviews made it a point to emphasize a certain indie-label obscurity to it. (Matt Conaway wrote for *AllMusic,* "With no major label throwing huge promotion dollars anywhere near his vicinity, Rasco is forced to do things the old fashioned way: word of mouth.")

Wolf's label was building a roster, but it was still a short distance away from actually making a name for itself—creating a brand, an identity, a rep. But just like Charizma and PBW were discovered through college radio, Wolf made a discovery of his own: The Lootpack's "Attack of the Tupperware Puppets" hit the airwaves while he was listening, and the song's murky, woozily tense sleigh-bell jazz sent him rushing to the phone to call the station's DJ so he could get the contact info for the group. After using his position in record distribution to order a thousand copies of the "Psyche Move" 12-inch on Crate Diggers Palace, Wolf met up with Otis Sr., Madlib, and the rest of the Lootpack crew and signed them up to Stones Throw. At the time, Wolf figured he'd just signed a dope crew with some solid potential. What he wound up with was one of the single most important, scene-defining catalysts in the entire hip-hop underground.

If there was one thing Wolf and Madlib could really connect over, it was a deep immersion in the wide-open possibilities of beatmaking. While Wolf still lived in the Bay Area, Madlib would come up from Oxnard to spend weeks recording in Wolf's home studio. And as Wolf kept putting together tracks for other rappers, as well as assembling the beats for his own full-length *My Vinyl Weighs a Ton,* he was firsthand witness to Madlib's working methods. Where some producers would take a week to make the beat for a single track, Madlib would just keep making beats, often finishing them after a first draft, until he'd accumulated somewhere in the neighborhood of twenty after a day's worth of work. It wasn't that Madlib was fickle or lazy—it's that he had a ton of ideas and a long-brewing plan of how to make them all work, coupled with a disinterest in lingering too long on a single beat and overworking it to death.

But first, he had to work out his influences. You can hear it clearly in 1999's *Soundpieces: Da Antidote,* Lootpack's first and to date only full-length album on Stones Throw. "Whenimondamic," first released as a single in 1998, is one of Madlib's simpler early beats, a bassline that resembles the rhythmic pattern from KRS-One's self-produced 1993 track "Return of the Boom Bap" but with a bit more melody to it, and drums that lift from EPMD's P-Funky 1989 "So What Cha Sayin'" rendered to sound older than its nine years. Oddly pitched vocal interjections and subtly layered-in electric piano keep it sounding like a subtle skewing of the usual boom-bap hip-hop angles; Madlib shrugs off his older work with the modesty of an always-looking-forward workaholic, but there's a sense he's toying with the precedent that his direct predecessors had laid down.

It's apparent on other cuts, too: "Long Awaited," featuring LA crew Dilated Peoples, takes the by-then-omnipresent siren-creak from the intro to ESG's "UFO" and pits it against an early '70s work of lounge jazz from the KPM library music label. (Library music—written and recorded by work-for-hire musicians for commercial licensing purposes, and available in a variety of styles from easy listening to jazz-funk to avant-garde experimental electronics—would become a cratedigger's bonanza once word of albums from British labels like De Wolfe, Chappell, and KPM made their way across the Atlantic.) "New Year's Resolution" drops in a soundbite from Gang Starr's '94 cut "Mass Appeal" as a brief rhythmic counterpoint to a beat primarily built around the baroque harpsichords and psychedelic orchestral jazz swing of David Axelrod's 1968 William Blake homage "Merlin's Prophecy." And one track, "Wanna Test," rode on a chop of Al Green's "I Wish You Were Here" that sounded like him stepping into RZA's shoes just to check out how they fit. Madlib's beats refracted hip-hop in on itself, samples of samples of samples.

In its own way, *Soundpieces: Da Antidote!* was Madlib's way of working through the question of indie rap's torch-carrying tendencies. Was it really nostalgia for a vanishing style that gangsta rap and "jiggy" pop crossover had threatened to eclipse? Or was it something more fundamentally postmodern and self-aware, the first defining moment of a career steeped in hip-hop as a more limitless way of mediating music's past? The Lootpack's record has the spirit of 1989 all over it— twenty-four tracks, stuffed with interstitial skits and jokey conceptual references — that are easily traced back to the oddball tendencies of Prince Paul's work with De La Soul. There's even a gear-nerd reference, simple but still something of an insider nod, in the intro, where Madlib's voice announces to a receptionist that "I have an appointment with Dr. SP at 1200 hours," which really only makes literal sense if you can imagine him actually treating his sampler as something he only visits intermittently instead of spending all of his waking hours tinkering with it.

And nothing got to Madlib's philosophy as a producer and a DJ quite like a twofer of tracks he cut with Lootpack in 1999 and 2000. The first, *Soundpieces* cut "Crate Diggin'," rode its rubbery beat like a circus wagon on oval wheels, Vanilla Fudge's overblown hippie-dip cavort through the Beatles' "Eleanor Rigby" tweaked for maximum zootedness. Madlib's the only Lootpack MC who actually raps on it, and the hook is all his, too: "Hey yo, how many know about crate diggin'? / What does crate diggin' mean to me? / Diggin' for them unordinary soundin' loops / Even if it's not clean to thee." Its sequel, the B-side to the 12-inch of a remix of Lootpack's "Weededed," is given the similarly straightforward title "The Loop Digga," and already pushes Madlib's sound of unpredictable spur-of-the-moment spontaneity into layers upon layers in the process of building a mental picture with beats.

Comedy-suspense synthesizers from an early '80s library record are interrupted by screeching tires when Madlib switches from an explanation of his style ("I'm the type of brother that don't like to hear the same thing / Over and over so I don't listen to the radio / I go beat shopping with my brothers or my lady, yo") to announce that "I'm out, I gotta go to the record store." His scattered internal monologue is set to an interstitial loop of Nucleus's 1973 jazz-prog cut "Roots" before announcing Medaphoar's guest verse with another library music sample flip, this time of Brian Bennett's 1978 cosmic funk synth instrumental "Solstice." And once Madlib actually arrives at the store, the beat switches up again as he flips through the crates, overwhelmed with possibility: David Axelrod, Steve Kuhn ("You know that got some Fender Rhodes on it"), Roy Ayers, Ornette Coleman, the music fan as listener turned collector turned creator. The track's not even four minutes and it's got enough samples and loops and ideas for at least five different songs.

That could be a side effect of Madlib's working method: quickly made tracks kept raw by a general disinterest in sprucing them up or mastering them to sound cleaner. But raw isn't sloppy, and quickly made isn't tossed off; it's like he just had a way of directly translating the particular essence of what he could glean from a recording, isolating the part most likely to leave an impression, building a beat from it, and efficiently translating just what it's like to get a piece of music stuck in your head. And as Madlib would prove over the next decade, both his record shelves and his imagination had limitless resources.

# 11 | *The Illest Villains*
## High Concepts and New Voices

**The deeper conceptual possibilities of hip-hop production let
two likeminded artists explore transformative alter egos.**

MADLIB HAD A PROBLEM: he didn't like the sound of his own voice. This
was more a personal idiosyncrasy than the kind of weakness that stood
out to others, and even during his early Lootpack years he sounded perfectly at home over his beats. His MCing was personable and heavy on
simple but evocative imagery—conscious without preachiness, funny
without buffoonery, and frequently quotable. (A highlight from Lootpack's "Hityawitdat": "I drop a pound of discussion and drop a rhyme to
leave you with a concussion / And have your whole crew commence to
hushin'.") There was something in his flow, in his voice, that didn't over-
exert itself too much: if anything, he sounded positively conversational,
hitting vocal emphases in ways that shifted from line to meter-altering
line as a counter-effect to his own beats' steadiness.

But the fact remained that Madlib had a certain self-consciousness
about the timbre of his voice, often drawing his own tongue-in-cheek
comparison to the rumbly baritone of soul icon Barry White. It didn't
always fit the loopy energy he was so easily able to express through his
beats; in a 2013 interview with *Wax Poetics* he described it as "low" and
"all tired-sounding." A delivery like that could definitely evoke a certain
stoned-but-lucid feeling, sativa-steeped illogic rearranged to make perfectly clear sense. Still, it left a relentlessly eclectic MC with one less
tool in his arsenal, a monotone where the rest of his work was kaleidoscopic.

So what would it mean to change it? Hip-hop was a genre where you
could make any amount of tweaks and alterations to a sample or a loop
or a break that you wanted, but the MC's voice itself was sacred. There
were exceptions, but usually they were confined to a certain region or a

particular niche, like the slowed-down, codeine-paced mixes that Houston's city-defining DJ Screw pioneered in the early '90s. And even then, those were remixes; the original voice could always be found elsewhere. It's not like the personality of the MC was altered in any way.

Still, Madlib worked at it, even before the first Lootpack album came out. He'd get in a certain headspace, often with the assistance of psychedelic mushrooms, and then let his psilocybin-fueled inspiration run wild. He'd make a beat, slow it down, and rap in his normal voice, albeit at a reduced enough pace that he'd match the slow-motion rhythm. Then, when he switched the beat back to its original tempo, his voice would sound pitched up but otherwise at a normally coherent speed, à la the old Alvin and the Chipmunks records. Madlib found a few advantages to this approach that went beyond just finding another spin on his voice—it freed him up to get a little more comedically explicit (and initially kept his mom from finding out it was actually him doing all those curse words)—and soon he'd come up with an entirely new character to represent that side of him: Quasimoto.

Quasimoto would eventually appear on a few Lootpack tracks, though it was a recording session circa 1997, a personal experiment never meant to be released, that Wolf overheard and encouraged Madlib to pursue further. Not only was the album's worth of material a bit more unorthodox and experimental in his choice of samples—leaning heavily on his jazz enthusiasms, melded into a more lo-fi and bass-heavy take on his early '90s East Coast influencers—but Madlib's sensibility was already starting to manifest itself in a more clearly idiosyncratic way than even his weirder Lootpack cuts were.

Soon, Madlib went from having Lootpack tracks that featured Quasimoto to Quasimoto tracks that featured Lootpack. "Discipline 99" was a nod to Madlib hero and avant-garde jazz piano great Sun Ra that had the helium-voiced alter ego deriding the limitations of other artists' styles while "Lord Quas keep the crowd from booin' / Always stay true 'n.'" A strange line—Quas wasn't actually a voice that could be reproduced for a live crowd, and for him to stay true would mean to play the role of a caricaturized invention—but he said it like he believed it, and why not believe it then?

The single that track appeared on, 1999's "Microphone Mathematics" 12-inch, also gave Quasimoto's unreal voice a surreal body. Three alien-like bipedal aardvark-esque creatures drawn by visual artist/producer Keith "DJ Design" Griego appeared on the sleeve art, and despite its nonspecific representation—it was originally just supposed to represent a general "bad character," with Quas himself depicted as a featureless Cadillac-passenger silhouette on the cover of 2000 debut *The Unseen*—the creature's adapted appearance as redrawn by Stones Throw in-house artist Jeff Jank soon became more immediately associated with the Quasimoto name. Madlib clicked with the new visual identity, as he recalls in the 2013 documentary *Our Vinyl Weighs a Ton: This Is Stones Throw Records:* "It sounded like what it looked like . . . a pig-faced Alf nigga." There was something a bit midnight-movie about it that clicked, too. Madlib's deep interest in René Laloux's 1973 psychedelic animated sci-fi film *La Planète sauvage,* aka *Fantastic Planet,* had lingered in his music; he'd even concocted his own alternate soundtrack to it, though the mournful orchestral acid funk of Alain Goraguer's original score was an often-sampled component in his beats as well. Now, Madlib had a visual representation of a figure that embodied his own excursions into the outer reaches.

*The Unseen* was the end product of a month on mushrooms and a deeper-than-previous dive into the increasingly far-flung margins of Madlib's rapidly expanding record collection. The formative inspirations were still audible; the kick-snare-bassline juxtapositions feinted at nods to early-to-mid-'90s NYC boom-bap, especially the jazz-laced strains of it that made albums like Nas's *Illmatic* and Gang Starr's *Daily Operation* sound tough and refined at the same time. But Madlib molded it from stranger stuff: Goraguer's *Planète sauvage* score mingled with jazz of every stripe from soul crossovers to cosmic freeform explorations, a gamut run from early post-bop to the slickest of late '70s fusion.

No concessions were made to purism, the generation-stretching gulf between classic drums/bass/piano/horn jazz combos and synthesized funk/rock futurism bridged with a logic that actually *sounded* like flipping through a loosely organized record collection. The lyrics bore that out, too, with total namedrop anthems "Return of the Loop Digga" and "Jazz Cats Pt. 1." The former was another record store travelogue, featuring an interlude dealing with a haplessly underinformed and outmatched clerk who doesn't know his Grant Green from his Stanley Cowell from his Chick Corea. The meat of the lyrics reveal even deeper dives, from David Axelrod ("I'm tackling gods and dogs on Holy Thursday") to a litany of names only experts were expected to know:

"Keeping Clifford Jordan on down to Willie Mason / The Propositions, Cassietta George, good for lacin'." The funny thing about Madlib listing those names is that as much as it seems like a deliberate breaking of the sample-spotter's code of silence, it almost stands out as a dare to other producers to make it all cohere.

And "Jazz Cats Pt. 1" was even more audacious in its tracing of influences: MCs are often encouraged to rap about what they know, but what Madlib knows most is music itself. And so his hip-hop was music about music about music, lyrics rattling off signifiers even faster than the beat does. "Jazz Cats Pt. 1" only samples four acknowledged artists— one selection by John Coltrane ("Central Park West," which appears as a snippet after the Quas voice mentions him), two from Cannonball Adderley's 1971 session *Black Messiah* ("Eye of the Cosmos" and "Circumference"), another two from Herbie Hancock's 1964 *Empyrean Isles* ("The Egg," which makes up the bulk of the beat, and "Oliloqui Valley"), and one from the enigmatic sax player Tyrone Washington (1974's "Universal Spiritual Revolt," one of the last things he recorded before disappearing from music completely).

But everyone he names in the lyrics is at least possible to connect to his sound, from the first-mentioned likes of Sun Ra to the borderline punchline/postscript nod to pop-crossover star sax player David Sanborn. Between those two points, he rolls out a litany of names that would keep any record store's jazz section well stocked: avant-garde and free jazz heroes like Albert Ayler, Art Ensemble of Chicago, and Paul Bley; bebop titans from Thelonious Monk and Dizzy Gillespie to Hampton Hawes and Lee Morgan; fusion greats Weather Report and George Duke—"Even Kool & the Gang got jazz for that ass," Madlib proclaims.

Many of these artists were considered incompatible or even at odds with each other by a contemporary if aging contingent of jazz critics and historians, a mental block that would still manifest in a high-profile way mere months later. Ken Burns's ten-episode *Jazz* miniseries, which debuted on PBS half a year after *The Unseen* came out, was pilloried for condensing everything that happened in the genre from 1961 onward into a single 108-minute concluding episode that depicted both Ornette Coleman's free jazz and Miles Davis's funk/rock crossover as betrayals of jazz's true spirit. Aesthetic-conservative talking heads like Wynton Marsalis and Stanley Crouch, who were featured in Burns's documentary as preservationists against this genre-fracturing mutation, would doubtlessly be mortified to hear Madlib mention '70s fusion superstars Weather Report in the same breath as pioneering bebop drummer Max Roach. Good. Keep 'em guessing. "There's plenty more that I could name," Madlib concludes, "but ya'll won't put them to use."

*The Unseen* held early signs of Madlib's broader musical interests, too: occasional excursions into reverb-soaked, murky basslined dub and reggae seeped through the margins of *The Unseen* like potently warm vapor. One of the most enjoyable surprises is a portion of Augustus Pablo's 1978 instrumental track "Unfinished Melody," a fluttering melodica drifting cheerfully over chiming bells and tendon-straining bass, opening "Goodmorning Sunshine" before a computer melody from Prince Jammy's digital-dub "Wafer Scale Integration" takes over, muffled beneath Madlib's kick-heavy drum programming to the point of becoming almost subliminal.

Did these disparate pieces flow together seamlessly? Not always, but that just made the eclecticism more arresting, a sort of cratedigger wire-fu that somehow becomes more thrilling when you can see the strings. Just the idea of "Green Power" putting George Russell, the scholarly modal theorist and composer who revolutionized how bebop was structured in the early 1950s, next to frictionless '70s/'80s smooth-fusion crossover notable Bobby Lyle, and connecting them with the vibes-and-kalimba percussive melody from a track by NYC Afro-jazz-funk crew Mandrill, felt like a lesson in musical deconstruction. *What else could you do from there?*

And the very presence of that manic, raconteurish Lord Quas voice—especially juxtaposed with Madlib's own natural delivery, which sounded not so much tired as it did bemused—had the effect of bending space around him, a sort of hip-hop theater that nodded in Prince Paul's skit-laden direction but dug even further back to the proto-rap performances of Melvin Van Peebles. Van Peebles is best known nowadays for his 1971 film *Sweet Sweetback's Baadasssss Song,* which kicked off a blaxploitation craze that his movie's deeper French New Wave influence, independent guerilla filmmaking, and Black Panther endorsement transcended. But Van Peebles, an accomplished poet, songwriter, director, and stage and screen actor, also wrote and performed in a number of stage plays and recorded a handful of albums— song / spoken word / poetry / comedy / theater hybrids that cast a satirical if empathetic eye to the postwar black working-class experience in America, with Van Peebles playing an entire cast of characters.

In a sense, Van Peebles's work was the last piece of *The Unseen*'s puzzle: Madlib sampled his recordings liberally, particularly 1971's *Ain't Supposed to Die a Natural Death*. And they were used to the point where the vocal interjections of all the characters Van Peebles played became call-and-responses or the backbone for Quasimoto's own ruminations. Beyond the similar titles that riffed off the Van Peebles performances they were sampling — "Come on Feet," "Put a Curse on You," "Good-morning Sunshine"—there was a shared sense of nodding to that tradition of musical poetry and character acting as a way to riff on a black American experience that had changed, but not in unrecognizable ways, over a generation. The sources were old, and the interjections came from someone else's voice. But it was the same world one way or another, even if you could hear the weathered vinyl crackle and the instruments hiss through another era's fidelity. It wouldn't be the last time Madlib drew on his influences to hide in plain sight, concealed under another time and another name.

• • •

By the end of 2000, the success of both the Lootpack's *Soundpieces* and Quasimoto's *The Unseen* fueled Wolf's notion that Madlib would provide a major portion of the Stones Throw sound. And in order to more easily work with the producer, Wolf was inspired to relocate the label to Los Angeles. The four biggest pillars of Stones Throw at the time — Wolf, Madlib, Jeff Jank, and general manager Eothen "Egon" Alapatt— all set up a headquarters in a house in the hills of the Mount Washington neighborhood. One of the house's more unusual features was an actual built-in bomb shelter, a space that previous owners had built in the 1950s to withstand nuclear attack; naturally, this became the Stones Throw in-house studio, which retained the "Bomb Shelter" identity but provided an entirely different plan for surviving into an uncertain future.

It was here, in the wake of *The Unseen*'s freedom-granting success, that Madlib made himself a few new musical acquaintances and united them under the banner of Yesterdays New Quintet. They were all jazz musicians — still amateurish and self-taught, but adventurous enough to fit Madlib's vision of a live-band post-bop in the spirit of experimental hip-hop. Ahmad Miller played the vibes, a bit more percussively and sparse than the melodic likes of Roy Ayers or Gary Burton, but his off-kilter timing was flavorful and meshed well with the similarly carefree keyboards of Joe McDuphrey. Bassist Monk Hughes and percussionist Malik Flavors made for a steady if unshowy soul jazz rhythmic back-bone, complementing the beat without overwhelming it and opting for maintaining the groove over going for solo showcases. And holding it all together was the man billed as Otis Jackson Jr., credited with playing an assortment of percussion and keyboards under his government name, as a nod to his musician father.

A clarification: in saying that "Madlib made himself a few new musical acquaintances," he actually *made* them, whole cloth, from his imagination. Miller, McDuphrey, Hughes, and Flavors were all Madlib working under assumed identities, playing all the instruments on his own and assembling them into an ensemble effort after the fact. Yester-days New Quintet first emerged through the 2001 album *Angles Without Edges,* an uncanny multitracked and studio-assembled representation of a group of up-and-coming players jamming together live. The mood was distinctly keyed into a hip-hop head's vision of 1970s soul jazz and early fusion; if the versions of the 1974 Maurice White–cowritten Ramsey Lewis hit "Sun Goddess" and Ramp's 1977 cut "Daylight" were only part of the picture, the remainder of the album's mid-tempo, break-focused idea of itself was the giveaway. Though Madlib came up through a jazz upbringing before even becoming aware of hip-hop as a youth, the Yes-terdays New Quintet project hung in a sort of netherworld of genre. His efforts to reverse-engineer a body of jazz music just to familiarize him-self with the ways his formative source material was played could only really manifest itself through the methodology of DIY beatmaking, a producer creating a Möbius strip of hip-hop by refracting himself.

The Yesterdays New Quintet concept grew even more ambitious in its tangle of acknowledgments, pseudonyms, and influences when Madlib released a collection of Stevie Wonder covers under the YNQ name in 2002, then proceeded to put out an increasingly focused and distinct number of singles and EPs for each "member" of the group through-out the next couple years: 2002's Joe McDuphrey Experience small-combo soul jazz *Experience EP* (introducing a new bassist, Russel Jenkins, another Madlib alter ego), Ahmad Miller's summery, mellow 2003 EP *Say Ah!* (now crediting the vibes player with flute and synthesizer as well), a 2004 full-length tribute to cosmic-funk great Weldon Irvine credited to Monk Hughes & the Outer Realm, and a percussion-heavy free jazz album that same year from Malik Flavors titled *Ugly Beauty*.

Those releases surrounded a stretch in Madlib's career where his jazz enthusiasms and bona fides had become so noteworthy that Blue Note let him dig around in their archives to remix and rework (or, in the words of a Lou Donaldson spoken interlude, "repossess") some selections from their catalog. *Shades of Blue* drew on a strong range of selections from hard bop to fusion, including Ronnie Foster's "Mystic Brew"—famously flipped by A Tribe Called Quest's "Electric Relaxation"—reimagined as a disco-adjacent party jam called "Mystic Bounce," and a partially live version of Horace Silver's "Song of My Father" that matched up Monk Hughes, Malik Flavors, and Joe McDuphrey up with actual non-Madlib musicians from funk group Connie Price and the Keystones.

At this time, Stones Throw was also starting to distinguish itself as a label that saw its hip-hop-based engagement with earlier music as a gateway toward approaching, preserving, and reviving the kinds of obscure jazz and soul records that had been a mainstay of DJ crates from the beginning. Egon's role in Stones Throw came after years of fascinated research into the work of mainstream-neglected but hip-hop-revered producers and composers like David Axelrod and Galt MacDermot. Egon actually spent much of the late '90s and early '00s working with MacDermot, composer of Broadway smash *Hair* and the musician behind deep-crate treasures like 1966's "Coffee Cold" and 1970's "Ripped Open by Metal Explosions." The gig came about on the heels of a wave of East Coast hip-hop producers—including Vic "V.I.C." Padilla from the Beatnuts and D.I.T.C. member Buckwild—realizing that MacDermot lived in Staten Island, had boxes of unsold copies of breakbeat-goldmine records like 1966's *Shapes of Rhythm* and 1969's *Woman Is Sweeter* gathering dust in his basement, and would strike up a rapport with the hip-hoppers who relished a chance to buy his records and pick his brain.

It was Egon who really started to dig the deepest. By 2001, a gig working with MacDermot's label Kilmarnock Records saw him help get the record catalog in order, track down original masters and hard-to-find acetates, and begin an effort in earnest to reissue some of Galt's rare and unreleased tracks. When *Up from the Basement* hit shelves in 2000, Egon's liner notes highlighted an idea of a record collector as archivist,

and in the context of the DJ, that meant someone who "shares new discoveries with an audience in the hopes of fostering a knowledge of the
music being played." No more steaming the labels off—this was a matter of acknowledging your sources openly, paying them respect, and giving them their flowers while they could still smell them.

When Egon hooked up with Stones Throw in 2000—he'd been in
correspondence with Wolf since the label emerged in '96—it didn't take
him long to transfer that curatorial, antiquarian sense to his new label.
And when an exhaustively researched compilation of rare and obscure
funk he assembled, *The Funky 16 Corners,* became an independent sensation for Stones Throw, it opened up the door for him to establish his
own imprint, Now-Again Records, dedicated to expanding the cratedigger sense of discovery into a full-fledged reissue label.

If Yesterdays New Quintet and Now-Again both posited the idea of
the record-collecting hip-hop enthusiast as a conduit for musical rediscovery—an extrapolation of the canon expansion that saw the *Ultimate
Breaks & Beats* standbys making room for the jazz-digger greats of the
East Coast, then the basement-raiding turntablists and MPC-wielding
obscurity-seekers out West—it also dovetailed with the growing movement to build a sort of shared musical knowledge as an identity of sorts,
a more benevolent, transformative, and progressive version of the old
vinyl-hoarding trope that saw a historical interest and fascination borne
through hands-on work.

It wasn't just listening to a band and affecting its aesthetic—it was
putting in the time, decoding the pieces, pulling them apart, and reassembling them that helped grow the knowledge of where this music
actually came from, what it first meant, and what else it could mean in
the hands of someone decades later. When an artist like Madlib used
that knowledge to build a new facade of his musical self with those old
formative records as a mediator, the opportunities for self-expression
ironically became even more wide open. Even more so when he got a
major chance to help an even more enigmatic and chameleonic artist
express himself.

• • •

Daniel Dumile was about ten years old when WHBI's Zulu Beats Show
changed everything for him. The London-born son of a Trinidadian
mother and a Zimbabwean father had moved with his family to Long

Island in the mid-'70s, and the same atmosphere that informed Prince
Paul and De La Soul was working its magic on him and his younger
brother Dingilizwe. In the hands of Zulu Nation's teenage phenom DJ
Afrika Islam, the Zulu Beats Show would become a kaleidoscopic showcase of hip-hop breaks that featured something extra: cut-ins of comedy
skits, movie clips, cartoons, and all sorts of strange and amusing drops.
The Dumile brothers would make it appointment listening in the early
'80s, and between that and the occasional glimpse at young local DJs
spinning practice sessions, their fascination with hip-hop was secured.

They came up with the name first: KMD, or Kausing Much Damage. It was a name for what they considered to be their hip-hop crew,
though what the crew actually did slowly shifted focus across the "four
elements" of hip-hop, moving from graffiti to breakdancing to their
eventual wheelhouse of rapping and DJing. By 1988, the teenage Dumile
brothers had given themselves aliases—Daniel was Zev Love X on the
mic, and Dingilizwe became MC/DJ Subroc—relocated with their
parents farther south along the island to Long Beach, New York, put
together demos, refined their craft, and met up with another up-and-
comer on the community talent show circuit who went by the name
MC Serch. KMD's introduction to the wider hip-hop world was auspi-
cious: when Serch's group 3rd Bass cut their cult classic "The Gas Face,"
Zev Love X got a booming special introduction from Don Newkirk and
a hard-knocking Prince Paul beat over which to rhyme his intricately
allusive verse. Dante Ross, the A&R rep who got De La Soul signed to
Tommy Boy, heard a similar potential in KMD and got them signed to
Elektra.

1991's *Mr. Hood* stood somewhere between those Zulu Beat Shows
the Dumiles had heard ten years back and the skit-laden sample-collage
narratives of the early De La Soul records; it even shared its May 14,
1991, release date with *De La Soul Is Dead*. Record shoppers picking
up a twofer would find some notable differences, though, with KMD's
through line of Afrocentrism and Nation of Islam doctrine woven
through the works more prominently than De La's more personal-as-
political approach. The group's logo, drawn by Zev Love X, was a grotesque racist cartoon caricature of a black "sambo"-style face with a red
circle/slash "no" sign over it, an anti-stereotype image addressed in the
track "Who Me?" ("In my logo you see us? / Whoever said that coon
was me?") that reinforced their lyrical themes of black consciousness

and uplift. That *Mr. Hood* felt overall good-natured throughout, and benefited from KMD's ear for comedic juxtapositions, made it a strong statement without coming across as humorless. When an album's titular foil is a square-sounding but belligerent thug sourced from a 1960s Spanish-language instructional record and Bert from *Sesame Street* kicks knowledge with the MCs, even the deepest Five Percenter references feel accessible, even welcoming.

But the follow-up wasn't what Elektra wanted. Like De La and countless other hip-hop acts who'd grown from youthful enthusiasm to industry-soured skepticism, KMD put some older-and-wiser edge and disillusionment into their second album and pushed its sound and imagery further than their major label was comfortable with. They called it *Black Bastards,* and the cover was the same sambo caricature Zev drew for the group's logo—only this time, as the subject of a literal game of Hangman, dangling from a noose on a gallows. Subroc in particular had hipped Zev to a certain us-against-the-world revenge narrative picked up from blaxploitation films—*Sweet Sweetback's Baadasssss Song* chief among them—and with third member Onyx receding from the group, the two Dumile brothers elevated each other into a harder, more irreverent version of KMD. In fact, Zev credited Subroc for much of his lyrical growth—a reversal of the usual big-brother dynamic, with the younger brother being the one bringing the fire new ideas and a finely honed style on the mic.

*Black Bastards* seemed prime for the grimier turn East Coast hip-hop would soon take in '93 with the breakthrough of groups like Wu-Tang Clan and Black Moon. ("Sweet Premium Wine" even samples dialogue from 1979's kung-fu film *World of the Drunken Master,* a RZA move before most people knew what RZA moves even were.) You can hear their lyrics growing rawer and closer to street level: weed takes on a significantly higher profile in the subject matter ("Smokin' That Shit"; "Contact Blitt"; "Suspended Animation"), Zev talks gunplay on "Get U Now," and "Plumskinzz (Oh No I Don't Believe It!)" takes the sex rhymes of *Mr. Hood* single "Peachfuzz" to more explicit ends—at least, once the abstract metaphors were untangled.

And the production evolved, too: if *Mr. Hood* was largely a series of off-kilter funk and soul flips, *Black Bastards* upped the influence of '60s and '70s soul jazz and free jazz to rival anything else coming out of New York at the time. The sibling production unit built the low-end slap of

"It Sounded Like a Roc" around the deep Cecil McBee basslines from Pharoah Sanders's album *Thembi,* drew from the piano/bassline melody of Bobbi Humphrey's "Blacks and Blues" to make "Plumskinzz" sound like sophisticated raunch, and jazz greats like Lee Morgan, Freddie Hubbard, and Cannonball Adderley added melodic elements to the album's murky if brisk drum samples. It still had its idiosyncrasies, though: excerpts from *The Blue Guerrilla,* Last Poets member Gylain Kain's solo spoken word album, were scattered through *Black Bastards* as a narrative thread commenting sardonically on black identity. And one track, the eventual lead single "What a Nigga Know?" (or "Niggy" in the radio edit), actually got its melodic refrain from Jody Watley's candy-sweet 1987 dance-pop smash "Looking for a New Love." It wouldn't be the last time Zev had a hand in turning an '80s R&B hit into something even the most hardcore hip-hop head could swear by.

But on April 23, 1993, it all fell under the heartbreaking category of What Could Have Been: Subroc was attempting to cross the stretch of Interstate 495 locally known as the Long Island Expressway on foot when a car struck and killed him. The album only had two songs left to be mixed and finished when the tragedy struck—3rd Bass member Pete Nice recalled Zev playing the nearly complete *Black Bastards* at Subroc's wake from a boombox set up beside his brother's casket—but a devastated Zev spent nearly a year completing it, and took pains to leave in as many remnants of Subroc's voice as he could. Even an outtake of him ad-libbing "What is you, stupid? Make my voice deeper!" was left in "Constipated Monkey." And on "Suspended Animation," the track that originally closed the album as intended, he gets the last line in a context turned tragic after the fact: "Subroc, my word is bond and I'm gone." After that, silence.

Nearly one year after Subroc's death, once the album was finally mastered and "What a Nigga Know?" hit shelves as a lead single, Elektra called Zev into the office. It was April 8, 1994, less than a month before the promoted May 3 release date, and label chairman Bob Krasnow had some news for Zev: the label was worried about media blowback over the album. The single would be decried in the following week's issue of *Billboard* by rap columnist Havelock Nelson for its title and the sleeve's usage of the KMD sambo logo ("Regardless of what the group was attempting to achieve with this imagery and the term, many in the black community will find them offensive. It's inexcusable that the executives at Elektra allowed these images to slip through"). Worse yet, the label had also received word that the "hangman" artwork had been leaked to another *Billboard* columnist, Terri Rossi, who would damn the entire project in her "R&B Rhythms" column shortly afterward as hateful: "To promote lynching is just plain evil. A holocaust is the same whether it is millions at a time or one at a time that ends up affecting millions . . . maybe [Zev] needs a refresher course on the entire civil rights movement . . . Martin Luther King is spinning in his grave."

Zev's protests to the contrary were clear: the character being hung wasn't promoting lynching, it was the death of "the whole concept and stereotype of our people being displayed as minstrels or servants or fools." And despite the side routes into sex, weed, and guns, *Black Bastards* wasn't a hardcore gangsta album, at least not in the same sense that other artists distributed under the Warner-Elektra-Atlantic umbrella like Dre, Snoop, or Tupac were; it was clear to any listener that the Afrocentric consciousness they exhibited on their first album had hardly receded. Elektra didn't buy it. Zev offered to change the artwork, but the decision had already been made: with parent company Time Warner still stinging from the "Cop Killer" controversy and the corporation's annual board of trustees meeting just a week out, *Black Bastards* was dropped from release. Elektra gave Zev back the masters, a check for $25,000, and their permission to try and shop it elsewhere. *Black Bastards* should've been the record that put KMD up into the ranks of the greats, an album that split the difference between the release-date-sharing *Midnight Marauders* and *Enter the Wu-Tang* in its combination of jazziness and rawness. But it never got a release date of its own.

"[He] seemed really unfazed by it," Dante Ross stated in an interview with *Rap Genius* in February 2013. "He said to me, 'I should get dropped more often every day . . . I'm gonna get $25,000 and my record back.'" And an editorial in the May 1994 issue of *The Source* depicted Zev as "only a little vexed when he stopped by *The Source* the evening he had been dropped, since he seemed confident about getting a new deal." But Zev soon learned that it was hard to shop an already-rejected album: "It was a dead album, everybody was scared of it. We shopped it and everybody shot it down." After even Pete Nice's cosign and Bobbito Garcia's tastemaking couldn't get him signed to their short-lived Columbia imprint Hoppoh Records, Zev gave up, started to split his time between New York and his family's home in Georgia, and vanished from hip-hop's radar. But if the KMD name was radioactive, and Zev Love X was no longer a name to check for, Daniel Dumile had an alias to spare. He alluded to it on "Figure of Speech," a KMD track from *Mr. Hood*: "Sounds are boomin', MCs shouts 'Doom is in the house!'"

The emergence of MF Doom was long in the making, shrouded in mystery and riddled with rumors. (Depending on the context, the "MF" stands for "Metal Face" or "Metal Fingers," the latter used for a long-running series of instrumental beat tapes, *Special Herbs,* he released throughout the 2000s.) The groundwork was laid as early as 1995: rapper and friend Kurious, who was the main beneficiary of the Hoppoh Records imprint before it went under, directed Doom to Bobbito's new indie label Fondle 'Em Records as a possible outlet for *Black Bastards*. But while four tracks from the album and their instrumentals eventually emerged under the title *Black Bastards Ruffs + Rares* in 1998, it was this new semi-incognito identity that got attention first.

There was very recent precedent for a move like Doom's: his fellow NYC-rooted, disillusioned golden era great Kool Keith had weathered the end of the Ultramagnetic MCs' heyday with the beginnings of a marathon-length solo career in the mid-'90s, going from his Fondle 'Em–launching collab in the Cenobites to his collaboration with Dan the Automator as Dr. Octagon. Both Doom and Dr. Octagon were villainous alter egos inspired by pulp media—Dumile's new persona came from cartoons, comic books, and UHF-aired monster movies, while Keith's fascination with both horror films and porno fueled 1996's *Dr. Octagonecologyst*—but Keith was always able to revert back to the version of himself that had existed on wax since the mid-'80s whenever he felt like it, which he did less than a year after Dr. Octagon's emergence for 1997's *Sex Style*. Zev Love X, whoever he was, didn't go on without Subroc. And when Doom finally appeared for the first time rapping in public at the Lower East Side Nuyorican Poets Café, he alternately wore pantyhose or a bandana over his face to obscure his identity.

The 1997 single "Dead Bent / Gas Drawls / Hey!" was Doom's return to recording, and if those in the know recognized the alias, the voice was a different matter. The abstraction was still there, but the voice was huskier and more weathered, and had the kind of relaxed-smartass delivery to it that made his cliché-busting, internal-rhyme-echoing punchlines register with deadpan wit. (From "Hey!": "I only play the games that I win at / And stay the same with more rhymes than there's ways to skin cats / As a matter of fact, let me rephrase: / With more rhymes than there's ways to fillet felines these days.")

His production pulled off a similar trick: the sources of his beats were instantly recognizable, but intentionally warped in ways that made the familiar sound hallucinogenic. "Dead Bent" turned a guitar riff from Isaac Hayes's 1969 psychedelic-soul hit version of Burt Bacharach and Hal David's "Walk on By" into a droning machine-shop whir as Doom crooned off-key parody lyrics to Atlantic Starr's goopy 1987 R&B / adult contemporary ballad "Always." "Gas Drawls" took a couple simple Fender Rhodes licks from Steely Dan's otherwise luxuriously smooth '77 *Aja* opener "Black Cow" and created a mood that felt like it was constantly teetering on the precipice of something wicked; naturally he couldn't resist dropping Donald Fagen's sung lyric "You were very high" into the mix. And for "Hey!" he flipped the kind of beat that would do Prince Paul proud with its sheer goofball audacity: its spooky droning organ, blaring horns, and titular shouted refrain came from the intro to the intro of the early '70s *New Scooby-Doo Movies* cartoon. Listen closely, and you can hear the easily startled Great Dane gulp "Aroo?"

In 1999, the same year he first started appearing in a metallic-looking mask that friend and graffiti artist Blake "KEO" Lethem made for him, Doom's album *Operation: Doomsday* expanded his reach and scope into phenomenon status. In retrospect, it sounds like a natural bridge between the Prince Paul / RZA school of cinematic audio worldbuilding and Madlib's idiosyncratic eclecticism, with clips from old *Fantastic Four* cartoons giving Doom the rapper a similarly wronged, vengeful despotism as Marvel Comics supervillain Doctor Doom and merging '60s four-color kitsch with hip-hop bravado. (Dr. Victor Von Doom's origin story involved the future dictator trying to build a machine that could communicate with a dead family member, only for the device to explode and disfigure him after a rival sabotaged it; the parallels to the *Black Bastards* saga aren't hard to draw.)

The beats got even more audacious, with more unlikely smooth '80s and '90s soul turned boom-bap: the Deele's L.A. Reid/Babyface–produced '87 R&B Top 10 hit "Shoot 'Em Up Movies" for "Red and Gold"; Sade's sophisti-pop gem "Kiss of Life" for "Doomsday"; the S.O.S. Band's 1986 Minneapolis-sound smash "The Finest" for a track of the same title. And, fuck it, why not sample the Beatles while he was at it—and in the weirdest possible manner, building around the tempo-

warping strings of "Glass Onion" for the meter-defying "Tick, Tick . . ."
The fact that the samples weren't very rare or esoteric was something
of a creative choice, though it was also a matter of practicality: as a producer on the move, Doom didn't always have a ton of obscure records
to work with, so he took the most obscure angles from what he already
had, a deliberately rugged and lo-fi counterpoint to the crowd-pleasing
pop-hit reworks that flooded late '90s mainstream rap.

As the conclusion to a decade that saw the rise of artists like Juggaknots, Company Flow, and Black Star anchor a powerful indie market for
underground hip-hop, *Operation: Doomsday* was a watershed—a giddily
creative, cathartic, endlessly playable record with miles of emotional
and philosophical depth beneath its comic-book surface. It caught on
strong in underground circles, and instead of piggybacking off Doom's
previous work with KMD, it started to eclipse it—a memorable, eccentric character dropping rimshot one-liners and knowledge with equal
panache—and might have become an even bigger indie hit if Fondle
'Em hadn't closed its doors in late 2001. (While the label never officially
signed Doom, thus giving him the freedom to release work on other
labels if he wanted, he wound up the label's most prolific and successful artist.) *Operation: Doomsday* would find homes on other labels in the
2000s—first, Sub Verse Music, a label founded by Company Flow member Bigg Jus that also put out a complete and expanded version of *Black
Bastards*—and then later on Doom's own Metal Face Records in a number of collector-edition formats, from an all 7-inch single version to a
deluxe package complete with lunchbox. And while the end of Fondle
'Em left Doom rootless for a year or two, the cult of the supervillain was
already big enough to make his next move closely monitored.

●   ●   ●

As Stones Throw's general manager, Egon had noticed that Madlib's fascination with re-creating the sounds of '60s and '70s jazz and soul were
rooted in a flagging interest in making straight-up hip-hop. And as liberating as it was for Madlib to add a few new twists to his musical arsenal—
along with the jazziness of YNQ, he'd also indulged his enthusiasm for
reggae and dub for the 2002 Trojan Records–cosigned mix *Blunted in the
Bomb Shelter*—Stones Throw was still counting on him to maintain at
least one foot in the style that brought him his first accolades. After an
attempt to get Lootpack back together petered out, Egon followed up

on a dream project Doom namedrop Madlib mentioned to the *Los Ange-les Times* in 2002, and used an old college-friend connection down in the same Atlanta suburb of Kennesaw where Doom lived to hit up the reclu-sive artist.

Doom had gone mostly dormant since *Operation: Doomsday* and was unfamiliar with Madlib or Stones Throw, but after Egon sent Doom a few of Madlib's records, the metal-faced villain found himself enthused to work with this new partner in crime. Stones Throw practically emp-tied their bank account getting Doom to fly out to the Bomb Shelter, but their tenuous financial situation wasn't about to jeopardize the proj-ect of a lifetime. Upon the arrival of Doom and a woman acting as his manager, Egon had to out-and-out distract the latter party out of threat-ening to pull the plug on the whole thing if a $1,500 payoff didn't mate-rialize. Meanwhile, Doom and Madlib hunkered down in the Bomb Shelter for their first in-person meeting and built themselves a working relationship that reinvigorated both artists, even though they spent far more time listening than speaking.

Madlib was making beats with an almost reflexive creative pro-cess. The Boss SP-303 Dr. Sample was a contraption about the size of a paperback book that ran for about $300 new in 2001, and it earned a significant amount of usage from producers in the '00s thanks to its combination of a decent-sized built-in effects library and a lo-fi but warm sound quality that made vinyl recordings sound evocatively gritty. Thanks to the simplicity of the SP-303, Madlib could record a sample, manipulate it, add effects, loop it, layer it, and move on to the next. And while many of them were halfway thought out or just exercises in mess-ing around, he exercised so many different ideas and drew from so many different sources that it was inevitable he'd have countless possibilities for Doom to pick from. These tracks—burned from the SP-303 straight to CD, and collected as *100 Beats* and *100 More Beats*—were the catalyst for Doom's lyrical ideas, hitting at a rate Doom recalled to *Spin* in 2019 of "one out of four, on average, [that] would stand out to me"—a solid quality-to-quantity ratio that eventually pushed their album to nearly two dozen tracks.

Doom would hang out in one part of the Stones Throw house, typ-ically puffing on Sour Diesel blunts on the deck outside and scribbling down verses, while Madlib made more beats in the Bomb Shelter. And by the time Doom had written lyrics to the handful of beats that clicked with him the most, Madlib would arrive with even more. They didn't so much converse with each other as they communicated through the music—as Doom put it during his own Red Bull Music Academy lecture in 2011, "He'd hear a joint and that's my conversation with him. Then I'd hear a beat and that's like what he's saying to me."

And since Madlib was drawing from more musical sources than ever before, the "conversations" he'd have with Doom became elaborately vivid. The album that would become *Madvillainy*—credited to the collective duo name Madvillain—took every sound Madlib picked up and made the whole cohere into a deeply idiosyncratic but unified two-man vision. The beats came from jazz and rock and soul and every unpredictable cross-pollination thereof, plus places even stranger than that.

"Meat Grinder" careened from the queasily lightheaded horns from Frank Zappa and the Mothers of Invention's "Sleeping in a Jar" to a mid-'70s library record that sounded like a drunk-and-high hula routine. "Rainbows" got its alternately slinky and stumbly layer of budget-jazz sleaze from the soundtrack to boobsploitation king Russ Meyer's 1968 strip club flick *Finders Keepers, Lovers Weepers!* (Doom actually sang along to it, to surreal effect.) Instrumental interludes like the Bollywood assemblage "Do Not Fire!" and the dulcimer boom-bap of "Sickfit" kept the vibe feeling like lo-fi transmissions from a world recognizable as the same one that mainstream hip-hop operated in, but several layers below the surface.

There were even in-jokes: if sampling that siren at the beginning of Quincy Jones's theme to *Ironside* was a well-worn hip-hop trope by 2002—the same year Quentin Tarantino used it for a famous series of music cues in *Kill Bill Vol. 1*—Madlib would just chop up alternately cheerful and suspenseful incidental music from one specific episode of the Raymond Burr drama instead. It sounded like he recorded the sample from a boom box sitting next to a TV set, but that only made "All Caps" more delirious.

And while there were touches of jazz on the record, they were deliberately odd ones—like the bassline from organist Lonnie Smith's "In the Beginning" turned into the muffled ambience for a deliberately off-beat drum break, or an abrupt, jumbled snippet of Freddie Hubbard in "Money Folder" dropped in as a sort of punchline cue after Doom's line "I don't think we can handle a style so rancid / They flipped it like Madlib did a old jazz standard." If any jazz musician came out sounding like themselves, it was fusion keyboard wizard George Duke, whose 1975 cut "Prepare Yourself" lent its soaring futurism toward "Operation Lifesaver AKA Mint Test"—and even with his sound left largely unmanipulated, it was in the service of a ninety-second, one-verse song about meeting a woman with halitosis.

The one track where Quasimoto actually appeared might hold another key to the album's identity. "Shadows of Tomorrow" liberally sampled dialogue from Sun Ra's 1974 science fiction movie musical *Space Is the Place,* concluding with the statement that "Equation wise, the first thing to do is to consider time as officially ended. We'll work on the other side of time." And if Madlib's lyrics were intricate chronological koans—"Today is the shadow of tomorrow / Today is the present future of yesterday / Yesterday is the shadow of today"—they also reflected the musical approach of *Madvillainy.* Something in Madlib's beats deliberately courted the sounds of malfunctioning, distorted transformation, of media that sounded like it did thanks to the ravages of age and time. This made a record fresh off the shelf feel like an old paperback or a yellowed newspaper from decades past, connecting with MF Doom's old-soul introspection and observational humor that dislodged the album from any idea of specificity in time and place.

At a time when mainstream hip-hop was slowly but surely abandoning sampling for the more lucrative, less cost-prohibitive options that original studio musicianship could offer, *Madvillainy* used sampling to come across like a paradox: here was an album that couldn't exist without the music of a recognizable past, but didn't sound like any particular moment in time. If sampling itself was increasingly considered a dated relic of hip-hop's old days, *Madvillainy* put forth the idea that the old days hadn't actually happened yet—and might not ever arrive.

These old sounds could feel comedic or nostalgic or unnerving, all while narrowing the gap between artistic profundity and low-budget pulp. But just by being sampled and manipulated with Madlib's first-draft-best-draft spontaneity—the musical equivalent of a Sharpie sketch that felt more alive and more real than a photograph—they became more about the particular intersection of a snippet of musical time manipulated by a voracious listener and beatmaker's of-the-moment thoughts, sampling used not to evoke a specific era or style but to nail down a particular space and personality. Madlib had his methods, and it's hard to imagine any other producer creating something like the beats on *Madvillainy*. But it's impossible to hear *Madvillainy*—not just Doom's allusive but dead-on evocative lyrics, but the voice-overs, the abrupt mood changes, the recursively mind-burrowing loops of unfamiliar music—without recognizing that Madlib didn't just collaborate with Doom, he was *inhabited* by Doom. Why stop at building a beat when you could build a world?

In November 2002, shortly after the first Madvillain sessions, Madlib took off for São Paulo, Brazil, on a gig for Red Bull Music Academy. RBMA started out in 1998 as a lecture series sponsored by the caffeinated vodka mixer of choice for clubbers of the era, a corporate patronage that gave independent and niche artists a chance to educate and entertain music students during a series of workshops and shows. (Aside from the presence of the beverage's logo in the lecture studio, the company was otherwise benevolently hands-off.) Madlib was there with a contingent of West Coast DJs: Cut Chemist, J. Rocc, and Babu. Concurrent with the lecture series, these beatmakers and DJs would also engage in a series of collaborative concerts with a number of veteran Brazilian percussionists, including Wilson das Neves, Joao Parahyba, and Ivan Conti—the latter of whom would go on to release a 2008 album with Madlib as Jackson Conti, the culmination of Madlib's long-running fascination with Conti's jazz-funk group Azymuth.

So while Madlib was in São Paulo, he made it a working vacation: instead of going clubbing, Madlib raided every record shop he could, seeking out anything that looked even remotely rare or unusual or exotic, Brazilian or otherwise. He then absconded to his hotel room with a CD/tape deck, a portable record player, and a the SP-303—a seat-of-the-pants makeshift portable studio—and made beat tape after beat tape, sometimes creating an entire slew of tracks based around samples lifted from a single LP. During his lecture and Q&A with Egon, Madlib espoused the inexpensive, DIY, easily accessible nature of the machinery he used— "Anybody could do a beat, you just got to use your brain"—and his adherence to this simple system would pay off major over the next few years.

That setup helped Madlib create a massive collection of beats in his São Paulo hotel room, a couple of which were slated for *Madvillainy*. "Strange Ways" was a wobbly string-driven loop from prog rockers Gentle Giant that sounded like a fourth-generation tape dub. "Raid" was one of the more notable Brazil-sourced loops, taking Osmar Milito E Quarteto Forma's "América Latina"—a jaunty bossa nova piece from the soundtrack to early '70s telenovela *Selva de Pedra*—and chopping its quintuple time signature up into a funky head-nodding 4/4. And there was also one other beat—a combination of two recordings by the legendary MPB singer Maria Bethânia, 1968's vocal jazz recording "Molambo" and 1971's downtempo orchestral ballad "Mariana Mariana"—that Madlib kept in his back pocket for later.

At this point, *Madvillainy* was nearly finished, and midway through the lecture, Egon dropped a bomb: the crowd were about to hear tracks from it for the first time in public. Madlib debuted portions of two cuts: a work of bottom-heavy, guitar-laced, scratch-drenched galumphing funk called "America's Most Blunted," and a continuation of Madlib's Yesterdays New Quintet live-played Stevie Wonder enthusiasms that turned 1968's *Eivets Rednow* instrumental curiosity "How Can You Believe" into the beyond-breezy "Great Day." Doom had already recorded verses for them—the kind of lines that showed off a comfortable rapport with Madlib's beats, ones that clearly fit Doom's long-standing appreciation of production that drew as heavily on comedic spoken-word and conceptual storytelling as it did on fat breaks. This, however, wouldn't be the only time anyone got to hear *Madvillainy* early.

Thanks to the constant foot traffic in the combination two-room suite he shared with Cut Chemist, Madlib had opened up his makeshift studio to all kinds of visitors. One of these visitors, nobody knows who, made off with a cassette copy of the near-finished album, and the contents inevitably leaked onto the internet in the early months of 2003. In the early 2000s, when both major and independent record labels were still struggling with the issue of how to prevent or at least circumvent online piracy, this leak could have killed *Madvillainy* dead—an ironic inverse of the *Black Bastards* fiasco, an album emerging against the creators' wishes. And for a while, both Doom and Madlib left the album on the back burner, acting under the assumption that the leak would drastically diminish the commercial prospects of a record that Stones Throw had banked on succeeding.

It wasn't all disastrous; the project had helped both artists to break out of their own respective blocks. Doom went on to create two albums in 2003 that added to his repertory of alter egos: King Geedorah, a hydra monster inspired by a Toho Studios Godzilla foe, acted as Doom's capo on his self-produced *Take Me To Your Leader,* while the small-time, Doom-envying goon Viktor Vaughan skulked his way battle-rapping through the ensemble beats of *Vaudeville Villain.* Madlib had other releases to sate listeners in the meantime, including the summer '03 release *Shades of Blue.* At the beginning of Madlib's remix of Donald Byrd's "Stepping into Tomorrow," we hear an intro from Madlib's erstwhile partner: "Party people: Doom here to let you know that I have no prior knowledge to any invasion . . . being planned or executed. And I have no ties to Madlib or any organizations affiliated. Thank you."

This was, thankfully, bullshit. In the fall of 2003, the two reconvened to salvage the album, and their solution to the leak just so happened to be a drastic but effective one: upon revisiting the original recordings, Doom decided that his delivery was too high-energy for the blunt-ash beats that Madlib had made for him, and rerecorded all his rhymes with a more laidback and confident voice, mellowing into the backdrop like someone who'd lived in it for far longer than just a year or so. On top of that, he recorded a couple new sets of lyrics, including a track called "Accordion" that Madlib audaciously sequenced as the album's first actual rap track once the introductory mood-setting soundbite-collage track "The Illest Villains" ran its course. The title came from the fact that the song featured Doom kicking lyrics over a wheezy accordion sampled from experimental Los Angeles producer Daedelus's 2002 track "Experience"—arguably the most unlikely hip-hop beat put to record by anybody of note to that date.

And when Egon stressed the duo about the fact that the album didn't seem to end in a satisfying way, Madlib pulled out that Maria Bethânia beat he'd made in Brazil nearly a year and a half before and gave it to Doom to record a new set of lyrics over. Just days before the completed album was due to turn in to the distributor, "Rhinestone Cowboy" became *Madvillainy*'s new closer, a whirlwind intricately boastful internal rhymes ("Known as the grimy limey, slimy, try me / Blimey! Simply smashing in a fashion that's timely / Madvillain dashing in a beat-rhyme crime spree") and direct allusions to the album's bootlegging that spun it as a sign of its highly anticipated demand ("It speaks well of the hyper base / Wasn't even tweaked and it leaked into cyberspace / Couldn't wait for the snipes to place / At least a track list in bold print typeface"). As last-minute additions go, they came up with one that the album couldn't live without.

*Madvillainy* was an underground smash: twelve of its twenty-two tracks were shorter than two minutes and none of the songs had traditional hooks or choruses, but it was so singularly unique and memorable both lyrically and production-wise that it became one of the most critically lauded hip-hop records of the decade, indie or mainstream. It sold over 150,000 copies, modest by mainstream music's platinum-or-bust standards, but successful enough to keep Stones Throw not just solvent but thriving. And if the old saying about the Velvet Underground was true for the rock world—that they only sold a fraction of the records that the popular bands did, but everyone who bought a copy started a band of their own—the echoes of *Madvillainy* would be heard everywhere by the end of the 2000s. Chain-toking stream-of-consciousness MCs and bedroom beatmakers fiddling with a Dr. Sample put out underground sensations of their own, from electronic/future-jazz musician Flying Lotus to the LA rap collective Odd Future. Even Thom Yorke of Radiohead singled out *Madvillainy* track "Raid" as a personal favorite on an iTunes Celebrity Playlist he put together in early 2007.

Still, for two artists who clicked so thoroughly, the partnership between Madlib and MF Doom never got its clamored-for sequel. They would still get together and trade ideas and record tracks, but despite occasional sophomore album promises, nothing really materialized; a 2008 release cheekily titled *Madvillainy 2* was actually a borderline-blasphemous exercise by Madlib where he put different beats beneath Doom's existing *Madvillainy* verses. And Doom himself would have a roller-coaster series of ups and downs after his Madlib collab. Following the paired success of *Madvillainy* and his other, self-produced 2004 release *MM . . . Food,* Doom had a watershed moment in 2005 when he had a featured verse on Gorillaz's hit album *Demon Days* and his collaboration with it-producer Danger Mouse, *The Mouse and the Mask,* fell just one slot short of making the Top 40 of the Billboard 200.

But other announced projects fell through—an album-length team-up with Wu-Tang Clan's Ghostface Killah, announced in 2006, resulted in all of three tracks over ten years—and controversy dogged his live shows when it was alleged, then later revealed, that he'd sent impostors to perform under the mask in his place. "I'm the writer, I'm the director," he told the *New Yorker* in 2009. "If I was to go out there without the mask on, they'd be like, 'Who the fuck is this?' . . . I might send a white dude next. Whoever plays the character plays the character . . . I'll send a Chinese nigga. I'll send ten Chinese niggas. I might send the Blue Man Group." A sampled voice at the beginning of Mad-villain's "Money Folder" stated that "the villain took on many forms," so don't say you weren't warned.

As for Madlib, immersed in others' pasts but never content to ruminate on his own, *Madvillainy* was a refresher. It acted as a conduit to help him reconnect with the idea that hip-hop didn't have to adhere to anybody's rules, not even his—which were always malleable with time, experience, and ever-expanding record crates. He'd put out another Quasimoto record, *The Further Adventures of Lord Quas,* in 2005, but he'd soon find out that his most vivid ideas came through the records he sampled, and that he didn't need to alter his voice to speak through his beats. But he still had plenty to offer to the voices of others.

# 12 | *Survival Test*
## *Hip-Hop as a Community*

**Hip-hop's tradition of producers finding their own voice through the music of others echoes through the work of a man who changed the lives of everyone who heard him.**

PEANUT BUTTER WOLF'S NEW LABEL wasn't even its planning phases yet when he got an unexpected phone call from Detroit. Michael Buchanan, a record store employee at Street Corner Music and burgeoning DJ better known as House Shoes, had recently picked up a gig in the D's underground hip-hop venue St. Andrews Hall, and used it to launch a campaign to spread the word about his city's woefully under-recognized scene as far as he could. So he got Wolf's number from a copy of *Peanut Butter Breaks* and gave him a call. Wolf was unsure when this call was, exactly—he ballparks it sometime in 1995—but he did recall the circumstances: House Shoes and Wolf played a brief game of pager tag, and after Wolf sent him a few copies of *Peanut Butter Breaks* for the store, House Shoes started raving about a Detroit-area producer named Jay Dee, playing Wolf tapes of the up-and-comer's beats over the phone.

Jay Dee was born James Dewitt Yancey on February 7, 1974, and like Madlib, was raised by parents who'd come up in music. His mother, Maureen "Ma Dukes" Yancey, was a student of classical music who sang opera, jazz, and gospel, while his father, Beverly Dewitt Yancey, played upright jazz bass and worked halftime shows touring with the Harlem Globetrotters. To that, add the fact of Jay's growing up in one of America's great experimental musical epicenters—home of the Electrifying Mojo's P-Funk-meets-Kraftwerk *Midnight Funk Association* radio show, which catalyzed three high school classmates in nearby Belleville to popularize a sound that loosely paralleled what Afrika Bambaataa and Egyptian Lover were doing on the coasts. But the techno records of Juan

Atkins, Derrick May, and Kevin Saunderson would define the sound of '80s black Detroit to the rest of the world long after NYC and LA were marked by sample-based hip-hop. Hip-hop was still a thing in the D, but outside the city's confines Jay was working largely in uncharted territory.

Yet he learned under a musician who could bridge that gap as good as anyone. Joseph "Amp" Fiddler was a super–session man who lived in Detroit, just a few blocks from where Jay lived. Fiddler acted as a sort of local guru to aspiring musicians—not a bad mentor to have, considering that by the turn of the '90s he had worked with both George Clinton and Prince. Like Flash, Jay was a sharp student who gravitated toward working with electronics and audio gear, and since he'd also started becoming formally trained in music starting in middle school—Ma Dukes remembers him as "an excellent cello player"—both his musical ear and his tech-head interests converged on Fiddler's recommended weapon of choice, the MPC. Jay had already spent the past couple years making his own pause-tape beats on a tape deck he'd actually disassembled, then put back together in a way that gave him more space to extend the sample source. Something as intuitive as an MPC would be child's play to him.

Fiddler remembers Jay as a quiet but studious and enthusiastic learner, as well as a counterintuitive, manual-ignoring experimenter: "When he first started making beats, he was just looping, but he had a particular way of doing it. Most people would start on the one of the kick, but he would start on the snare or the hi-hat or some other shit and just fit it into the equation, like a mathematician." Jay also gravitated toward a fascination with mistakes and imperfection, recalling himself that "when I hear mistakes in records [it's] exciting for me. Like, 'Damn, the drummer missed the beat in that shit. The guitar went off key for a second.' I try to do that in my music a little bit, try to have that live feel."

And the most important thing Jay did in building his beats was to completely reject quantization. The "quantize" function on the MPC was a sort of assist mode for producers who manually tapped out their beats on the machine's punch-button grid: if some kick or snare or other rhythmic element was just a bit off-beat, the MPC could "snap" it into place so it would sound perfectly metronomic. By bypassing this feature, Jay had the freedom to let the internal rhythms that drove his fingers call all the shots, and it led him to drastically change the parameters for how hip-hop rhythms could work: he not only built his own breaks one beat at a time, but had total control over how loose and live he could make them sound.

This was the secret weapon dating back to his earliest cuts. Listen to 1994's "Now" by the Detroit group Da' Enna C.—one of the first commercial releases he ever did a beat for—and you can already hear him using extra dropped-in kicks to boost the simple drum loop he lifted from Gladys Knight & the Pips' "Who Is She (and What Is She to You)." That technique had begun to flourish a couple years earlier, when a classmate and rapper known as T3 (nee R. L. Altman) would join Jay at Fiddler's studio, and the two would work on material for a group project that they'd eventually name Slum Village. In 1992, the embryonic version of the group, which also included a third rapper named Baatin (born Titus Glover), was signed to a deal by R&B local R. J. Rice and Detroit Pistons big man turned entrepreneur John Salley. After Salley split when he was traded to the Miami Heat, Rice relocated his studio operation into his house, and hosted Slum Village's early workshopping as they began to piece together a demo.

But even before that crew's vision was fully realized, Fiddler was starting to rave about Jay's abilities to anyone who would listen—one of whom was Q-Tip. Fiddler was playing keyboards with George Clinton & the P-Funk All Stars when they shared a Lollapalooza '94 bill with A Tribe Called Quest, and after talking up Jay's beatmaking prowess during conversations at every stop on the tour, Fiddler finally invited him backstage when Lollapalooza hit Detroit. Jay handed Tip the demo tape himself, and soon it became a fixture on Tribe's tour bus. As Q-Tip recalled to Red Bull Music Academy in 2013, Tribe were doing some concurrent shows with De La Soul, and after having a *holy shit* epiphany listening to the Slum Village demo on his system, Tip convinced De La's Trugoy to give it a listen, too. As the first person outside Tribe to hear the tape, Plug Two's verdict was an irreverent but honest declaration that "he sounds like your shit but just . . . *better.*"

Tip had a new artist to champion, and plenty of friends to refer him to. The Pharcyde wanted Q-Tip to produce their second album, but when Tip turned out to be unavailable for the work, he recommended Jay Dee and set up a bit of minor confusion in the process. "We didn't even believe Jay Dee existed," Slimkid3 told *Fader* in 2006. "Q-Tip's name is Jonathan Davis, [so] we thought it was Q-Tip pretending that was his little spin-off name." Mistaken identity notwithstanding, the beats Jay gave them all became highlights of *Labcabincalifornia,* the group's archetypal "difficult second album" maturation effort. The album initially confused early champions of *Bizarre Ride II the Pharcyde* and earned lukewarm reviews from *Spin* ("mid-tempo muddle") and the *Los Angeles Times* ("the casually delivered, low-key narratives nearly vanish into the background"). And even laudatory reviews, from *Rap Pages* to *Vibe* to *The Source,* downplayed Jay's identity as a contributor if they even dropped his name at all.

But *Labcabincalifornia* became a slow-burn classic-in-retrospect, and it earned a place as Jay Dee's first real brush with a receptive hip-hop community outside Detroit. Real heads knew: the intricate Stan Getz bossa nova recursion in "Runnin'," the backwards-swimming, compacted-snare bass glow of "Drop," and combination of chisel-sharp percussion and elegiac piano (sourced from a Vince Guaraldi Trio recording from *A Boy Named Charlie Brown*) in "Splattitorium" weren't just a break from the mainstream, they were a break from familiarity itself. And one cut from *Labcabincalifornia* was so off-kilter in its brilliance that it shook hip-hop's preeminent live drummer to his core.

The Roots were openers for the Pharcyde during the latter crew's tour, and the first song off *Labcabincalifornia* was also the first song in their setlist, a track called "Bullshit." Ahmir "Questlove" Thompson tells the story often: during the tour's North Carolina stop, he had to leave right after the Roots' set to do an interview with a college radio station. But on his way out of the club, something stops him in his tracks: "I'm hearing the vibration of the kick drum, and it was the most life-changing moment I ever had. Like, I had to get out of the car and run back in the club to make sure, like, 'Did I hear that?' Whereas [the snare and hi-hat rhythm] was normal, it sounded like the kick drum was played by like a drunk three-year-old. And I was like, 'Are you allowed to do that?'" The next day, Questlove got the Pharcyde to play him the *Labcabincalifornia* beat tape, and it was as though every restraint he put on himself in the process of becoming a musical perfectionist was suddenly severed: "I just never heard someone not give a fuck and that, to me, was the most liberating moment."

Soon, demand for Jay's beats was stirring up competitiveness and collaboration alike. An early post-Pharcyde shot came with the analog keyboard ether frolic/snare-kick clinic he concocted for Busta Rhymes's "Still Shining"—a strong deep cut off 1996's Busta's solo debut *The Com-*

*ing.* The combination of Busta's diabolical, emphatic leonine flow and Jay's calm but off-kilter grooves clicked instantly, a contrasting but complementary juxtaposition which let Jay indulge his stranger inspirations over successive years. They were usually deep cuts rather than major hits, but one track cut from *The Coming* might've changed all that. If it weren't for Busta's reluctance to cosign a track that included some lyrical shots at Tupac, we could've gotten Jay Dee doing a beat for a Notorious B.I.G. verse; as it stood, "The Ugliest" and its subtly sinister bass bounce were left to the archives.

Meanwhile, De La Soul had hit the reset button with *Stakes Is High,* their first album without Prince Paul and their first major opportunity to create a primarily self-produced record. But Q-Tip was still looking to get Jay some work—at this point, he was Jay's de facto manager—and played Posdnous a beat tape that included a masterful flip of a 1974 Ahmad Jamal track, "Swahililand," that turned the emphatic horn exclamations of the song's crescendo into a ruminative refrain. The bassline Jay brewed up took the same loop and pared back every frequency except the lowest end of the EQ, turning it into a muddy but rich slab of bass and creating two completely disparate sonic elements out of the same couple bars—a trick he often pulled when differentiating between the percussive loop for a rap track's verses and the melodic one for its hook. Drop in an MPC-punched drum beat that took full advantage of Jay's ability to concoct a hip-hop beat that *swung* instead of just bumping, and you've got the kind of track that could anchor an entire album.

This forced Pos into a poker ace's bluff: the De La member figured if he showed too much enthusiasm for it, Q-Tip would wind up claiming it for himself. So he stoically concealed how geeked out he was over it, downplayed the track's strengths, and then snuck off to another room where Tip couldn't hear him so he could call up Trugoy and go nuts over the prospect of using it. The gambit worked, and the beat became the title cut to *Stakes Is High.*

Still, Tip still had plenty of opportunity to pick the cream of Jay Dee's beats: concurrent with the making of A Tribe Called Quest's fourth album *Beats, Rhymes, and Life* in 1996, Tip formed a producers' collective with Jay and Ali Shaheed Muhammad, calling the unit "The Ummah" after an Arabic word for "community." Their first collaborative work would immediately become their most controversial: in following up *Midnight Marauders* more than two and a half years after that album insinuated itself into listeners' minds as an impossible-to-top classic, *Beats, Rhymes, and Life* was a marked stylistic change behind the boards: smoother, more relaxed, almost minimalist compared to its densely rich predecessor.

The frayed nerves that were developing between Tip and fellow Tribe MC Phife might have added to a mood that listeners considered something of a downer, and the lyrics were taking a turn for the defensive and disillusioned, but Jay Dee's beats took much of the brunt of blame for the album's vibe: among lukewarm-to-negative reviews, *AllMusic* dismissed the production as "skeletal," *Spin* played up how "dark" and "lonely" it sounded (while attributing it all to Muhammad), and the *Washington Post,* while laudatory, warned that "some of the youthful bounce is gone." Fan response wasn't any better. Bloggers and message-board posters still snipe at each other to this day over whether Jay Dee's beats hastened A Tribe Called Quest's falloff. And even Hanif Abdurraqib's 2019 love letter to the group, *Go Ahead in the Rain,* recollects his initial reaction as so let down that he'd constantly fast-forward through the disappointing tracks on his tape dub even though it meant taking off his gloves in finger-freezing Midwest weather. With a more sympathetic contemporary ear, he wrote of that fourth album, "Being good is only a failure if you've been impossible three times in a row."

In that sense, and in many different ways to come, Jay Dee's career was a constant battle against doubt. Here he was innovating a sound that built whole new rhythmic landscapes out of techniques few had even considered, earning the respect of some of the most musically adventurous groups in hip-hop. And yet not only did a vocal contingent of fans and critics run cold to his work, they often failed to recognize it as his work in the first place. Q-Tip lamented that "with Ummah, just because I was the face, people would automatically assume sometimes . . . that I produced it or that I did the beat when it was [Jay Dee]." Part of that came from Jay's tendency to prefer the studio to the spotlight, but he'd also faced his share of rejection as well: the release that finally came from the conversations House Shoes had with Peanut Butter Wolf was a 1997 collection called *Jay Dee Unreleased,* an EP Wolf helped press for House Shoes' label that consisted entirely of Jay Dee remixes he'd done on spec that labels subsequently rejected.

And in one memorable case of loose attribution, the production for Janet Jackson's Q-Tip–featuring 1997 single "Got 'til It's Gone"—

credited to Jackson, Jimmy Jam, and Terry Lewis—was unmistakably indebted to the Ummah's neo-soul sound. Jam and Lewis admitted to *Rolling Stone* in 2015 that "[the Ummah] had done a remix of a Brand New Heavies song ['Sometimes'] that had a feel to it I just loved. I thought if I could come up with something with that feel with Janet, and then put a Joni Mitchell sample over it, that would be a magic combination, taking things from different eras and weaving it together." The track was a #1 R&B hit, but the attribution left both Tip and Jay fuming, with the former calling it a style bite ("They heard some shit that we were doing and were trying to copy it I guess") and the latter stating that "we all collaborated on this track, made it happen. . . . When it came out, it said produced by someone else." When the Ummah remixed the song in a way that simultaneously amplified and warped their characteristic sound, they called it "Jay Dee's Revenge Mix."

But there was one album that did nothing but boost Jay Dee's reputation on the boards. Even with the leading lights of alt-rap cosigning him, Jay saw to it that he could still bring up the other artists who had his back before he ever stepped foot outside Detroit. And so he recorded another demo with T3 and Baatin in his home studio over the course of 1996–'97, a grip of one-take, two-mic raps set to a metronomic click track that they all had to get right on the first try since they were being recorded to DAT tapes. *Fan-Tas-Tic Vol. 1* was finished in a week, and if the MCing has occasional moments of flows scrambling to fit the odd rhythmic emphases, the tracks were all intricately assembled showcases of Jay's instantly recognizable style. Plus it threw in a curveball that served as one of hip-hop's greatest moments of breaking sampling's fourth wall: "I Don't Know" featured T3 and Baatin spitting lines that were completed by James Brown soundbites ("No time for acting [*funky*] with me / You best believe that you won't [*do it*]") where that familiar and well-traveled hip-hop source was slotted in a mode somewhere between Dickie Goodman's "Flying Saucer" and DJ Premier's cut-up messages.

The whole affair was decidedly lo-fi and loosely distributed. The original run consisted of two hundred cassettes, complete with covers printed at Kinkos, that the group brought to a St. Andrews Hall show and sold out immediately. This not only built a legend around this rare holy grail of an album, but added some grimy, underground character to the beats that gave it additional *where did this come from???* mystique, especially when it was copied as a second-generation dub. Before the decade was out, it had become a legendary bootleg that went from a local buzz-building effort to an international hip-hop head secret handshake.

Its sequel, *Fantastic, Vol. 2,* was recorded just a year later in an attempt to capitalize on the buzz, and featured appearances by everyone from Q-Tip and Busta Rhymes to Death Row / Dogg Pound alumni Kurupt and Chicago conscious rapper Common. The album was completed in 1998 for A&M Records, but because Jay couldn't ever catch a break, A&M went under and was dissolved into the conglomerate Interscope Geffen A&M Records. Slum Village were left in the lurch for another two years, and an album that could've been one of the earliest landmarks of hip-hop in neo-soul mode was delayed until July of 2000 and dropped on the short-lived, Santa Monica–based fledgling indie label Good Vibe Recordings. Thanks to the delay, *Fantastic Vol. 2* came across instead like a victory lap.

Questlove's mind-rearranging experience with Jay Dee's beats had led him to seek the producer out, having drawn heavily (and with acknowledged attribution) from the percussive style that Jay had developed on the MPC. For a hip-hop producer to drastically rewire the way a live drummer played was nearly unheard of; that it came during the recording sessions for R&B superstar D'Angelo's long-simmering second album *Voodoo* was a coup in itself. And when Questlove formed a like-minded collective of artists—including D'Angelo; fellow neo-soul stars Bilal and Erykah Badu; rappers Q-Tip, Common, Black Star (Mos Def and Talib Kweli); and *Voodoo* musicians James Poyser, Roy Hargrove, and Pino Palladino—Jay became the beatmaking powerhouse of the crew that would come to be called the Soulquarians. Between early 1999 and the summer of 2001, Jay would contribute memorably to career-highlight records by the Roots ("Dynamite" from *Things Fall Apart*), Q-Tip (the lion's share of *Amplified,* including Top 40 hit "Vivrant Thing"), Common (most of *Like Water for Chocolate,* with Grammy-nominated "The Light" becoming one of hip-hop's greatest love songs), Erykah Badu (whose *Mama's Gun* track "Didn't Cha Know?" garnered Jay another Grammy nom), and Bilal (where *1st Born Second* had Jay rubbing elbows with Dr. Dre).

Ask Questlove, though, and he'll probably tell you that Jay's biggest feat during that period was the time he performed an impossible work of alchemy for a Black Star track. "Little Brother" is still an underrated song: it was never released as a single and only surfaced on the sound-track recording for Norman Jewison's half-remembered 1999 Denzel Washington–starring Rubin Carter biopic *Hurricane*. And the track's success rode heavily on its sample source. Roy Ayers's 1971 song "Ain't Got Time" had only ever been sampled twice before, and even then, in thin fragments: by Diamond D in 1992 as an opening flourish on Show-biz & A.G.'s "Hard to Kill," and then by Pete Rock two years later as an interstitial loop on his 1994 album with C.L. Smooth, *The Main Ingredi-ent*. The reason for this was simple: despite Roy Ayers and his resonant vibraphone being a popular source for samples, there isn't a single four-bar stretch on "Ain't Got Time" where Ayers's voice isn't present to the point of distraction.

But Jay was so intent on capturing its essence that he took minus-cule samples—a second, half a second, a split-second blip of a note or a drumbeat—and "micro-chopped" his way into an entirely new recon-struction of the song's instrumental portions, playing it out by hand on the MPC and making it sound like a seamless new loop. Questlove wit-nessed this beat's creation, and then was crestfallen to learn that Jay was reluctant to even let it see the light of day: "His favorite thing was to take whatever Pete Rock or Premier did, sometimes Tip, and figure out how he would do it, but he would never let those tapes out. . . . I'm like, 'Well, why?' He's like, 'No, I don't want people to feel a certain way.' Like, he knew he was on some next shit, but he was so humble about it, he didn't want to alienate [other producers]." Pete Rock was an idol, and Jay didn't want to show him up. The only way that beat made it to Black Star was by accident, as Jay unthinkingly left it on a beat tape he later gave to Talib Kweli.

His peers knew Jay was brilliant, but the charts didn't. As the '90s gave way to the 2000s, sampling had receded in the mainstream thanks to punishing, high-dollar sample-clearance costs and the emerging popu-larity of purely synthesized Southern rap beats. But even if he was gifted an unlimited budget, it was that "mellow" neo-soul vibe that put Jay's beats at odds with the mainstream the most. This frustrated Jay: after Q-Tip made a habit of comparing Slum Village to A Tribe Called Quest's successors, Jay spent years simmering about how it pigeonholed him musically when he was more of a boho-meets-hood duality, a between-two-coasts sensibility that was more nuanced than his "backpacker" rep allowed. "It's kinda fucked up because the audience we were trying to give to were actually people we hung around," he remarked. "Me, myself, I hung around regular ass Detroit cats. Not the backpack shit that people kept putting out there like that. I mean, I ain't never carried no goddamn backpack. But like I said, I understand to a certain extent. I guess that's how the beats came off on some smooth type of shit. And at that time . . . there was a lot of hard shit on the radio so our thing was we're gonna do exactly what's not on the radio."

But without that radio support, it soon seemed like the underground was where he had to make his way. In 2002, his string of critical and commercial hits for MCA artists like Common and the Roots earned him what seemed like free rein from the label to indulge in two projects close to his heart: *48 Hours,* a full-length collaboration with Detroit rappers Frank n Dank, and a solo album, tentatively titled *Pay Jay.* Getting the Frank n Dank album through the major-label gauntlet was headache enough: Jay had created a whole slate of beats, only to have them rejected by the label, ostensibly because the cost of clearing the samples outweighed the likelihood of the album having any commercial hit potential. Jay rerecorded the whole thing using live instruments—heavy on analog synthesizers—but despite its retro-futuristic style, one that presented a distinctly Detroit twist on g-funk and could hold its own along anything the Neptunes and Timbaland could send to #1, MCA shelved it indefinitely.

*Pay Jay* was even more of a detour: despite being best known as a producer, Jay considered himself a double threat, and decided that he was more interested in showing off his street-minded personality on the mic over productions by other beatmakers he admired. He'd already started calling himself by a new name, J Dilla—claimed to be a way to avoid being confused with producer/mogul Jermaine "J.D." Dupri—and now here he was delegating beats to others. It was put on ice for the same reason *48 Hours* was: MCA A&R and Dilla advocate Wendy Goldstein left the label for Capitol, and her remaining projects, Dilla included, were shuffled off into some dusty corner to molder. After all, who'd want to hear him rap about his sexual conquests and his new Cadillac Escalade, even over beats by Pete Rock? Or House Shoes? Or Madlib?

• • •

House Shoes was hanging around at an Alkaholiks show when Madlib was DJing for them; as hip-hop crews are wont to do, they all decided to go record shopping together. Still in Dilla-advocate mode, Shoes took the opportunity to play "Stakes Is High" for Madlib, who was duly impressed. A year later, Madlib copped *Fan-Tas-Tic Vol. 1* and had his suspicions confirmed: he'd found a kindred spirit. "It was completely different from my stuff but still the same, you know?" he told *Urb* in their March 2004 issue. "Like it's always raw and soulful and it never sounds too computerized." That impression lingered, and it proved to be something that would help drag him out of the rut he'd found himself in post–*The Unseen,* when he was halfway to abandoning rap entirely for his one-man jazz band works. The Beat Junkies' J. Rocc passed Madlib a beat tape, and something just clicked: "I can't rap to too many other people's beats, and I can barely rap to my own. But when I hear his shit, there's just something to it that I connect with. I could just write to it all day."

That writer's block–breaking catalyst wasn't just a practice exercise: Madlib actually burned a CD of his lyrical excursions rhyming over Dilla beats, christening it *Jaylib* with marker on the disc. One of those tracks was his twenty-first-century mutation of Grandmaster Flash & the Furious Five's "The Message," which turned Melle Mel's lyrics outward ("It's not worth it sometimes / It makes me wonder if we're all goin' under") over a Dilla beat sourced from an unlikely but fitting guitar/bass loop from Anglo-French art-poppers Stereolab. (The track Dilla sampled, "Come and Play in the Milky Night," was released in 1999, just a year before he first used the beat for Busta Rhymes' "Show Me What You Got"—proof that he didn't have to dig that far back in time to find uncharted turf.) Peanut Butter Wolf pressed a three-hundred-count run of unofficial "white label" 12-inch copies, and inevitably it made it into enough DJ crates that Dilla heard it was circulating.

"The Message" wasn't necessarily an invitation, but Dilla took it like one. He'd spent the last couple years pushing the boundaries of what people expected from him: 2001's *Welcome 2 Detroit,* his self-produced solo debut as a producer/MC for BBE Records, was a full-on conceptual rap travelogue of his city's musical spirit that gave full rein not just to his neo-soul breaks, but to some next-phase evolutionary turns toward unexpected prog, psych, and electro sources. (You thought one of hip-hop's most Detroit-rooted producers *wasn't* going to nod Kraftwerk's way? Check out "B.B.E. [Big Booty Express].") Later that year, after the umpteenth time being hassled by cops for being black and well dressed in an imported SUV, Dilla cut a single with a familiar title: "Fuck the Police," a scathing diatribe against racial profiling that combined his immaculate drum programming with deceptively lighthearted-sounding woodwinds lifted from a library record. The timing might have stifled its airplay potential—the single dropped literally one week after the attacks of September 11, 2001, when national sympathy for police and other emergency service workers was at an all-time high—but it positioned him as the kind of artist who could bridge the club-friendly, boho-conscious, and hardcore underground scenes when most other artists were staking claims in just one of those territories.

Meanwhile, as his time with MCA wound down, Dilla had found himself both steered toward and independently pursuing even further-flung ideas. Common's 2002 album *Electric Circus* saw the MC, struck with the spirit of Jimi Hendrix while recording at Electric Lady Studios, pushing Dilla and the rest of the Soulquarians to give him the most experimental beats they were capable of: scowling post-OutKast acid funk ("Electric Wire Hustle Flower"), artsy haunted-house psych ("New Wave," featuring guest vocals from Stereolab's Lætitia Sadier), space-walk Moog bounce ("Star * 69," which sported a chorus featuring both Bilal and Prince), even a sort of tri-generational Dr. Buzzard's Original Savannah Band–style big band disco version of neo-soul ("I Am Music"). It was an ambitious, brilliant mess that critics either adored or outright loathed, and with no Top 40 showing for either the album or its only single (the largely conventional Neptunes-produced R&B ballad "Come Close"), the industry saw it as stark proof that rap this weird couldn't sell. *Electric Circus* moved less than three hundred thousand units a year after it was released. For comparison, 50 Cent's *Get Rich or Die Tryin'*, which came out two months after *Electric Circus*, went six times platinum in the same span.

But at this point Dilla was getting used to making music for the benefit of himself and the niche of heads who would follow him to the ends of the earth. That liberated him to create music like his 2003 *Ruff Draft* EP, a beats-for-their-own-sake release which he described as "stuff for me to drive around and listen to." With no expectations, filters, or overwork, the EP was completed in a week and filled with some of the weirdest shit *anybody* was doing at the time. "Let's Take It Back" was built around abstract fluttering keyboard melodies that sounded like a synthesizer imitating rainfall on a campfire. "The $" got both melody and bassline from what sounded like an aluminum cello. And "Nothing Like This" punted a "We Will Rock You"–esque boom-boom-bap drum cadence into the reverb stratosphere while backwards acid rock guitar harmonized with his awestruck, zoned-out yet exclamatory sing-raps ("All I need. In. My. Life is / There is. Noth. Ing. Like this").

While his willingness to experiment meant his newest phase of production style would fit an underground sensibility well, his actual enthusiasm for the potential to work with Madlib dated back further, all the way to the early Soulquarian years. In another anecdote, Questlove recalls getting a 2:00 a.m. call from Dilla sometime around 1999. From the tone of Dilla's voice, Questlove assumed something was wrong—a beat tape leaked, or he'd read a negative message-board post on Okayplayer. "He's like . . . 'I'm fucked up, man. I met my match, shit's fuckin' with me.' And I was like, 'What?' He said, 'Dog, man . . . Lootpack.'" Dilla had been so thrown by the way Madlib flipped beats on *Soundpieces* that he'd had some kind of existential crisis, and Questlove started calling the album "Dilla's kryptonite."

Dilla himself explained it to *Urb* in 2004: "Just to know that Madlib did that stuff on the SP1200 freaked me out because the only cat I knew that could really freak that machine was Pete Rock. That album was crazy. Me and my partners rode that shit for the longest time. As soon as I popped my deal with MCA, I went looking for him." In a 2003 interview with Dutch producer Y'skid, Dilla tracks their earliest collaborative efforts to the eventually shelved *Pay Jay*—"I flew him out [to Detroit], we laid like six tracks"—but after that was put on the back burner, "The Message" only re-stoked the enthusiasm to work with Madlib. "He sent me a CD of twelve songs with vocals, cuts, it was like an *album*. But all [my] beats. So I'm like, 'No, that's impossible.' So I just called him, like . . . 'Don't take this the wrong way, but what's goin' on? I'm hearin' about this white label 12-inch with this Jay Dee beat and you're rhymin' . . . [but] I just dropped it and said, 'Look, if we're gonna do it, let's do it official.'"

This kicked off a mutually enthusiastic and focused collaboration, though the time spent was largely thanks to their unwieldy way of trading ideas: the two artists had enough trust and faith built up that they'd be sending each other some top-tier beats, so instead of meeting at a studio they wound up exchanging tracks through the mail between their two cities. (The leadoff cut and only coproduction credit, "L.A. to Detroit," hints as much.) They both stuck to Madlib's two-track, no-overdub plan—no messing with the beats, period—and would alternate between Dilla rapping on Madlib's tracks and vice versa. The Madlib tracks Dilla picked out—including a bunch from the same tireless sessions that would provide the bulk of *Madvillainy*'s beats—were characteristically grimy. There were melting string-section drones on "The Mission," hissing buzzes and a horn riff that sounded like a stuck cog in a piece of funk machinery on "McNasty Filth," Bollywood soundtrack melodies spun into panic-attack intensity in "Survival Test." While Dilla usually sounded best as a rapper over his own productions—nobody flows quite over a beat like the artist who made it in the first place—he took well to Madlib's, his blunt lyricism barely concealing the sly counter-beats and rhythmic responses he used in his delivery.

But the Dilla beats that Madlib picked were raw and off-kilter, too, as if the former was pushing the latter to indulge his weirdest ideas. "Nowadayz" was a minimalist boom-clap set against a seething organ drone and tension-building bassline, a steady if handmade-sounding foundation where Madlib could be at his most conversational since the beat's organic presence made it part of the conversation. "The Heist" sported some of the nastiest synths ever heard on a rap track, sourced in part from notorious British electronic-industrial experimentalists Throbbing Gristle's 1979 album *20 Jazz Funk Greats*. (That title was ironic until Dilla got ahold of it.) "React" turned a clip of an electric violin from UK prog rockers Gentle Giant's 1971 track "Plain Truth" into a refractory melodic spasm, sounding less like a loop than a Möbius strip. And "Raw Addict," all muffled, bleary bass frequencies and staccato drum patterns, sounded like an especially head-nod-worthy flat tire. They were all exhibitions of Dilla's tendency to build variations on a rhythm and a break instead of looping the same four bars, but with a couple exceptions—the beat to "Starz" sounded like (but sadly wasn't) a bona fide club-rap hit—they still felt claustrophobic and a bit uncomfortable, perfect for Madlib's idiosyncratic style.

*Champion Sound* remains, by Madlib's admission, one of his favorite albums he ever made. And despite its commercial failure, even by indie standards—Egon described it as having "absolutely and utterly flopped"—the contingent of critics and buyers who were fans of both producer/MCs made it a cult classic, a rare example of two do-it-all hip-hop artists actually riffing off each others' styles. There was even a sequel not far from either of their minds; all that they needed was some free time. It seemed like a strong likelihood from the outside, since Dilla's commitments to creating tracks for other artists was emptying out. After the MCA deal dissolved, so did the Soulquarians, and many of the core members of the group either went on extended hiatus (including Bilal, Q-Tip, and D'Angelo) or branched out into different styles—Mos Def going rock crossover on *The New Danger,* Erykah Badu turning *Worldwide Underground* into a free-flowing live jam session, and the Roots feinting toward radio pop crossover on *The Tipping Point.* The indie-leaning, experimental-minded Stones Throw looked to be Dilla's home for the foreseeable future. But he'd been dealing with far more than just low record sales and a continued severing from mainstream hip-hop.

He wasn't willing to elaborate at first. In the March 2004 *Urb* profile, Dilla explained that he'd been ill, but claimed it was because "I'd ruptured my kidney from being too busy and being stressed out and not eating right." It was a credible explanation—everyone who knew Dilla had witnessed just how deeply focused his work ethic was, to the point where he'd lose track of time and when he needed to eat. He went on to state that actually working on music was therapeutic: "When I'm doing it, there's no pain, no nothing—just connections, feeling. If I'm sick, I do music; then I don't feel sick."

But the truth was something more disconcerting: upon coming home from doing gigs in Europe, he complained to his mother that he felt under the weather, maybe with a cold or the flu. When things got worse, Ma Dukes rushed him to the emergency room of Bon Secours Hospital in Detroit's Grosse Point neighborhood, where doctors discovered that his blood platelet count—typically somewhere in the mid-hundreds for a healthy adult—was less than ten. James Yancey had thrombotic thrombocytopenic purpura (TTP), a blood disease where his small blood vessels were becoming filled with clots that were consuming his platelets. No cure was available.

• • •

Even with his life upended by his diagnosis, Dilla never stopped making beats. By early 2004 he had moved to Los Angeles at the behest of Common, who figured the sunshine and change of scenery would do him good. The two collaborators and friends lived together in the same house, and while Dilla could only bring a bare-bones version of his setup out west—he left a massive record collection and a home studio back in Detroit, and was largely limited to a portable sampler/turntable setup when he had to stay in the hospital—he worked around his limitations, or took advantage of them, or just outright bypassed them. Soon he was making beat tapes again, mostly short experiments filled with beats he figured were too out-there for rappers to rhyme over, and he played one of them—a twenty-two-minute collection he gave the name *Donuts*—for Madlib and Peanut Butter Wolf during a car ride. Wolf's immediate instinct was that it deserved a commercial release.

*Donuts,* the last album Dilla created and released in his lifetime, has grown to represent the man and his vision more than just about anything else he did. That it was created under the most agonizing circumstances imaginable—fleshed out from its initial twenty-two-minute form into something twice as long and more elaborate during extended hospital stays starting in the summer of 2005—might have something to do with it. When a work of art is created by somebody who knows they're dying, it's easy to dig as deep as you can inside that work in search of some sign of its creator's state of mind. It's not hard to infer, even on an album where every voice is a sampled portion of someone else's words, many of which are chopped into unrecognizable portions. At one point, there's a stutter-loop sample of contemporary rapper Jadakiss shouting "'s'dat real," and with all the noise and context swirling around it, the phrase sounds uncannily like it's been mutated into "death's real." It could be the environment at work: *Donuts* was completed in Los Angeles's Cedars-Sinai Medical Center, the same hospital where Eazy-E died of AIDS and the Notorious B.I.G. succumbed to his gunshot wounds.

But there's something else haunting the record, both physically and spiritually. In the former's case, actually making the music for *Donuts* was a strenuous exercise—especially when his physical condition began to deteriorate, and he needed his mother's help moving from his bed to a chair and back, having her massage his hands just so he'd be able to operate the Boss SP-303 he'd complete his tracks on. Think of the implications of this: any other musician in a field playing any other kind of instrument would, under these physical conditions, barely be able to play or perform. The sampling machinery that allowed Dilla to express himself with a clarity and creativity that seemed boundless was still able to serve as a direct line from his thoughts to his art, even when it hurt to move. His beats had rarely sounded more vibrant, more alive.

And they'd rarely sounded so *everywhere*. If one's reaction to their own looming mortality is to take stock, Dilla not only drew from his life and everything he'd learned, he condensed every possible future he could have made for himself into the album's kaleidoscopic scope of sound. Breaks and samples that he and other producers had flipped countless times before—like the metallic guitar-distortion siren from ESG's "UFO," or Mountain's Woodstock performance of "Long Red" and its two-ton drum break and "Louder! Got that?" stage patter—meshed with left-field sources from the worlds of prog, psychedelic funk, primitive synth, and art rock. Working with 45 RPM 7-inch records was a bookend to his musical life. Ma Dukes recalled that even when he was barely old enough to walk, he'd join his father in spinning records in Detroit's Harmonie Park: "He'd have his arms full of 45s—his little arms, you know, fit right through the holes." And so a host of lo-fi '70s soul breaks, sourced from 45s that his mother and local friends brought him, echoed fundamental hip-hop source material that happened to coincide with a three-year window of Dilla's 1974 birth year, breaks that were formative for both his genre and his own life.

If *Donuts* was loaded with ideas to the point of it sounding like a life flashing before your ears, the truncated breaks and micro-chopped loops sounded like that life replayed in fast-forward. Dilla had always worked fast; his beat for A Tribe Called Quest's 1996 track "Get a Hold" took less than fifteen minutes to make, and might have taken even less time if he hadn't been frustrated over getting the drums just right. But now, he was chopping things up so that they sounded deliberately fragmentary and abruptly, jarringly snapped into pieces, loops that were made to be broken. One track, "Waves," draws its beats from 10cc's 1973 doo-wop throwback/parody "Johnny, Don't Do It"—but it's almost completely unrecognizable, having been slowed down and broken up into its component beats. The drums sound steady, but they're overlaid with vocals that sound like monosyllabic, wordless stammers. (The only legible word, "Johnny," happens to be the first name of Dilla's younger brother, who performs as Illa J.) And with the exception of "Glazed," a repetitive horn blast / vibraphone riff that grinds itself into your forebrain like a car alarm, none of the loops really resolves neatly, while the songs don't so much segue or blend into each other as they just smack into each other. Despite the fact that the album is sequenced as one big loop, with the last track ("Donuts [intro]") segueing into the first ("Donuts [outro]"), even that end-to-beginning loop itself isn't seamless, hitching between the rejoined halves like a needle skipping a groove.

And the mood of the album told it all: manic and almost silly one moment, mournful and nostalgic the next, ruminative and meditative in both quiet reflection and heavy, speaker-rattling intensity. *Donuts* brought a full spectrum of emotion that turned the works of other artists into the inward-looking, outwardly reassuring message that this one producer, a man revered by his peers, knew why he was loved and wanted to bring that love full circle. It was a thank-you letter to the music world, cut out and assembled from the words the music world gave him.

Many of Dilla's friends heard *Donuts* as a farewell message when it came out, just three days before he passed away on February 10, 2006. Many more said their own goodbyes on record over the next couple years: the Roots with their 2006 tribute "Can't Stop This," which reworked Dilla's *Donuts* track "Time: The Donut of the Heart"; J. Rocc's *Thank You Jay Dee* mixes that the DJ assembled annually from 2006 through 2009; the 2007 Busta Rhymes tribute mixtape with Mick Boogie, *Dillagence;* Erykah Badu lacing remembrances throughout her 2008 *New Amerykah Part One (4th World War)* album; Q-Tip and De La Soul and Talib Kweli all paying homage throughout the years. Eventually, Dilla became the most eulogized hip-hop artist since Tupac and Biggie, and it was increasingly difficult to find artists who *didn't* want a piece of his legacy somewhere or another; even big-budget Def Jam cocaine-trade rappers like Rick Ross and Pusha T paid lyrical tribute to him nearly a decade after his passing.

The legacy of James Yancey—of Jay Dee or Dilla or however you care to remember him—is hard to untangle nowadays. While his passing revealed just how much he meant to producers of just about every decade and region, it also complicated things when it came to who got paid and what got released. A fractious battle between two different parties— the lawyer and accountant who served as executors of Dilla's estate in one corner, Dilla's family heirs (Ma Dukes, Dilla's two daughters, and his brother John) and their advocate Egon in the other—made it difficult for the Yancey family to get reimbursed for Dilla's work. Eventually the scuffle over the rights to release Dilla's music posthumously, including the lost MCA album that would eventually be released as *The Diary,* led to a changing of the guard in the estate and the opportunity for Egon to set up a company dedicated to keeping tabs on future profits from Dilla's intellectual property. In a nod to the MCA album's original title, the company was called Pay Jay.

On top of that, Egon had left his position at Stones Throw in 2010, and refocused his working relationship with Madlib into a sort of auteurist label called Madlib Invasion. According to Egon, "We're at a point where the sustainability of a record company at a large level is in question, but the idea that artists like Madlib can sustain a career and release music is possible . . . there are projects that need extra push and those that don't, such as those done for spiritual reasons because that's how Madlib and Dilla make music. Music needs to go into the world."

And Madlib was clearly rattled by the whole ordeal that Dilla's legacy went through before his family and the artistic community could finally have its say. After establishing a sizeable Madlib Invasion catalog over the course of a two years, centered around a thirteen-volume collection of archival and brand-new beats under the banner of *Madlib Medicine Show,* the ridiculously prolific producer had a chance to reflect on his own legacy, especially considering how much of an archive of unheard and unreleased music he'd built up.

Madlib was always deeply self-conscious about his music and refused to let others hold more control over it than he did, dating back to the time the engineer who mixed the first Lootpack album cleaned up all the lo-fi idiosyncrasies Madlib left on the demo tape. So his response was decidedly *can't take it with you:* "I'm gonna burn it down before I die, a little Lee Perry action," he stated in a 2014 profile with *Dazed & Confused,* referring to the fire that the legendary reggae producer allegedly set to burn down his Black Ark Studio. "Ain't nobody exploiting my shit. If I was dying in [a] hospital I'd tell my son to go and burn it. Don't think I'm going to get exploited like they're doing to Dilla."

• • •

Can you invoke a producer's spirit just by flipping beats the same way he did? Once it became known just how Dilla made his unquantized, loose, "drunk"-sounding beats, the opportunity arose to try and piggyback off his ideas, a technique that could've been construed as biting before Yancey's death meant it could be done as tribute instead. Dilla's own perspective on the idea of people biting his style was fairly sanguine: the 2003 Y'skid interview had him admitting that "when I hear that shit, it makes me wanna go make something—but *not* make something like what I've just heard . . . they take the inspiration and do the exact same thing, I don't understand that. What I feel when I make music is energy. I'm not thinking about [DJ] Premier when I make beats. I'm not thinking about Pete Rock. I love their work, I love Dre, I love Timbaland . . . [but inspiration] is how I feel for the day. I don't understand how the shit comes through me—when I feel the urge to work, it just happens." In other words, it's the end result of one particular life experience hearing and spinning and chopping records, an individual experience that can't be imitated or duplicated. Use the same equipment, pull from the same crates, use the same technique, and you still wouldn't be able to counterfeit how Dilla translated what he heard to what he thought to what he made.

This highlights one of the core realities of sample-based music, particularly hip-hop: even in a genre that incorporates a whole continuum of traditions and draws from a shared knowledge of fundamentals—all concerned with how *other artists' music* is reinterpreted—the producer or beatmaker or DJ is still expected to create a *self* from those works, where even someone who owns tens of thousands of records is still able to take pieces from a few of them and rearrange them and juxtapose them in ways literally nobody else could. That's often why so many efforts to literally recapture his sound feel false—an unconscious unlearning of everything a producer used to make their own identity first.

To get an idea of just how difficult this is, let's talk about the producer who got much of the credit for repopularizing sample-based beats in mainstream hip-hop—like Dilla, a Midwestern producer/MC who emerged out of a post–Native Tongues milieu to put his own stamp on the genre. Like Dilla, he prided himself on an ability to straddle classic golden-era hip-hop traditions and popular success among a more materialistic mainstream—in his own words, "first nigga with both a Benz and a backpack"—but unlike Dilla, Kanye West made a bigger splash on the charts and the popular consciousness, spending only a couple years in relative obscurity before emerging as a phenom alongside fellow sample-flipper genius Just Blaze in the production duties for Jay-Z's 2001 masterpiece *The Blueprint*.

Kanye's ear for beats wasn't particularly esoteric or revolutionary;

his first notable early trademark, the sped-up/pitched-up usage of R&B hooks that earned the label "chipmunk soul," had already been used to ghostly effect by RZA on mid-'90s tracks like GZA's "Shadowboxin'" and Wu-Tang Clan's "For Heaven's Sake." What Kanye *did* have was an ability to pull deep cuts from well-known artists—the Doors ("Five to One" on Jay-Z's "The Takeover"), Chaka Khan ("Through the Fire" on his own "Through the Wire"), Curtis Mayfield ("Move on Up" for "Touch the Sky")—and get at them from an approach that preserved the source material's familiarity while coming at it from a completely different rhythmic angle.

Like just about any sample-based producer working at the same time Dilla was, Kanye respected his Detroit peer with a particular reverence. The two initially crossed paths when Kanye was slated to contribute a beat to *Pay Jay,* and Dilla eventually picked the fuzz-bass assault "We F'ed Up," which West originally put together as an alternate beat for "The Takeover" in case the Doors sample couldn't be cleared. Even if Dilla was a quiet, innovative introvert and Kanye was an extroverted, spotlight-bathing synthesist, they seemed to click well. During the making of *Be,* Common's 2005 album with Kanye handling the lion's share of beats and Dilla pitching in for two of them, all three artists would hang out and shoot the breeze. As Kanye recalled in a BBC radio interview, "One of the best days of my life was when [Dilla] handed me a record with drums on it. I was so honored."

But when Kanye was hired to produce the majority of 2007's *Finding Forever,* Common's first album since Dilla's passing, some things just failed to fall into place. Kanye was the main musical force behind *Be,* and everything just felt *right;* even if Dilla's work on *Electric Circus* remains underappreciated to this day, Kanye helping Common rebound with a tight, fundamentally sound return-to-form effort was enough to give both Chicago artists some characteristically definitive entries in their discographies. But *Finding Forever* is where Common and Kanye made a concerted effort to reproduce the Soulquarian-era Dilla sound in earnest, and it's the audio equivalent of a trip to the uncanny valley. It sounds like Kanye's straining out of his wheelhouse to be more slippery and abstract and grimy than he was capable of up to that point, but without Dilla's adventurousness or moments of inspired dissonance. The drums are too clean, the bass too mellow and atonal, the low end not quite low enough. Compounding this is the fact that there's an actual

Dilla beat on *Finding Forever,* "So Far to Go," that makes the Kanye tracks sound weak in direct, easy-to-hear comparison.

It's interesting to note where both artists went from there. Common juggled acting gigs, schlepped through a poorly received follow-up *Universal Mind Control,* then reconnected with longtime friend and producer No I.D. to reestablish himself as one of the sharpest, most humane veteran rappers in the game. Kanye's first big production job post–*Finding Forever,* meanwhile, was a pop-art supernova of a 2007 solo album called *Graduation,* where he expanded his stylistic palette to incorporate electro-house, singer-songwriter rock, and synthpop while still sounding like he was working in his own mode—arena-sized drums and hooks for days and malleable but resonant versions of what could qualify as soul. Then he went minimalist and mournful through Auto-Tune and drum machines on *808s and Heartbreak;* threw his reputation into confused, sometimes-awed tumult; and went on to become one of the most *most* artists of the 2010s, a contentious driver of celeb machinery capable of unfathomable genre-crumbling surprise on record and mortifying, embarrassing troll-job outbursts in the media, social or otherwise.

By the time Madlib worked with him on 2016's *The Life of Pablo* single "No More Parties in LA," the vintage funk-soul beat that Madlib worked up for Kanye and guest rapper Kendrick Lamar—a lo-fi juggling of elements from songs by '70s deep funk icons Junie Morrison, Johnny Guitar Watson, and Larry Graham—was said to have centered the loose cannon Kanye a bit, and critics made a point of sounding how much like the "old Kanye" he sounded. Maybe it was just a case of a megastar happy to relax over a beat that didn't need to prove anything to anyone.

But Madlib revealed something deeper with the beats he made in the latter half of the 2000s—that there was something about Dilla's music that was hard to shake from the mind, even during a concerted effort to make something more individualistic. There were personal reasons, of course: the second Quasimoto album, 2005's *The Further Adventures of Lord Quas,* was intended to be a sort of visual companion piece to Dilla's upcoming *The Shining,* with Jeff Jank cartoon street scenes intentionally echoing each other to fit into a continuous landscape. But Dilla's half of the piece was transferred from *The Shining* to *Donuts,* and the two albums became united in a different way: Dilla's final album of his lifetime, and the last album that featured Madlib as a full-time MC.

With scarce exceptions, Madlib dedicated himself entirely to speaking with his beats.

And he spoke to Dilla in the fifth and sixth volumes of his *Beat Konducta* beat-tape collection. This was a series that, starting in 2006, had already explored some of the best instrumental ideas of Madlib's career, including the eclectic lo-fi hip-hop iconoclasm of *Vol. 1–2: Movie Scenes* and the Bollywood-warping *Vol. 3–4: Beat Konducta in India.* Released as individual volumes in 2008 and collected as an album-length twofer in early 2009, *Vol. 5–6: A Tribute to . . .* is undisguised in its appreciation and homage; each of the album's brief but thoughtfully assembled tracks are given titles that speak to some deeper knowledge, whether upfront nods ("The Mystery [Dilla's Still Here]"; "The Main Inspiration [Coltrane of Beats]"; "First Class [The Best Catalogue]") or allusive in-jokes and personal references ("Never Front [Ears Up]"; "Rolled Peach Optimos [Call Day]"; "Suffer [Concentration]").

But as a tribute, it's slipperier than that. You hear shades of Dilla's sonic ideas: his signature siren drop, sourced from Mantronix B-side "King of the Beats," that he started to use in the early '00s; the same James Brown soundbites he turned into "I Don't Know" punchlines; basslines that hum melodically with the buzz of old analog synthesizers; loops truncated and folded in on each other counterintuitively à la *Donuts.* Yet the comedic soundbites, the slow-burning builds from ambient haze to subwoofer rumbles, and the unexpected detours from genre to genre belong to Madlib. He's not so much doing what Dilla would do, exactly, but doing the kinds of things that hearing Dilla freed Madlib up to try himself, taking one little piece of his friend's vision and carrying it with him forever. And if hip-hop's proven anything, it's that sometimes one little piece is all you need.

# Epilogue
## Breaks and Echoes

GRANDMASTER FLASH isn't so much a traditional album-release-cycle kind of artist these days—he's more of a presence, emerging in the spotlight every so often to provide a reminder of hip-hop's fundamentals and act as one of the living links to the origins of the genre. As a semi-fictional version of him acts as the mentor to the purely fictional Get Down Brothers hip-hop crew in Baz Luhrmann's late '70s Bronx period piece *The Get Down,* the actual Flash served as associate producer and coached the actors on the finer details of hip-hop style as it existed during its origins. He was inducted into the Rock and Roll Hall of Fame in 2007 along with the Furious Five, and was awarded Sweden's Polar Music Prize in 2019 alongside German classical violinist Anne-Sophie Mutter. He remains a regular presence on the international music festival circuit.

Thirty years after he broke out with *3 Feet High and Rising* and twenty years after *A Prince among Thieves* realized his wildest artistic ambitions, Prince Paul has continued to release music in sporadic but counterintuitively fascinating ways: the 2016 Tropicália-tinged Brazilian crossover crew BROOKZILL!, 2012's father-and-son comedy-rap opus *Negroes on Ice* (which inverts the songs-to-skits ratio so that it's the latter that form the bulk of the record), and 2007's mind-bending funk / new wave Bernie Worrell team-up Baby Elephant. While his early work with De La Soul might be hard to find on streaming services thanks to copyright and royalty issues, you can still find it if you know where to look, and as of spring 2019 negotiations are still being hammered out. Paul still does frequent DJ gigs across the United States, though whether or not he still gets mad at his records is up in the air.

Aside from the 2017 HBO docu-series *The Defiant Ones,* chronicling his come-up alongside Jimmy Iovine in the record biz, Dr. Dre's been pretty low-profile in the music world since the release of 2015's *Compton.* In business terms, he's been hit by a series of setbacks: a jury ruled against Dre and Iovine to the tune of over $25 million when former business partner Steven Lamar sued them over royalties for three different models of Beats headphones, and Apple pulled the plug on the Dre-starring/exec-produced online series *Vital Signs* for being too laden with sex, drugs, and violence. Even when he's not on the mic or behind the boards, Dre keeps getting caught up in odd reflections of the controversies that plagued him decades before. But as long as his name keeps appearing in executive producer credits for Kendrick Lamar and Anderson .Paak records, he'll never be more than half a step away from a well-crafted hit.

In a May 2019 interview with Craig Jenkins for *Vulture,* jazz/hip-hop/IDM beat creator Flying Lotus invoked something he remembered Madlib saying about longevity in hip-hop: "You're a producer for six years. That's it." Not only did FlyLo use that remark as an opportunity to find a blessing in his own career's continuing creative dividends, he inadvertently pointed out the fact that Madlib's had more than three times that long to keep at the cutting edge. For someone who can have his discography described as the accumulated work of an actual quarter century, Madlib's by no means faded—slowed down, sure, but only after putting out project after project, solo or collaborative, up through the mid-2010s. Taking a three-year sabbatical after "No More Parties in LA" gave him his highest profile beat ever felt like an uncharacteristic move, but coming back with *Bandana,* his second album with gangsta rapper Freddie Gibbs after the 9mm-in-35mm cinematic sweep of *Piñata,* was a strong way to break his silence.

• • •

In 2015, Memphis hip-hop great and Oscar winner Juicy J produced a track for Harlem-based rapper A$AP Rocky titled "Wavybone." On the mic, it's a fascinating blur of multiple cities' regional rap styles turned into nationwide argot: with the Three 6 Mafia producer/MC joined in guest-verse duty by Port Arthur's long-standing Texas-wide standard-bearers UGK, the southern/southwestern influence of Rocky's flow is put into a sort of cosigned kinship by its elder statesmen. It's what Juicy

J does behind the boards that brings up a fascinating tangle of its own: the track samples "Heaven & Hell," RZA's instrumental for a Raekwon track as covered by Brooklyn funk group El Michels Affair. RZA's beat for the original "Heaven & Hell" was built around "Could I Be Falling in Love," a 1974 recording by singer Syl Johnson cowritten and produced by Willie Mitchell in Memphis's Hi Records.

This is what sampling can bring out in music: a beneath-the-surface narrative of genres and generations carrying across time, musical ideas and interpretations refracting across each other, all in the service of a referential art form you don't actually need to understand the reference to enjoy. Music's in a weird space right now: a lot of it feels intangible, even ephemeral, when the idea of actually buying an album and poring over its liner notes to immerse yourself in its world is a thing of the past. But the fact that sampling is still a common practice in hip-hop feels like a testament to the power of deep-dive knowledge and stylistic recontextualization, especially at a time when the music industry's still trying to re-center itself around the tenuous profit-making possibilities of streaming services and other non-purchase-based models.

This epilogue's being written on the cusp of summer 2019, and it's not hard to find artists using new permutations of sample culture—or old ones used skillfully, for that matter. One of the most talked-about and notoriously genre-busting songs of the year, Lil Nas X's country-crossover rap track "Old Town Road," is based heavily around Nine Inch Nails' minimalist, ambient/industrial 2008 instrumental "34 Ghosts IV"—a collision of four genres at once creating a song that's become nigh-on inescapable. Tyler, the Creator's *IGOR* incorporates samples throughout the album's entirety—everything from Krautrock synth-jockeys Cluster to soul icon Al Green—but he uses them as part of a seamless whole that's hard to separate from the future-funk keyboard chords and drum programming he pulls from other means. And across all genres of hip-hop and R&B, the site WhoSampled.com counts well over four thousand different songs from 2018 that use samples, including Top 40 hits by 21 Savage ("A Lot"), Drake ("Nice for What"), Kanye West ("Ghost Town"), Lil Wayne ("Uproar"), and J. Cole ("ATM").

So, no: sampling isn't going away anytime soon. Not when twenty-something Dilla-inspired bedroom beatmakers punch up evocative soul-jazz gems for "chill beats to study and relax to" playlists on YouTube, or DIY makers create zero-budget loop-based beats on portable studios just to be heard. Especially not when archival reissue labels keep finding obscure old sounds that haven't been chopped yet. It's long expanded well past the scope of hip-hop, of course—you could write books as big as this one on sampling's role in R&B, dance music, even rock. But that's the thing about DJ culture, and the sample culture that came from it: there will always be another beat, another way to loop, another break waiting to shake speakers into another phase of creation.

# Acknowledgments

There are so many people I want to thank for this book, starting with my family—Mom and Dad, who encouraged my enthusiasm for music just by having it on in the car all the time; my stepfather David Rich, who taught me that there was a whole huge world of music from Sun Ra to Jorge Ben far beyond the radio; and my big brother Damian, who pulled me deep into hip-hop once Grandmaster Flash, Run-D.M.C., and the Beastie Boys sparked my interest as a kid. (He makes beats himself, and has been an invaluable resource when it comes to learning the ins and outs of DJing and producing.)

I've also got countless thanks to all the friends and fellow writers I've found through this lifelong obsession with music: Charles Aaron, Nitsuh Abebe, Dart Adams, Hilton Als, Jessica Armbruster, Sarah Askari, Ian Babineau, Chris Barrus, Stuart Berman, Andy Beta, James Blount, Jonathan Bogart, Jay Boller, Jen Boyles, Regina Bradley, Tom Breihan, Jonah Bromwich, Daphne Brooks, David Brothers, Donna Brown, Marty Brown, Todd Burns, Mairead Case, Jeff Chang, Dan Charnas, Hayden Childs, Nate Chinen, Robert Christgau, Amy Coddington, Anthony Cohan-Miccio, Aaron Cohen, Brian Coleman, Daniel Cooper, Del Cowie, Raymond Cummings, Michael Daddino, Geeta Dayal, Melody and Stephen Deusner, Chris DeVille, Martin Douglas, Mike Duquette, Steacy Easton, Chuck Eddy, Ali Elabaddy, Dan Epstein, Stephen Thomas Erlewine, Chris Estey, kris ex, Tom Ewing, Jerard Fagerberg, Kathy Fennessy, Reed Fischer, Anna Forsher, Phil Freeman, Jay Williams Friedman, Nathaniel Friedman, Andrew Gaerig, Jeff Gage, Deneen Gannon, Noah Goodbaum, Michael Grasso, Julia Gray, Jayson Greene, David Grossman, Shuja Haider, Rahawa Haile, Robert Ham,

Jack Hamilton, dream hampton, Nick Hanover, Keith Harris, Jess Harvell, Eric Harvey, Rob Harvilla, Kenan Hebert, Will Hermes, Kevin Hoffman, Marc Hogan, Jessica Hopper, Kaleb Horton, Brian Howe, Hua Hsu, Steve Huey, Charles Hughes, Thomas Inskeep, Kate Izquierdo, Craig Jenkins, Maura Johnston, Mike Joseph, Britt Julious, Rafi Kam, Tom Keiser, Andy Kellman, Kim Kelly, Zach Kelly, Nicole Kessler, J. Edward Keyes, Kate Koliha, Josh Kortbein, Jody Beth LaFosse, Scott Lapatine, Jeremy Larson, Kallen Law, Michael Legan, Joan and Matt LeMay, Bruce Levenstein, Catherine Lewis, Zachary Lipez, Tigger Lunney, Brian MacDonald, Erin MacLeod, Melissa Maerz, Ian Manire, Jill Mapes, Greil Marcus, Marc Masters, Ian Mathers, Michaelangelo Matos, Jen Matson, Evan McGarvey, Mike McGonigal, Kembrew McLeod, James McNally, Nick Minichino, Evan Minsker, Chris Molanphy, Marcus J. Moore, Vanessa Moore Ardolino, Mike Mullen, Evan Nabavian, Evie Nagy, Michael Nelson, Frank Nieto, Chris O'Leary, Sach Orenstein, Luis Paez-Pumar, Alex Pappademas, Jill Passmore, Jenn Pelly, Liz Pelly, Dan Perry, Lisa Jane Persky, Amanda Petrusich, Amy Phillips, Leonard Pierce, Scott Plagenhoef, Thomas Pluck, Ann Powers, Ned Raggett, Ian Rans, David Raposa, Bridgette Reinsmoen, Simon Reynolds, Matt Rice, Mark Richardson, Jody Rosen, David Roth, Kelly Savage, Fred "Freddy Fresh" Schmid, Todd Schneider, Pete Scholtes, Zach Schonfeld, Susannah McNeely Schouweiler, Will Schube, Shea Serrano, Scott Seward, Jeff Shaw, Philip Sherburne, Maria Sherman, Rachel Shimp, Al Shipley, Brad Shoup, Mark Sinker, Jes Skolnik, Jay Smooth, Laura Snapes, Alfred Soto, Anton Spice, Katherine St. Asaph, Tyina Steptoe, Tucker Stone, Andy Sturdevant, Jessica Suarez, Andrea Swensson, Austin Swinburn, Joe Tangari, Rob Tannenbaum, Greg Tate, Benjamin Tausig, Conrad Teves, Lindsey Thomas, Paul Thompson, Dave Tompkins, Pete Tosiello, Gabriela Tully Claymore, Scott Von Doviak, Oliver Wang, Eric Weisbard, Jeff Weiss, RJ White, Carl Wilson, Sean Witzke, Douglas Wolk, Mark Yarm, Noah Yoo, Annie Zaleski, Andy Zax, and Lindsay Zoladz. You could pick any one of these people at random and have a conversation about music and culture that'd give you some legit hope in this world, so look up their bylines when you can.

Additional thanks to my editors Erik Anderson and Kristian Tvedten at the University of Minnesota Press, along with my agent Philip Turner.

Special thanks to all the artists and musicians who inspire me not just as a fan but as a writer. An incomplete list: Open Mike Eagle, Eothen "Egon" Alapatt, Questlove, J-Zone, El-P and Killer Mike, Jean Grae, Quelle Chris, Pharoahe Monch, billy woods, Serengeti, Chrissy Shively, Renee "Reverend Dollars" Jarreau, Stephen "Zilla Rocca" Zales, Chris Schlarb, Jason Forrest, Sean McPherson, and Dylan Hicks.

Rest in peace to Raghav Mehta, Rashod Ollison, and Reggie "Combat Jack" Osse.

# Notes

## Introduction

**ix**    Daniel Hamm: Andy Beta, "Blood and Echoes: The Story of *Come Out,*
*Steve Reich's Civil Rights Era Masterpiece,*" *Pitchfork,* April 28, 2016.

**ix**    "People are destroyed": James Baldwin, "A Report from Occupied Territory," *The Nation,* July 11, 1966.

**ix**    Reich agreed: Beta, "Blood and Echoes."

## 1. Wheels of Steel

**9**    "We started reaching": Bill Brewster and Frank Broughton, *Last Night a*
*DJ Saved My Life: The History of the Disc Jockey* (New York: Grove Press,
2000), 235–36.

**16**    "I was asked": Ibid., 238.

## 2. Change the Beat

**21**    "I just anticipated": Bill Brewster and Frank Broughton, *Last Night a DJ*
*Saved My Life: The History of the Disc Jockey* (New York: Grove Press,
2000), 251–52.

**23**    In a handwritten list: Chris Salewicz, *Redemption Song: The Ballad of Joe*
*Strummer* (New York: Faber and Faber, 2006), 279.

**30**    "Man with drum": Jeff Mao, "Arthur Baker," *Red Bull Music Academy,* September 2007.

**35**    "It was this amazing thing": Kembrew McLeod, *Creative License: The Law*
*and Culture of Digital Sampling* (Durham, N.C.: Duke University Press,
2011), 112–13.

**36**    In fact, the *Voice:* Michael Hill, "Licks: Rap-Off," *Village Voice,* October 11,
1983.

## 3. Funky Drummer

**39**    "The phone would": Grandmaster Flash with David Ritz, *The Adventures of Grandmaster Flash: My Life, My Beats* (New York: Broadway Books, 2008).

**44**    "If you were": easymobee, "THE MOST INFLUENTIAL RECORDS IN HIP HOP: Fusion Beats Vol. 2 (Bozo Meko Records circa 1980–81)," Instagram, July 6, 2015, www.instagram.com/p/4zu_UgHwt2.

**52**    "The lyrics are too": Jill Cuniff, "Public Enemy: *Yo! Bum Rush the Show*," *Thrasher,* December 1987.

## 4. Synthetic Substitution

**68**    Paul wound up unhappy: Angus Batey, "The Magic Number," *HipHop.com,* April 7, 2009.

**69**    "a deep record collection": Larry Fitzmaurice, "5-10-15-20: Prince Paul," *Pitchfork,* October 25, 2012.

**71**    "new wave to Public Enemy's punk": Robert Christgau, "Consumer Guide," *Village Voice,* March 28, 1989.

**71**    "psychedelic": Michael Azerrad, "3 Feet High and Rising," *Rolling Stone,* March 23, 1989, and "De La Soul's Hippie-Hop," *Rolling Stone,* May 4, 1989.

**75**    "They're pulling the greatest": Jonathan Croyle, "On This Date: The Controversial Beastie Boys Play the War Memorial in 1987," Syracuse.com, April 10, 2017.

**78**    "I went to Tower Records": Beats 1, "Mike D & Adam 'Ad-Rock' Horovitz from Beastie Boys [FULL INTERVIEW," YouTube, uploaded September 8, 2015, www.youtube.com/watch?v=svorqE9tnYo.

**79**    "Man, we was mad": Batey, "Magic Number."

## 5. Talkin' All That Jazz

**83**    "this is the first generation": Nelson George, *Hip Hop America.* London: Penguin Group (USA), 1998.89–90.

**83**    "You cannot substitute": Frank Owen, "Bite This," *Spin,* November 1989.

**84**    "you spend 12 seconds": Ibid.

**84**    His appearance at the New Music Seminar: Ibid.

**85**    "You can have that": Ryan Proctor, "Old to the New Q&A (Part Three): Daddy-O," *Old to the New,* September 11, 2013, www.oldtothenew.wordpress.com.

**87**    "I must be": Jeff Mao, "Q-Tip," *Red Bull Music Academy,* June 2013.

**88**    "A completely original": "A Tribe Called Quest: *People's Instinctive Travels and the Paths of Rhythm*," *The Source,* June 1990.

**88**    "Sampling gives young blacks": Owen, "Bite This."

**89**    "At first": Jaeki Cho, "Prince Paul Tells All: The Stories behind His Classic Records (Part 1)," *Complex,* December 8, 2011, www.complex.com.

**99**    "I was leery": Bill, Adler, liner notes to *Guru's Jazzmatazz Volume 1* by Guru, Chrysalis 0946 3 21998 2 9, F2 21998, CD, 1993.

## 6. Constant Elevation

**102**   "I guess by now": Touré, "Public Enemy: *Muse Sick-n-Hour Mess Age,*" *Rolling Stone,* July 14, 1994.

**105**   "Why you trying": Jaeki Cho, "Prince Paul Tells All: The Stories behind His Classic Records (Part 2)," *Complex,* December 11, 2011, www.complex.com.

**111**   "The piano is detuned": The RZA, *The Wu-Tang Manual* (New York: Riverhead Books, 2005), 191.

**111**   "I was like": Thomas Golianopoulos, "Chain Reaction," *Scratch Magazine,* March/April 2006.

**113**   Instead of "buying a car": The RZA, *The Tao of Wu* (New York: Riverhead Books, 2009), 112.

**114**   "one for each voice": Ibid., 117.

**114**   "Ghost's voice": Ibid., 119.

**114**   "money, fame, and ego": Ibid., 134.

**114**   "I'd spent two years": Ibid., 135.

**115**   "like it grew": Ibid., 136.

**116**   Incidentally, Pete Rock: David Ma, "As One of Hip-Hop's Most Respected Producers, Pete Rock Wants to Continue Forever," *Wax Poetics,* September 18, 2008.

**120**   "I tried to make": Andrew Mason, "The Memoirs of Prince Paul," *Wax Poetics,* Spring 2002.

## 7. Funky Enough

**127**   "Greg blamed": Dave Stelfox, "Nightclubbing: Uncle Jamm's Army," *Red Bull Music Academy Daily,* October 31, 2017.

**128**   "I had never": Tim Sanchez, "Exclusive: Greg Mack Breaks Down the History of 1580 KDAY," *AllHipHop*, December 30, 2013.

**129**   "In the back": Red Bull Music Academy, "Uncle Jamm's Army: Pioneers of the Modern Party," YouTube, uploaded October 27, 2017, www.youtube.com/watch?v=ohZ3WIS3qBo.

**129**   "When we first": Ibid.

**129**   "The Long Beach Insanes": Jeff Chang, *Can't Stop Won't Stop: A History of the Hip-Hop Generation* (New York: St. Martin's Press, 2005), 508.

**129** "angry, disillusioned, unloved": Patrick Goldstein, "Can Rap Survive Gang War?" *Los Angeles Times,* August 24, 1986.

**130** "We need to give it": Ibid.

**135** "Me and Dre": Chris Ziegler, "Arabian Prince: Women and Partying and Freaks," *L.A. Record,* August 19, 2008, www.larecord.com.

**141** "It's not the same": Kasper Hartwich, "Vanilla Ice denies Ripping Off Queen and David Bowie's Under Pressure," YouTube, uploaded March 12, 2013, www.youtube.com/watch?v=a-1_9-z9rbY.

**142** "because the group": Brian Coleman, *Check the Technique, Volume 2: More Liner Notes for Hip-Hop Junkies* (Everett, Mass.: Wax Facts Press, 2014), 239.

**142** "then you'll barely": Ibid., 240.

**143** "with Bomb Squad": Ibid., 242.

**143** But it was an even more: Chris Wilder, "Album of the Year 1991: NWA— *Niggaz4life,*" *The Source,* January 1992.

**143** there was a *Rolling Stone:* Arion Berger, "*Niggaz4Life,*" *Rolling Stone,* July 11, 1991.

## 8. G Thang

**145** "defined, shaped, and expanded": "George Clinton, Bootsy Collins, and Bernie Worrell," *Our Voices with Bev Smith,* BET, 1991.

**145** "We're not upset": Ibid.

**146** "Artists aren't allowed the luxury": George Clinton, *Brothas Be, Yo Like George, Ain't That Funkin' Kinda Hard on You? A Memoir* (New York: Atria Books, 2017), 295.

**147** "I don't give": Gerrick D. Kennedy, *Parental Discretion Is Advised: The Rise of N.W.A and the Dawn of Gangsta Rap* (New York: Atria Books, 2017), 162.

**148** "I got all you": Eazy-E Ruthless Records, "Ice Cube Pump It Up Clip that Led Dr Dre to Assault Dee Barnes," YouTube, uploaded December 1, 2016, www.youtube.com/watch?v=IJe7otZRW88.

**148** "deserved it": Alan Light, "N.W.A.: Beating Up the Charts," *Rolling Stone,* August 8, 1991.

**148** "They've started believing": Ibid.

**149** "Eazy-E, MC Ren": dream hampton, "Niggaz, Please," *Village Voice,* July 23, 1991.

**150** "If [N.W.A.] were offended": Ronin Ro, "There Goes Round 2," *The Source,* June 1992.

**155** "They had the worst": Kennedy, *Parental Discretion Is Advised,* 152–53.

**156** "the words don't exist": Ibid., 199.

**157** "shot *at*": Ronin Ro, "Moving Target," *The Source,* November 1992.

**159** "I was a young producer": Shawn Setaro, "Dr. Dre Perfected G-Funk, but He Didn't Invent It—Gregory Hutchinson Did," *Complex,* July 11, 2017.

**163** "With 'Dre Day'": Tony Best, "Musician Colin Wolfe Built Beats with Dr. Dre for *The Chronic,* N.W.A's *Niggaz4Life,* and Jimmy Z's *Muzical Madness,*" *Wax Poetics,* June 3, 2014.

## 9. Aftermath

**169** "The music was": Chuck Philips, "Rap Defense Doesn't Stop Death Penalty," *Los Angeles Times,* July 15, 1993.

**170** "These are my boys": Peter A Berry, "Woman Who Accused Tupac Shakur of Rape Recalls 1993 Assault in Hotel Room," *XXL,* January 31, 2018.

**170** "taking something from": "Tupac Shakur," *Arsenio Hall Show,* March 8, 1994.

**170** "they knew me": Kevin Powell, "Ready to Live," *Vibe,* April 1995.

**171** "blues record": Tupac Shakur, *Tupac: Resurrection, 1971–1996* (New York: Atria Books, 2003), 166.

**171** "I knew I could": Ibid., 186.

**173** "the vengeful Tupac": Powell, "Ready to Live."

**175** "Me and Snoop": "Jermaine Dupri," *Drink Champs,* October 25, 2017, www .youtube.com/watch?v=ssU_xN6wOg8.

**177** "He said you can't": Rob Marriott, "Last Testament," *Vibe,* November 1996.

**178** "I don't want": Kevin Powell, "Live from Death Row," *Vibe,* February 1996.

**179** "I have no mercy": Marriott, "Last Testament."

**180** "My decision was based": Ibid.

**180** "[Death Row's] whole business": Ronin Ro, "Escape from Death Row."*Vibe,* October 1996.

**181** The working title: Nathan Slavik, "Tupac Was Working on 'One Nation' Album with Outkast, DJ Premier, and More When He Died," *DJBooth. net,* February 12, 2018.

**185** "A lot of rappers": Alex Pappademas, "Icon: Dr. Dre," GQ, October 2007.

## 10. The Loop Digga

**193** "We were supposed": Jeff Weiss, "The Madlib Mystique," *LA Weekly,* June 24, 2010.

**193** "My pops had me": Jeff Mao, "A Conversation with Madlib," *Red Bull Music Academy,* April 2016.

**199** "I was like": Jeff Chang, liner notes to *Quannum Presents Solesides Greatest Bumps,* Quannum Projects QP 022-2, CD, 2002.

**201** "In the '80s": Tom Murphy, "DJ Shadow Isn't So Sure That *Introducing* Was the First 100 Percent Sample-Based Record," *Westword,* September 26, 2013.

**202** "Just being in here": *Scratch*, directed by Doug Pray (New York: Palm Pictures, 2001).

**206** In a disaster-courting twist: "Peanut Butter Wolf," *Questlove Supreme,* Pandora, March 20, 2019.

**206** "With no major label": Matt Conaway, "Rasco—*Time Waits for No Man,*" *AllMusic,* July 1998.

## 11. The Illest Villains

**210** "low" and "all tired-sounding": Jeff Mao, "Mythic Crates," *Wax Poetics,* Fall 2013.

**221** "Regardless of what": Havelock Nelson, "The Rap Column," *Billboard,* April 16, 1994.

**222** "To promote lynching": Terri Rossi, "R&B Rhythms," *Airplay Monitor,* March 1994.

**222** "the whole concept": John Schechter, "Corporate Hysteria," *The Source,* June 1994.

**222** "[He] seemed really": "Dante Ross Podcast," *Outside the Lines with Rap Genius,* February 19, 2013, https://genius.com/posts/1666-New-podcast-dante-ross-34.

**222** "only a little vexed": Schecter, "Corporate Hysteria."

**222** "It was a dead album": Brian Coleman, *Check the Technique, Volume 2: More Liner Notes for Hip-Hop Junkies* (Everett, Mass.: Wax Facts Press, 2014), 293.

**226** "one out of four": Will Gottsegen, "*Madvillainy* at 15: MF Doom on the Legacy of His Classic Madlib Collaboration," *Spin,* March 25, 2019.

**227** "He'd hear a joint": Jeff Mao, "DOOM," *Red Bull Music Academy,* November 2011.

**229** "Anybody could do a beat": Eothen Alapatt, "Interview: Madlib," *Red Bull Music Academy,* 2002.

**232** Even Thom Yorke: Scott Colothan, "Thom Yorke Lists His Favourite New Sounds," *Gigwise,* January 24, 2007.

**232** "I'm the writer": Ta-Nehisi Coates, "The Mask Of Doom," *The New Yorker,* September 14, 2009.

## 12. Survival Test

**235** "an excellent cello player": Ronnie Reese, "Son of Detroit: The Oral History of J Dilla," *Wax Poetics,* June/July 2006.

**235** "When he first started": Ibid.

**235** "when I hear mistakes": Alvin Blanco, "Still Lives Through," *Scratch,* February 2006.

**236** "he sounds like": Jeff Mao, "Q-Tip," *Red Bull Music Academy,* June 2013.

**236** "We didn't even believe": Eothen Alapatt et al., "J Dilla: Shine On," *The Fader,* December 2006.

**237** "mid-tempo muddle": Sia Michel, "The Pharcyde—*Labcabincalifornia,*" *Spin.* December 1995.

**237** "the casually delivered": Steve Hochman, "Album Reviews : ** The Pharcyde, 'Labcabincalifornia,' Delicious Vinyl," *Los Angeles Times,* November 18, 1995.

**237** "I just never": Jeff Mao, "Questlove," *Red Bull Music Academy,* June 2013.

**238** The gambit worked: Reese, "Son of Detroit."

**239** AllMusic dismissed the production: John Bush, "A Tribe Called Quest— *Beats, Rhymes, and Life,*" *AllMusic,* n.d.

**239** *Spin* played up: Will Hermes, "A Tribe Called Quest—*Beats, Rhymes, and Life,*" *Spin,* September 1996.

**239** the *Washington Post:* Richard Harrington, "A Tribe Called Quest, *Beats, Rhymes, and Life,*" *Washington Post,* August 28, 1996.

**239** "Being good is only": Hanif Abdurraqib, *Go Ahead in The Rain: Notes to A Tribe Called Quest* (Austin: University of Texas Press, 2019), 102.

**239** "with Ummah": "Exclusive: Q-Tip Interview," *moovmnt.com,* April 19, 2009, www.moovmnt.com/2009/04/19/exclusive-q-tip-interview.

**240** "[The Ummah] had done a remix": Steve Appleford, "Jimmy Jam and Terry Lewis: Our Life in 15 Songs," *Rolling Stone,* October 9, 2015.

**240** "they heard some shit": "Exclusive: Q-Tip Interview."

**240** "we all collaborated": dunya a, "Dilla Interview 2003 Part 1 of 4," YouTube, uploaded March 23, 2008, www.youtube.com/watch?v=YKGm3wc3qOE.

**242** "His favorite thing": Mao, "Questlove."

**243** "Me, myself, I hung around": Anslem Samuel, "J Dilla, The Lost Interview [circa 2004]," *XXL,* February 10, 2010.

**244** "It was completely different": Martin Turenne, "High Fidelity," *Urb,* March 2004.

**245** "stuff for me": Don Hogan, "Do the Math," *Rime,* republished on *Stones Throw,* May 1, 2003.

**246** "He's like . . .": "Peanut Butter Wolf," *Questlove Supreme,* Pandora, March 20, 2019.

**246** "I flew him out": dunya a, "Dilla Interview 2003 Part 1 of 4."

**247** *Champion Sound* remains: Alapatt et al., "J Dilla."

**247** "absolutely and utterly flopped": Jordan Ferguson, *Donuts* (New York: Bloomsbury, 2016), 74.

**250** "He'd have his arms": Reese, "Son of Detroit."

**252** "We're at a point": Laurent Fintoni, "Give Them What They Want: The 10-Year Mission to Release J Dilla's Legendary Lost Solo Album," *Fact,* March 29, 2016.

**253** "when I hear that shit": dunya a, "Dilla Interview 2003 Part 1 of 4."

**254** "One of the best days": Timmhotep Aku, "Fantastic Voyage," *The Source,* April 2006.

# Bibliography

ALONG WITH ARTICLES AND WORKS directly referenced as citations, I've compiled a list of every single resource I've consulted during the writing of this book. While I've done all due diligence to cite specific quotations when not attributed in the body of the text, further reading and viewing of the works listed has also contributed significantly to this book, and I recommend all of it as further reading.

Certain publications and resources deserve special mention.

The Adler Hip Hop Archive, collected digitally through Cornell University, has been an invaluable resource throughout, especially in its accumulated press clippings and coverage of hip-hop in the 1980s.

The works of Bill Brewster and Frank Broughton, especially their collaborative books *Last Night a DJ Saved My Life: The History of the Disc Jockey* and *The Record Players: DJ Revolutionaries,* provided numerous insights into the ins and outs of club culture as it pertained to hip-hop's early DJ roots.

Grandmaster Flash's autobiography with David Ritz, *The Adventures of Grandmaster Flash: My Life, My Beats,* is as thorough an insight to the personal, professional, and artistic life of the superstar DJ as you could ever want, a crucial resource in understanding the formative years of an artist who's not often given to dwelling on the past.

Brian Coleman's two-volume (and, hopefully, counting) series *Check the Technique* has proven not just resourceful but inspirational, the sort of oral-history deep dives into albums like *AmeriKKKa's Most Wanted, 6 Feet Deep,* and *Black Bastards* that this book would be all the poorer without. That goes double for his encouragement.

Gerrick D. Kennedy's book *Parental Discretion Is Advised: The Rise of N.W.A and the Dawn of Gangsta Rap* was an exhaustive resource that helped send me off in a bunch of different directions in search of ideas, and on its own it's an endlessly compelling look at how West Coast hip-hop came to be.

Corporate patronage can be fickle, but the work that Yadastar did with Red Bull Music Academy (for whom, full disclosure, I've written before) brought two decades' worth of firsthand insight from artists and music journalists that any publication could envy.

Firsthand interviews were difficult to land, but my brief yet illuminating conversation with Eothen "Egon" Alapatt was a gift, and he came across as the kind of person with whom you could kill a few hours just geeking out over underheard records. I hope I can find an excuse to do so more often.

## Periodicals

"2 Musicians Sue Rapper." *Variety,* March 16, 1993.

"A Tribe Called Quest: *People's Instinctive Travels and Paths of Rhythm.*" *The Source,* June 1990.

Abbey, John. "Introducing Melvin Bliss." *Blues & Soul,* issue 131, March 26, 1974.

Adler, Jerry. "The Rap Attitude." *Newsweek,* March 19, 1990.

Agoston, Peter. "Charizma & Peanut Butter Wolf." *Elemental Magazine,* February 2004.

Aku, Timmhotep. "Fantastic Voyage." *The Source,* April 2006.

Akwanza. [MC Ren interview]. *Rap Pages,* February 1994.

Alapatt, Eothen. "Blunted on Beats." *Wax Poetics,* Spring 2004.

Alapatt, Eothen, et al. "J Dilla: Shine On." *The Fader,* December 2006.

Aletti, Vince. "Golden Voices and Hearts of Steel—Review of the Rap Party at the Ritz." *Village Voice,* March 18, 1981.

Aletti, Vince. "Licks: Furious," *Village Voice,* July 20, 1982.

Anson, Robert Sam. "To Die Like a Gangsta." *Vanity Fair,* March 1997.

Azerrad, Michael. "3 Feet High and Rising." *Rolling Stone,* March 23, 1989.

Azerrad, Michael. "De La Soul's Hippie-Hop." *Rolling Stone,* May 4, 1989.

Baldwin, James. "A Report from Occupied Territory." *The Nation,* July 11, 1966.

Bangs, Lester. "The White Noise Supremacists." *Village Voice,* April 30, 1979.

Baraka, Ras. "Mo' Dialogue: Ice Cube." *The Source,* September 1991.

Barrow, Jerry L. "Dr. Dre *Vibe* Cover Story." *Vibe,* August/September 2010.

Berger, Arion. "*Niggaz4Life.*" *Rolling Stone,* July 11, 1991.

The Blackspot. "Stakes Is High." *Vibe,* September 1996.

Blackwell, Mark. "Niggaz4Dinner." *Spin,* September 1991.

Blanco, Alvin. "Still Lives Through." *Scratch Magazine,* February 2006.

Blanning, Lisa. "The Crate Mass Experiment." *The Wire,* August 2009.

Boyer, Edward J. "Celebrities Use Airwaves to Take On Street Violence." *Los Angeles Times,* October 10, 1986.

Bozza, Anthony. "Dr. Dre." *Rolling Stone,* December 9, 1999.

Brown, Ethan. "My Name Is Prince . . . and I Make Beats." *The Source,* April 1999.

Cagle, Jess, and John Callan. "All Hell Breaks Loose at a Run-D.M.C. 'Raising Hell' Rap Concert in California." *People,* September 1, 1986.

Carter, Kelley L. "Jay Dee's Last Days: Serious Illness Couldn't Stop Drive to Make Music." *Detroit Free Press,* May 2, 2016.

Chang, Jeff, and Mike Nardone. "Saturday Nite Fresh: An Interview with Uncle Jamm's Army." *Rap Pages,* December 1994.

Chennault, Sam. "The Beat Goes On." *SF Weekly,* November 26, 2003.

Chonin, Neva. "A Dilly of a Career." *SFGate,* November 1, 1998.

Christgau, Robert. "1981 Pazz & Jop: The Year the Rolling Stones Lost the Pennant." *Village Voice,* February 1, 1982.

Christgau, Robert. "Consumer Guide." *Village Voice,* March 28, 1989.

Coates, Ta-Nehisi. "The Mask of Doom." *New Yorker,* September 14, 2009.

Coleman, Brian. "Hammers of the Gods: Celebrating the Technics 1200, the Weapon of Choice That Makes Every DJ's Day." *XX,* Fall 1998.

Coscarelli, Joe. "Dr. Dre Apologizes to the 'Women I've Hurt.'" *New York Times,* August 21, 2015.

Cuniff, Jill. "Public Enemy: *Yo! Bum Rush the Show.*" *Thrasher,* December 1987.

Da Ghetto Communicator. "Nas: Queens B-boy Brings Back the Bridge." *Vibe,* April 1994.

Dennis, Reginald C. "Tim Dog: Nightmare on Webster Avenue." *The Source,* September 1991.

Detrick, Ben. "The Dirty Heartbeat of the Golden Age." *Village Voice,* November 6, 2007.

"Eazy E: Temporary Insanity." *The Source,* July 1993.

Eshun, Ekow. "The Rap Trap." *The Guardian,* May 26, 2000.

ex, kris. "Nas, 'It Was Written.'" *Vibe,* September 1996.

Flores, Louis. "Dee Barnes Interview." *The Source,* December 1992.

Frazier, Kelly, et al. "Spiritualized." *Real Detroit Weekly,* March 19, 2006.

Gale, Ezra. "Liquid Liquid Haven't Lost Their Edge." *Village Voice,* March 23, 2011.

George, Nelson. "Flash Is Bad." *Village Voice,* April 7, 1987.

Gold, Jonathan. "N.W.A: A Hard Act to Follow." *LA Weekly,* May 5, 1989.

Golianopoulos, Thomas. "Chain Reaction." *Scratch Magazine,* March/April 2006.

Goldstein, Patrick. "Can Rap Survive Gang War?" *Los Angeles Times,* August 24, 1986.

Haden-Guest, Anthony. "We Happy Few." *New York*, April 4, 1983.

hampton, dream. "Niggaz, Please." *Village Voice,* July 23, 1991.

hampton, dream. "R-E-S-P-E-C-T." *The Source,* May 1991.

Harrington, Richard. "A Tribe Called Quest, *Beats, Rhymes, and Life.*" *Washington Post,* August 28, 1996.

Harrington, Richard. "De La Soul's Mind-Bending Rap." *Washington Post,* May 18, 1989.

Harrington, Richard. "Run-DMC and the Rap Flap." *Washington Post,* August 29, 1986.

Hermes, Will. "A Tribe Called Quest—*Beats, Rhymes, and Life.*" *Spin,* September 1996.

Hiatt, Brian. "N.W.A: American Gangstas." *Rolling Stone,* August 27, 2015.

Hilburn, Robert. "Rap 'Message' Jumps Out in a Flash." *Los Angeles Times,* March 27, 1983.

Hilburn, Robert. "Striking Tales of Black Frustration and Pride Shake the Pop Mainstream." *Los Angeles Times,* April 2, 1989.

Hill, Michael. "The Clash at the Clampdown." *Village Voice,* June 10, 1981.

Hill, Michael. "Licks: Rap-Off." *Village Voice,* October 11, 1983.

Hochman, Steve. "Album Reviews : ** The Pharcyde, 'Labcabincalifornia,' Delicious Vinyl." *Los Angeles Times,* November 18, 1995.

Hochman, Steve. "Compton Rappers versus the Letter of the Law: FBI Claims Song by N.W.A Advocates Violence on Police." *Los Angeles Times,* October 5, 1989.

Holmstrom, John. "Death to Disco Shit!" *Punk,* January 1976.

Hunt, Dennis. "Liberating Rap with Jazz Sound: Freestyle Fellowship Adds Riffs to Rhymes." *Los Angeles Times,* June 29, 1993.

Knoedelseder, William, Jr. "Record Industry Probe Examines Small N.J. Firm: East, West Coast Grand Juries Looking into Sugar Hill Label." *Los Angeles Times,* March 31, 1986.

Leland, John. "Public Enemy: Noise Annoys." *Village Voice*, April 21, 1987.

Leland, John. "The Big Steal." *The Face,* March 1988.

Leland, John. "Public Enemy: Noise Annoys." *Village Voice,* April 21, 1987.

Light, Alan. "New Faces of 1991: De La Soul." *Rolling Stone,* April 18, 1991.

Light, Alan. "N.W.A: Beating Up the Charts." *Rolling Stone,* August 8, 1991.

Loder, Kurt. "Grandmaster Flash, 'The Message.'" *Rolling Stone,* September 16, 1982.

Lorrel, Elyse. "Ear to the Street." *The Source,* October 1991.

Ma, David. "In the Beginning." *Wax Poetics,* Spring 2017.

"Mail." *Vibe,* August 1995.

Mao, Jeff. "Behind the Boards: The Legacy of Marley Marl." *ego trip*, issue 12, 1998.

Mao, Jeff. "Mythic Crates." *Wax Poetics,* Fall 2013.

Marriott, Rob. "Last Testament." *Vibe,* November 1996.

Mason, Andrew. "Mad Skills." *Scratch Magazine*, Spring 2005.

Mason, Andrew. "The Memoirs of Prince Paul." *Wax Poetics,* Spring 2002.

McCord, Mark. "Once upon a Time in the Boogie Down Bronx." *Wax Poetics,* issue 27, February 2008.

Miller, Chuck. "Two Turntables and a Microphone: The Story of Grandmaster Flash and the Furious Five." *Goldmine,* December 6, 1996.

Morris, Chris. "Building the Perfect Beastie Album." *Billboard,* September 9, 1989.

Mullen, Brendan. "Down for the Good Life." *LA Weekly,* June 21, 2000.

Murphy, Bill. "Phantom Menace: Remix Mag Interview with Madlib and Engineer Dave Cooley." *Remix Magazine,* republished on *Stones Throw,* May 5, 2005.

Murphy, Keith. "The Love Movement." *Vibe,* February 2007.

Nelson, Havelock. "The Rap Column." *Billboard*, April 16, 1994.

Noakes, Tim. "A Rare Encounter with Madlib." *Dazed & Confused,* December 2013.

Owen, Frank. "Bite This." *Spin,* November 1989.

Owen, Frank. "Hanging Tough." *Spin,* April 1990.

Palmer, Robert. "Funk Takes a Provocative Turn." *New York Times,* November 21, 1982.

Pappademas, Alex. "Icon: Dr. Dre." *GQ,* October 2007.

Pareles, Jon. "Defiance and Rage Hone a Debut Rap Album." *New York Times,* May 10, 1987.

Pareles, Jon. "Disco: Rap Group at the Ritz." *New York Times,* September 12, 1984.

Pemberton, Andy. "Trip Hop." *Mixmag,* June 1994.

Philips, Chuck. "N.W.A's Dr. Dre Target of Suit by Host of Rap Show." *Los Angeles Times,* July 23, 1991.

Philips, Chuck. "Rap Defense Doesn't Stop Death Penalty." *Los Angeles Times,* July 15, 1993.

Philips, Chuck. "Tupac Shakur: 'I Am Not a Gangster.'" *Los Angeles Times,* October 25, 1995.

Philips, Chuck. "The Violent Art, Violent Reality of Dr. Dre." *Los Angeles Times,* December 15, 1992.

Powell, Kevin. "*2Pacalypse Now*." *Vibe,* February 1995.

Powell, Kevin. "Little Big Man." *Vibe,* December 1993/January 1994.

Powell, Kevin. "Live from Death Row." *Vibe,* February 1996.

Powell, Kevin. "Ready to Live." *Vibe,* April 1995.

Reese, Ronnie. "Son of Detroit: The Oral History of J Dilla." *Wax Poetics,* June/July 2006.

Rim, Joan. "Boyz 'N Court." *The Source,* December 1991.

Ro, Ronin. "Escape from Death Row." *Vibe,* October 1996.

Ro, Ronin. "Moving Target." *The Source,* November 1992.

Ro, Ronin. "There Goes Round 2." *The Source,* June 1992.

Roberts, Gerard "kidkanevil." "Cover Story: Madlib (ft. DOOM)." *Bonafide,* issue 9, October 2014.

Rogers, Charles E. "Grandmaster Flash: Messages." *Rock & Soul,* October 1986.

Rossi, Terri. "R&B Rhythms." *Airplay Monitor,* March 1994.

Serv One. "Charizma & Peanut Butter Wolf." *Vapors,* February 2004.

Shecter, Jon. "Corporate Hysteria." *The Source,* June 1994.

Shecter, Jon. "Real Niggaz Don't Die." *The Source,* September 1991.——. "Corporate Hysteria." *The Source,* June 1994.

Snowden, Don. "Sampling: A Creative Tool or License to Steal? The Controversy." *Los Angeles Times,* August 6, 1989.

Tingen, Paul. "Fairlight: The Whole Story." *Audio Media,* January 1996.

Torres, Andre. "The Architect." *Scratch Magazine,* Summer 2004.

Torres, Andre. "Astral Traveler." *Wax Poetics,* Fall 2013.——. "The Architect." *Scratch Magazine,* Summer 2004.

Touré. "Public Enemy: *Muse Sick-N-Hour Mess Age.*" *Rolling Stone,* July 14, 1994.

Turenne, Martin. "High Fidelity." *Urb,* March 2004.

Van Nguyen, Dean. "Kindred Soul." *Wax Poetics,* Summer 2013.

Weingarten, Marc. "Grooving on Artistic Freedom." *Los Angeles Times,* January 20, 2002.

Weingarten, Marc. "The Woo-Hah!!–ing of the Age of Aquarius." *Village Voice,* June 26, 2001.

Wilder, Chris. "Album Of The Year 1991: NWA—*Niggaz4life.*" *The Source,* January 1992.

Wilson, Elliott. "KMD." *4080,* Vol. 2, #6, 1994.

## Books

Abdurraqib, Hanif. *Go Ahead in The Rain: Notes to A Tribe Called Quest.* Austin: University of Texas Press, 2019.

Brewster, Bill, and Frank Broughton. *Last Night a DJ Saved My Life: The History of the Disc Jockey.* New York: Grove Press, 2000.

Brewster, Bill, and Frank Broughton. *The Record Players: DJ Revolutionaries.* New York: Black Cat, 2010.

Chang, Jeff. *Can't Stop Won't Stop: A History of the Hip-Hop Generation.* New York: St. Martin's Press, 2005.

Charnas, Dan. *The Big Payback: The History of the Business of Hip-Hop*. New York: New American Library, 2010.

Clinton, George. *Brothas Be, Yo Like George, Ain't That Funkin' Kinda Hard on You? A Memoir*. New York: Atria Books, 2017.

Coleman, Brian. *Check the Technique: Liner Notes for Hip-Hop Junkies*. New York: Villard, 2007.

Coleman, Brian. *Check the Technique, Volume 2: More Liner Notes for Hip-Hop Junkies*. Everett, Mass.: Wax Facts Press, 2014.

Cummings, Alex Sayf. *Democracy of Sound: Music Piracy and the Remaking of American Copyright in the Twentieth Century*. New York: Oxford University Press, 2013.

Edwards, Paul. *The Concise Guide to Hip-Hop Music: A Fresh Look at the Art of Hip-Hop, from Old-School Beats to Freestyle Rap*. New York: St. Martin's Griffin, 2015.

Ferguson, Jordan. *Donuts*. New York: Bloomsbury, 2016.

Fricke, Jim, and Charlie Ahearn. *Yes Yes Y'all: The Experience Music Project Oral History of Hip-Hop's First Decade*. Boston: Da Capo Press, 2002.

George, Nelson. *Hip Hop America*. London: Penguin, 1998.

Grandmaster Flash with David Ritz. *The Adventures of Grandmaster Flash: My Life, My Beats*. New York: Broadway Books, 2008.

Kennedy, Gerrick D. *Parental Discretion Is Advised: The Rise of N.W.A and the Dawn of Gangsta Rap*. New York: Atria Books, 2017.

LeRoy, Dan. *Paul's Boutique*. New York: Continuum, 2006.

Marshall, Wayne. "Kool Herc." In *Icons of Hip Hop: An Encyclopedia of the Movement, Music, and Culture*, ed. Mickey Hess. Westport, Conn.: Greenwood, 2007.

McLeod, Kembrew. *Creative License: The Law and Culture of Digital Sampling*. Durham, N.C.: Duke University Press, 2011.

Rodgers, Nile. *Le Freak: An Upside Down Story of Family, Disco, and Destiny*. New York: Spiegel & Grau, 2001.

The RZA. *The Tao of Wu*. New York: Riverhead Books, 2009.

The RZA. *The Wu-Tang Manual*. New York: Riverhead Books, 2005.

Salewicz, Chris. *Redemption Song: The Ballad of Joe Strummer*. New York: Faber and Faber, 2006.

Schloss, Joseph G. *Making Beats: The Art of Sample-Based Hip-Hop*. Middletown, Conn.: Wesleyan University Press, 2014.

Shakur, Tupac. *Tupac: Resurrection, 1971–1996*. New York: Atria Books. 2003.

Shapiro, Peter. *Turn the Beat Around: The Secret History of Disco*. New York: Faber and Faber, 2005.

## Websites

Aciman, Alexander. "Meet the Unassuming Drum Machine That Changed Music Forever." *Vox,* April 16, 2018.

Alapatt, Eothen. "Interview: Madlib." *Red Bull Music Academy,* 2002.

Ali, Reyan. "Madlib Muses on Methods behind His Madness." *Spin,* March 20, 2014.

Appleford, Steve. "Jimmy Jam and Terry Lewis: Our Life in 15 Songs." *Rolling Stone,* October 9, 2015.

Batey, Angus. "Enter the Golden Age: BDP, Public Enemy, Eric B & Rakim 30 Years On." *The Quietus,* February 27, 2017.

Batey, Angus. "The Magic Number." *HipHop.com,* April 7, 2009.

Batey, Angus. "Recycled Riffs: Samples of Music Biz Justice." *The Guardian,* June 23, 2011.

Berry, Peter A. "Woman Who Accused Tupac Shakur of Rape Recalls 1993 Assault in Hotel Room." *XXL,* January 31, 2018.

Best, Tony. "Musician Colin Wolfe Built Beats with Dr. Dre for *The Chronic,* N.W.A's *Niggaz4Life,* and Jimmy Z's *Muzical Madness.*" *Wax Poetics,* June 3, 2014.

Beta, Andy. "Blood and Echoes: The Story of *Come Out,* Steve Reich's Civil Rights Era Masterpiece." *Pitchfork,* April 28, 2016.

Blue, Ruza. "Ruza 'Kool Lady' Blue on Kraftwerk." *Electronic Beats,* November 12, 2012.

Bristout, Ralph. "Poetry, Power, Pistols: An Oral History Of 2Pac's 'Me Against the World.'" *Revolt.TV,* March 14, 2016.

Burgess, Omar. "DJ Quik Reveals the Secret to Working with Dr. Dre." *HipHopDX,* December 3, 2013.

Bush, John. "A Tribe Called Quest—*Beats, Rhymes, and Life.*" *AllMusic,* n.d.

Cantor, Paul. "How the 1995 Source Awards Changed Rap Forever." *Complex,* August 3, 2015.

Cho, Jaeki. "Prince Paul Tells All: The Stories behind His Classic Records (Part 1)." *Complex,* December 8, 2011.

Cho, Jaeki. "Prince Paul Tells All: The Stories behind His Classic Records (Part 2)." *Complex,* December 11, 2011.

Clinton, George. "Can't C Me" commentary. *Genius,* 2013.

Coleman, Brian. "1580 KDAY: And the Beat Goes On." *BrianColemanBooks.com,* January 7, 2016.

Coleman, Brian. "Interview: Rodger Clayton." *Red Bull Music Academy Daily,* October 31, 2017.

Coleman, Brian. "Prince Paul Interview." *BrianColemanBooks.com,* April 9, 2016.

Colothan, Scott. "Thom Yorke Lists His Favourite New Sounds." *Gigwise,* January 24, 2007.

Conaway, Matt. "Rasco—*Time Waits for No Man.*" *AllMusic,* July 1998.

Couchman, Doug, and Chris Dearcangelis. "The Production of Public Enemy: Gear, Sampling and Embracing Distortion." *Reverb,* March 1, 2016.

Cowie, Del F. "Nas: Battle Ready." *Exclaim,* December 1, 2004.

Croyle, Jonathan. "On This Date: The Controversial Beastie Boys Play the War Memorial in 1987." *Syracuse.com,* April 10, 2017

Davey D. "Interview w/ DJ Kool Herc: 1989 New Music Seminar." *Davey D's Hip Hop Corner,* n.d.

Davey D. "Interview w/ Grandmaster Flash: Hip Hop's Innovator." *Davey D's Hip Hop Corner,* September 1996.

Diaz, Brandon: "How Zev Love X Became DOOM: A Supervillain Origin Story." *The Hundreds,* March 2, 2017.

Dombal, Ryan. "?uestlove: 15 Years." *Pitchfork,* August 19, 2011.

Drake, David. "DJ Quik Tells All: The Stories behind His Classic Records." *Complex,* April 24, 2012.

easymobee. "The Most Influential Records in Hip Hop: Fusion Beats Vol. 2 (Bozo Meko Records circa 1980–81)." *Instagram,* July 6, 2015.

Ettelson, Robbie. "Pete Rock: The Unkut Interview." *Unkut,* April 30, 2008.

Ettelson, Robbie. "Ultimate Breaks and Beats: An Oral History." *Cuepoint,* March 13, 2015.

ex, kris. "Slum Village—*The Fan-Tas-Tic Box Set.*" *Pitchfork,* June 4, 2016.

"Exclusive: Q-Tip Interview." *moovmnt.com,* April 19, 2009.

Fintoni, Laurent. "15 Samplers That Shaped Modern Music—and the Musicians Who Use Them." *Fact,* September 15, 2016.

Fintoni, Laurent. "For Stones Throw Records, a Love of Hip-Hop Sparked 20 Years of Musical Conversations." *The Fader,* November 14, 2016.

Fintoni, Laurent. "Give Them What They Want: The 10-Year Mission to Release J Dilla's Legendary Lost Solo Album." *Fact,* March 29, 2016.

Fitzmaurice, Larry. "5-10-15-20: Prince Paul." *Pitchfork,* October 25, 2012.

Gottsegen, Will. "*Madvillainy* at 15: MF Doom on the Legacy of His Classic Madlib Collaboration." *Spin,* March 25, 2019.

Hall, John. "Interview with Peanut Butter Wolf." *The Hundreds,* August 18, 2010.

Harling, Danielle. "Dr. Dre Says after 27 Years of Working on Music He's Taking a Break." *HipHopDX,* November 14, 2011.

Heimlich, Adam. "DJ Shadow: The Shadow Sheds Light." *Salon,* September 23, 1998.

Hogan, Don. "Do the Math." *Rime*, republished on *Stones Throw,* May 1, 2003.

Horowitz, Matt. "Interview: Dave Cooley." *Grown Up Rap,* September 12, 2017.

"House Shoes' 10 Favorite Sample Flips." *egotripland,* October 1, 2012.

Ing, Matt. "Interview with Big Hutch." *Fazer Magazine,* June 3, 2010.

Isenberg, Daniel: "DJ Muggs Tells All: The Stories behind His Classic Records (Part 1)." *Complex,* January 26, 2013.

Jank, Jeff. "History of Lord Quas." *Stones Throw,* January 25, 2009.

JayQuan. "Grandmaster Flash Interview." *The Foundation,* June 2002.

JayQuan. "Get Funky, Make Money and Ya Don't Stop: The Story of Duke Bootee aka Ed Fletcher." *The Foundation,* February 2007.

Jenkins, Craig. "There's Nothing Flying Lotus Can't Do." *Vulture,* May 24, 2019.

Jones, Pete "DJ." "How Hip-Hop Emerged." *The Foundation,* September 2005.

Jones, Tracy. "Uncle Jamm's Army Was the West Coast's Real-Life Answer to *The Get Down.*" *LA Weekly,* September 7, 2016.

Kovar, Sweeney. "Amen, Brother: Breakbeat Lou and The Legacy of 'Ultimate Breaks and Beats.'" *Passion of the Weiss,* November 21, 2014.

Louis, Steven. "'I Just Want to Make Music with My Middle Finger Up': An Interview with DJ Muggs." *Passion of the Weiss,* August 14, 2018.

Ma, David. "As One of Hip-Hop's Most Respected Producers, Pete Rock Wants to Continue Forever." *Wax Poetics,* September 18, 2008.

MacAdams, Torii. "Dâm-Funk Breaks Down the Freaky Influence of Electro Pioneers Uncle Jamm's Army." *Noisey,* October 26, 2017.

Mao, Jeff. "A Conversation with Ice-T." *Red Bull Music Academy,* October 28, 2017.

Mao, Jeff. "A Conversation with Madlib." *Red Bull Music Academy,* April 2016.

Mao, Jeff. "Arthur Baker." *Red Bull Music Academy,* September 2007.

Mao, Jeff. "DOOM." *Red Bull Music Academy,* November 2011.

Mao, Jeff. "Q-Tip." *Red Bull Music Academy,* June 2013.

Mao, Jeff. "Questlove." *Red Bull Music Academy,* June 2013.

McKinnon, Matthew. "When We Were Ruthless: An Interview with Jerry Heller." *Cuepoint,* February 17, 2015.

Meline, Gabe. "Remembering the Time Tupac Shakur Sued the Oakland Police for $10 Million." *KQED.org,* June 16, 2016.

Monroe, Jazz, and Amy Phillips. "Dr. Dre TV Show Dropped by Apple Due to Violence, Sex: Report." *Pitchfork,* September 24, 2018.

Montesinos-Donaghy, Daniel. "Our Vinyl Weighs a Ton: We Went to a Q&A with Stones Throw Founder Peanut Butter Wolf." *Vice,* April 1, 2014.

Murphy, Keith. "Full Clip: Ice Cube Breaks Down His Entire Catalogue." *Vibe,* October 8, 2010.

Murphy, Sean. "BrooklynBio: The Mystery of Grandmaster Flowers." *Brooklyn Music,* July 2, 2009.

Murphy, Tom. "DJ Shadow Isn't So Sure That *Entroducing* Was the First 100 Percent Sample-Based Record." *Westword,* September 26, 2013.

Nathan, Bobby. "Sample This! Drum Machine and Sampler Museum." *Bobby-Nathan.com,* n.d.

Pattinson, Chris. "Exclusive: Prince Paul Breaks Down Gravediggaz '6 Feet Deep' Track-by-Track." *HipHopSite.com,* July 25, 2013.

Peltz, Jonathan. "Peanut Butter Wolf on '90s vs. 2010s Hip-Hop: 'The Commercial Music's Worse Now.'" *Miami New Times,* April 25, 2014.

"Photos: Making *Madvillainy.*" *Stones Throw,* March 1, 2004.

Pierznik, Christopher. "The Day Hip-Hop Died." *Medium,* February 26, 2015.

Proctor, Ryan. "Old to the New Q&A (Part One): Daddy-O." *Old to the New,* September 1, 2013.

Proctor, Ryan. "Old to the New Q&A (Part Two): Daddy-O." *Old to the New,* September 5, 2013.

Proctor, Ryan. "Old to the New Q&A (Part Three): Daddy-O." *Old to the New,* September 11, 2013.

Rabin, Nathan. "Steve 'Steinski' Stein." *AV Club,* June 24, 2008.

Reid, Shaheem. "Puff Daddy Clarifies Infamous 1995 Source Awards Speech on 'Drink Champs.'" *Revolt.TV,* November 25, 2016.

Reyes, Andres. "DJ House Shoes Interview." *Certified Hiphop,* March 17, 2007.

Ryce, Jeff. "Reginald C. Dennis: Death of a Dynasty Pt 1." *HipHopDX,* May 27, 2008.

Samuel, Anslem. "J Dilla, The Lost Interview (circa 2004)." *XXL,* February 10, 2010.

Sanchez, Tim. "Exclusive: Greg Mack Breaks Down the History of 1580 KDAY." *AllHipHop,* December 30, 2013.

Schraeder, Adrian. "Madlib." *Urban Smarts,* October 14, 2004.

Serota, Maggie. "De La Soul's Catalog Withheld from Streaming Platforms amid Dispute with Tommy Boy." *Spin,* March 1, 2019.

Setaro, Shawn. "Dr. Dre Perfected G-Funk, but He Didn't Invent It—Gregory Hutchinson Did." *Complex,* July 11, 2017.

Shipley, Al. "Dr. Dre's 'The Chronic': 10 Things You Didn't Know." *Rolling Stone,* December 15, 2017.

Skillz, Mark. "Straight No Chaser: DJ Hollywood." *Hip Hop 101A,* May 9, 2007.

Slavik, Nathan. "Tupac Was Working on 'One Nation' Album with Outkast, DJ Premier, and More When He Died." *DJBooth.net,* February 12, 2018.

Smooth, Jay. "Mr. Magic and Mister Cee: Hip Hop History 101." *HipHopMusic. com,* n.d.

Sorcinelli, Gino. "Paul C. McKasty: The Legend, the Tragedy, the Story of an Era." *Micro-Chop,* Sep 20, 2017.

Spice, Anton. "Their Vinyl Weighs a Ton: Stones Throw Boss Peanut Butter Wolf on the Records That Have Defined the Label." *Vinyl Factory,* April 3, 2014.

Stelfox, Dave. "Nightclubbing: Uncle Jamm's Army." *Red Bull Music Academy Daily*, October 31, 2017.

Stewart, Jesse. "Retaining a New Format: Jazz-Rap, Cultural Memory, and the New Cultural Politics of Difference." *Critical Studies in Improvisation,* November 6, 2014.

Strauss, Justin. "Interview: Justin Strauss with Fab 5 Freddy." *Ace Hotel,* March 2018.

Strauss, Matthew. "Dr. Dre and Jimmy Iovine Lose $25 Million Beats Lawsuit." *Pitchfork,* June 27, 2018.

Sullivan, Caroline. "How We Made: Jiggs Chase and Ed Fletcher on 'The Message.'" *The Guardian,* May 27, 2013.

Thurm, Eric. "Prolific Producer Prince Paul on Almost Being Fired, De La Soul Classics, and Working with His Son." *AV Club*, March 18, 2013.

Tompkins, Dave. "Return to the World As A Thought." *360HipHop,* January 2001.

Weiss, Jeff. "DJ Quik: Trials and Tribulations of a West Coast Legend." *LA Weekly,* June 2, 2011.

Weiss, Jeff. "Having Already Influenced Every Rapper You Like, Freestyle Fellowship Are Back." *LA Weekly,* September 27, 2011.

Weiss, Jeff. "The Madlib Mystique." *LA Weekly,* June 24, 2010.

Weiss, Jeff. "The Making of *The Chronic*." *LA Weekly,* November 19, 2012.

Weiss, Jeff. "Searching for Tomorrow: The Story of Madlib and DOOM's *Madvillainy*." *Pitchfork,* August 12, 2014.

Westhoff, Ben. "How Tupac and Biggie Went from Friends to Deadly Rivals." *Noisey,* September 12, 2016.Weiss, Jeff. "The Making of *The Chronic*." *LA Weekly*, November 19, 2012.

Wicks, Sam. "Interview: DJ Yella." *RNZ,* December 2, 2015.

Wood, Evan. "Inside LA's Early Hip-Hop Scene with Egyptian Lover." *Frank151,* April 2016.

Zekri, Bernard. "Key Tracks: 'Change the Beat.'" *Red Bull Music Academy Daily,* September 19, 2017.

Ziegler, Chris. "Arabian Prince: Women and Partying and Freaks." *LA Record,* August 19, 2008.

## Album Liner Notes

Adler, Bill. Liner notes to *Guru's Jazzmatazz Volume 1* by Guru. Chrysalis 0946 3 21998 2 9, F2 21998, CD, 1993.

Alapatt, Eothen. Liner notes to *Up from the Basement (Unreleased Tracks Vol. 1)* by Galt MacDermot. Kilmarnock KIL2000-4, CD, 2000.

Batey, Angus. "Ultramagnetic MC's—Critical Beatdown: An Oral History."

Liner notes to *Critical Beatdown* reissue by Ultramagnetic MCs. Next Plateau Records / Roadrunner Records 168 618 297-2, CD, 2004.

Chang, Jeff. Liner notes to *Quannum Presents Solesides Greatest Bumps*. Quannum Projects QP 022-2, CD, 2002.

Hsu, Hua. Liner notes to *What Does It All Mean? 1983–2006 Retrospective)* by Steinski. Illegal Art IA116, CD, 2008.

McClaren, Malcolm. Liner notes to *Duck Rock* by Malcolm McClaren. Charisma MMLP1, LP, 1983.


## Video and Television

"Tupac Shakur." *The Arsenio Hall Show.* Syndicated. March 8, 1994.

Beats 1. "Mike D & Adam 'Ad-Rock' Horovitz from Beastie Boys [FULL INTERVIEW]." YouTube, uploaded September 8, 2015.

*The Defiant Ones.* Directed by Allen Hughes. HBO, 2017.

dunya a. "Dilla Interview 2003 Part 1 of 4." YouTube, uploaded March 23, 2008.

Eazy-E Ruthless Records. "Ice Cube *Pump It Up* Clip That Led Dr Dre to Assault Dee Barnes." YouTube, uploaded December 1, 2016.

"George Clinton, Bootsy Collins, and Bernie Worrell." *Our Voices with Bev Smith.* BET, 1991.

"Jermaine Dupri." *Drink Champs*, October 25, 2017.

Kasper Hartwich, "Vanilla Ice Denies Ripping Off Queen and David Bowie's Under Pressure." YouTube, uploaded March 12, 2013.

KevinIntensity. "Mini-Documentary on 'Sampling' circa 1989." YouTube, uploaded January 12, 2011.

Red Bull Music Academy. "Uncle Jamm's Army: Pioneers of the Modern Party." YouTube, uploaded October 27, 2017.

Sway's Universe. "Hip-Hop Icons, Ultramagnetic MC's Celebrate the 30 Year Anniversary of 'Critical Beatdown.'" YouTube, uploaded October 10, 2018.

"Tupac Shakur." *Arsenio Hall Show,* March 8, 1994.

Vox. "How J Dilla Humanized His MPC3000." YouTube, uploaded December 6, 2017.


## Film

*Birth of a Nation 4\*29\*1992.* Directed by Matthew McDaniel. New York: Third World Newsreel, 1993.

*Founding Fathers: The Untold Story of Hip Hop.* Directed by Ron Lawrence and Hassan Pore. New York: DVS Filmworks and Highlife Entertainment, 2009.

*Juice.* Directed by Ernest R. Dickerson. Hollywood, Calif.: Paramount Pictures, 1992.

*Our Vinyl Weighs a Ton: This Is Stones Throw Records.* Directed by Jeff Broadway. Los Angeles: Stones Throw Records, 2013.

*Scratch.* Directed by Doug Pray. New York: Palm Pictures, 2001.

*Straight Outta Compton.* Directed by F. Gary Gray. Universal City, Calif.: Universal Pictures, 2015.

*Synthetic Substitution: The Life Story of Melvin Bliss.* Directed by Earl Holder. N.p.: Peripheral Enterprises, 2011.

*Wild Style.* Directed by Charlie Ahearn. New York: First Run Features, 1982.

## Radio and Podcasts

"Common." *Questlove Supreme,* Pandora, February 21, 2018.

"Dante Ross Podcast." *Outside the Lines with Rap Genius,* February 19, 2013.

"DJ Quik: 'Flamboyant? Every Now and Then.'" *Microphone Check,* NPR, January 30, 2015.

"Hank Shocklee: 'We Had Something to Prove.'" *Microphone Check,* NPR, April 16, 2015.

"Jermaine Dupri." *Drink Champs,* October 25, 2017.

"Kool Herc: A Founding Father of Hip Hop." *Fresh Air,* NPR, March 30, 2005.

"Marley Marl on the Bridge Wars, LL Cool J, and Discovering Sampling." *Microphone Check,* NPR, September 12, 2013.

"Peanut Butter Wolf." *Questlove Supreme,* Pandora, March 20, 2019.

"Prince Paul." *The Cipher,* March 16, 2015.

# Selected Discography

This DISCOGRAPHY includes many of the albums and singles mentioned in this book, as well as a number of other essential records worth checking out.

## Introduction

The Beatles. *The Beatles,* Apple Records SWBO-101, 1968.
Buchanan and Goodman. "The Flying Saucer," Luniverse 101, 1956.
The Dramatics. "In the Rain / (Gimme Some) Good Soul Music," Volt VOA-4075, 1972.
Madvillain. "Money Folder / America's Most Blunted," Stones Throw Records STH 2064, 2003.
Reich, Steve. *Early Works,* Elektra, Nonesuch 9 79169-2, 1987.

## I. The Grandmaster

A Number of Names. "Sharevari," Capriccio Records P-928, 1981.
The Art of Noise. *Into Battle with the Art of Noise,* ZTT ZTIS 100, 1983.
The Art of Noise. "Beat Box," ZTT ZTIS 108, 1984.
The Art of Noise. *Who's Afraid of the Art of Noise,* ZTT ZTTIQ2, 1984.
Babe Ruth. *First Base,* Harvest/EMI SHSP 4022, 1972.
Bad Brains. *I against I,* SST Records SST 065, 1986.
Bambaataa, Afrika. *Death Mix—Live!!!* Paul Winley Records 12X33-10, 1983.
Bambaataa, Afrika, & Soulsonic Force. "Planet Rock," Tommy Boy TB 823, 1982.
Bambaataa, Afrika, & Soulsonic Force. "Looking for the Perfect Beat," Tommy Boy TB-831, 1983.
Beastie Boys. "Rock Hard," Def Jam Recordings DJ 002, 1984.
Beastie Boys. "She's on It," Def Jam Recordings 44-05292, 1985.

Beastie Boys. *Licensed to Ill,* Def Jam Recordings FC 40238, 1986.

Biz Markie. *Goin' Off,* Cold Chillin' 1-25675, 1988.

Blondie. "Rapture," Chrysalis CHS 2485, 1981.

Blondie and Freddie. "Yuletide Throw Down," Flexipop 015(a), 1981.

Boogie Down Productions. *Criminal Minded,* B-Boy Records BB 4787, 1987.

Boogie Down Productions. *By All Means Necessary,* Jive 1097-1-J, 1988.

Boogie Down Productions. *Man & His Music,* B-Boy Records BB 1-2000, 1988.

Booker T. & the M.G.'s. *Melting Pot,* Stax STS 2035, 1971.

Brother D with Collective Effort. "Dib-Be-Dib-Be-Dize / How We Gonna Make the Black Nation Rise?" Clappers Records CL-0001, 1980.

Brown, James. *Sex Machine,* King Records KS-7-1115, 1970.

Brown, James. *In the Jungle Groove,* Polydor 829 624-1 Y-2, 1986.

Captain Rock. "Cosmic Blast," NIA Records NI 1244, 1984.

The Jimmy Castor Bunch. *It's Just Begun,* RCA Victor LSP-4640, 1972.

Chic. *Chic,* Atlantic SD 19153, 1977.

Chic. *C'est Chic,* Atlantic SD 12909, 1978.

Chic. *Risqué,* Atlantic SD 16003, 1979.

Chubb Rock. *Chubb Rock Featuring Hitman Howie Tee,* Select Records SEL 21624, 1988.

Ciccone Youth. "Burnin' Up / Tuff Titty Rap / Into the Groovy," New Alliance Records NAR 030, 1986.

The Clash. *Sandinista!* CBS FSLN1, 1980.

The Clash. "The Magnificent Seven," CBS A1133, 1981.

The Clash. "Radio Clash," CBS A1797, 1981.

Coffey, Dennis, and Detroit Guitar Band. *Evolution,* Sussex SXBS 7004, 1971.

Commodores. *Machine Gun,* Motown M6-798S1, 1974.

DJ Hollywood. "Shock, Shock, the House," Epic 48 50885, 1980.

DJ Hollywood. *Rarities,* Ol' Skool Flava OSF CD 4012, 1995.

Double Dee & Steinski. *Mastermixes,* not on label, 1984.

Double Dee & Steinski. *Lesson 1, 2 & 3,* Tommy Boy TB 867, 1985.

Dyke & the Blazers. "Let a Woman Be a Woman—Let a Man Be a Man," Original Sound OS-89, 1969.

Eno, Brian, and David Byrne. *My Life in the Bush of Ghosts,* Sire SRK 6093, 1981.

EPMD. *Strictly Business,* Fresh Records LPRE-82006, 1988.

Eric B. & Rakim. "Eric B. Is President / My Melody," Zakia Records ZK 014, 1986.

Eric B. & Rakim. *Paid In Full,* 4th & Broadway BWAY 4005, 1987.

Eric B. & Rakim. *Follow The Leader,* UNI Records UNI-3, 1988.

ESG. *ESG,* 99 Records 99-04 EP, 1981.

ESG. *Come away with ESG,* 99 Records 99-003LP, 1983.

Fab 5 Freddy / Beside. "Change the Beat," Celluloid CEL 156, 1982.

Funk Inc. *Funk Inc.,* Prestige PRST10031, 1971.

Grandmaster Flash. *They Said It Couldn't Be Done,* Elektra 60389-1, 1985.

Grandmaster Flash. *The Source,* Elektra 60476-1, 1986.

Grandmaster Flash. *Ba-Dop-Boom-Bang,* Elektra 60723-1, 1987.

Grandmaster Flash and the Furious Five. "Superrappin'," Enjoy Records 6001, 1979.

Grandmaster Flash and the Furious Five. "Freedom," Sugar Hill Records SH-549, 1980.

Grandmaster Flash and the Furious Five. "The Birthday Party," Sugar Hill Records SH-555, 1981.

Grandmaster Flash and the Furious Five. "The Adventures of Grandmaster Flash on the Wheels of Steel," Sugar Hill Records SH-557, 1981.

Grandmaster Flash and the Furious Five. "It's Nasty (Genius of Love)," Sugar Hill Records SH-569, 1981.

Grandmaster Flash and the Furious Five. *The Message,* Sugar Hill Records SH-268, 1982.

Grandmaster Flash and the Furious Five. "The Message," Sugar Hill Records SH-584, 1982.

Grandmaster Flash and the Furious Five. "Scorpio," Sugar Hill Records SH-590, 1982.

Grandmaster Flash and the Furious Five. *The Message,* Sugar Hill Records SH 268, 1982.

Grandmaster Flash and the Furious Five. *On the Strength,* Elektra 60769-1, 1988.

Grandmaster & Melle Mel. "White Lines (Don't Don't Do It)," Sugar Hill Records SH 465, 1983.

Grandmaster Flowers. "Brooklyn Park Jam (restored)," uploaded by Tape Deck Wreck, YouTube.

Fatback. *Fatback XII,* Spring Records SP-1-6723, 1979.

G.L.O.B.E. and Whiz Kid. "Play That Beat Mr. D.J.," Tommy Boy TB 836, 1983.

Grasso, Francis. "Legends of Vinyl Presents The Sanctuary Francis Grasso 1971 'The Full Recording,'" uploaded by legendsofvinylTM, YouTube.

Hancock, Herbie. "Rockit (Extended Dance Version)," Columbia 44-03978, 1983.

Headhunters. *Survival of the Fittest,* Arista AL 4038, 1975.

The Honey Drippers. "Impeach the President / Roy C's Theme," Alaga Records AL-1017, 1973.

Bob James. *Two,* CTI Records CTI 6057 S1, 1975.

The J.B.s. "The Grunt," King Records 45-6317, 1970.

James, Bob. *Two,* CTI Records CTI 6057 S1, 1975.

The Jimmy Castor Bunch. *It's Just Begun,* RCA Victor LSP-4640, 1972.

Kool G Rap & DJ Polo. "It's a Demo / I'm Fly," Cold Chillin' CC 101, 1986.

Kraftwerk. *Trans-Europe Express,* Capitol Records SW-11603, 1977.

Kraftwerk. *Computer World,* Warner Bros. Records HS 3549, 1981.

The Kryptic Krew featuring Tina B / Afrika Bambaataa & the Jazzy 5. "Jazzy Sensation," Tommy Boy TB 812, 1981.

Lightnin' Rod. *Hustlers Convention,* United Artists Records UA-LA156-F, 1973.

Liquid Liquid. *Optimo,* 99 Records 99-11 EP, 1983.

LL Cool J. "I Need a Beat," Def Jam Recordings DJ001, 1984.

LL Cool J. *Radio,* Def Jam Recordings BFC 40239, 1985.

Mancuso, David. *The Loft,* Nuphonic NUX 136CD, 1999.

Mancuso, David. *The Loft,* Nuphonic NUX 154CD, 2000.

Mandrill. *Composite Truth,* Polydor 8F 5043, 1972.

Markham, Pigmeat. "Here Comes the Judge / The Trial," Chess 2049, 1968.

Marley Marl. *In Control, Volume 1,* Cold Chillin' 1-25783, 1988.

McLaren, Malcolm. *Duck Rock,* Charisma MMLP1, 1983.

MC Shan. "Beat Biter," Bridge Records BD-001, 1986.

MC Shan. *Down by Law,* Cold Chillin' CCLP 500, 1987.

Melle Mel & Duke Bootee. "Message II (Survival)," Sugar Hill Records SH-594, 1982.

Michael Viner's Incredible Bongo Band. *Bongo Rock,* Pride PRD-0028, 1973.

The Mohawks. *The Champ,* Pama Records PMLP 5, 1968.

Moulton, Tom. "The Sandpiper, Fire Island, New York, USA—1974," uploaded by Reuben Turner, Soundcloud.

Moulton, Tom. *Philadelphia International Classics: The Tom Moulton Remixes,* Harmless HURTXCD 112, 2012.

Public Enemy. "Public Enemy #1," Def Jam Recordings 44-06719, 1987.

Public Enemy. *Yo! Bum Rush The Show,* Def Jam Recordings FC 40658, 1987.

Public Enemy. *It Takes a Nation of Millions to Hold Us Back,* Def Jam Recordings FC 44303, 1988.

Public Enemy. "Fight the Power (Extended Version)," Motown MOT-4647, 1989.

Public Enemy. *Fear of a Black Planet,* Def Jam Recordings C 45413, 1990.

Public Enemy. *Apocalypse 91 . . . The Enemy Strikes Black,* Def Jam Recordings C2 47374, 1991.

Queen. "Another One Bites the Dust," EMI 5102, 1980.

Quick Quintin & M.C. Mello J. "The Classy M.C.'s," Barnes Records BR 817, 1985.

Rammellzee vs. K-Rob. "Beat Bop," Tartown Record Co. TT001, 1983.

Run-D.M.C. "It's Like That / Sucker M.C.'s (Krush Groove 1)," Profile Records PRO-7019, 1983.

Run-D.M.C. *Run-D.M.C.,* Profile Records PRO-1202, 1984.

Run-D.M.C. *King of Rock,* Profile Records PRO-1205, 1985.

Run-D.M.C. *Raising Hell,* Profile Records PRO-1217, 1986.

Shanté, Roxanne. "Roxanne's Revenge," Pop Art Records PA-1406, 1984.

Slick Rick. *The Great Adventures of Slick Rick,* Def Jam Recordings FC 40513, 1988.

Steinski. *What Does It All Mean? (1983–2006 Retrospective),* Illegal Art IA116, 2008.

Sugarhill Gang. "Rapper's Delight," Sugar Hill Records SH-542, 1979.

Sugarhill Gang. "8th Wonder," Sugar Hill Records SH-553, 1980.

T La Rock & Jazzy Jay. "It's Yours," Partytime Records / Def Jam Recordings PT 104, 1984.

Tackhead. "Mind at the End of the Tether," On-U Sound DP 15-12, 1985.

Tackhead. "What's My Mission Now?" On-U Sound DP 13-12, 1985.

Time Zone. "World Destruction," Celluloid CEL 176, 1984.

Tom Tom Club. *Tom Tom Club,* Sire SRK 3628, 1981.

Ultramagnetic MCs. *Critical Beatdown,* Next Plateau Records Inc. PLCD 1013, 1988.

Various Artists. *Disco Par-r-r-ty,* Spring Records SPR 6705, 1974.

Various Artists. "Flash It to the Beat / Fusion Beats (Vol. 2)," Bozo Meko Records, 1980.

Various Artists. *The Thing with Two Heads (Music Inspired By),* Pride, PRD-0005 ST, 1972.

Michael Viner's Incredible Bongo Band. *Bongo Rock,* Pride PRD-0028, 1973.

Wesley, Fred, and the J.B.'s. *Damn Right I Am Somebody,* People PE 6602, 1974.

Yes. *90125,* ATCO Records 79-0125-1, 1983.


## II. The Prince

3rd Bass. *The Cactus Album,* Def Jam Recordings CK 45415, 1989.

3rd Bass. *Derelicts of Dialect,* Def Jam Recordings C2 47369, 1991.

The 45 King. *Master of the Game,* Tuff City TUF LP 5553, 1988.

The 45 King. *45 Kingdom,* Tuff City TUF LP 0563, 1990.

The Arsonists. *The Session,* Fondle 'Em FE003, 1996.

Artifacts. *Between a Rock and a Hard Place,* Big Beat 92397-2, 1994.

A Tribe Called Quest. *People's Instinctive Travels and the Paths of Rhythm,* Jive 1331-2-J, 1990.

A Tribe Called Quest. *The Low End Theory,* Jive 1418-2-J, 1991.

A Tribe Called Quest. *Midnight Marauders,* Jive 01241-41490-2, 1993.

Audio Two. "Make It Funky / Top Billin'," First Priority Music FPM 2938, 1987.

Banbarra. "Shack Up," United Artists Records UA-XW734-Y, 1975.

Beastie Boys. *Paul's Boutique,* Capitol Records CDP 7 91743 2, 1989.

Beastie Boys. *Love American Style EP,* Capitol Records V-15483, 1989.

Beastie Boys. *Paul's Boutique,* Capitol Records CDP 7 91743 2, 1989.

Beastie Boys. *Check Your Head,* Grand Royal / Capitol Records CDP 7 98938 2, 1992.

Beastie Boys. *Ill Communication,* Grand Royal / Capitol Records C2 7243 8 28599 2 5, 1994.

The Beatnuts. *Intoxicated Demons The EP,* Relativity / Violator Records 88561-1114-2, 1993.

The Beatnuts. *The Beatnuts,* Relativity / Violator Records 8856101179-2, 1994.

Big Daddy Kane. *It's a Big Daddy Thing,* Cold Chillin' 9 25941-2, 1989.

Big Daddy Kane. *Taste of Chocolate,* Cold Chillin' 1–26303, 1990.

Black Moon. *Enta da Stage,* Wreck Records NRV 2002-2, 1993.

Bliss, Melvin. "Reward / Synthetic Substitution," Sunburst Records SU-527, 1973.

Boogie Down Productions. *Sex and Violence,* Jive 01241-41470-2, 1992.

Brand Nubian. *One for All,* Elektra E2 60946, 1990.

Brand Nubian. *In God We Trust,* Elektra 9 61381-2, 1992.

Burdon, Eric, and War. "Spill the Wine / Magic Mountain," Polydor 2001 072, 1970.

The Jimmy Castor Bunch. *It's Just Begun,* RCA Victor LSP-4640, 1972.

The Cenubites. *The Cenubites,* Fondle 'Em FE 001, 1995.

Chef Raekwon. *Only Built 4 Cuban Linx . . . ,* Loud Records / RCA 07863-66663-1, 1995.

Common Sense. *Resurrection,* Relativity 88561-1208-2, 1994.

Crazy Wisdom Masters. *The Payback EP,* Black Hoodz BH006, 1999.

Cypress Hill. "Latin Lingo," Ruffhouse Records 44 74478, 1992.

Davis, Miles. *Doo-Bop,* Warner Bros. Records 9 26938-2, 1992.

De La Soul. "Plug Tunin' / Freedom Of Speak," Tommy Boy TB 910, 1988.

De La Soul. "Jenifa (Taught Me) / Potholes in My Lawn," Tommy Boy TB 917, 1988.

De La Soul. "Plug Tunin' / Freedom of Speak," Tommy Boy TB 910, 1988.

De La Soul. *Buddy & Ghetto Thang,* Tommy Boy TB 943, 1989.

De La Soul. *3 Feet High and Rising,* Tommy Boy TB 1019, 1989.

De La Soul. *Buddy & Ghetto Thang,* Tommy Boy TB 943, 1989.

De La Soul. *De La Soul Is Dead,* Tommy Boy TB 1029, 1991.

De La Soul. *Buhloone Mind State,* Tommy Boy TBCD 1063, 1993.

Deda. *The Original Baby Pa,* BBE RR0028LP, 2003.

Dr. Octagon. *Dr. Octagon,* Bulk Recordings CD902, 1996.

Eric B. & Rakim. "Paid in Full (Seven Minutes of Madness—The Coldcut Remix)," 4th & Broadway 12 BRW 78, 1987.

Eric B. & Rakim. *Let the Rhythm Hit 'Em,* MCA Records MCA 6416, 1990.

Eric B. & Rakim. *Don't Sweat the Technique,* MCA Records MCA-10594, 1992.

Diamond and the Psychotic Neurotics. *Stunts, Blunts, & Hip Hop.* Chemistry Records LTD, P2-13934, 1992.

Digable Planets. *Reachin' (a New Refutation of Time and Space),* Pendulum Records / Elektra 9 61414-2, 1993.

Digable Planets. *Blowout Comb,* Pendulum Records 7243 8 30654 2 4, 1994.

Felice, Dee, Trio. *In Heat,* Bethlehem Records BS-10,000, 1969.

Gang Starr. *No More Mr. Nice Guy,* Wild Pitch Records WPL2001, 1989.

Gang Starr. "Words I Manifest." Wild Pitch Records WP1012, 1989.

Gang Starr. "Jazz Thing." Columbia CAS 2137, 1990.

Gang Starr. *Step in the Arena.* Chrysalis F2 21798, 1990.

Gang Starr. *Daily Operation.* Chrysalis F2 21910, 1992.

Gang Starr. *Hard to Earn.* Chrysalis F2–28435, 1994.

Genius/GZA. *Liquid Swords,* Geffen Records GEFD-24813, 1995.

Ghostface Killah. *Ironman,* Razor Sharp Records / Epic Street EK 67729, 1996.

Gravediggaz. *6 Feet Deep,* Gee Street 314-524 016-2, 1994.

Gravediggaz. *The Pick, the Sickle, and the Shovel.* Gee Street / V2 63881-32501-2, 1997.

Guru. *Guru's Jazzmatazz Volume 1,* Chrysalis F2 21998, 1993.

Handsome Boy Modeling School. *So . . . How's Your Girl?* Tommy Boy TB1258, 1999.

InI. *Center of Attention,* Soul Brother Records INICD 001, 2002.

The Invitations. "Hallelujah / Written on the Wall," DynoVoice Records 206, 1965.

Jay-Z. *Reasonable Doubt,* Priority Records / Roc-A-Fella Records P2 50592, 1996.

The Jaz. *To Your Soul,* EMI USA CDP 7 93320 2, 1990.

Jeru tha Damaja. *The Sun Rises in the East,* Payday/FFRR 697-124-011-2, 1994.

The Jimmy Castor Bunch. *It's Just Begun,* RCA Victor LSP-4640, 1972.

The Juggaknots. *The Juggaknots,* Fondle 'Em FE002, 1996.

Jungle Brothers. *Straight Out the Jungle,* Warlock Records WAR2704, 1988.

Jungle Brothers. *Done by the Forces of Nature,* Warner Bros. Records 9 26072-1, 1989.

Jungle Brothers. *J. Beez wit the Remedy,* Warner Bros. Records 9 26679-2, 1993.

Kelly, Herman, & Life. *Percussion Explosion!* Electric Cat ECS-225, 1978.

Killarmy. *Silent Weapons for Quiet Wars,* Wu-Tang Records / Priority P2 50633, 1997.

Kool G Rap & D.J. Polo. *Road to the Riches,* Cold Chillin' 9 25820-2, 1989.

Kool G Rap & D.J. Polo. *Wanted: Dead or Alive,* Cold Chillin' W2 26165, 1990.

KRS-One. *Return of the Boom Bap,* Jive 01241-41517-2, 1993.

Leaders of the New School. *A Future Without A Past . . . ,* Elektra 9 60976-2, 1991.

Leaders of the New School. *T.I.M.E.—The Inner Mind's Eye,* Elektra 9 61382-1, 1993.

Lord Finesse. *Return of the Funky Man.* Giant Records, PRO-A-5202, 1992.

Lord Finesse & DJ Mike Smooth. *Funky Technician,* Wild Pitch Records WPL 2003, 1990.

Main Source. *Breaking Atoms,* Wild Pitch Records WPD 2004, 1991.

Main Source. *Fuck What You Think,* Wild Pitch Records WPL-2012, 1994.

Manzel. "Sugar Dreams / Midnight Theme," Fraternity Records 3422, 1979.

Markie, Biz. *Goin' Off,* Cold Chillin' 9 26575-1, 1988.

Markie, Biz. *The Biz Never Sleeps,* Cold Chillin' 9 26003-1, 1989.

Markie, Biz. *I Need a Haircut,* Cold Chillin' 9 26648-2, 1991.

Markie, Biz. *All Samples Cleared!* Cold Chillin' 9 45261-2, 1993.

Method Man. *Tical,* Def Jam Recordings 314 523 839-2, 1994.

Mikey D & the L.A. Posse. "I Get Rough / Go for It," Public Records PA 012, 1987.

Mikey D & the L.A. Posse. "My Telephone," Public Records PA 008, 1987.

Mobb Deep. *The Infamous,* Loud Records 66480-2, 1995.

M.O.P. *To the Death,* Select Street Records 2-21648, 1994.

Nas. *Illmatic,* Columbia CK 57684, 1994.

Nas. *It Was Written,* Columbia CK 67745, 1996.

Nasty Nas. *Half Time,* Ruffhouse Records 44 74777, 1992.

The Notorious B.I.G. *Ready to Die,* Bad Boy Entertainment 78612-73000-2, 1994.

O.C. *Word . . . Life,* Wild Pitch Records E2-30928, 1994.

Ol' Dirty Bastard. *Return to the 36 Chambers: The Dirty Version,* Elektra 61659-2, 1995.

Organized Konfusion. *Organized Konfusion,* Hollywood BASIC HB-61212-2, 1991.

Organized Konfusion. *Stress: The Extinction Agenda,* Hollywood BASIC HB-61406-1, 1994.

Parliament. *Osmium,* Invictus ST-7302, 1970.

Play Hard featuring Gangster "B." "Cold Waxin' the Party," Alexadon Records AR-1522, 1988.

P.M. Dawn. *Of the Heart, of the Soul, and of the Cross: The Utopian Experience,* Gee Street 314-510 276-2, 1991.

Prince Paul. *Psychoanalysis (What Is It?),* WordSound WSCD010, 1996.

Prince Paul. *A Prince among Thieves,* Tommy Boy TBCD 1210, 1999.

Prince Paul. *Politics of the Business,* Razor & Tie RTS917-2, 2003.

Prince Paul. *Itstrumental,* Female Fun Records FEM013, 2005.

Prince Paul. *The Redux,* not on label, 2017.

Prince Rakeem. "Ooh I Love You Rakeem," Tommy Boy TB 968, 1991.

Public Enemy. "Shut 'Em Down," Def Jam Recordings 44–74165, 1991.

Public Enemy. *Muse Sick-n-Hour Mess Age,* Def Jam Recordings 523 362-2, 1994.

Queen Latifah. *All Hail the Queen,* Tommy Boy TBCD 1022, 1989.

Queen Latifah. *Nature of a Sista',* Tommy Boy TB 1035, 1991.

Queen Latifah. *Black Reign,* Motown 374 636 370-2, 1993.

Redman. *Whut? Thee Album,* Rush Associated Labels OK 52967, 1992.

Redman. *Dare Iz a Darkside,* Rush Associated Labels 314 523 846-2, 1994.

Resident Alien. *Mr. Boops,* Dew Doo Man Records / Columbia CSK 73970, 1991.

Resident Alien. *It Takes a Nation of Suckers to Let Us In,* not on label, 1991.

Resident Alien. *Mr. Boops,* Dew Doo Man Records / Columbia CSK 73970, 1991.

Rock, Chris. *Roll with the New,* DreamWorks Records DRMD-50008, 1997.

Rock, Chris. *Bigger & Blacker,* DreamWorks Records DRMD-50055, 1999.

Rock, Chris. *Never Scared,* Geffen Records B000325000, 2005.

Rock, Pete, & C.L. Smooth. *All Souled Out,* Elektra 9 61175-2, 1991.

Rock, Pete, & C.L. Smooth. *Mecca and the Soul Brother,* Elektra 9 60948-2, 1992.

Rock, Pete, & C.L. Smooth. *The Main Ingredient,* Elektra 61661-2, 1994.

The Roots. *Organix,* Remedy Recordings REMEDY01CD, 1993.

The Roots. *Do You Want More?!!!??!* DGC DGCD-24708, 1995.

The Roots. *Illadelph Halflife,* DGC DGCD-24972, 1996.

RZA. *RZA as Bobby Digital—In Stereo,* Gee Street / V2 63881-32521-2RE, 1998.

Salt-N-Pepa. *Blacks' Magic,* Next Plateau Records Inc. PL-1019, 1990.

Salt-N-Pepa. *Very Necessary,* Next Plateau Records Inc. 828 392-2, 1993.

Skull Snaps. *Skull Snaps,* GSF Records GSF-S-1011, 1973

Slick Rick. *Behind Bars,* Def Jam Recordings P2-23847, 1994.

Smith, Lonnie Liston, & the Cosmic Echoes. *Expansions,* Flying Dutchman BDL1-0934, 1975.

Stetsasonic. "Just Say Stet," Tommy Boy TB 975, 1985.

Stetsasonic. *On Fire,* Tommy Boy TBLP-1012, 1986.

Stetsasonic. *In Full Gear,* Tommy Boy TBLP 1017, 1988.

Stetsasonic. *Blood, Sweat, & No Tears,* Tommy Boy TBCD 1024, 1991.

Stezo. *Crazy Noise,* Fresh Records LPRE-82011, 1989.

Super Lover Cee & Casanova Rud. *Girls I Got 'Em Locked,* Elektra 9 60807-1, 1988.

Too Poetic. "Poetical Terror / God Made Me Funky," Tommy Boy / DNA International Records TB 930, 1989.

Too Poetic. *Droppin' Signal EP,* Chopped Herring Records CH2PO3T1C01, 2015.

A Tribe Called Quest. *People's Instinctive Travels And The Paths Of Rhythm,* Jive 1331–2-J, 1990.

A Tribe Called Quest. *The Low End Theory,* Jive 1418–2-J, 1991.

A Tribe Called Quest. *Midnight Marauders,* Jive 01241-41490-2, 1993.

Tricky vs. Gravediggaz. *The Hell E.P.,* 4th & Broadway 12 BRW 326 DJ, 1995.

Trouble Funk. *Drop the Bomb,* Sugar Hill Records SH 266, 1982.

Ultramagnetic MCs. "Ego Tripping / Funky Potion," Next Plateau Records Inc. NP 50051, 1986.

Ultramagnetic MCs. "Give the Drummer Some," Next Plateau Records Inc. NP 50091, 1989.

Us3. *Hand on the Torch,* Blue Note 0777 7 80883 2 5, 1993.

Various Artists. *Ultimate Breaks & Beats: The Complete Collection,* Street Beat Records SBR 1740, 2006.

Various Artists. *Blue Break Beats: Volumes One–Four,* Blue Note 7243 5 23182 2 3, 1999.

Various Artists. *Ultimate Breaks & Beats: The Complete Collection,* Street Beat Records SBR 1740, 2006.

The Winstons. "Color Him Father / Amen, Brother." Metromedia Records, MMS-117, 1969.

Wu-Tang Clan. "Protect Ya Neck / After the Laughter Comes Tears." Wu-Tang Records PR 234, 1992.

Wu-Tang Clan. *Enter the Wu-Tang (36 Chambers),* Loud Records / RCA 07863 66336-2, 1993.

Wu-Tang Clan. *Wu-Tang Forever,* Loud Records/RCA 07863-66905-2, 1997.

## III. The Doctor

2Pac. *2Pacaplypse Now,* Interscope Records 91767-2, 1991.

2Pac. *Strictly 4 My N.I.G.G.A.Z . . . ,* Interscope Records CDL 50604, 1993.

2Pac. *Me against the World,* Interscope Records 92399-2, 1995.

2Pac. "California Love," Death Row Records DRR 7003, 1996.

2Pac. *All Eyez on Me,* Interscope Records / Death Row Records 314-524 204-2, 1996.

2Pac. "California Love," Death Row Records DRR 7003, 1996.

2Pac. "How Do U Want It," Death Row Records/Interscope Records 422–854 653–1, 1996.

2Pac. *R U Still Down? (Remember Me),* Jive / Amaru Records 01241-41628-2, 1997.

50 Cent. *Get Rich or Die Tryin',* Shady Records / Aftermath Entertainment / Interscope Records 0694935442, 2003.

The 7A3. *Coolin' in Cali,* Geffen Records GHS 24209, 1988.

Aaliyah. *One in a Million,* Blackground Enterprises / Atlantic 92715-2, 1996.

Aaliyah. *Aaliyah,* Blackground Records 7243 8 10082 2 5, 2001.

Above the Law. *Livin' Like Hustlers,* Ruthless Records / Epic E 46041, 1990.

Above the Law. *Black Mafia Life,* Ruthless Records/Giant Records 9 24477-2. 1992.

Above the Law. *Uncle Sam's Curse,* Ruthless Records 88561-5524-2, 1994.

Arabian Prince. *Innovative Life—The Anthology—1984–1989,* Stones Throw Records STH2192, 2008.

Steve Arrington's Hall of Fame. *I,* Atlantic 80049–1, 1983.

Blackstreet. *Another Level,* Interscope Records INTD-90071, 1996.

Body Count. *Body Count,* Sire / Warner Bros. Records 9 26878-2, 1992.

Bone Thugs-N-Harmony. *E. 1999 Eternal,* Ruthless Records / Relativity 88561-5539-2, 1995.

Busta Rhymes. *The Big Bang,* Aftermath Entertainment / Interscope Records B0006748-02, 2006.

C.I.A. *Cru' in Action!* Kru-Cut Records MRC-1004, 1987.

Clinton, George. *Atomic Dog,* Capitol Records V-8603, 1982.

Clinton, George. *Computer Games,* Capitol Records ST-12246, 1982.

Clinton, George. *The Cinderella Theory,* Paisley Park 9 25994-2, 1989.

Clinton, George. *Hey Man . . . Smell My Finger,* Paisley Park PRO-A-6537, 1993.

Clinton, George. *Sample Some of Disc Sample Some of D.A.T. Volume 1,* AEM Record Group AEM 25701-2, 1993.

Clinton, George. *Sample Some of Disc Sample Some of D.A.T. Volume 2,* AEM Record Group AEM 25741-2, 1993.

Clinton, George, & the P-Funk Allstars. *T.A.P.O.A.F.O.M.,* Epic 48 38332, 1996.

Cybotron. *Enter,* Fantasy F-9625, 1983.

Cypress Hill. *Cypress Hill,* Ruffhouse Records / Columbia CK 47889, 1991.

Cypress Hill. *Black Sunday,* Columbia / Ruffhouse Records CK 53931, 1993.

Davy DMX. "One for the Treble (Fresh)," Tuff City / CBS Associated Records 4Z9 04955, 1984.

Davy DMX. "The DMX Will Rock," Tuff City TUF 120003, 1985.

Del tha Funkeé Homosapien. *I Wish My Brother George Was Here,* Elektra 9 61133-2, 1991.

Dezo Daz. "It's My Turn," Techno Hop Records THR-19, 1987.

Digital Underground. "Doowutchyalike," Tommy Boy / TNT Records TB 932, 1989.

Digital Underground. *Sex Packets.* Tommy Boy / TNT Records TBCD 1026, 1990.

Digital Underground. *Sons of the P,* Tommy Boy / TNT Recordings TBCD 1045, 1991.

Digital Underground. *The "Body-Hat" Syndrome,* Tommy Boy / TNT Recordings TBCD 1080, 1993.

Disco Daddy & Captain Rapp. "The Gigolo Rapp," Rappers Rapp Disco Co. RR-1989, 1981.

DJ Quik. *Quik Is the Name,* Profile Records PCD-1402, 1991.

DJ Quik. *Way 2 Fonky,* Profile Records PCD-1430, 1992.

DJ Quik. *Safe + Sound,* Profile Records PRO-1462-2, 1995.

The D.O.C. *No One Can Do It Better,* Ruthless Records / Atlantic 91275-1, 1989.

Dog, Tim. *Penicillin on Wax,* Ruffhouse Records / Columbia CK 48707, 1991.

Tha Dogg Pound. *Dogg Food,* Death Row Records / Interscope Records P2 50546, 1995.

Dr. Dre. *'85 Live!* not on label, 1985.

Dr. Dre. *'86 in the Mix!* not on label, 1986.

Dr. Dre. "Deep Cover." Epic / Solar ZAS 4520, 1992.

Dr. Dre. *The Chronic,* Interscope Records / Death Row Records / Priority Records P2 57128, 1992.

Dr. Dre. *The Aftermath*, Aftermath Entertainment / Interscope Records INTD-90044 1996.

Dr. Dre. *2001*, Aftermath Entertainment / Interscope Records 069490486-2, 1999.

Dr. Dre. *Compton (A Soundtrack by Dr. Dre)*, Aftermath Entertainment /Interscope Records B0023912-02, 2015.

Eazy-E. *Eazy-Duz-It*, Ruthless Records / Priority Records SL57100, 1988.

Eazy-E. *5150 Home 4 tha Sick*, Ruthless Records / Priority Records PCDS 53815, 1992.

Eazy-E. *It's on (Dr. Dre) 187um Killa*, Ruthless Records 88561-5503-2, 1993.

Eazy-E. *Str8 Off tha Streetz of Muthaphukkin Compton*, Ruthless Records 483576 2, 1995.

Egyptian Lover. *Egyptian Lover 1983–1988*, Stones Throw Records STH2350, 2016.

Elliott, Missy "Misdemeanor." *Supa Dupa Fly*, The Goldmind, Inc. / EastWest Records America 62062-2, 1997.

Elliott, Missy "Misdemeanor." *Da Real World*, The Goldmind, Inc. / EastWest Records America 62232-2, 1999.

Elliott, Missy "Misdemeanor." *Miss E . . . So Addictive*, Elektra / The Goldmind, Inc. 62639-2, 2001.

Elliott, Missy "Misdemeanor." *Under Construction*, Elektra / The Goldmind, Inc. 62813-2, 2002.

Eminem. *The Slim Shady LP*, Interscope Records / Aftermath Entertainment INTD-90287, 1999.

Eminem. *The Marshall Mathers LP*, Interscope Records / Aftermath Entertainment 069490629-2, 2000.

Eminem. *Relapse*. Interscope Records / Aftermath Entertainment B0012863-02, 2009.

The Firm. *The Album*, Aftermath Entertainment / Interscope Records INTC-90136, 1997.

Funkadelic. *One Nation under a Groove*, Warner Bros. Records BSK 3209, 1978.

Funkadelic. *Uncle Jam Wants You*, Warner Bros. Records WB 56 712, 1979.

The Game. *The Documentary*, Aftermath Entertainment / G Unit / Interscope Records B0003562-02, 2005.

Goodie Mob. *Soul Food*, LaFace Records 73008-26018-2, 1995.

Goodie Mob. *Still Standing*, LaFace Records 73008-26047-2, 1998.

Hashim. "Al-Naafiysh (The Soul)," Cutting Records CR-200, 1983.

Hayes, Isaac. *Hot Buttered Soul*, Enterprise ENS-1001, 1969.

Haywood, Leon. *Come and Get Yourself Some*, 20th Century Records T-476, 1975.

Hudson, Ronnie, and the Street People. "West Coast Poplock," Street People Record Co. BD 1002, 1982.

Ice Cube. *AmeriKKKa's Most Wanted,* Priority Records CDL57130, 1990.

Ice Cube. *Kill at Will,* Priority Records CDS 7238, 1990.

Ice Cube. *Death Certificate,* Priority Records CDL 57155, 1991.

Ice Cube. *The Predator,* Priority Records P2–57185, 1992.

Ice Cube. *Lethal Injection,* Priority Records P2 53876, 1993.

Ice-T. "Cold Wind-Madness / The Coldest Rap," Saturn Records SAT-1002, 1983.

Ice-T. "Dog'n the Wax (Ya Don't Quit—Part II) / 6 In The Mornin'," Techno Hop Records THR-13, 1986.

Ice-T. *Rhyme Pays,* Sire 9 25602-2, 1987.

Ice-T. *Power,* Sire 9 25765-1, 1988.

Ice-T. *The Iceberg (Freedom of Speech . . . Just Watch What You Say),* Sire 1-26028, 1989.

Ice-T. *O.G. Original Gangster,* Sire / Rhyme $yndicate Records 9 26492-2, 1991.

Jay-Z. *In My Lifetime, Vol. 1,* Roc-A-Fella Records 314 536 392-2, 1997.

Jay-Z. *Vol. 2 . . . Hard Knock Life,* Roc-A-Fella Records 314 558 902-2, 1998.

Jay-Z. *Vol. 3 . . . Life and Times of S. Carter,* Roc-A-Fella Records 314 546 822-2, 1999.

Jay-Z. *Kingdom Come,* Roc-A-Fella Records B0008045-02, 2006.

Jive Rhythm Trax. *Jive Rhythm Trax,* Jive JL 6–8135.

J.J. Fad. *Supersonic—The Album,* Ruthless Records / ATCO Records 7 90959-4, 1988.

Junior M.A.F.I.A. *Conspiracy,* Big Beat / Atlantic 92614-2, 1995.

Kokane. *Funk upon a Rhyme,* Ruthless Records 88561-5512-2, 1994.

The Lady of Rage. "Afro Puffs," Death Row Records / Interscope Records 95841–2, 1994.

Lamar, Kendrick. *Section 80,* Top Dawg Entertainment, 2011.

Lamar, Kendrick. *good kid, m.A.A.d city,* Top Dawg Entertainment / Aftermath Entertainment / Interscope Records B0017534-02, 2012.

Lamar, Kendrick. *To Pimp a Butterfly,* Top Dawg Entertainment / Aftermath Entertainment / Interscope Records B0022958-02, 2015.

Lamar, Kendrick. *Damn,* Top Dawg Entertainment / Aftermath Entertainment / Interscope Records B0026716-02, 2017.

Mack, Craig. *Project: Funk Da World,* Bad Boy Entertainment 78612-73001-1, 1994.

Makaveli. *The Don Killuminati (The 7 Day Theory),* Interscope Records / Death Row Records INTD-90039, 1996.

MC Ren. *Kizz My Black Azz,* Ruthless Records / Priority Records PCDS 53802, 1992.

MC Ren. *Shock of the Hour,* Ruthless Records 88561-5505-2, 1993.

Mellow Man Ace. *Escape from Havana,* Capitol Records C1-91295, 1989.

Mellow Man Ace. *The Brother with Two Tongues,* Capitol Records CDP 7 94608 2, 1992.

Michel'le. *Michel'le,* Ruthless Records 91282-2, 1989.

Noreaga. *N.O.R.E.,* Penalty Recordings PENCD 3077-2 1998.

Notorious B.I.G. "Big Poppa / Who Shot Ya? / Warning," Bad Boy Entertainment 78612-79020-1, 1995.

Notorious B.I.G. *Life after Death,* Bad Boy Entertainment 78612-73019-2, 1997.

N.W.A. "Panic Zone / Dope Man / 8-Ball," Ruthless Records MRC-1034, 1987.

N.W.A. *Straight Outta Compton,* Ruthless Records / Priority Records CDL57102, 1988.

N.W.A. *100 Miles and Runnin',* Ruthless Records / Priority Records EVL7224, 1990.

N.W.A. *Efil4zaggin,* Ruthless Records /Priority Records CDL 57126, 1991.

N.W.A. and the Posse. *N.W.A. and the Posse,* Macola Record Co. MRC-LP-1057, 1987.

Ohio Players. *Pleasure,* Westbound Records WB 2017, 1972.

OutKast. *Southernplayalisticadillacmuzik,* LaFace Records 73008-26010-2, 1994.

OutKast. *ATLiens,* LaFace Records 73008-26029-2, 1996.

OutKast. *Aquemini,* LaFace Records 73008-26053-2, 1998.

OutKast. *Stankonia,* LaFace Records/Arista 73008-26072-2, 2000.

P-Funk All Stars. *Urban Dancefloor Guerillas,* CBS PZ 39168, 1983.

P-Funk All Stars. *Dope Dogs,* Hot Hands HOTH MC 1, 1995.

Parliament. *Mothership Connection,* Casablanca NBLP 7022, 1975.

Parliament. *The Clones of Dr. Funkenstein,* Casablanca NBLP 7034, 1976.

Parliament. *Funkentelechy vs. the Placebo Syndrome,* Casablanca NBLP 7084, 1977.

Parliament. *Motor Booty Affair,* Casablanca NBLP 7125, 1978.

Parliament. *GloryHallaStoopid (Pin the Tale on the Funky),* Casablanca NBLP 7195, 1979.

Parliament. *Trombipulation,* Casablanca NBLP 7249, 1980.

Puff Daddy & the Family. *No Way Out,* Bad Boy Entertainment 78612-73012-2, 1997.

Schoolly D. *Schoolly-D,* Schoolly-D Records SD-114, 1985.

Schoolly D. *Saturday Night!—The Album,* Schoolly D Records SD-117, 1986.

Snoop Dogg. *Doggystyle,* Death Row Records / Interscope Records 1CD 92279, 1993.

Snoop Dogg. *Tha Doggfather,* Death Row Records / Interscope Records INTD-90038, 1996.

Snoop Dogg. *Tha Blue Carpet Treatment,* Geffen Records B0008132–02, 2006.

Stereo Crew. "She's a Skag," Epic 49-05921, 1986.

Steve Arrington's Hall of Fame. *I,* Atlantic 80049-1, 1983.

Terminator X. *Terminator X & the Valley of the Jeep Beets,* P.R.O. Division / Columbia CK 46896, 1991.

Toddy Tee. "Batterram," Epic 49-05294, 1985.

Too $hort. *Don't Stop Rappin',* 75 Girls Records and Tapes DH 1988, 1985.

Too $hort. *Players,* 75 Girls Records and Tapes DH 1990, 1987.

Too $hort. *Raw, Uncut And X-Rated,* 75 Girls Records and Tapes DH 1991, 1987.

Too $hort. *Born To Mack,* Dangerous Music DM 1534, 1987.

Too $hort. *Players,* 75 Girls Records and Tapes DH 1990, 1987.

Too $hort. *Raw, Uncut And X-Rated,* 75 Girls Records and Tapes DH 1991, 1987.

Too $hort. *Life Is . . . Too $hort,* Zomba / Dangerous Music 1149–2-J, 1988.

Tragedy. "LA, LA," 25 to Life Entertainment / Dolo Records TTL 1012-4, 1996.

Twilight 22. "Electric Kingdom," Vanguard SPV 68, 1983.

Uncle Jamm's Army. "Dial-a-Freak / Yes, Yes, Yes," Freak Beat Records UJA 1001, 1983.

Uncle Jamm's Army. "Naughty Boy," Freak Beat Records UJA-1002, 1985.

Various Artists. *Juice (Original Motion Picture Soundtrack),* SOUL MCAD-10462, 1991.

Various Artists. *Poetic Justice (Music from the Motion Picture),* Epic Soundtrax EK 57131, 1993.

Various Artists. *Murder Was the Case (The Soundtrack),* Death Row Records 92484-2, 1994.

Various Artists. *Above the Rim (The Soundtrack),* Interscope Records / Death Row Records 6544-92359-2, 1994.

Various Artists. *Murder Was the Case (The Soundtrack),* Death Row Records 92484-2, 1994.

Various Artists. *Friday (Original Motion Picture Soundtrack),* Priority Films / New Line Cinema P2 53959, 1995.

Warren G. *Regulate . . . G Funk Era,* Violator Records / Rush Associated Labels 314-523-335-2, 1994.

World Class Wreckin' Cru. "Slice / Kru Groove," Kru-Cut Records KC-001, 1984.

World Class Wreckin' Cru. "Surgery," Kru-Cut Records KC-002, 1984.

World Class Wreckin' Cru. "Bust It Up 2 + 1," Kru-Cut Records KC-005, 1985.

World Class Wreckin' Cru. "Juice," Kru-Cut Records KC 003, 1985.

World Class Wreckin' Cru. *World Class,* Kru-Cut Records KC 004, 1985.

World Class Wreckin' Cru. "Bust It Up 2 + 1," Kru-Cut Records KC-005, 1985.

World Class Wreckin' Cru. *Rapped in Romance,* Epic E 40324, 1986.

Wright, Charles, & the Watts 103rd Street Rhythm Band. *Express Yourself,* Warner Bros. Records WS 1864, 1970.

Zapp. *Zapp,* Warner Bros. Records BSK 3463, 1980.

Zapp. *Zapp II,* Warner Bros. Records 9 23583-1, 1982.
Zapp. *Zapp III,* Warner Bros. Records 9 23875-1, 1983.

## IV. The Beat Konducta

Aceyalone. *All Balls Don't Bounce,* Capitol Records CDP 7243 8 30023 2 0, 1995.
Adderley, Cannonball. *The Black Messiah,* Capitol Records SWBO-846, 1971.
Tha Alkaholiks. *21 & Over,* Lout Records 07863 66280-2, 1993.
Tha Alkaholiks. *Coast II Coast,* RCA 07863 66446-2, 1995.
Tha Alkaholiks. *Likwidation,* Loud Records LOUD 1814-2, 1997.
A Tribe Called Quest. *Beats, Rhymes, and Life,* Jive 01241-41587-2, 1996.
A Tribe Called Quest. *The Love Movement,* Jive J2 1638, 1998.
Atwood-Ferguson, Miguel. *Mochilla Presents Timeless: Suite for Ma Dukes—The Music Of James "J Dilla" Yancey,* Mochilla MOCD017, 2010.
Axelrod, David. *Song of Innocence,* Capitol Records ST 2918, 1968.
Axelrod, David. *Songs of Experience,* Capitol Records SKAO-338, 1969.
Axelrod, David. *David Axelrod,* Mo Wax MWR141CD, 2001.
Badu, Erykah. *Baduizm,* Universal Records / Kedar Entertainment UD 53027, 1997.
Badu, Erykah. *Mama's Gun,* Motown 012 153 259-2, 2000.
Badu, Erykah. *Worldwide Underground,* Motown B0000739-01, 2003.
Badu, Erykah. *New Amerykah: Part One (4th World War),* Universal Motown / Control Freaq Records B0010800-02, 2007.
Badu, Erykah. *New Amerykah Part Two: Return of the Ankh,* Universal Motown B0014023-02, 2010.
Beat Junkies. *Classic Material Volume One,* Beat Junkie Sound BJS-001, 2001.
Bilal. *1st Born Second,* Interscope Records 069493009-2, 2001.
Blackalicious. *Melodica,* Solesides SS003, 1994.
Blackalicious. *A2G EP,* Quannum Projects / 3-2-1 Records T21 CD 1085, 1999.
Blackalicious. *Nia,* Mo Wax MWR 112CD, 1999.
Black Star. *Mos Def & Talib Kweli Are Black Star,* Rawkus RWK 1158-2, 1998.
Boogie, Mick, Presents Busta Rhymes + J Dilla. *Dillagence,* not on label, 2007.
The Brand New Heavies. "Sometimes," FFRR BNHCD 8, 1997.
Busta Rhymes. *The Coming,* Elektra / Flipmode Entertainment / Violator Records 61742-2, 1996.
Busta Rhymes. *Anarchy,* Elektra / Flipmode Entertainment 62517-2, 2000.
Busta Rhymes. *Genesis,* J Records / Flipmode Records 80813-20009-2, 2001.
Busta Rhymes. *It Ain't Safe No More . . . ,* J Records 80813-20043-2, 2002.
Busta Rhymes. *The Big Bang,* Aftermath Entertainment / Flipmode Entertainment / Interscope Records / Violator B0006748-02, 2006.
Captain Murphy. *Duality,* not on label, 2012.

Charizma & Peanut Butter Wolf. "My World Premiere," Stones Throw STH 2001, 1996.

Charizma & Peanut Butter Wolf. *Circa 1990–1993,* Stones Throw Records STH2331, 2014.

Common. *One Day It'll All Make Sense,* Relativity REK 11535, 1997.

Common. *Like Water for Chocolate,* MCA Records 088 111 970-2, 2000.

Common. *Electric Circus,* MCA Records 088 113 114-2, 2002.

Common. *Be,* Geffen Records / G.O.O.D. Music B0004670-02, 2005

Common. *Finding Forever,* Geffen Records / G.O.O.D. Music B000938202, 2007.

Common. *Nobody's Smiling,* Def Jam Recordings / ARTium Recordings B0021165-02, 2014.

Company Flow. *Funcrusher Plus,* Rawkus RWK 1134-1, 1997.

Conti, Jackson. *Sujinho,* Mochilla MOCD-003, 2008.

The Coup. *Kill My Landlord,* Wild Pitch Records WPD-2014, 1993.

The Coup. *Genocide & Juice,* Wild Pitch Records/EMI E2–29273, 1994.

The Coup. *Steal This Album,* Dogday Records / Polemic Records DDR-4600, 1998.

Da' Enna C. "You Can't Use My Pen," Uptop Entertainment 941201, 1994.

Daedelus. *Invention,* Plug Research PR340202CD, 2002.

D'Angelo. *Voodoo,* Virgin / Cheeba Sound 7243 8 48499 2 4, 2000.

Danger Doom. *The Mouse and the Mask,* Epitaph 86775-2, 2005.

Dee, Jay. *Welcome 2 Detroit,* BBE BBEBGCD001, 2001.

Dee, Jay. "Fuck the Police," Up Above Records UA 3017-1, 2001.

Dee, Jay. *Ruff Draft EP,* Mummy Records MUM002, 2003.

De La Soul. *Stakes Is High,* Tommy Boy TB 1149, 1996.

De La Soul. *Art Official Intelligence: Mosaic Thump,* Tommy Boy TB 1361, 2000.

De La Soul. *AOI: Bionix,* Tommy Boy TB 1362, 2001.

De La Soul. *The Grind Date,* Sanctuary Records 06076-87526-2, 2004.

De La Soul. *Smell the Da.I.S.Y. (Da Inner Soul of Yancy),* not on label, 2014.

Del the Funky Homosapien. *No Need for Alarm,* Elektra 61529-2, 1993.

Dilla, J. *Donuts,* Stones Throw Records STH2126, 2006.

Dilla, J. *The Shining,* BBE BBECD076, 2006.

Dilla, J. *Jay Stay Paid,* Nature Sounds NSD 142, 2009.

Dilla, J. *The Diary,* Pay Jay Productions / Mass Appeal MSAP0032, 2016.

DJ Q-Bert. *Demolition Pumpkin Squeeze Musik,* not on label, 1994.

DJ Q-Bert. *Wave Twisters—Episode 7 Million: Sonic Wars within the Protons,* Galactic Butt Hair Records GBH0007-2, 1998.

DJ Rels. *Theme for a Broken Soul,* Stones Throw Records STH2087, 2004.

DJ Shadow. *What Does Your Soul Look Like,* Mo Wax MW027, 1994.

DJ Shadow. *Endtroducing. . . . . ,* Mo Wax / FFRR 697-124 123-2, 1996.

DJ Shadow. *The Private Press,* MCA Records 088 112 937-2, 2002.

DJ Shadow. *The Outsider,* Universal Motown B0007443-02, 2006.

DJ Shadow & Cut Chemist. *Brainfreeze,* Sixty7 Recordings, 1999.

DJ Shadow & Cut Chemist. *Product Placement,* ONE29 Recordings CS 2002, 2001.

DJ Shadow & Cut Chemist. *Product Placement on Tour,* Pillage Roadshow Productions PRSCD-001, 2004.

DJ Shadow & Cut Chemist. *The Hard Sell,* Pillage Roadshow Productions HS001, 2007.

DJ Shadow & Cut Chemist. *The Hard Sell (Encore),* Pillage Roadshow Productions HS002, 2008.

DJ Shadow / DJ Krush. "Lost and Found (S.F.L.) / Kemuri," Mo Wax MW 024, 1994.

DJ Shadow and the Groove Robbers. "In/Flux / Hindsight," Mo Wax MW 014, 1993.

DJ Shadow and the Groove Robbers / Asia Born. "Entropy / Send Them," Solesides SS-001, 1993.

Faddis, Jon. *Youngblood,* Pablo Records 2310 765, 1976.

Fanatik. *Phanaik Beats,* Stones Throw Records STH 2002, 1996.

Fanatik. *Nothin but a Beat Thang,* Stones Throw Records STH 2012, 1997.

Fiddler, Amp. *Waltz of a Ghetto Fly,* Genuine / PIAS America PIASA 29, 2004.

Flavors, Malik. *Ugly Beauty,* Stones Throw Records STH 2072, 2004.

Flying Lotus. *Los Angeles,* Warp Records WARPCD165. 2008.

Flying Lotus. *Cosmogramma,* Warp Records WARPCD195, 2010.

Flying Lotus. *Until the Quiet Comes,* Warp Records WARPCD230, 2012.

Flying Lotus. *You're Dead!* Warp Records WARPCD256, 2014.

Frank-N-Dank. *48 Hours,* Delicious Vinyl DV9067-CD, 2013.

Freestyle Fellowship. *To Whom It May Concern . . . ,* Sun Music SM-1001, 1991.

Freestyle Fellowship. *Innercity Griots,* 4th & Broadway 162-444 050–2, 1993.

Gibbs, Freddie, & Madlib. *Piñata,* Madlib Invazion MMS-024, 2014.

Gibbs, Freddie, & Madlib. *Bandana,* Madlib Invazion, 2019.

Goraguer, Alain. *La Planète Sauvage (Bande Sonore Originale),* Pathé 2C 066-12698, 1973.

Gorillaz. *Demon Days,* Virgin 7243 8 73838 2 1, 2005.

Hancock, Herbie. *Empyrean Isles,* Blue Note BST 84175, 1964.

Hieroglyphics. *3rd Eye Vision,* Hiero Imperium HI8473, 1998.

Hubbard, Freddie, & Ðlhan MÐmaroÐlu. *Sing Me a Song of Songmy (A Fantasy for Electromagnetic Tape),* Atlantic SD 1576, 1971.

Hughes, Monk, & the Outer Realm. *A Tribute to Brother Weldon,* Stones Throw Records STH2092, 2004.

Invisibl Skratch Piklz. "Invisbl Skratch Piklz vs. Da Klamz Uv Deth," Asphodel ASP 0106, 1996.

Invisibl Skratch Piklz. *The Shiggar Fraggar Show! Vol. 5,* Hip Hop Slam HHS-001, 1998.

Invisibl Skratch Piklz. *The Shiggar Fraggar Show! Vol. 4,* Hip Hop Slam HHS-003, 1999.

Invisibl Skratch Piklz. *The Shiggar Fraggar Show! Vol. 3,* Hip Hop Slam HHS-007, 1999.

Invisibl Skratch Piklz. *The Shiggar Fraggar Show! Vol. 2,* Hip Hop Slam HHS-009, 1999.

Invisibl Skratch Piklz. *The Shiggar Fraggar Show! Vol. 1,* Hip Hop Slam HHS-015, 2000.

Invisibl Skratch Piklz. *Shiggar Fraggar 2000,* Hip Hop Slam HHS-016, 2000.

Jackson, Janet. "Together Again / Got 'til It's Gone (Ummah Jay Dee's Revenge Mix)," Virgin V25D-38623, 1997.

Jackson, Otis. "Beggin' for a Broken Heart / Message to the Ghetto," MEGA Records MR-1220, 1974.

Jackson, Otis. *The Art of Love.* Crate Diggas Palace TEG-2824, 2006.

Jaylib. *Champion Sound,* Stones Throw STH2062, 2003.

Jaylib / Madlib. "The Message / LAX to JFK," not on label, 2002.

Jay-Z. *The Blueprint,* Roc-A-Fella Records 314 586 396-2, 2001.

Jay-Z. *Unplugged,* Roc-A-Fella Records 314 586 614-2, 2001.

Jay-Z. *The Black Album,* Roc-A-Fella Records B0001528-02, 2003.

Jay-Z. *The Blueprint² The Gift & the Curse,* Roc-A-Fella Records 440 063 381-2, 2002.

J.Rocc. *Play This (One),* Stones Throw Records STH2054, 2003.

J.Rocc. *Cold Heat Funk Mix.* Now-Again Records NA5021, 2006.

J.Rocc. *Thank You Jay Dee,* Stones Throw Records Podcast 1, 2006.

J.Rocc. *Thank You Jay Dee, Act 2,* Stones Throw Records Podcast 17, 2007.

J.Rocc. *Thank You Jay Dee, Act 3,* Stones Throw Records Podcast 29, 2008.

J.Rocc. *Thank You Jay Dee, Act 4,* Stones Throw Records Podcast 43, 2011.

J.Rocc. *Some Cold Rock Stuf,* Stones Throw Records STH2233, 2011.

J.Rocc. *Beats on Tap(e),* Stones Throw Records STH2365, 2014.

Kain. *The Blue Guerrilla,* Juggernaut Records JUG ST/LP 8805, 1970.

Kat, Phat. "Dedication to the Suckers," House Shoes Recordings HSR4001, 1999.

Kat, Phat. *The Undeniable LP (Detroit Edition),* Barak Records BRKP501, 2003.

King Geedorah. *Take Me to Your Leader,* Big Dada Recordings BDCD051, 2003.

KMD. *Mr. Hood,* Elektra 60977-2, 1991.

KMD. *Black Bastards Ruffs + Rares,* Fondle 'Em FE-83, 1998.

KMD. *Bl_ck B_st_rds,* Sub Verse Music / Metal Face Records SVM 15, 2001.

Kweli, Talib, & Madlib. *Liberation,* Blacksmith Music 0 9026 63160 21, 2006.

Latyrx. *The Album,* Solesides SS008, 1997.

Lifers Group / Charizma & Peanut Butter Wolf. "Short Life of a Gangsta / Red Light, Green Light," Hollywood Basic PRCS-10301-1, 1993.

Lifers Group / Shadow. "Real Deal (Shadow Remix) / Lesson 4," Hollywood BASIC ED 5567, 1991.

Lootpack. *Psyche Move,* Crate Diggas Palace GLP96-2421, 1996.

Lootpack. *Soundpieces: Da Antidote,* Stones Throw Records STH2019, 1999.

Lootpack. *The Lost Tapes,* Traffic Entertainment Group TEG-2416 CD, 2004.

MacDermot, Galt. *Shapes of Rhythm—Woman Is Sweeter,* Kilmarnock KIL2000-6, 2001.

MacDermot, Galt. *Up from the Basement (Unreleased Tracks, Volumes 1 & 2),* Kilmarnock KIL-2002-2, 2002.

Madlib. *Blunted in the Bomb Shelter,* Antidote ANTCD102, 2002.

Madlib. *Shades of Blue,* Blue Note 7243 5 36447 2 7, 2003.

Madlib. *Vol. 1–2: Movie Scenes,* Stones Throw Records STH 2133, 2006.

Madlib. *Vol. 3–4: Beat Konducta in India,* Stones Throw Records STH 2177, 2007.

Madlib. *WLIB AM: King of the Wigflip,* Rapster Records RR0070CD, 2008.

Madlib. *Vol. 5–6: A Tribute to . . . ,* Stones Throw Records STH 2205, 2009.

Madlib. *Madlib Medicine Show: The Brick,* Madlib Invazion MMSBOX101, 2012.

Madlib & Doom. "Avalanche," Madlib Invazion MMS030, 2016.

Madvillain. "Money Folder / America's Most Blunted," Stones Throw Records STH 2064, 2003.

Madvillain. *Madvillainy,* Stones Throw Records STH 2065, 2004.

Madvillain. *Madvillainy 2: The Madlib Remix,* Stones Throw Records STH 2198, 2008.

Mantronix. "Join Me Please . . . (Home Boys—Make Some Noise)," Capitol Records V-15386, 1988.

McDuphrey, Joe, Experience. *Experience EP,* Stones Throw Records STH 2049, 2002.

Metal Fingers. *Presents Special Herbs: The Box Set Vol. 0–9,* Nature Sounds NSD-120, 2006.

MF Doom. "Dead Bent / Gas Drawls / Hey!" Fondle 'Em FE008, 1997.

MF Doom. "Greenbacks / Go with the Flow," Fondle 'Em FE-0082, 1997.

MF Doom. *Operation: Doomsday,* Fondle 'Em FE-86 CD, 1999.

MF Doom. *MM.. Food,* Rhymesayers Entertainment RSE0051-2, 2004.

MF Doom. *Born Like This,* Lex Records LEX069CD, 2009.

MF Doom. *Gazzillion Ear,* Lex Records LEX079EP, 2010.

Miller, Ahmad. *Say Ah!* Stones Throw Records STH2050, 2003.

Mix Master Mike. *Anti-Theft Device,* Asphodel ASP 0985-2, 1998.

Odd Future. *The Odd Future Tape,* OFWGKTA, 2008.

Odd Future. *Radical,* OFWGKTA, 2010.

Odd Future. *The OF Tape Vol. 2,* Odd Future Records 88691 95478 2, 2012.

Oh No. *The Disrupt,* Stones Throw Records STH2097, 2004.

Oh No. *Exodus into Unheard Rhythms,* Stones Throw Records STH2143, 2006.

Oh No. *Dr. No's Oxperiment,* Stones Throw Records STH 2165, 2007.

Paris. *Sleeping with the Enemy,* Scarface Records SCR007-100-2, 1992.

Peanut Butter Wolf. *Peanut Butter Breaks,* Heyday Records PBB 001, 1994.

Peanut Butter Wolf. *Step on Our Ego's?* Southpaw Records SP-008, 1996.

Peanut Butter Wolf. *Lunar Props EP,* 2 Kool TKT 17, 1996.

Peanut Butter Wolf. *My Vinyl Weighs a Ton,* Stones Throw Records STH 2017, 1998.

The Pharcyde. *Bizarre Ride II the Pharcyde,* Delicious Vinyl DV2 1803, 1992.

The Pharcyde. *Labcabincalifornia,* Delicious Vinyl 61044-71812-2, 1995.

Q-Tip. *Amplified,* Arista 07822-14619-2, 1999.

Q-Tip. *The Renaissance,* Universal Motown B0012213-02, 2008.

Quasimoto. *Microphone Mathematics,* Stones Throw Records STH 2021, 1999.

Quasimoto. *The Unseen,* Stones Throw Records STH 2025, 2000.

Quasimoto. *The Further Adventures of Lord Quas,* Stones Throw Records STH2110, 2005.

Quasimoto. *Yessir Whatever,* Stones Throw Records STH2326, 2013.

Rasco. *Time Waits for No Man,* Stones Throw Records STH2014, 1998.

Ra, Sun. *The Heliocentric Worlds of Sun Ra, Vol. 1,* ESP Disk 1014, 1965.

Ra, Sun. *The Heliocentric Worlds of Sun Ra, Vol. 2,* ESP Disk 1017, 1966.

Ra, Sun. *Space Is the Place,* Blue Thumb Records BTS 41, 1973.

The Roots. *Things Fall Apart,* MCA Records MCAD-11948, 1999.

The Roots. *Phrenology,* MCA Records 088 112 996-2, 2002.

The Roots. *The Tipping Point,* Geffen Records B0002573-02, 2004.

The Roots. *Game Theory,* Def Jam Recordings B0007222-02, 2006.

The Roots. *Rising Down,* Def Jam Recordings B0011138-02, 2008.

The Roots. *Dilla Joints,* not on label, 2010.

Shadow. *Hip Hop Reconstruction from the Ground Up,* not on label, 1991.

Simpson, Guilty. *OJ Simpson,* Stones Throw Records STH2243, 2010.

Slum Village. *Trinity (Past, Present, and Future),* Capitol Records 2435-38911-2, 2002.

Slum Village. *Fan-tas-tic Box,* Ne'Astra Music Group, 2016.

Souls of Mischief. *93 'til Infinity,* Jive 01241-41514-2, 1993.

Souls of Mischief. *No Man's Land,* Jive 01241-41551-2, 1995.

Sound Directions. *The Funky Side of Life,* Stones Throw Records STH2124, 2005.

Stereolab. *Cobra and Phases Group Play Voltage in the Milky Night,* Elektra 62409-2, 1999.

Sweatshirt, Earl. *Earl,* OFWGKTA, 2010.

Sweatshirt, Earl. *Doris.* Columbia / Tan Cressida / Odd Future Records, 88883 75170 2, 2013.

Sweatshirt, Earl. *I Don't Like Shit, I Don't Go Outside: An Album by Earl Sweatshirt,* Columbia 88875069272, 2015.

Sweatshirt, Earl. *Some Rap Songs,* Tan Cressida / Columbia 19075898042, 2018.

Swift, Rob. *Presents Soulful Fruit,* Stones Throw Records STH2007, 1997.

A Tribe Called Quest. *Beats, Rhymes And Life,* Jive 01241-41587-2, 1996.

A Tribe Called Quest. *The Love Movement,* Jive J2 1638, 1998.

The Turntablist. *Super Duck Breaks . . . The Saga,* Stones Throw Records STH 2046, 2002.

Tyler, the Creator. *Goblin,* XL Recordings XLLP529, 2011.

Tyler, the Creator. *Wolf,* Odd Future Records 88765453842 DG1, 2013.

Tyler, the Creator. *Cherry Bomb,* Odd Future Records 88875 08464 2, 2015.

Tyler, the Creator. *Scum Fuck Flower Boy,* Columbia 88985441132, 2017.

UNKLE. *Psyence Fiction,* Mo Wax MW085CD, 1998.

Van Peebles, Melvin. *Brer Soul,* A&M Records SP 4161, 1969.

Van Peebles, Melvin. *Ain't Supposed to Die a Natural Death.* A&M Records SP-4223, 1971.

Van Peebles, Melvin. *Sweet Sweetback's Baadasssss Song (An Opera),* Stax STS-3001, 1971.

Van Peebles, Melvin. *Don't Play Us Cheap (Original Cast & Soundtrack Album),* Stax STS 2-3006, 1972.

Van Peebles, Melvin. *What the . . . You Mean I Can't Sing?!* Atlantic SD 7295, 1973.

Van Peebles, Melvin. *As Serious as a Heart-Attack,* A&M Records SP-4326, 1974.

Various Artists. *Project Blowed,* Project Blowed / Grand Royal PB-21310 1995.

Various Artists. *Jay Dee Unreleased EP,* House Shoes Recordings SHOES 001, 1997.

Various Artists. *Solesides Greatest Bumps,* Quannum Projects QP 022-2, 2000.

Various Artists. *The Hurricane (Music from and Inspired by the Motion Picture),* MCA Records 088 170 116-2, 2000.

Various Artists. *The Funky 16 Corners,* STH 2038, 2001.

Various Artists. *Keepintime: A Live Recording,* Mochilla MOCD-001, 2004.

Vaughn, Viktor. *Vaudeville Villain,* Sound-Ink. / Traffic Entertainment Group TEG 2409, 2003.

Vaughn, Viktor. *(VV:2) Venomous Villain,* Insomniac, Inc. INS 1005, 2004.

West, Kanye. *Get Well Soon . . . ,* Roc-A-Fella Records / The Heavy Hitters / Hustle, 2002.

West, Kanye. *The College Dropout,* Roc-A-Fella Records B0002030-02, 2004.

West, Kanye. *Graduation,* Roc-A-Fella Records B0009541-02, 2007.

West, Kanye. *The Life of Pablo,* G.O.O.D. Music / Def Jam Recordings, 2016.

The X-Ecutioners. *X-Pressions,* Asphodel 0977, 1997.

Yesterdays New Quintet. *Angles without Edges,* Stones Throw Records STH2042, 2001.

Yesterdays New Quintet. *Stevie,* Stones Throw Records STH2086, 2004.

## Epilogue

21 Savage. *I Am > I Was,* Slaughter Gang 190759221228, 2018.

Baby Elephant. *Turn My Teeth Up!* Godforsaken Music DDS 85010, 2007.

Brookzill! *Throwback to the Future,* Tommy Boy TB-182-2, 2016.

Cole, J. *KOD,* Dreamville / Interscope Records / Roc Nation BOO28487-02, 2018.

Drake. *Scorpion,* Young Money Entertainment / Cash Money Records / Republic Records, 2018.

Johnson, Syl. *Diamond in the Rough,* Hi Records SHL32805, 1974.

Lil Nas X. "Old Town Road," not on label, 2018.

Lil Wayne. *Tha Carter V,* Young Money B0029310-02, 2018.

El Michels Affair. *Enter The 37th Chamber,* Fat Beats FB-5127-2, 2009.

.Paak, Anderson. *Malibu,* OBE ERE218, 2016.

.Paak, Anderson. *Oxnard,* Aftermath Entertainment / OBE, 2018.

.Paak, Anderson. *Ventura,* Aftermath Entertainment 019029 6904929, 2019.

Prince Paul & DJ Pforreal. *Negroes on Ice,* Green Streets Entertainment GSE-748, 2013.

Rocky, A$AP. *At.Long.Last.A$AP,* RCA Records / Polo Grounds Music / A$AP Worldwide 88843-07775-2, 2015.

Prince Paul & DJ Pforreal. *Negroes On Ice,* Green Streets Entertainment GSE-748, 2013.

Tyler, the Creator. *IGOR,* Columbia, 2019.

West, Kanye. *Ye,* Def Jam Recordings B0028730-02, 2018.

# Index

Page numbers in *italics* refer to illustrations.

Hollywood (DJ), 4, 5, 14, 16
Hollywood Basic (record label), 200, 205
Home Boys Only (H.B.O.; band), 132–33
Homeless Derilex (band), 206
Honey Drippers (band), 47
"Honky Tonk Women" (Rolling Stones), 65
*Hooked* (*To the Extreme*; Vanilla Ice), 140
Hoppoh Records, 222, 223
Horn, Trevor, 41
Horovitz, Adam "Ad Rock," 75, 76, 78
Horror City (band), 117, 119
"Hot Pants" (James Brown), 49
House of Pain (band), 108, 113, 119
House Shoes (Michael Buchanan), 234, 239, 243–44
Howard, Ronald Ray, 168–69
"How Can You Believe" (Stevie Wonder), 230
"How I Could Just Kill a Man" (Cypress Hill), 153–54, 167
"How Not to Get Jerked" (KRS-One), 105
"How We Gonna Make the Black Nation Rise" (Brother D), 27
Hsu, Hua, 42
Hubbard, Freddie, 195, 221, 227
Hubbard, Leonard "Hub," 99
Hudson, Ronnie, 124
Hughes, Monk (Madlib alter ego), 216, 217
Hugo, Chad, 184
"The Human Abstract" (David Axelrod), 203
Human League (band), 29
Humphrey, Bobbi, 221
"The Humpty Dance" (Digital Underground), 146
Hunts Point Palace (nightclub), 11
*Hurricane* (film), 242
*Hustlers Convention* (record album), 17
Huston, Paul, 66

Hutch, Richard, 158
Hutch, Willie, 158
"Hyperbolicsyllabicsesquedalymisti" (Isaac Hayes), 152

"I Am Music" (Common), 245
"I Can't Go for That" (Hall and Oates), 70
"I Can't Help It" (Michael Jackson), 100
Iceberg Slim (writer), 124
Ice Cube (O'Shea Jackson; rapper), 113, 138, 154, 169, 176–77, 195, 197; George Clinton's collaborations with, 164; D.O.C. mocked by, 148; Dr. Dre and, 133, 142, 143, 147, 164, 165, 178, 187; Nation of Islam influence on, 147; as N.W.A. member, 134–35, 137, 138, 156, 166; solo career of, 141–42, 143
"Ice Ice Baby" (Vanilla Ice), 140, 155
Ice-T (Tracy Marrow; rapper), 98, 124, 132, 161, 169
"I Desire" (Salt-N-Pepa), 64
"I Don't Know" (Jay Dee), 240, 256
"If I Die 2Nite" (Tupac Shakur), 176
"If I Ruled the World" (Nas), 116
"If You Think I'm Jiggy" (Lox), 183
"I Get Around" (Digital Underground), 170
"I Get Rough" (Mikey D and the L.A. Posse), 73
*IGOR* (Tyler, the Creator), 259
"I Got That Feelin'" (DJ Quik), 151
"I Got You (I Feel Good)" (James Brown), 48
"I Just Want to Be" (Cameo), 151
"I Know What Boys Like" (Waitresses), 183
"I Know What Girls Like" (Puff Daddy), 183
"I Like It" (Emotions), 72
*Ill Communication* (Beastie Boys), 101
"The Illest Villains" (Madvillain), 231
"I'll House You" (Jungle Brothers), 86

"I Wish You Were Here" (Al Green),
208

Jackson, Al, Jr., 6
Jackson, Ayanna, 170
Jackson, Janet, 239–40
Jackson, Johnny Lee (Johnny "J"), 177
Jackson, Michael, 28, 78, 100, 204
Jackson, Michael W. ("Oh No"), 193
Jackson, O'Shea. *See* Ice Cube
Jackson, Otis, 193, 196, 206
Jackson, Otis, Jr. *See* Madlib
Jackson, Reggie, 15
Jackson 5, 77
Jadakiss (rapper), 249
"Jailhouse Rap" (Fat Boys), 128
Jam, Jimmy, 240
Jamal, Ahmad, 95, 97, 238
James, Bob, 34, 62, 88
James, Mark "The 45 King," 94
James, Rick, 124, 139
"Jam-Master Jammin'" (Run-D.M.C.),
40
Jank, Jeff, 212, 215, 255
Jay, Jazzy, 9, 32, 37, 44
Jay Dee. *See* J Dilla
*Jay Dee Unreleased* (compilation
album), 239
*Jaylib* (J Dilla and Madlib), 244
Jay-Z (rapper), 89, 115, 183, 185, 253
Jaz (rapper), 89
*Jazz* (television series), 213
"Jazz Cats Pt. I" (Quasimoto), 212–13
*Jazzmatazz* (Guru), 98–99, 163
"Jazz Thing" (Gang Starr and Branford
Marsalis), 95, 110
"Jazzy Sensation" (Afrika Bambaataa
and the Jazzy Five), 30
*J Beez with the Remedy* (Jungle
Brothers), 103
J.B.'s (band), 48–49, 51–54, 109
J Dilla (Jay Dee; James Dewitt
Yancey): critical response to, 237,
242–43; early years of, 234–35,
250; experimental bent of, 238–39,

244–47; illness and death of, 248,
249, 251; influence of, 251–53,
255–56; posthumous work of,
254–55; quantization eschewed by,
235–36; Questlove and, 240–41; as
Ummah member, 238–40
Jenkins, Craig, 258
Jenkins, Ruseel (Madlib alter ego), 216
Jeru tha Damaja (rapper), 101
Jewison, Norman, 242
Jimenez, Romeo "DJ Romes," 194
Jimmy Jam, 124
Jimmy Z. (rapper), 162–63
Jive Records, 87
Jive Rhythm Trax (band), 127
"J.O.B." (Prince Paul), 118
Joel, Billy, 68
"Johnny Don't Do It" (10cc), 250
"Johnny Ryall" (Beastie Boys), 77
Johnson, Mario "Chocolate," 140, 155
Johnson, Syl, xi, 54, 259
Jolicoeur, David "Trugoy," 68, 70–71,
86, 116–17, 236
Jones, Derrick "D-Nice," 46
Jones, Grace, 16
Jones, Mick, 23
Jones, Pete DJ, 13–14
Jones, Quincy, 98, 158, 172, 181, 196,
227
Jones, Quincy, III (QD III), 164, 178
Jones, Russell (Ol' Dirty Bastard), 108,
113
Jones, Stan "the Guitar Man," 138
Jones, Tom, 62
J. Roce (DJ), 229
J. Sumbi (rapper), 196
J-Swift (producer), 196
Juggaknots (band), 118, 119, 225
*Juice* (film), 167–68
Juice Crew, 46, 47, 48, 55
"Juicy" (Notorious B.I.G.), 83, 116
"Juicy Fruit" (James Mtume), 83, 116
Juicy J (producer and rapper), 258–59
Jungle Brothers, 86–87, 92, 102, 103,
107, 118

Young, Andre. *See* Dr. Dre
Young, Doug, 148
Young, Tyree, 139
"Young Niggaz" (Tupac Shakur), 172
"You Showed Me" (Turtles), 81, 196, 199
"Youthful Expression" (A Tribe Called Quest), 88
Y'skid (producer), 246, 253
"Yuletide Throw Down" (Fab 5 Freddy and Blondie), 32

Zapp (band), 27, 124, 128, 129, 151, 172, 178
Zappa, Frank, 203, 227
Zev Love X (Daniel Dumile), 72, 218–23
ZTT Records, 41
Zulu Beats Show (radio program), 218–19
Zulu Nation (activist group), 8–9, 65, 92

**Nate Patrin** is a freelance music critic and journalist who has been listening to hip-hop since the mid-'80s and writing about it—and many other genres—since the mid-'90s, starting with his high school newspaper. Since then he has contributed to dozens of publications, from his hometown Minneapolis/St. Paul alt-weekly *City Pages* to websites including *Pitchfork, Red Bull Music Academy, Bandcamp Daily,* and *Stereogum.*